MW00941389

# THE MUSLIM DISCOVERY
# OF AMERICA

*Wishing you warmest regards
and success,*

*Frederick William Dame*

*Patriotic, Steadfast, and True.*

*April, 2013*

# THE MUSLIM DISCOVERY

# OF AMERICA

Frederick William Dame

With a Commendatory Preface by

Don Fredrick

and

Foreword by

Pamela Geller

**Bibliographical Information of the Deutsche Nationalbibliothek**
This publication is listed in the Deutsche Nationalbibliographie of the
Deutsche Nationalbibliothek;
detailed bibliographical information
can be accessed under http: //dnb.d-nb.de

© 2013 Frederick William Dame
Printing and Production: BoD – Books on Demand
ISBN 978-3-8482-3863-7

# DEDICATION

I dedicate this book to my dearest Elisabeth.

She knows all of the reasons why.

# TABLE OF CONTENTS

## CHAPTER ONE
### Preview to Understanding

## CHAPTER TWO
### The Pre-Columbian Era

# CHAPTER THREE

## Claims that Muslims Discovered The New World

# CHAPTER FOUR

## Muslims in America 1500-1800

## CHAPTER FIVE

### Islam and America 1800-2000

## CHAPTER SIX

### Muslims in America Organize

## CHAPTER SEVEN

A Case of Cultural Jihad and Geographical Taqiyya

## CHAPTER EIGHT

Islamization and Jihad Continue in theTwenty-First Century

## CHAPTER NINE

Willful Blindness Continues in the Twenty-First Century

## CHAPTER TEN

Blueprint and Prognosis

# COMMENDATORY PREFACE

by

## Don Fredrick

On April 6, 2009 Barack Hussein Obama addressed the Turkish parliament and declared that the United States has been "enriched by Muslim-Americans." He offered a "deep appreciation for the Islamic faith, which has done so much over the centuries to shape the world—including in my own country." Obama's remark no doubt led some skeptical critics on a search to find any shred of evidence that Islam has "shaped the United States"—although some might argue that Muslims "reshaped" the New York skyline on September 11, 2001. (Others might argue that by "my own country" Obama was referring to Kenya or Indonesia.)

Obama also said, "We do not consider ourselves a Christian nation or a Jewish nation or a Muslim nation" – a statement totally at odds with the history of the United States and the beliefs and traditions of its citizens. Obama noted, "We consider ourselves a nation of citizens bound by ideals and a set of values." Those values, however, are primarily Judeo-Christian values – a fact which contradicts his prior sentence. That contradiction did not matter to Obama, however, because he was eager to please the citizens of Turkey and other Muslims around the world. He had no trouble casually disowning America's history and heritage, even though he resisted disowning his minister, Reverend Jeremiah Wright, for two decades of racist and anti-American sermons.

i

Two months later, in an interview on the French television network *Canal Plus*, Obama claimed that American Muslims would make the United States "...one of the largest Muslim countries in the world." Although Obama had made it a point to state that the United States is not a Christian or a Jewish nation, he was perfectly willing to state that it was on its way to becoming a Muslim nation.

If Obama was relying on population figures, he was mistaken. If, for example, one counts Jews in America, they would make up the largest "Jewish country" in the world other than Israel—but Obama has never claimed that the United States was "one of the largest Jewish countries in the world." Depending on the source, the number of Muslims in the United States is estimated to be between 1.8 and 8 million people. The 1.8 million figure, from the Pew Research Center, is likely closer to the truth than 8, and would make the United States the 48th largest Muslim nation.

Obama's "largest Muslim countries" remark is like a white person trying to "talk ghetto" or evocative of those who say, "I'm not racist... I have black friends too!" But millions of Islam's followers are not satisfied with the ranking of the United States as the 48th largest Muslim country; they want it to be the world's largest Muslim country. To that end, Obama told *Canal Plus* that Americans "...have to educate [themselves] more effectively on Islam" and "...there's got to be a better dialogue and a better understanding between the two peoples."

Meanwhile, Muslims are doing their best to educate Americans on the subject of Islam by working to insert into history books a multitude of facts about their religion/ideology—many of which happen to be false. Hence, we turn to Frederick William Dame's *The Muslim Discovery of America*. Mr. Dame examines "Islam's goal of world domination," "the myth that Mohammed is a direct descendant of Adam" and his self-appointed prophet status, and "the various pre-Columbian Muslim claims of their discovery of America." The claims of early global exploration by Muslims have some basis in truth, of course, but the amount of exaggeration and outright falsehoods is stunning. Mr. Dame addresses—and refutes—those claims. He reviews the history of Muslims in the American Colonies, "the myths of Arab-Islamic maps and inventions, the origin of slavery, slavery in the American Colonies, and the presentation of some documented, randomly chosen individual Muslims who lived in early America."

Dr. Youssef Mroueh is one of the sources of claims that Muslims have a long history in the United States, preceding Christopher Columbus and other European explorers. To the average person, Mroueh's claims may make some sense. But if one researches those claims (and author Dame is most assuredly a thorough researcher) they evaporate on close examination. Mroueh claims, "A careful study of the names of the native Indian tribes revealed that many names are derived from Arab and Islamic roots and origins..." Mr. Dame responds, "There is no truthful fact behind his allegations. It is all creeping *al-taqiyya*. Dr. Mroueh is a liar." (Mr. Dame is refreshingly blunt.) As an extreme example of the "We were here first!" claim, Muslims argue that the name Islamorada, Florida has Islamic origins. That is nonsense. "The name Islamorada, (Isla morada)," writes Mr. Dame, "means *purple island*, designated by the early Spanish explorers in the area.

The English pronunciation is *aisle-a-more-AH-dah*. The name has no Arabic-Islamic origin." (That the first five letters in the name spell "Islam" is apparently proof enough for Muslims to claim Florida as their own.) The town of Allakaket, Alaska apparently sounds enough like "Allah" to enable Mroueh to claim that Alaska has a Muslim past, but Mr. Dame points out that "Allakaket is a Koyukuk Indian name meaning *mouth of the Alatna River.*" Mroueh has dug up hundreds of such "Muslim names," and Mr. Dame demonstrates that they have nothing to do with an Arab-Islamic heritage.

In 1996, there were even attempts by Mroueh and others "to claim the One Thousand Year Anniversary of the Muslim (Islam) Discovery of America." Mr. Dame writes, "Based on the exposé of the true roots of the above historical, geographical and linguistic place names and those that Dr. Mroueh cited as reasons to call for a millennium celebration of the arrival of Muslims in America, we can conclude that the whole listing was nothing more than the Muslim exercise of *taqiyya*. There was and there is no reason for an international call to celebrate any Muslim arrival in the Americas five centuries before Columbus, unless the goal is to rewrite history and to delude people into believing that the foundation of cities and places in America owe their existence to Muslims, Mohammed's dogma of world domination, and Islam. ...The reason that Islamic internet sites conduct such creeping, slimy Islamic claims is because they are intent on convincing unknowledgeable persons that wherever a Muslim set his foot, that land belongs to Islam. It does not matter when this happened. As such, the Islamic logic of expansion is that whenever and wherever a Muslim appears in a foreign land, regardless of the historical age, it is only logical according to the Koran that that land must become Islamic, otherwise Allah would never have made it possible for that Muslim discoverer or explorer to be physically present in said new country."

Readers of *The Muslim Discovery of America* will encounter perhaps the longest name ever given to any human being: Amr bin Lahyo bin Harath bin Amr ul-Qais bin Thalaba bin Azd bin Khalan bin Babalyun bin Saba. They will also learn of what may have been the first Muslim "honor killing" on the North American continent—the death of Mohawk Indian Princess Lotowana (Princess "Sparkling Water") at the hand of a Hudson River Valley resident, an Egyptian Muslim named Norsereddine, who is himself "honored by Islamic historians as the first permanent Arab Muslim settler in New York." (For most people, using a dart "poisoned with snake venom" to kill the woman who rejected his romantic advances might be enough to have a stalker's name crossed off their "honorable persons" list, but Islam was apparently no more forgiving in the Catskill Mountains in the 16th century than it is today. One need only spend a few moments at AtlasShrugs.com to find reports of modern day Muslim "honor killings" in the United States that the mainstream media seems content to ignore.)

No discussion of Muslims and the earliest days of the United States can proceed without noting the years of treaties with the Barbary kingdoms—treaties which essentially called for paying tribute to Muslim pirates in exchange for their not raiding US cargo ships. Ultimately, President Thomas Jefferson "sent American warships to the Mediterranean," and the Marines landed on "the shores of Tripoli." More than 200 years later, Muslim pirates still raid cargo ships—although they now do so off the coast of Somalia. (Speaking of Thomas Jefferson, he did not, as Obama has claimed, host the first iftar dinner in the White House. Notes Mr. Dame: "Jefferson was interested in talking to the ambassador over the piracy being conducted against American merchant ships by Tunisia, but otherwise could not have cared anything about Islam. It was the Islamic fasting month of Ramadan and the temporary envoy said that he could not come to dinner during the day. Jefferson was polite and delayed the dinner a few hours to sunset. There was no special menu. President Jefferson changed the time of the dinner from the usual 3:30 pm to sunset." Sharing a meal with a Muslim is certainly not the equivalent of arranging a special celebratory feast with an Islamic menu. In any event, President Thomas Jefferson's interest was not accommodating Muslims. His interest was nothing more than putting an end to their acts of vicious piracy.)

The history of the United States includes its regrettable period of slavery that lasted approximately 150 years from 1619 to the end of the American Civil War. Vast numbers of slaves were Muslims, and those who were not were also rounded up by Muslim slave traders in Africa and sent across the Atlantic Ocean to work in American agriculture.

Of particular interest to some readers may be Mr. Dame's mention of colonist Royall Tyler and his descriptions of the slave trade in his 1797 novel, *The Algerian Captive*. The cruel treatment of slaves by some American plantation owners pales in comparison to their treatment by the Muslim traders. The modern-day beheadings conducted by Muslim terrorists may seem almost merciful when compared to the Muslim traders' treatment of escaped slaves, who were "burned at the stake, or impaled on huge iron hooks or large wooden poles shoved up the rectum and extruding out of the slave's neck. One of the Muslim's favorite methods of dealing with runaway slaves or those who insulted Islam, Mohammed, or the Muslim ruler was public crucifixion. In their own minds the beys, deys and bashaws of the Barbary States were only doing Allah's and Mohammed's will."

By 1895 President Grover Cleveland was protesting the massacre of Armenian Christians by Turkish Muslims, writing that the United States was an agent "of the Christian world (to ensure that) conduct of Turkish government as will restrain fanatical brutality, and if this fails (the) duty is to so interfere as to insure against such dreadful occurrences in Turkey as have lately shocked civilization..." The genocide of Christians by Muslims continued, and Cleveland later reported to Congress that the Turks did not end the killing: "We have been afflicted by continued and not unfrequent reports of the wanton destruction of homes and the bloody butchery of men, women, and children, made martyrs to their profession of Christian faith." (More than a century later, Obama broke his 2008 campaign promise to the Armenian people that, as president, he would officially refer to the slaughter of 1.5 million people as genocide. In his speech in Turkey, Obama merely referred to the killings as "terrible events"—as if to assign blame to both sides. He even said, "Our country still struggles with the legacy of our past treatment of native Americans." Obama cannot admit that Muslims kill Christians, but he can condemn Americans for killing Indians.)

After a review of American Muslims in the nineteenth century, Mr. Dame examines Islamic movements in the twentieth century. He "analyzes a case study of cultural jihad and geographical taqiyya," and dissects "Islamic logic behind the claiming of land and islamization of the United States of America." Those readers who are not familiar with "taqiyya" would be wise to pay close attention to Mr. Dame's explanation, as it is one of the main processes by which Islam is being spread. "Taqiyya" is supported by two other Muslim/Islamic doctrines of lying. One doctrine is called "kitman", which means lying by not telling the complete truth, i. e., leaving certain aspects out of a situation that would explain the complete happening. The other doctrine is called "tawriya" which allows a Muslim to lie in all circumstances. All three doctrines, "taqiyya", "kitman", and "tawriya", are permissible for the advancement of Islam. (Anyone who is fascinated by the secrets behind magicians' tricks will appreciate learning what Muslims have up their sleeves.)

We learn that Muslims established the Red Crescent in Detroit in 1920 "because Muslims have a penchant, indeed a psychological proneness, for being insulted when they see a cross or hear the word cross." One year later *Muslim Sunrise*, "the oldest and longest-running Muslim magazine," began publication. "Under the motto *One God, One Imam, One Destiny* the Universal Islamic Society was established in Detroit Michigan in 1926 by Dues Muhammad Ali, the so-called mentor of Marcus Garvey." "Nation of Islam (NOI) Wallace Ford (Fard Muhammad) founded the Nation of Islam in Detroit, Michigan 1933."

One cannot review Islam in America without reviewing terrorism in America, and the book reports on the many domestic terrorist acts that have occurred since September 11, 2001. It is by no means a short list. Mr. Dame points out the "increased activity of jihad and creeping Islam in the United States..." and explains "the Islamic framework and guiding principles with which Islam conducts an undermining of American culture..." He concludes with a list of methods by which Americans can "fight against the Islamization and the mosqueing of the United States of America." Some readers may wonder if, in fact, the United States may someday become "…one of the largest Muslim countries in the world." If enough Americans read *The Muslim Discovery of America*, that will not happen.

*Don Fredrick*
July, 2012

Don Fredrick is the author of the novel, *Colony 14*; the economic primer, *What You Don't Know About Economics Can Hurt You*; and *The Obama Timeline*, the most comprehensive compilation of information about the life of Barack Obama and his actions in the Oval Office. His web site, www.colony14.net, includes essays by Frederick William Dame.

# FOREWORD

## by

## Pamela Geller

This book is the record of a colonization. As these pages demonstrate, it is not an ordinary colonization, but it is a colonization nonetheless. It was not initiated by an invading army, and so far has not resulted in a political transformation, although it is certainly aiming at that. It started slowly, with a trickle of individuals into this country, but in recent decades, especially the ten years since the 9/11 attacks, it has rapidly picked up speed, such that Muslims are now daily growing more assertive, and making their intentions for the United States known more clearly every day.

And so here we are, over ten years later—ten years after it was raining bodies on 9/11, and we have Muslim footbaths in universities and airports. We have textbooks that read like a CAIR press release on Islamic history. We have Islamic anti-Semitism infecting the whole soul of the world. We have the mosqueing of the workplace and the public school. We have the United States Treasury Department giving seminars in sharia finance.[1] We have a Muslim Brotherhood-linked Congressman.

As *The Muslim Discovery of America* shows, Islamic supremacists are more aggressive in the United States today than they have ever been. They're building large mega-mosques

---

[1] Pamela Geller, *US Treasury Submits To Islam*, AtlasShrugs.com, November 4, 2008.

in communities where the local Muslims can neither fill nor afford them. They're demanding—and receiving—special privileges for Muslims in workplaces, and special installations for Islamic prayers in public universities and public schools, as well as in airports and other public facilities.

They're bringing back prayer in public schools—but only for Muslims, while insisting that Christians, Jews, Hindus, and Buddhists and other religious groups can assert no such Constitutional privilege under our law: they are seeking special legal status for Islam. Islamic law places Muslims in a special class, giving them rights that non-Muslims do not have, and the demands for these special accommodations are all in the service of bringing Islamic law here and asserting its primacy over American law.

They're shutting down the national debate that we urgently need to have about Islam and Islamization. They're demonizing as "bigots," "racists," and "Islamophobes" anyone who suggests any anti-terror measure, or who challenges the Muslim community in the US about its tolerance of evil.

They're working as hard as they can to shut down the rapidly growing anti-sharia movement nationwide, and to prevent any more states from passing anti-sharia laws like the one that Kansas Governor Sam Brownback signed in May 2012. They're working to muzzle free speech, criminalizing criticism of Islam by means of "hate speech" laws they will manipulate to shut up their opponents and anyone who dares speak out against their Islamization agenda. This is in line with the international war on free speech that is being pursued by the Organization of Islamic Cooperation (OIC).

The Muslim Brotherhood, a global organization dedicated to the establishment of Islamic political law in all the countries of the world, is also working through its supposedly "moderate" front organizations like the Muslim American Society (MAS) and the Council on American-Islamic Relations (CAIR), which tries to intimidate Americans into being afraid to oppose jihad activity or even report suspicious behavior by Muslims. These very organizations have infiltrated senior levels of the Department of Defense, the Department of State, the Department of Homeland Security, the Department of Justice, et al., with the aim of advancing their agendas and making them law.

Muslims are working in the United States now to make sure that Islam dominates, by destroying our constitutional freedoms. The Muslim Brotherhood, according to a captured internal document of that international pro-sharia organization, is dedicated in America to "a kind of grand jihad in eliminating and destroying the Western civilization from within and 'sabotaging' its miserable house by their hands and the hands of the believers so that it is eliminated and Allah's religion is made victorious over all other religions."[2]

Omar Ahmad, the co-founder and longtime board chairman of the nation's leading "Muslim civil rights group," the Council on American-Islamic Relations (CAIR), also once let the mask slip in a speech he gave to a Muslim audience in California in 1998. Ahmad said, "Islam isn't in America to be equal to any other faith, but to become dominant. The Koran

---

[2] Mohammed Akram. *An Explanatory Memorandum on the General Strategic Goal for the Group in North America*, May 22, 1991, Government Exhibit 003-0085, US vs. HLF et al. is available for public download at http://www.investigativeproject.org/documents/misc/20.pdf.

should be the highest authority in America, and Islam the only accepted religion on earth."[3]

CAIR spokesman Ibrahim Hooper expressed the same desire in a 1993 interview: "I wouldn't want to create the impression that I wouldn't like the government of the United States to be Islamic sometime in the future."[4]

And one of the leading Muslim spokesmen in the United States, the imam Siraj Wahhaj, who in 1991 became the first Muslim cleric to give an invocation to the United States Congress, has warned that the US will fall unless it "accepts the Islamic agenda." He has also said, "If only Muslims were clever politically, they could take over the United States and replace its constitutional government with a caliphate."[5]

The march of Islamic supremacists enjoined by their leftist enablers has been going on for decades, long before 9/11, under the radar screen: quiet, unnoticed, stealthy. Muslim Brotherhood front groups had prepared both political and cultural initiatives in anticipation of jihad attacks. And so they were at the ready on 9/11 to direct the efforts of our most senior government and law enforcement agencies—that one of their utmost concerns had to be not initiatives in the Islamic community to teach against the beliefs that inspired and

---

[3] Spencer, Robert. *Stealth jihad: How Radical Islam Is Subverting America Without Guns Or Bombs*, Regnery Publishing Inc., Washington, D.C.: 2008, p. 16.

[4] Pamela Geller, *Illinois Governor's Hamas Council Exclusive: Pamela Geller reveals Muslims tied to terrorists giving advice to state government*, at http://www.wnd.com/2011/09/344713/.

[5] Spencer, Robert. *The Politically Incorrect Guide to Islam and the Crusades*, Regnery Publishing, Inc., Washington, D.C.: 2005, pp. 44-45.

motivated the attacks, but rather preventing a backlash against Muslims. Yet no such backlash ever materialized. But the fallacious meme, "anti-Muslim backlash," became a familiar mantra on the airwaves, in print media, and from the silver-tongued stealth jihadists. Anyone who spoke out against the Muslim colonization of America was accused of fueling this "backlash."

Do you want to live in a country where you could be put to death for saying what you think about Islam? Or any other religion?

Do you think this is impossible in America? If you do, consider this: in places where Islamic law reigns supreme, there is no freedom of speech. Right now there are non-Muslims in prison in Pakistan and awaiting death for blasphemy. This is Islamic law, and this is the Islamic law that Muslims want to bring to the United States.

Every citizen must now work to defend America's constitutional government and stop the Muslim colonization of America in its tracks. Every free citizen must join this fight. The separation of mosque and state is essential to preserving American freedom and our way of life. Yet the Islamic supremacists have made real inroads. Over the last few years, we have seen the encroachment of Islam on the secular marketplace. It is now up to us – to everyone who is reading this book – to act upon what it shows, before it is too late.


*Pamela Geller*
September, 2012

Pamela Geller is the founder, editor, and publisher of Atlas Shrugs.com and Executive Director of the American Freedom Defense Initiative (AFDI) and Stop the Islamization of America (SIOA). She is the author of *The Post-American Presidency: The Obama Administration's War on America*, with Robert Spencer, and *Stop the Islamization of America: A Practical Guide for the Resistance*. In addition, she is a columnist for World Net Daily (wnd.com), Big Government and Big Journalism, and American Thinker, as well as various other publications.

*ABC*, *CNN*, *Fox's Hannity*, *Geraldo At Large*, *Huckabee*, *NBC Nightly News*, *The O'Reilly Factor*, and other news and information television stations regularly invite Pamela Geller to appear on their programs and news broadcasts. She has been the subject of a profile by *The New York Times* and a documentary by *60 Minutes*.

# ACKNOWLEDGEMENT

Critical and constructive assistance is absolutely necessary for the writing and completion of any book. It is fortunate that such persons with an objective eye and opinion have assisted me in the research and compilation of material essential for the execution of these two volumes. They are the personnel of the Pfalzbibliothek, Bezirksverband Pfalz, Bismarckstrasse 17, 67655 Kaiserslautern, Federal Republic of Germany. I give them full credit and appreciation by naming them: Frau Renate Flesch, Direktorin der Abteilungsleitung, Einkauf, Veranstaltungen (Director of the Library Division, Purchases, and Events); Frau Claudia Germann, Leiterin für Austellungen, EDV, Katologisierung (Director for Exhibitions, Electronic Data Processing, Cataloging); Frau Elisabeth Erb, Auskunft, Fernleihe (Information, Interlibrary Loans); Herr Fabian Striehl, Ausleihe, Zeitschrift Verwaltung (Library Loans, Newspapers and Magazines); and Frau Tina Koplin, Auskunft, Fernleihe (Information, Interlibrary Loans).

I also thank Don Fredrick of *The Obama Timeline* for the kind words in his Commendatory Preface. His advice, criticisms, and suggestions have made positive contributions to this book. His *The Obama Timeline* at www.colony14.net is of the utmost importance in understanding the continuing, active history of the Barack Hussein Obama years.

I owe immense gratitude to Pamela Geller for her availability, time, and willingness to write the Foreword to this book. I also express my gramercy for the permission to quote many of her articles at length.

All Americans should be thankful that Pamela Geller is the astute researcher and reporter about how Islam and the progressives are destroying the *Constitution for the United States of America* and with it the American Republic. One can always depend on Pamela Geller for the truth concerning creeping sharia, creepy Islam, and present-day American and international politics. The examples of creeping sharia and the islamization of America presented in Chapters Eight and Nine were selected out of almost 1000 incidences that can be found in internet sources, but not in the so-called mainstream media. They are representative of the open and surreptitious activities that are undertaken by Islamists every day all across the United States of America.

The source of the cover photograph for this book in which the devout are only showing their respect to the reader is http://www.signofourtime.com/archives/330/muslimsholddayprayercapitolhill. It has been freely republished at a number of internet sites.

All books are like a perfect painting. Somewhere there is a mistake. *The Muslim Discovery of America* is no different. The author takes full responsibility for any deficiencies in the manuscript. Such imperfections are not wonted and no slightness is intended. Some capitalizations of words are intentional for emphasis or meaning, like American Colonies meaning the thirteen original colonies.

The author is responsible for the design of the book from cover to cover.

*Frederick William Dame*
December, 2012.

# CHAPTER ONE

# Preview to Understanding

## Introduction

Originally, this book was to appear as only a short book summary concerning Islam and the United States of America. It has become a full-length book about the Muslim discovery of America, specifically, the United States of America. As such, the book will serve as an incentive and a starting point for further research. The *modus operandi* is *in medias res*. There are no pseudo-intellectual formulations. This work is the representation of the situation as the author has researched and analyzed the facts, all of which are documented.

There is no special emphasis on political correctness. The author believes that in being politically exact, one does not have to lie and one does not have to brainwash the reader. In being politically exact, this author uses language that is straightforward to present behaviors, ideas, policies, genders, cultures, disabilities, races, and ideologies as they were in history and as they are today. There is no trespassing over the boundaries of commentary into a language of meaningless nothings. Words in a language have definite meanings. There is truly no use in presenting gobbledygook. For example, if a politician's stance on a certain issue is dumb, then it is dumb. Period! There is no sense in saying that *the politician's stance is in such an ambience that one might want to consider the possibilities of the statements made in an atmosphere of*

1

*academic sensibilities concerning the relative quotients of intellectual relationships with those statements made by the political colleagues who do not necessarily, yet who also might agree or disagree on the matter at hand in an atmosphere of cordiality and mutual respect for differing opinions.*

*The Muslim Discovery of America* has ten chapters. Chapter One presents a review of the literature and an explanation of terms that will be used throughout the book.

Chapter Two discusses Islam's goal of world domination. Attention is paid to the myth that Mohammed is a direct descendant of Adam and the questionability of Mohammed's raison d'être as a self-appointed prophet.

Chapter Three examines the various pre-Columbian Muslim claims of their discovery of America. It covers the years from approximately 880 to 1500. Succinctly, it presents a discussion of the pre-Columbian theories concerning the assertions that Muslims discovered America approximately 600 years before Christopher Columbus made landfall on San Salvador, Bahamas, on 12 October 1492.

Chapter Four covers the period of the settlement of the American Colonies to the establishment of the United States of America and its emergence on the world scene as an independent nation. The themes will include the myths of Arab-Islamic maps and inventions, the origin of slavery, slavery in the American Colonies, and the presentation of some documented, randomly chosen individual Muslims who lived in early America. This was an age when there was little implementation of Islamic dogma in the United States of America. The appearance of Islam and Muslims was a cultural idiosyncrasy, a novelty, in the American Colonies. Although there was scant Muslim immigration and Muslim settlements were scarce, there were important diplomatic engagements with Islamic lands. A major war was conducted due to the threats of Islamic countries and their destruction of commercial exchanges and sailing routes between the United States of America and Europe.

Chapter Five inspects the founding of initial Islamic movements from the first decade of the nineteenth century to the beginnings of the twentieth century. An overview of Muslim historical personages will be presented.

Chapter Six explores the rediscovery of America by Islamic movements in the twentieth century. This was a time when the Islamic population experienced a great increase due to immigration, conversion to Islam, and a high birth rate among Islamic adherents.

Chapter Seven analyzes a case study of cultural jihad and geographical taqiyya. The Islamic logic behind the claiming of land and islamization of the United States of America is scrutinized.

Chapter Eight inquires into the present status of Muslims in America since the Islamic terrorist attack on the World Trade Center on September 11, 2001. The time period covered will be the first decade of the twenty-first century.

Chapter Nine takes up where Chapter Eight closes. The content shows the increased activity of jihad and creeping Islam in the United States of America beginning with the second decade of the twenty-first century.

Chapter Ten explains the Islamic framework and guiding principles with which Islam conducts an undermining of American culture and its twenty-point program to institute Islam as the controlling force in America politics. The ultimate goal is the takeover of American society and government. A prognosis for the future of Islam in the United States of America is presented. The background of this forecast is the present Islamic organizations in the United States of America, particularly the Council on American Islamic Relations (CAIR), established in June of 1994 by the Muslim Brotherhood. The chapter closes with suggestions on how to combat and stop the Islamic takeover of the United States of America from within.

Unless otherwise stated, the use of the term America will mean that part of North America that became the United States of America. When the word Muslim is written, the reader should also comprehend the word Islam, considered by the majority of people to be a world religion. Likewise, when the word Islam or one of its goals like the establishment of sharia law occurs, the reader should also comprehend the terminology Muslim.


## Review of the Literature

All reviews of literature that are used in writing an academic book are subjective. The selection of the literature used in *The Muslim Discovery of America* is no exception. Nevertheless, this author has divided the literature review into the five sections with listed serious and quasi-serious sources.

4

The literature concerning Islam and America that this author calls fairy-tale literature is not presented. There is no special separation of books from periodicals and internet sources, except for section five. Literature will have meaning only to the degree that the reader is willing to read its contents and take part in the conversation the author is presenting to the public. The following literatures are politically correct in that they are not apologetic. They present the truth about Islam.

## I. A General Background on Islamic History

*Behind the Veil*, an electronic book at http://answering-islam.org/BehindVeil/index.html, retrieved on 12.01.2012.

Bostom, Andrew G. editor. *The Legacy of Islamic Antisemitism From Sacred Texts to Solemn History*, Prometheus Books, Amherst, New York: 2008.

Bostom, Andrew G. editor. *Sharia versus Freedom The Legacy of Islamic Totalitarianism*, Prometheus Books, Amherst, New York: 2012.

Bostom, Andrew G. editor. *The Legacy of Jihad Islamic Holy War and the Fate of Non-Muslims*, Prometheus Books, Amherst, New York: 2005.

Lewis, Bernard. *The Arabs in History*, Oxford University Press, Oxford, England: 2003.

O'Leary, De Lacy. *Arabic Thought and Its Place In Western History*, Routledge & Kegan Paul, Ltd., London: 1954.

O'Neill, John J. *Holy Warriors Islam and the Demise of Classical Civilization*, Felibri Publications, 2010 at jonplotinus@googlemain.com.

Pipes, Daniel. *Slaves, Soldiers and Islam The Genesis of a Military System*, Yale University Press, New London, Connecticut: 1981.

Pirenne, Henri. *Mohammed and Charlemagne*, translated from the French by Bernard Miall, Barnes and Noble, New York: 1956.

Richardson, Don. *Secrets of the Koran Revealing Insights into Islam's Holy Book*, Regal Books, Ventura California: 2003.

Salemi, Peter. *The Plain Truth About Islam* at http://www.british-israel.ca/Islam.htm.

Spencer, Robert. *Did Mohammed Exist? An Inquiry into Islam's Obscure Origins*, ISI Books, Wilmington, Delaware: 2012.

Warraq, Ibn, editor and translator. *The Quest for the Historical Muhammad*, Prometheus Books, Amherst, New York: 2000.

Warraq, Ibn, editor and translator. *What the Koran Really Says: Language, Text, and Commentary*, Prometheus Books, Amherst, New York: 2002.

Warraq, Ibn, editor. *Leaving Islam: Apostates Speak Out*, Prometheus Books, Amherst, New York: 2003.

Warraq, Ibn, editor. *The Origins of The Koran: Classic Essays on Islam's Holy Book*, Prometheus Books, Amherst, New York: 1998.

Warraq, Ibn. *Defending the West: A Critique of Edward Said's Orientalism*, Prometheus Books Amherst, New York: 2007.

Warraq, Ibn. *Which Koran?: Variants, Manuscripts, and the Influence of Pre-Islamic Poetry*, Prometheus Books Amherst, New York: 2007.

Warraq, Ibn. *Why I Am Not a Muslim*, Prometheus Books, Amherst, New York: 1995.

Warraq, Ibn. *Why the West is Best: A Muslim Apostate's Defense of Liberal Democracy*, Encounter Books, New York: 2011.

Ye'or, Bat. *Eurabia: The Euro-Arab Axis*, Fairleigh Dickinson University Press, Madison, New Jersey: 2005.

Ye'or, Bat. *Islam and Dhimmitude: Where Civilizations Collide*, Fairleigh Dickinson University Press, Madison, New Jersey: 2001.

Ye'or, Bat. *The Decline of Eastern Christianity: From Jihad to Dhimmitude; seventh-twentieth century*, Fairleigh Dickinson University Press, Madison, New Jersey: 1996.

Ye'or, Bat. *The Dhimmi: Jews and Christians Under Islam*, Fairleigh Dickinson University Press, Madison, New Jersey: 1985.

## II. Pre-Columbian Evidence of Muslims in America

There are no enormous literature sources regarding the pre-Columbian Islamic discovery of America. What literature there is must remain extremely questionable. Nevertheless, the theories that can be considered as serious, although with some questionable elements are found in the literature listed below.

Fell, Howard Barraclough (Barry). *America B. C.: Ancient Settlers in the New World*, Quadrangle Books, New York: 1976.

Fell, Howard Barraclough (Barry). *Bronze Age America*, Little, Brown, Boston: 1982.

Fell, Howard Barraclough (Barry). *Saga America,* Times Books, New York: 1980.

Ghanea Bassiri, Kambiz. *A History of Islam in America: From the New World to the New World Order*, Cambridge University Press; 2010, chronicles the Muslim presence in America across five centuries.

M'Bow, Amadou Mahtar; Kettani, Ali. *Islam and Muslims in the American continent*, Center of Historical, Economical and Social Studies, Beirut: 2001.

Pimienta-Bey, Jose V. *Muslim Legacy in Early Americas* at http://www.imamreza.net/eng/imamreza.php?id=2028, retrieved 15.01.2012.

Sezgin, Fuat. *The Pre-Columbian Discovery of the American Continent by Muslim Seafarers*, Institute for the History of Arabic-Islamic Studies, Johann Wolfgang Goethe University, Frankfurt am Main: 2005, at www.uni-frankfurt/fb13/igaiw, retrieved on 16.01.2012.

Van Sertima, Ivan. *They Came Before Columbus*, Random House, New York: 1976.

von Wuthenau, Alexander. *Unexpected Faces in Ancient America,* Crown Publishers, New York: 1975.

## III. Muslims in America: 18th, 19th, and 20th Centuries

Alford, Terry. *Prince Among Slaves,* Harcourt Brace Jovanovich, New York: 1977. This work recounts the documentation done by William Brown Hodgson on Bilali Muhammad, who wrote a book on Islamic Law in America; Umar ibn Said who wrote a thirteen-page autobiography in Arabic and engaged in taqiyya by feigning a conversion to Christianity; and Abdul Rahman Ibrahim Sori who wrote two autobiographies and two copies of the Fatiha.[1] Hodgson also translated five chapters of the Koran that were written by an unknown slave of Georgetown, South Carolina.

Cooper, James, wrote about Salih Bilali in William Brown Hodgson's *Notes on North Africa,* Wiley and Putnam, New York: 1844. Therein Bilali recounts his remembrance of Africa and the Fula language.

Curtis IV, Edward E. *Encyclopedia of Muslim-American History,* Facts on File Inc., New York: 2010. This is a good book with interesting facts.

Curtis IV, Edward E. *Muslims in America: A Short History,* Oxford University Press, Oxford, 2009. The history is too short.

---

[1] The *Fatiha* is the first sura (chapter) with seven verses in the Koran that stress Allah's lordship and mercy and is a prayer for Allah's guidance. It is recited seventeen times a day.

Dwight, Theodore Jr. *Condition and Character of Negroes in Africa, Methodist Quarterly Review*, January 1864, pp. 77-90. Dwight writes of the former slave Lamen Kebe and his knowledge of teaching.

Koszegi, Michael A., and Melton, J. Gordon, eds. *Islam In North America A Sourcebook*, Garland Publishing, New York: 1992. This book tries to be independent in its views. However, there is no criticism of Islam and its policies towards women, ethics, and adversaries.

Smith, Jane I. *Islam in America*, Columbia University Press, New York: 1999, 2009. The discussion of African-American Muslims is comprehensible. However, the whole book is an attempt to make a controversial threat to America's existence non-controversial. As such, it is a whitewashing of Islam that neglects the terror aspect in Mohammed's life and in the Koran.

## IV. Islam in America: Transition from the 18th to the 19th Century

Allison, Robert J. *The Crescent Obscured: The United States and the Muslim World, 1776–1815*, Oxford University Press, Oxford: 1995.

Gawalt, Gerard W. *America and the Barbary Pirates: An International Battle Against an Unconventional Foe,* at http://memory.loc.gov/ammem/collections/jefferson_papers/mtj prece.html, retrieved on 12.02.2012.

Kidd, Thomas. S. *American Christians and Islam - Evangelical Culture and Muslims from the Colonial Period to the Age of*

*Terrorism*, Princeton University Press, Princeton, New Jersey: 2008.

## V. Concerning the Islamic Threat to America

<u>Internet Sites</u>

- http://allaboutMohammed.com/islamic-jurisprudence.html.
- http://answering-islam.org/BehindVeil/btvintro.html.
- http://answering-islam.org/Quran/Themes/jihad_passages.html.
- http://answering-islam.org/Terrorism/by_the_sword.html.
- http://archive.frontpagemag.com/readArticle.aspx?ARTID= 297.
- http://atlasshrugs2000.typepad.com/. All contemporary articles and archived articles.
- http://atlasshrugs2000.typepad.com/atlas_shrugs/2010/10/fu ll-text-wilders-in-berlin.html.
- http://bigpeace.com/ndarwish/2010/08/26/sharia-for-dummies/#more-20945.
- http://creepingsharia.wordpress.com/. All contemporary articles and archived articles.
- http://divine-ripples.blogspot.com/.
- http://divine-ripples.blogspot.com/2011/02/obama-saudi-operative-to-facilitate.html.
- http://hauns.com/~DCQu4E5g/koran.html#Koran.
- http://islamexposed.blogspot.com/.

11

- http://kitmantv.blogspot.com/2010/06/first-comes-saturday-then-comes-sunday.html.
- http://loganswarning.com/. All contemporary articles and archived articles.
- http://projectshiningcity.org/fp518.php.
- http://righttruth.typepad.com/right_truth/, wherein there are daily reports and respective essays on Islam as well archived material.
- http://vladtepesblog.com/?p=24380.
- http://web.archive.org/web/20070610042932/
- http://wikiislam.net/wiki/Main_Page, and the links and articles therein.
- http://www.aish.com/jw/s/48969486.html.
- http://www.answering-islam.org/Silas/slavery.htm.
- http://www.barkati.net/english/#01.
- http://www.cis.org/articles/2002/back802.html.
- http://www.colony14.net/id41.html, *The Obama Timeline*. It has monthly news reports as well as respective essays.
- http://www.faithfreedom.org/.
- http://www.faithfreedom.org/index.htm.
- http://www.flex.com/~jai/satyamevajayate/index.html.
- http://www.godtube.com/watch/?v=JE01BMNU.
- http://www.inquiryintoislam.com/2010/07/why-is-islam-so-successful.html.

- http://www.islammonitor.org/.

- http://www.islammonitor.org/index.php?option=com_conte nt&task=view&id=3897&Itemid=67.

- http://www.islam-watch.org/articles.htm.

- http://www.islam-watch.org/Nosharia/PreventEuropeIslamization1.htm.

- http://www.islam-watch.org/Warner/Taqiyya-Islamic-Principle-Lying-for-Allah.htm.

- http://www.islamweb.net/emainpage/index.php?page=articl es&id=134284. All of it is a form of al-taqiyya.

- http://www.jewishencyclopedia.com/articles/11305-names-of-god#164.

- http://www.jihadwatch.org/. All contemporary and archived articles.

- http://www.jihadwatch.org/2010/07/sharia-in-new-jersey-muslim-husband-rapes-wife-judge-sees-no-sexual-assault-because-husbands-religio.html.

- http://www.jpost.com/MiddleEast/Article.aspx?id=207415.

- http://www.mideastweb.org/islamhistory.htm.

- http://www.nationalreview.com/articles/243587/ban-burqa-claire-berlinski.

- http://www.nationalreview.com/articles/244803/muslims-mainstream-media-madness-clifford-d-may?page=1.

- http://www.politicalislam.com/. Very revealing!

- http://www.prophetofdoom.net/Prophet_of_Doom_Letter_t o_the_Reader.Islam.

- http://www.san.beck.org/1-12-NorthAfricato1700.html.

- http://www.senate.gov/~schumer/SchumerWebsite/pressroo m/press_releases/PR02009.html, retrieved on 15.01.2012. Schumer: *Saudis Playing Role in Spreading Main Terror Influence in United States* – Original Charles Schumer Press Release September 10, 2003.

- http://www.shiloahbooks.com/download/Muslim%20Histor y.pdf.

- http://www.shiloahbooks.com/download/Muslim%20Histor y.pdf. A great deal of this is questionable!

- http://www.stormfront.org/forum/t746826-14/#post8648916. Although too oriented towards all-white societies, the website does have some revealing facts on the truths behind Islam:

- http://www.thememriblog.org/.

- http://www.youtube.com/watch?v=Ib9rofXQl6w&feature= player_embedded.

- https://theislamicstandard.wordpress.com/tag/asabiyyah/.

Books

Gaubatz, David P. and Sperry, Paul. *Muslim Mafia*, WND Books, New York: 2009.

Geller, Pamela. *Stop the Islamization of America   A Practical Guide to the Resistance*, WND Books, New York: 2011.

McCarthy, Andrew C. *The Grand Jihad How Islam and the Left Sabotage America*, Encounter Books, New York: 2010.

McCarthy, Andrew C. *Willful Blindness A Memoir of the jihad.* Encounter Books, New York: 2008.

## Presentation of Terms

Through the book there will be the use of certain terms that relate to Islam. They are herewith presented alphabetically with commentary concerning the truthfulness of their meaning.

**Abrogation** Abrogation means that if there is a contradiction in the Koran, a later verse supersedes the earlier verse. The earlier verse is still correct and the latter verse does not contradict it. The earlier verse can be used to present the positive side of Islam, while the latter verse can be used to call Muslims to jihad. For example, jihad supersedes tolerance. Jihad is the other side of the coin of active world domination. Suras may contradict each other on the one side, but on the other side, they are still true. This is Islamic dualism.[2]

**Allah** Generally speaking, the terminology *Allah* has been accepted as the name of God among the Western World, Christian Arabs, and Muslims. The word has been in the English language since approximately 1584. It is a terrible acceptance and wrong translation that came into being. This author considers it the worst translation mistake in the history of literature. Allah should have remained Allah. To say that

---

[2] This is a must read: http://www.politicalislam.com/blog/statistical-islam-part-5-of-9-abrogation-and-dualism-dec-3-2010/, retrieved on 21.01.12.

15

Allah is the same as God is an insult to God! The knowledge of Islam, the Koran, Allah, and Mohammed (570-632) in the Western World and the English-speaking countries was, and still is, greatly deficient. Indeed, this is what Islam and its *scholars* desire. Have no knowledge of Islam, the Koran, Allah, and Mohammed. Just accept them!

There are two likely sources of the nomenclature *Allah.* The first possible origin is that the Islamic/Arabic term *Allah* is a derivative contraction of *al-ilāh*, (the true deity) from the Hebrew word *'Elōah* (God). This is the origin that Islam and its Muslims prefer to accept and justify. The more commonly used formal form is *Elohim*, a special usage to depict a reserved formality of respect at a distance, that can be roughly translated from the Hebrew to mean *the strong one, the powerful one.* In the Christian Bible *Elohim* is translated as God. However, *Elohim* can also mean angel or human (Second Book of Moses 4:16). The Jewish usage is that *Elohim* is *the Creator and Judge.* The terminology JHWH (*Jahweh, Yahweh*)) is considered to mean *the compassionate aspect of God. Allah* as a development from *'Elōah (Elohim)* was used by Christians in the pre-Islamic age before the end of the 3rd century AD, the time in which Arabic began to develop as a language. The etymological fact is that the origin of the substantive *al-ilāh* is neither Islamic nor Arabic. It is Hebraic. When Muslims argue that this is the source of the nomenclature Allah, they are saying at the same time that they stole the term from the Hebrew (Jewish) culture. The Koran lists ninety-nine names for Allah. Some Muslim authorities claim that there are more than ninety-nine names. In reality, these are not names. They are attributes.

The second possible and most probable origin of the term *Allah* that borders on 100 percent accuracy is that *Allah* comes from the worship of the moon. This is the origin that Islam and Muslims do not like to hear. At first, it seems far-fetched, but scrutiny and archaeological excavations prove that in North and South Arabia, even in the times of Mohammed, the dominant cult worshiped the Moon-god *Sin* (*Suen* in Mesopotamia), the title of which was *al-ilāh*, i.e., *the deity*. Notice the similarity with the Hebrew word *'Elōah*, but the differences in meaning. Another name was Hubal. This meant that *al-ilāh* was the highest god of all moon deities, of which there were approximately 360 in Arabia. The term was shortened to *Allah*, the name of a pagan god in pre-Islamic times. Professor Carlton S. Coon says that "... under Mohammed's tutelage, the relatively anonymous (Southern Arabic) *Ilah*, became *Al-Ilah*, The God, or *Allah*, the Supreme Being" of the moon-gods.[3]

Mohammed never defined who *Allah* was in the Koran because, having been brought up in the religion of the moon-god, he knew that the Arabs had a concept of who Allah was. All that Mohammed did was transform *Ilah* to *Al-ilah* and into *Allah* and proclaim the term as the collectivity of all of the moon-gods.[4] Why? Because Mohammed said that he had been told to do so by Allah. The pagan Arabs never charged Mohammed with worshiping an *Allah* different from their

---

[3] Coon, Carleton S. *Southern Arabia*, Smithsonian Institute, Washington, D.C.: 1944, p. 398.

[4] Coon, p. 399.

17

moon-god *Allah-Hubal*. The Holy Bible rightly says that such worship is idolatry.[5]

The Jews refused to accept Mohammed as the successor prophet to Jesus Christ because of this moon-god cult. Because the Jews refused Mohammed, he developed an implacable hatred against them and pursued this hatred until the end of his life. Because all Muslims are to emulate Mohammed, they must continue the adoration of the moon-god Allah-Hubal and share Mohammed's hatred of the Jews.[6] The origin of Allah is in the Arabian heathen deities. Allah is not from the Bible! Allah is Hubal and Hubal is Allah! Therefore, Islam is Hubalism!

The historical facts show that:

➢ Stars were used as pagan symbols of the daughters of *Allah-Hubal*. They are *Lat, al-Uzza,* and *Manat*.

➢ Suras 53:19-20. The Koran told Muslims to worship *al-Lat, al-Uzza,* and *Manat*. Those suras, called *The Satanic Verses,* have been abrogated out of the present Koran.

➢ The Arab tribes gave the moon-god different titles: *Sin (Suen), Hubal, Ilumquh, Al-ilah.*

➢ The title *al-ilāh* (the deity) was used for the Moon-god.

➢ The word *Allah* was derived from *al-ilāh*.

➢ *Allah* was only one of many Meccan gods in the Kaaba.

---

[5] Deuteronomy 4:19; 17:3; II Kings 21:3-5.

[6] Consult the complete discussion of this aspect in Gibbon, Edward. *The History of the Decline and Fall of the Roman Empire*, David Womersley, editor, 3 Vols., Penguin, New York: 1994, Chapter 50.

➤ The pagan *Allah* was a high god in a pantheon of 360 deities worshipped at the Kaaba.

➤ The Muslims placed a statue of *Hubal* on top of the Kaaba; at that time *Hubal* was considered the moon-god.

➤ The Kaaba was the *house of the moon-god* and the name *Allah* eventually replaced that of *Hubal* as the name of the moon-god.[7]

➤ Approximately 400 years before Mohammed's birth, a man named Amr bin Lahyo bin Harath bin Amr ul-Qais bin Thalaba bin Azd bin Khalan bin Babalyun bin Saba, a descendant of Joktan[8] and king of Hijaz (the northwestern section of Saudi Arabia, which encompassed the cities of Mecca and Medina), had placed a Hubal idol onto the roof of the Kaaba. This idol was one of the chief deities of the ruling Quraysh tribe. The idol was made of red agate. It had the form of a human being. However the right hand had been broken off and had been replaced with a golden hand. After the idol was moved inside the Kaaba, seven arrows were placed in front of it. They were used for divination.[9]

---

[7]    http://www.theologyweb.com/campus/archive/index.php/t-52114.html, retrieved on 25.02.2012. http://www.leaderu.com/wri/articles/islam-singh.html, retrieved on 21.01.12. http://www.faithfreedom.org/Articles/skm 30804.htm, retrieved on 21.01.12. Read also Moshay, G.J.O. *Who Is This Allah?* Dorchester House, Bucks, United Kingdom: 1994.

[8] According to the Second Book of Moses, 10:25, Joktan was a descendant of Noah's son Shem and the great-great-great uncle of Abraham.

[9]    Sarwar, Hafiz Ghulam. *Muhammad: the Holy Prophet*, Muhammah Ashraf, Lahore, Pakistan: 1961, pp.18-19.

Dr. N. A. Newman, in the conclusion to a study of early Christian-Muslim controversies, states, "Islam proved itself to be ... a separate and antagonistic religion which had sprung up from idolatry."[10] Islamic scholars claim the concept that Allah is a moon-god is a religious fantasy created by those who are anti-Islam. Yet, archeological-cultural-etymological research proves that Allah was first used as a title of a moon-god. Some critics consider this position antiquarian, just as the origin of god is not exactly known. Although some scholars have traced the etymology back to the South Arabian *Ilah*, the title of the moon-god, this presentation of historical fact is also considered antiquarian.

If this position is antiquarian, then Islam is antiquarian because it is founded on a truth (?) that is antiquarian. The critics and scholars argue that Nabataean inscriptions show that Allah (*Ilah*) means *god* and not *moon-god*.[11] However, Nabataean inscriptions show that the Nabataean use of god was not the Jewish and Christian meaning of God. The Arab-Islam conception from the Nabataean belief was oriented toward the moon. The final word on the matter comes from the renowned professor of history and Islamic scholar Caesar E. Farah (1929-2009). "There is no reason, therefore, to accept the idea that Allah passed to the Muslims from the Christians and Jews."[12]

---

[10] Newman, N. A. editor. *Three Early Christian – Muslim Debates*, Ibri, Hatfield, Pennsylvania: 1994, p. 719.

[11] Guillaume, Alfred. *Islam*, Penguin, Harmondsworth, England: 1990, p.7.

[12] Farah, Caesar. *Islam: Beliefs and Observations*, Barrons, New York: 1987, p. 28.

**Fig. 1. The moon-god Hubal from all four sides.** Note the crescent moon carved on Hubal's chest. Hubal was the chief god of all of the 360 gods (sun and moon gods) revered by the pagan Arabs in the Kaaba. Source: http://www.biblebelievers.org.au/images/muslim.jpg, retrieved 28.02.2012. The image is in the public domain.

If, however, Allah did come from the Jews, and is not a moon-god, then

➤ Why were the main idols deified by the pagan Arabians those with a symbol of the moon on their chest?

➤ Why did Mohammed's tribe, the Quraysh tribe, have as their symbol the crescent moon?

➤ Why is the crescent moon the symbol of Islam?

➤ Why is the crescent moon placed on top of the mosques and minarets?

➤ Why is a crescent moon found on flags of Islamic nations?

➤ Why do Muslims fast only throughout Ramadan, the month that begins with a crescent moon and ends with a crescent moon in the sky?

➤ Why is the Islamic year based on a lunar calendar?

➤ Why do Islamic pilgrims to Mecca kiss the *Hadschar al Aswad* (black stone) in the Kaaba and worship *Yamin Allah* as a sign of meteorite worship that Mohammed claimed was the *Yamin Allah*, the right hand of the moon-god?

➤

**Fig. 2. Worshiping *Yamin Allah*** at the *Hadschar al Aswad* (black stone). The terminology *Yamin Allah* is Arabic for *the right hand of Allah*. When one kisses the *Hadschar al Aswad* (Black Stone) that person is doing Islam. This means that the person is performing Islam. The proper way to kiss the *Hadschar al Aswad* is to place one's hands on the wall of the Ka'ba in the same position as when one performs prostration while praying (sajdah). If it is not physically possible to kiss the *Hadschar al Aswad* the person can just touch it. If this is not possible it is permissible to point to it and blow a kiss. Mohammed loved stones, especially black ones. For him a black stone was a better friend than a dog.
Source: http://www.bibliotecapleyades.net/imagenes_mistic/meteorite13.jpg, retrieved on 28.02.12. The image is in the public domain.

The *Hadschar al Aswad* is sacred to the Muslims because they believe that it came from the moon and was given to them by Hubal, their moon-god. Why did Mohammed kiss this black stone if Allah was a different god than Hubal?[13] If Allah was/is different from Hubal, then Mohammed would have been committing blasphemy and Muslims are committing blasphemy by joining other gods with Hubal. When Muslims pay homage to *Yamin Allah* they are saying that they swear the stone is from the moon-god Hubal.

This author contends that nowadays *Allah* is neither the Christian God nor the *Elohim* of the Jews. Discussions with Muslims support this contention. Avid Muslims have told the author that there is only *Allah*. There is no Christian God and there is no Jewish *Elohim*. Because Jews, Christians, and all other religious adherents are non-believers in Islam, they cannot really have a God, and if they claim that they do have a God, that God is anti-Allah. *Allah* is for the Muslims only and for those who convert to Islam. The non-believers, therefore, have no god. Muslims argue that the pre-Islamic Christians and Jews made their God and *Elohim* into a farce. Muslims claim that the Islamic belief developed the nomenclature *Allah* from *'Elōah* (*'Elohim*) in order to make the Hebrew God pure, because Muslims contend that Islam is the purest of all religions. Yet, because the Islamic *Allah* sanctions evil against non-believers, which is held to be sacred by the Koran and the behavior of Mohammed, such immoral acts have no ethical core and, therefore, cannot be a religion in the sense of the

---

[13]  http://answering-islam.org/BehindVeil/index.html was retrieved on 25.02.2012. Click from there.

morality and ethics of the Judeo-Christian religious world. The conclusion is that Islam is not a religion! It is an ideology containing religious phraseology and at best quasi-reformed paganism. As such, it was never enlightened and it was never tolerant. Likewise, it will never be enlightened and it will never be tolerant!

Many Islamic sources voice a great deal of illogical arguments to prove that Allah is not a moon-god. It is fact that Islamic internet sites have to go far out of the way of logic and archaeology to prove that Allah is comparable to the Christian and Jewish God. After 1,600 years of believing in the one Allah (Hubal), Islamic dogma has no choice but to attempt to prove that Allah exists and the Jewish and Christian God do not.[14]

Muslims quote the Koran 41:37: "And among His signs are the night and the day and the sun and the moon; do not make obeisance to the sun nor to the moon; and make obeisance to Allah Who created them, if Him it is that you serve."

The sura should be understood with caution. It has a double meaning. Major translations of the Koran 41:37 that this author knows use the word *worship* instead of *obeisance*. *Obeisance* means *to bow, to lie face down as if one is in humiliation or adoration*. *Worship* means *to show reverent love and allegiance to a deity*. Therefore, if the Arabic word means to prostrate, then the Muslims are not showing *reverent love and allegiance to a deity*.

---

[14]    http://www.islamic-awareness.org/Quran/Sources/Allah/moongod.html, retrieved on 26.02.2012.

Meaning 1: Muslims will argue that this sura is proof that their Allah is the same as the Christian and Jewish God. However, Muslims also know that Allah and the moon-god Hubal are one and the same pagan deity. The meaning behind this sura of the Koran is this: when you prostrate, do not prostrate to the object the sun or to the object the moon, but prostrate to Allah, the name of a particular god considered by the pagan Arabs to be the highest god among the 360 gods that the pagan Arabs honored in the Kaaba. This was prostrating to the deity of the moon, the supreme moon-god, in this case to Allah, another term for the moon-god Hubal. Do the Muslims not say that Allah is the greatest of all the (360) gods? The Israelites knew Yahweh is Elohim. The Arabs knew Allah is Hubal.

Meaning 2: The second aspect concerning Koran 41:37 is that the verse shows that Jewish and Christian influences have taken over Mohammed's teaching. These influences subtly converted Mohammed's moon-god Hubal (Allah) into the Supreme God of all without Mohammed realizing what had happened. However, Mohammed's and the Muslims' scapegoat argument is that Mohammed never mentions Hubal in the Koran. The reason for the non-mention is that Mohammed knew that all Arabs knew that Allah was Hubal. For Muslims today it is still Allah is Hubal! Otherwise, they are apostates!

The symbol of this moon-god, the crescent moon, did not come into existence with the Ottoman Turks! It was constantly found on ancient pottery or artifacts of worship. It has been shown that "the worship of the moon-god *Suen* (also called *Nanna* or *Asimbabbaar*) was the most wide-spread religion in the Middle East.[15] Islam adopted the crescent moon as its pagan, religious symbol because of the pre-Arabic tradition of revering their moon-god(s). In Mesopotamia, the word *Suen* was transformed into the word *Sin* by the Sumerians as their favorite name for the moon-god.[16] Is it possible that worshipping the moon-god Allah-Hubal is a sin? The Old Testament condemns the worship of the moon-god because it caused Israel to commit idolatry.[17]

While the name of the moon-god was *Sin*, his title was *al-ilah* meaning *the deity*. *Ilah* is a generic Arabic word for *god* or *deity*. "The god *Il* or *Ilah* was originally a phase of the Moon God."[18] The pre-Islamic Arabs shortened *al-ilah* to Allah. Children were given the name *Alla(h)*. Mohammed's father and uncle had a form of *Allah* as part of their names. "Similarly, under Mohammed's tutelage, the relatively anonymous Ilah, became Al-Ilah, The God, or Allah, the Supreme Being."[19] Yet, the origin was the moon-god. Mohammed used Allah as a collective terminology for pre-Islamic pagan deities and ordered that his followers worship all of them with one title: Allah. Therefore, Ibn Warraq is correct when he states, "Islam

---

[15] Hall, Mark. *A Study of the Sumerian Moon-god, Nanna/Suen*, University of Pennsylvania Press, Philadelphia: 1985, is the best study of this topic.

[16] http://www.bible.ca/islam/islam-photos-moon-worship-archealolgy.htm, retrieved on 29.02.2012, and Potts, Austin. *The Hymns and Prayers To The Moon-god, Sin*, Dropsie College, Philadelphia Pennsylvania: 1971, p. 2.

[17] *Deuteronomy* 4:19; 17:3; *Second Kings* 21:3-5 and others.

[18] Coon, p. 398.

[19] Coon, p. 398.

also owes the term *Allah* to the heathen Arabs. We have evidence that it entered into numerous personal names in Northern Arabia and among the Nabataeans. The terminology Allah occurred among the Arabs of later times, in theophorous names, and on its own."[20]

The Hebrew YHWH, (modern Jehovah), has a meaning like *he who causes to exist* or *who gives life*, whereby the idea of the root word is probably *to breathe*, and hence, *to live*.[21] There is no comparable meaning in the terminology Allah, Hubal, or Allah-Hubal. Allah-Hubal must be accepted as being static and not vigorous with life.

The hajj pilgrimage, fasting for a complete month during the hours of daylight, and praying five times a day facing towards Mecca were also pagan rituals.[22]

---

[20] Warraq, Ibn. *Why I Am Not A Muslim*, Prometheus, Amherst, New York: 1995, p. 42.

[21] http://www.jewishencyclopedia.com/articles/11305-names-of-god#164, retrieved on 27.02.2012.

[22] Armstrong, Karin. *Jerusalem: One City, Three Faiths*, Balantine Books, New York: 1996, p. 221. "Each year the tribes would assemble from all over the peninsula to take part in the arduous and intricate rites of the *hajj* pilgrimage, Christian Arabs alongside the pagans. By Muhammad's time, the Ka'bah was dedicated to the Nabataean deity Hubal and surrounded by effigies of the Arabian pantheon, but it may well originally have been the shrine of Allah, the high god." Ramadan denotes the environment of intense heat, scorched ground, and a shortness of food rations. Prior to Islam Ramadan was the month Natiq, which came in the dry season. http://en.wikipedia.org/wiki/Ramadan#cite_note-1, retrieved on 22.02.2012. *Salah* is Arabic for the ritual communication with Allah, praying. Praying has occurred in all cultures, pagan and non-pagan. The ritual of praying is that a Muslim must face Mecca and pray five times a day. A *fatwa* (juristic

Mohammed never attacked Hubal because he knew that Allah and Hubal were the same. The Meccans worshipped Allah (Hubal) in the Kaaba because it

- was the deity of Mohammed's tribe, the Quraysh,

- was the main heathen god,

- was the same heathen god Mohammed and the pagan Arabs worshipped,

- was the same heathen god Mohammed proclaimed,

- was the same heathen god that the pagan Arabs had worshipped for centuries.

Just as the Israelites knew Yahweh as Elohim, the pagan Arabs knew Hubal as Allah and vice-versa. The fact that Mohammed proclaimed that Allah is the name does not make a difference.

**Al-Taqiyya** "The word *al-Taqiyya* literally means: *the concealing or disguising of one's beliefs, convictions, ideas, feelings, opinions, and/or strategies at a time of imminent danger (decided by the Muslim), whether now or later in time, to save oneself from physical and/or mental injury.*"[23] A good English word is *dissimulation*. *Al-Taqiyya* is a behavior in Islam that allows a Muslim to tell the truth, to lie, to be moral, to be immoral, to be ethical, to be unethical, to obey the law, or to commit crimes as long as the Muslim is protected and the spread of Islam is assured. A Muslim would call *al-Taqiyya* the

---

ruling) issued in Turkey stated that a Turkish Muslim has to pray only three times a day.

[23] http://www.al-islam.org/encyclopedia/chapter6b/1.html, retrieved on 21.01.2012.

*process of holy deception* as dictated by Mohammed! Deception is not a sin when it advances Islam. Deception against the non-believers is essential because non-believers do not understand the dual ethics of Islam.

A Muslim must not lie to another Muslim unless it makes the other Muslim feel good. A Muslim must not lie unless there is no other possible way of achieving the Muslim's goal. Islamic Arabic is the only language in the world that has the concept of al-taqiyya. Who tries to convince the world that Islam is a religion of peace? Muslims! Who tries to convince the world that jihad is not the real Islam? Muslims! For Muslims jihad is at the core of Islam. For the non-believers they will believe that *jihad* means *inner struggle* only.

Closely allied to al-taqiyya is the use of **kitman**, which means *leaving out part of the truth about something*. It is like taking a partial oath to tell the truth, but not the whole truth. Many times in public discussions, Muslims will argue that the truth about jihad is that it is nothing more that the inner struggle. Muslims will not tell you the complete spectrum and ramifications of jihad.

A second al-taqiyya-allied strategy is **muruna.** Muruna means *flexibility,* as in Barack Hussein Obama will show Russia more muruna after his re-election. On Victory Day in Egypt there were two million Egyptians chanting *To Jerusalem we march, martyrs by the millions.* Sheikh Yusef Abdallah al-Qaradawl is an Islamic leader who appeared before the two million chanters and egged them on with the strategy of muruna that the Egyptian Muslim Brotherhood developed in 1989 during a meeting with other Islamic leaders in the Middle East.

29

The muruna strategy sanctions the use of deception and lying because it has the same final result desired by the Koran and Mohammed: the dominance of sharia law throughout the world. Part of the muruna strategy is a so-called doctrine of balance. This means that there can be a balance between good and evil, and if the good and evil conflict with each other, Muslims make the priority as to when they put evil ahead of good for the sake of an interest, and determine when an evil deed is forgiven for the sake of an interest.[24] These lying strategies are encompassed by *tawriya*, the doctrine of lying in all circumstances.

Arabic is the language of Islam. As such, Arabic is an integral part of the world-conversion politics of Islam. Arabic is a vanguard language opposed to non-Muslim cultures and non-Arabic languages, mainly those of the Western World.

**Arab** In an Akkadian language record of the 9th century BC called the Monolithic Inscriptions, the term Arab appears for the first time in documented history. The origin of the nomenclature rests with three possibilities.

1.     The term Arab comes from a man named Yarab (also spelled Yarrob, Ya'rob, Yarrob, or Yar'ub, or Yaarub), the grandson of the biblical Eber and son of the biblical Joktan. Some Arabic accounts say that he is the grandson of Jokton. (Yarrob bin Yashjub bin Qahtan). Yarab was an ancestor of the Himyarite kings of Yemen.[25] Thus, Yarrob *is the forefather and thus founder of al-'Arab al-'Ariba (the arab arabs, pure arabs)*,

---

[24]    http://www.therightscoop.com/walid-shoebat-explains-islamic-muruna, retrieved on 17.02.2012.

[25]    van Donzel, E. J. *Islamic Desk Reference, compiled from the Encyclopaedia of Islam*, E. J. Brill, Leiden: 1994, p. 483.

normally identified with the Qahtanites and the two main tribes the Himyar and the Kahlan.[26] Some sources contend that Yarab was the first to person to speak Arabic. This is the reason why the language is named after him.[27] Arabic language specialists credit him with being the founder of the Kufic script.[28]

2.      Another view is that the Arab people were really the GhArab, which in the Semitic language means *west*, because the Arabs were located in the west of Mesopotamia. GhArab was changed into the short form Arab.

3.      The term Arabs and the people come from the Ishmaelites, the descendants of Ishmael, the oldest son of Abraham, who were located in the Arabah Valley. This valley runs in a north-south direction from the Sea of Galilee to the Dead Sea and ends in the Gulf of Aqaba.

The word Arab is found often in the Semitic languages. Its word-root means *west*, *sunset*, *desert*, *mingle*, *merchant*, and *raven*. It is also possible that the word-root means *moving around*, thus shading into the word *nomadic*.[29]

---

[26] Prentiss, Craig R. *Religion and the creation of race and ethnicity: an introduction.* NYU Press, New York: 2003, p. 172.

[27] Sperl, Stefan; Shackle, C.; Awde, Nicholas. *Qasida Poetry in Islamic Asia and Africa: Classical traditions and modern meanings - Volume 20 of Studies in Arabic literature*, E. J. Brill, Leiden: 1996, pp. 138, 209.

[28] Sperle and Shackle. p. 136. Thackston, Wheeler McIntosh. *Album prefaces and other documents on the history of calligraphers and painters: Volume 10 of Studies in Islamic art and architecture*, E. J. Brill, Leiden, 2001, p. 7.

[29] Grunebaum, G. E. von. *Classical Islam: A History 600 A.D. - 1258 A.D.,* Aldine Publishing Company, Chicago: 1970, p. 16.

**Claiming of land** As used in this book the claiming of land or making land claims means that someone makes a declaration of desired control over areas of property including bodies of water. That declaration is often in legal terms. Nowadays the land claim is used with respect to disputed property. The phrase is generally used with respect to disputed or unresolved land claims. In the days of exploration, discovery, and colonialism, a person could claim a piece of land for himself, in the name of a government, and most often, in the name of the monarch. The process involved nothing more than to state that the land was being claimed in the name of King XYZ or Queen XYZ, regardless of the fact that aboriginal natives *possessed* (occupied) the land before the arrival of the explorers. This was usually sanctioned and notarized by a priest, or by the previous emission of a royal charter. The act of claiming land was made law by the placement of the mother country's flag affixed to the flag pole into its soil. In modern times land claims by country are no longer possible, except when one country invades another and claims that the land invaded had always belonged to the invader. A prime example is the claim by Palestinians that Israel belongs to the Palestinians because it has always belonged to them, which is not the historical case.

**Denial of Islam** If a Muslim claims that s/he is an apostate and the goal is to save oneself or to deny any allegiance to Islam for the purpose of not endangering Islam, then that person is really advancing her/himself and Islam. This situation has serious consequences for the United States of America. All government officials, congresspersons, judges, and service personnel, municipal servants, etc., must take an oath to support the *Constitution for the United States of America*. Yet those persons who are Muslims know that Islam and sharia take precedence over all of the systems of law. Therefore, such an oath of office taken by a Muslim in the United States of America is meaningless. Taking this fact into consideration, it is a very convincing argument that no Muslim should occupy a position of public office at any level of government in the United States of America. This would not be discrimination on the part of the United States of America, but discrimination established by Islam itself, for Islam states that Islam is supreme.

**Dhimmi and dhimmitude** The word *dhimmi* means *one whose responsibility has been taken*. The dhimmi exist only in the dogma of Islam and the rules of the sharia. A dhimmi is a non-Muslim who loses all responsibilities of his/her own and is placed under protection and receives rights of residence in return for the obligated payment of taxes to the Islamic government because that person has been subdued. Islam proclaims that the dhimmis are equal to Muslims under the sharia laws of property, contract, and obligation, but there is no guarantee that their rights will be upheld. **Dhimmitude** is the Islamic system in which conquered peoples are placed.

**Discovery** Discovery means nothing more than finding something that is new, or something that has always been present, but it was not known to be present. Discovery is closely related to the term exploration, particularly when one culture makes initial incursions into the geographical area of a different people and intrudes on their culture. In the Age of Discovery, which is also called the Age of Exploration (15th to

17<sup>th</sup> centuries), the Chinese and the Europeans discovered the new continents and adjoining lands like islands, the peoples of these new continents, and their adjoining lands, although they and their populations had already existed for millennia.

**Exploration** As used in this book the exploration of the New World has to do with investigating, examining, studying, or searching throughout or ranging over a region of the earth for the purpose of discovery.

**Hadith** A hadith is an act, saying, or unspoken approval that is validly or invalidly ascribed to Mohammed. The Sunni (Abu Bakr- and Umar-sourced hadiths) and Shia (Ali-sourced hadiths) divisions of Islam have their own hadith collections.

**Islam** is usually defined as *the religion of the Muslims*. This author contends that it is an ideology couched in a religious disguise. The term *Islam* comes from the Arabic *islām*, meaning *resignation, surrender, and submission*, with the connotation that surrender is made *to the will of Allah*. The Arabic term *islām* comes from the word root *aslama*, meaning *he resigned or surrendered*, which in turn is related to *salima*, meaning *he was safe*, and the well-known term *salām*, which comes from the Jewish *shalom*. In the seventeenth century the term *Islam* was understood to mean an orthodox Muslim. By about 1817, it became part of the English language with *The Revolt of Islam*, a poem in twelve cantos by Percy Bysshe Shelley (1792-1822). In Islam the person resigns and gives surrender and submission to a moon-god. In Judaism the ethical person is an individual who is freethinking, not coerced, and unimpressed. Freedom in Judaism and Christianity liberates people from domination by cults. Freedom is a political

34

principle that is to be sanctified and consecrated to God, but not to *Allah*. In Islam's goal of world domination the basic stages of Islam are that Muslims first set out to conquer foreign lands in hope of gaining riches, territory, slaves, and then total world domination.[30]

**Islamic ethics** This is a seeming contradiction in terms. There is an Islamic ethic and a non-Islamic ethic. Therefore, Islamic ethics are of a fundamental dualism. Dualism in Islam is the basis of that dogma's view of ethics. For example, for the Muslims, Islam is peace. But the Koran says that for the kafirs[31] (non-believers), Islam is war. The Sira, the traditional Muslim biographies of Muhammad about his life and Islam's early period, and the Koran show that Islam as a peaceful religion was a failure. Integrity is not possible in a dualistic system. Because Islamic ethics are dualistic in their nature there is no integrity in Islam. If it is a virtue to lie, regardless of the reason for lying, then there can be no integrity.

**Jihad** is based on ethical dualism. The goal is to force the non-believer to submit to Islam. Mohammed attacked his enemies in order to force them to submit to the Moon-god Allah-Hubal. The rejection of Allah-Hubal is the logic for killing the non-believer. As such, jihad is a defensive measure because the offensive behavior comes from the non-believers.

**Kafir (Kaffir)** This term originally referred to an ancient Iranian people who lived in Nuristan in Afghanistan,

---

[30] Read http://answering-islam.org/Authors/Arlandson/ultimate_goal.htm, retrieved on 21.01.2012.

[31] The Koran spellings are Kafir, Kuffar, and Kufr It is used 470 times in 451 different verses.

35

possibly named as such because they planted seeds for crop growing and covered them with earth. The word root *K-F-R* is a pre-Islamic term that means *to cover*. For Muslims the term transposes into a *non-believer* because a person hides or covers the self from the true religion: Islam. Islam first applied the term to the Meccans who at the beginning refused to submit to Islam. In Old Arabic *kafir* means *unthankful*.

**Mosque** is the term for *a place of prayer or worship*. It is not a church. There is an early spelling *muskee*, or *moskee*, which is borrowed from the Middle French *mosque*, itself coming from Italian *moschea*, which is an alliteration of *moscheta*, and this in turn is from Spanish *mezquita*, a transliteration from the Arabic word *masjid* as it comes from *sajada*, meaning *he prayed*. In early Middle English we also find *moseak* and *moseache*, dating from the early fifteenth century.

**Muslim** (also **Moslem**) is the terminology for a believer in Islam, which is the ideological teaching of Mohammed and the Koran. The word *Muslim* literally means *one who professes submission to the belief of Islam*. Its root is *aslama*, meaning *he resigned, he submitted*. Where a Muslim is there is Islam. Where Islam is, the people have to be forced to become Muslims.

Regardless of what attribute is being used by the most pious Muslim who always and ever tries to imitate the life of Mohammed, we know that from Mohammed on the Muslims have justified all of their evilness as being the divine will of Allah: from *jihad* to *dhimmitude*, from honor killings to discrimination against women and so-called non-believers. By claiming that all of the evils committed by believers in the ideology of Islam are the will of Allah, the original Hebrew-culture God (*'Elōah*) was stripped of all of its moral and ethical essence. The justifications for these evils are all in the Koran, as written down by the questionable merchant person and pedophile Mohammed, who took the child Aisha as his bride when she was six years old and consummated the marriage when she was nine. Whether or not the Koran allows it, or whether or not the Islamic law (sharia) that is in conformity with the Koran allows it, pedophilia is pedophilia! If Mohammed is a prophet, he is one with many blemishes, to say it truthfully.

**Muslim brotherhood/sisterhood** All Muslims are brothers and sisters, but each in their segregated group.

**Salafism** This movement in Sunni Islam considers that only the generation of Mohammed and the three following generations, are the orthodox Islam. All other branches of Islam are not the true dogma and must not be observed. Therefore, it is closely related to Wahhabism, which, indeed as a movement is extremely close to Salafist Islam. It is a literal and purist presentation of Islamic dogma. Salafists are prime jihadists, although everyone who believes in Islam is a jihadist, either active or passive.[32]

**Shiites** or Shias are the followers of Shia Islam. Shia is the abbreviated form of the historic Islamic phrase *Shī'atu 'Alī*,

---

[32] http://www.fas.org/sgp/crs/misc/RS21695.pdf, retrieved on 21.01.2012.

meaning *followers of Ali, faction of Ali,* or *party of Ali.*[33] Shiites believe in the Koran and the messenger Mohammed. They believe that only Allah can choose a leader of Islam. They pay homage to Ali as the legal successor to Mohammed. Ali was the first imam, a leader of a mosque and Muslim community. The Shiites claim that Mohammed selected Ali to be his successor. Ali was seen as being without error and infallible (having no sin). Ali is known as the perfect man, just like Mohammed.

**Sunni Islam** are the Sunni Muslims, in Arabic *'Ahl ūs-Sunnah wa āl-Jamā'ah,* meaning *people of the tradition of Mohammed* as well as the consensus of the umma, the world community of Islam. We know them in English as Sunni Muslims, Sunnis or Sunnites. This is orthodox Islam. The word *Sunnah* in Arabic means *the sayings and actions of Mohammed.* They are recorded in hadiths, a so-called collection of narratives concerning Mohammed, what he did and what he said. The hadiths are considered to be accurate and authentic as coming from Mohammed. The hadiths and the Koran are the basis of Sunni law. The hadiths are written in *Sahih Bukhari* (870), *Sahih Muslim* (875), *Sunan al-Sughra* (915), *Sunan Abu Dawood* (888), *Jami al-Tirmidhi* (892), and *Sunan ibn Majah* (887).

**Political correctness** On the one hand, this author takes the standpoint that political correctness is a form of lying and even more so, a form of brainwashing. Political correctness

---

[33] *The New Encyclopædia Britannica,* 15th Edition, Encyclopædia Britannica, Inc., Chicago, Illinois: 1998, Vol. 10, p. 738; *The Term* Shia *in Quran and Hadith,* Al-islam.org, retrieved on 06.03.2012.

uses behavior, ideas, language, and policies in such a manner as to not make any offense regarding age-related situations, belief, culture, disability, gender, ideology, occupation, race, religion, or sexual orientation. This is often observed to such an excessive extent that the realities of life are buried in useless phrases. Thus political correctness is negative. On the other hand, this author takes the standpoint that political incorrectness is positive because it includes behavior, language, and ideas that are not constrained by any perceived properness or regard about expressing bias or offending age-related situations, belief, culture, disability, gender, ideology, occupation, race, religion, or sexual orientation. One can be politically incorrect without being insulting. Political incorrectness is the truth!

**Sharia law** The teachings of the Koran, Mohammed, and the sharia are the foundation of Islam. There is really no other kind of law in Islamic countries because laws in Islamic countries must conform to the principles and rules of sharia law. sharia law comes from the guidelines written in the Koran, from the examples established by Mohammed, and from the Sunnah (custom), the exact words, the habits, the practices, and the silent sanctions of Mohammed or those attributed to him.

**Slavery** In Islam all references to a person freed from slavery are with the terminology *free slave*. There is not one reference that says that humankind is one unit. All references to humankind are dualistic: Muslims vis-à-vis kafirs. Contrary to popular belief and acceptance, Islam was the prime source of the re-institution of slavery. Mecca was a large distribution center for slaves.[34] Without Islam and Mohammed there would have been no post-Roman Empire slavery.[35]

**Wahhabism** originated with Sheikh Muhammad ibn Abd al-Wahhab (Muhammad ibn Abd al-Wahhab ibn Sulaiman ibn Ali ibn Muhammad ibn Ahmad ibn Raschid at-Tamim, 1703-1792), an Arabian fundamentalist and extremist Islamist who founded the Wahhabi movement in the eighteenth century. The Sheikh made a pact with Muhammad bin Saud to establish the first Saudi empire and thus began a dynastic alliance between both families, who today share the power in Saudi Arabia. The Saudi family is responsible for the political matters and the Wahhab family is responsible for the religious matters. Wahhabism is a movement to purge Islam of all impurities and matters that are not original to pure Islam. Wahhab claimed that all additions to Islam after the third century (ca. 950 AD) were false and must be eliminated from Islamic life. A true Muslim is one who adheres strictly to the original teachings of Mohammed and the Koran.[36] The present King of Saudi Arabia, Abdullah bin Abdul-Aziz Al Saud, is a devout Wahhabite.

---

[34] Crone, Patricia. *Meccan Trade and the Rise of Islam*, Georgia Press, Piscataway, New Jersey: 2004, p. 80.

[35] O'Neill, John J. *Holy Warriors Islam and the Demise of Classical Civilization*, Felibri Publications, jonplotinus@googlemail.com., pp. 149f.

[36] http://www.fas.org/sgp/crs/misc/RS21695.pdf, retrieved on 21.01.2012. http://www.sultan.org/articles/wahabism.html, http://atheism.about.com/od/ islamic sects/a/wahhabi.htm, both retrieved on 21.01.12.

# CHAPTER TWO

# The Pre-Columbian Era

## The Koran and World Domination

There is no possible way that Mohammed (c. 570-632), real name Abū Al-Qāsim Mohammed Ibn 'Abd Allāh Ibn 'Abd Al-Mut-Ṭalib Ibn Hāshim, the self-appointed Arabian prophet and self-named founder of Islam,[37] would have known the size of the world, its various continents and its peoples, to say nothing of their beliefs. However, Mohammed would not have cared, for Mohammed definitely believed that Islam should and would dominate the world, regardless of the size and expanse, as well as the rise of forces against Islamic expansion and domination. Of course, Muslims claim that because he was a prophet Allah-Hubal would have given him this information.

---

[37] The meaning of the name is interesting. *Abū Al-Qāsim* means *the father of Qasim* (Quasim has numerous meanings: the spreader of things to people; the separator who divides good from evil, the unifier who fits things together.) *Mohammed* means *the praised one. Ibn 'Abd Allāh* means *son of the servant of Allah. Ibn 'Abd Al-Mut-Ṭalib* means *son of the servant searched by his own will, who needs nothing and no one, but everyone needs him. Ibn Hāshim* means *son of Hashim.* Hashim is the name of Mohammed's great-grandfather for whom the clan Banu Hashim is named. It is one of the oldest and most honorable clans of the Quraish Arabian tribe, mainly because Mohammed was a member of this tribe. *Hashim* means *crusher of evil* as well as *broker. Banu* is a feminine appellation for females meaning respected *noblewoman.* It could also mean noble, used for both a man and a woman. In Nepalese *Banu* means the *sun.* The present author has found no explanation for the association of the feminine name *Banu* for women with the masculine name *Hashim.*

41

There are three fundamental verses in the Koran that state the unequalled omnipotence of Islam over all other religions. It is thus accepted fact that Mohammed did realize that there would be other cultural groupings outside of his limited, knowable, physical, geographic location. The pertinent suras are:

Sura 9:33 *He it is Who hath sent His messenger with the guidance and the Religion of Truth, that He may cause it to prevail over all religion, however much the idolaters may be averse.*

COMMENT: Judaism and Christianity were the most important beliefs against which Mohammed competed and conducted his crusades. The rhetoric that he uses is vitriolic. Islam is superior to them and will prevail over them. Mohammed introduced the idea of a crusade long before the Europeans used this form of politics to free the Holy Land from the evil Mohammedans (c. 1095-c. 1272). The basis of sura 9:33 is violence and war. Previously, in sura 9:29 the word *fight* is used. It is in this context that sura 9:33 must be understood. Muslims must fight Jews and Christians who do not submit to Islam, whether by conversion or by paying the tax to be second-class citizens, which was really below any citizenship status. This is the policy that the Muslims must use when Mohammed is no longer alive. Mohammed died in 632. The Muslims adopted the policy of sura 9:29. Islam teaches and Muslims believe that the only available choices for Jews and Christians are that Jews and Christians must fight and consequently die, or pay a tax for protection, which is no Islamic guarantee that their lives will be spared in the long run, or convert to Islam.

<u>Sura 48:28</u> *He it is Who hath sent His messenger with the guidance and the religion of truth, that He may cause it to prevail over all religion. And Allah suffices as a Witness.*

COMMENT: This sura repeats sura 9:33. Again Islam is supposed to triumph over all religions. War against the unbelievers is always present in Islam. Because Mohammed was victorious in his extermination of those who refused to believe in Allah-Hubal, Islamic terrorists and all Muslims consider Mohammed an inspiration.

<u>Sura 61:9</u> *He has sent His messenger with the guidance and the true religion, and will make it dominate all religions, in spite of the idol worshipers.*[38]

COMMENT: Islam will triumph over its adversaries in warfare. By the time this sura was communicated, Mohammed had replaced Jesus Christ as the savior of the world because Mohammed says that it is so. Mohammed has become the anti-Christ and his power is not based on salvation through grace, but through violence, treachery, evilness, and warfare.

It is a fundamental rule of Islamic philosophy that if a land has at one time in history belonged to Islam, it is the will

---

[38] Sura 61:9 was most likely issued after the Battle of Uhud in March of the year 625. A'la Maududi, Sayyid Abdul. *The Meaning of the Qur'an*, Vol. 5, Markazi Maktaba Islami Publishers, New Delhi: 2006, pp. 487, 489. Mohammed led the Muslims against the Meccans at the Battle of Uhud, March 16, 625. The Meccans won, but they did not decimate Mohammed's army which defeated the Meccans on March 31, 627 near Medina in the Battle of the Trench also known as the Battle of Ahzab, as well as the Battle of the Confederates and the Siege of Medina. Thereafter Islam became firmly established in the region. The Meccans were relegated to a position of little importance. http://en.wikipedia.org/wiki/Battle_of_the_Trench, retrieved on 21.01.2012

of Allah-Hubal that it shall always belong to Islam. Thus, Islam claims that Spain must be reconquered, because it belonged to Islam seven hundred years, from 711 with the invasion by Tariq ibn Ziyad (???-720), to the *Reconquista* in 1492 under the leadership of Ferdinand II (1452-1516) and Isabella I. (1451-1504).[39] Moreover, there is also the argumentation that wherever a Muslim sets his foot, that land belongs to Islam, for Allah-Hubal sent him there as a messenger to insure the expansion of Islam. We find the following statement fourteen times in the Koran: "And to Allah belongs the kingdom of the heavens and the earth." The logic is that Allah-Hubal created the heavens and the earth (suras 5:17; 120) and therefore everything belongs to him. Because Muslims are Allah's servants, they are to prostrate themselves and show awe, respect and obedience to Allah and Mohammed upon the soil to which Allah has directed them. That is the Islamic land claim for Allah and Islam.[40]

Islamic scholars believe that these three verses quoted above are the prophecies that unflinchingly prove that Islam will become the only world power. These verses have been used to spread Islamic violence repeatedly. The verses have also been used to lay claims to land that Islam never knew existed. As such, the Islamic logic of expansion is that whenever and wherever a Muslim appears in a foreign land, regardless of the historical age, it is only logical according to

---

[39] This is no surprise. http://atgsociety.com/2011/03/muslims-aim-at-reconquering-spain/, retrieved on 11.03.2012.

[40] Murata, Sachiko. *The Tao of Islam: a sourcebook on gender relationships in Islamic thought*, State University of New York Press, Albany, New York: 1992, pp. 129 ff.

the Koran that that land must become Islamic, otherwise Allah would never have made it possible for that Muslim discoverer or explorer to be physically present in said new country. This viewpoint is so encompassing that it is retroactive so as to include all places where a Muslim was before there was Islam, for Islam maintains that only Islam is the complete and valid religion. Therefore, it encompasses all time and places. With this Islamic logic as the raison d'être of discovery, exploration, and land claiming, it is only obvious that all geographical landmasses of the world will eventually become dominated by Islam because Allah and Mohammed will it.

## The Ishmael Connection

In order to justify his (self-) calling as a prophet, Mohammed had to prove his genealogical relationship to Abraham. Therefore, he declared that he was a direct descendant of Ishmael. In *Genesis* 17:18, we read that Abraham pleaded for the future of his son Ishmael, saying, "If only Ishmael might live under your blessing." God answered in *Genesis* 17:20-21, "As for Ishmael, I have heard you; I will surely bless him ... (and) will make him into a great nation. But my covenant I will establish with Isaac, whom Sarah will bear to you." In *Genesis* 21:12-13 we read that God reaffirmed Isaac as the first heir, "It is through Isaac that your offspring will be reckoned. I will make him (Ishmael) into a nation also, because he is your offspring." Mohammed stated that since the Jews had soiled their Book, Allah decreed to Mohammed via the Angel

Gabriel that they must be punished and that Mohammed would be the last of the prophets and become the savior of the world.[41]

There are many Muslim genealogical lines that link Mohammed as a direct descendant of Ishmael. Perhaps the best known follows this genealogy.[42]

1 Abraham Hanifa (AS) was the father of

2 Isma'il (AS) was the father of

3 Kedar was the father of

4 'Adnaan was the father of

5 Ma'add was the father of

6 Nizaar was the father of

7 Mudar was the father of

8 Ilyaas was the father of

9 Mudrikah was the father of

10 Khuzaimah was the father of

11 Kinaanah was the father of

12 Al-Nadr was the father of

13 Maalik was the father of

14 Quraysh was the father of

---

[41] Richardson, Don. *Secrets of the Koran Revealing Insights Into Islam's Holy Book*, Regal Books, Ventura, California: 2003. This aspect is explored at length, particularly on pp. 30-63.

[42] http://genesisden.musicdot.com/genealogy.htm, retrieved on 31.01.2012. http://myafrica.wordpress.com/2006/10/02/is-ishmael-the-father-of-prophet-Mohammed/, retrieved on 31.01.2012.

15 Ghaalib was the father of

16 Lu'ayy was the father of

17 Ka'ab was the father of

18 Murrah was the father of

19 Kilaab was the father of

20 Qusayy was the father of

21 'Abd Manaaf was the father of

22 Haashim was the father of

23. 'Abdul Muttalib was the father of

24 'Abdullah was the father of

25 Mohammed


The Islamic historian Mohammed ibn Ishaq (704-767/768) and early biographer of Mohammed gives the direct genealogy of Mohammed back to Adam.[43]

The following list has a total of forty-nine generations. Being lenient and allowing forty years as a generation places Adam's creation approximately in the year 1410 before the birth of Christ, which is really quite difficult to believe when knowing the history of the world and the discovery of the first humans in Africa. However, the point is that for Mohammed to claim authority from God (not Allah?), there has to be proof

---

[43] http://genesisden.musicdot.com/genealogy.htm, retrieved on 31.01.2012. See other discussions of Mohammed's genealogy and proofs that they are all faked in Guillaume, Alfred translator of *The Life of Mohammed*, 10th edition, Oxford University Press, Karachi: 1995.

that he has a direct lineage in order to be a prophet and a holy person. Islamic logic claims that the fact that all non-Muslims are non-believers proves the truth of the lineage of Mohammed.

1. Adam, father of

2. Sheeth, father of

3. Yaanish, father of

4. Qaynan, father of

5. Mahlil, father of

6. Yard, father of

7. Akhnookh, father of

8. Mattooshalakh, father of

9. Lamk, father of

10. Nooh, father of

11. Saam, father of

12. Arfakhshadh, father of

13. Shaalikh, father of

14. Aybar, father of

15. Faalikh, father of

16. Raa'oo, father of

17. Saaroogh, father of

18. Naahoor, father of

19. Tarih, father of

20. Ibraheem, father of

21. Ismaa'eel, father of

22. Naabit, father of

23. Yashjub, father of

24. Ya'rub, father of

25. Tayrah, father of

26. Naahoor, father of

27. Muqawwam, father of

28. Udd (Udad?), father of

29. 'Adnaan, father of

30. Ma'add, father of

31. Nizaar, father of

32. Mudar, father of

33. Ilyaas, father of

34. Mudrika, father of

35. Khuzayma, father of

36. Kinaana, father of

37. al-Nadr, father of

38. Malik, father of

39. Fihr, father of

40. Ghaalib, father of

41. Lu'ayy, father of

42. Ka'b, father of

43. Murra, father of

44. Kilaab, father of

45. Qusayy, father of

46. 'Abdu-Manaaf, father of

47. Haashim, father of

48. 'Abdul-Muttalib, father of

49. 'Abdullaah, father of

50. Mohammed

When we add the Islamic-believed logic that "starting from Adam (down to) the last Messenger of Allah, every person Allah has sent for the guidance of mankind with the key ... *there is none to be obeyed other than Allah, i.e., the sovereignty of Allah followed by the name of the particular person declaring him to be a Messenger of Allah,* ... and that every Messenger was sent to a particular region of the earth, to a particular people for their guidance in a certain point in the process of evolution of mankind, and our leader was sent for the guidance of the whole mankind for all time to come ... to prevail ... over all other ways of life," [44] then every Muslim is a Messenger of Allah and wherever a Muslim is located, Islam had/has an Allah-given ordainment to be established in that region of the earth and to be supreme over all other beliefs.

---

[44] Panni, Mohammad Bayazeed Khan. *The Five Itemized Agenda for Establishing Islam.* The article is difficult to read because of the faulty English. See http://www.hezbuttawheed.com/component/content/article/1-displayhome/6-thefiveitemedagendaforestablishingislam that was retrieved on 31.01.2012.

This logic is the basic starting point for making claims that Muslims and Islam were the first to discover and occupy the various geographical parts of the world because they had an Allah-given command. It is not important that other peoples were already living in these regions which Mohammed, Islam, and Muslims never knew existed. It is not important that lands were claimed in the name of ruling monarchs, regardless of their home country. It is not at all important that international laws regulated and still regulate the claims to international territories.

It is important that Islamic demagogues maintain that Islam is Allah's and Mohammed's perfect guide to make the world subservient to the will of Allah and the will of Mohammed. There are no other options. Nothing can happen without the knowledge and consent of Allah. Therefore Allah, via Mohammed, gave his consent that every Muslim is a Messenger of Allah. Allah, via Mohammed, gave his consent that regardless of where a Muslim is located, Islam had/has an Allah-given commandment to be established in that region of the earth. Allah, via Mohammed, decreed that Islam is to be totally supreme over all other beliefs to the extent that all other beliefs are to be exterminated by jihad and the establishment of Islamic law, known as sharia law.

# CHAPTER THREE

# Claims that Muslims Discovered
# The New World

## Prelude

There are a number of assertions that Muslims (Islam) discovered the New World. Practically 99 percent of all Islamic sources place the emphasis on the fact that Muslims as a force of spreading Islam were at the fore of discovery and exploration. Because the persons who believe in Islam's Allah, their moon-god, are called Muslims, the terms *Islam* and *Muslims* are inseparable and thus as messengers of Allah they made geographical discoveries. Therefore, not only did Muslims discover the New World, Islam was a part of the discovery as well. The Muslim (Islam) assertions of discovering the New World are listed in chronological order.

## ➢ Claim 1: The Appearance of Kufic Arabic in America

In *Saga America*, Dr. Barry Fell contends that in addition to the Vikings landing in northeastern North America, there were North Africans (Berbers), Phoenicians, Arab-Iberians, and Arabs who made landfalls in North America.

Dr. Fell says that the Pima people of the American Southwest possessed a vocabulary that contained words of Kufic Arabic origin, Yet examples of such words are not available. Kufic Arabic is the ancient calligraphic form of Arabic writing. Arabs claim this script was their invention and they named it after the place where it was invented: Kufa, Iraq. However, the script is a modification of Nabataean script and was thus known in Mesopotamia approximately one hundred years before the establishment of the city of Kufa. Kufic Arabic was already in use in the Arabian Peninsula before Islam was started by Mohammed.[45] The first Korans were written in Kufic Arabic. Dr. Fell also uncovered an early rock carving (undated) in Inyo County, California, with the inscription *Yasus ben Maria* (Jesus, Son of Mary).[46] Only Arab scholars have attested that this is the correct translation of the inscription. Dr. Fell also claimed that he had discovered the existence of Muslim (Libyan Muslim) schools in Nevada, Colorado, New Mexico, and Indiana dating back to 700-800 which taught arithmetic, agricultural sciences, geometry, etc.[47] However, Islamic schooling consisted in the study of the Koran, Mohammed's life, and sharia law. Interest in science only began in the eleventh and twelfth centuries. Keith Fitzpatrick-Matthews, an angry archaeologist and an opponent of pseudoarchaeology, dismisses Dr. Barry Fell's *discoveries* as fringe archaeology.[48]

---

[45]http://www.caroun.com/Calligraphy/aCalligraphyGeneral/Kufic/KuficScript.html, retrieved on 23.01.2012.

[46] Fell, Barry. *Saga America*, Times Books, New York: 1980, p. 173.

[47] Fell, *Saga America*, pp. 296-340.

[48] Fitzpatrick-Matthews, Keith. *Barry Fell. Cult and Fringe Archeology*, no page, 28 March 2006, available at http://kjmatthews, retrieved on 23.01.2012.

In his books *America B. C.: Ancient Settlers in the New World*, *Saga America*, and *Bronze Age America* Dr. Fell argues that the first people who came to America were not necessarily white people only, but were a mixture of North Africans (Berbers), Phoenicians, Iberians (Moors), and even Arabs. According to Dr. Fell, these peoples were interracial mixtures of the tribe of Dan, the thirteenth tribe of the Israelites. They came to Britain in settlement waves and these population waves reached America long before Christopher Columbus discovered the West Indies in 1492. The theory continues that Israelites (Arabs contend that Israelites were pre-Arabian Arabs) had already begun leaving the area of Israel-Judea long before the Babylonian Exile, sometimes called the Second Exodus, in 586 BC.[49] Indeed, they had begun to establish settlements in Greece, Troy, Spain, and portions of Europe as early as 1700 BC. Fell expands his theory to maintain that groups crossed the Atlantic approximately 3000 years ago and began to colonize America. They came from the Iberian Peninsula via the Canary Islands with trade winds and settled along the New England coast, established villages, temples, and even Druidic circles. They were followed by Phoenician traders from Spain, who spoke Punic and wrote in a script called Iberian. Dr. Fell says that some, along with Egyptian traders, stayed in North America and became part of the Abenaki/Micmac Indians.[50] Dr. Fell

---

[49] This should not be confused with the First Exodus in the thirteenth century BC when Moses led his people, the Israelites, out of Egyptian captivity.

[50] The Wabanaki (Wabenaki) are officially known as the Ab(e)naki, a confederation of Algonkian-speaking Indian tribes in the northeast of North America that formed for resistance and protection against the Iroquois League, especially the Mohawk Indians. They were decimated by the

claims that some words in the Wabanaki (Abenaki/Micmac) languages have their roots in Arabic.[51] Dr. Fell also claims that a marking dated approximately 700 AD has been found in Nevada. The text reads *Nabi 'llh Mohamed* (Mohammed is the Prophet of Allah). This is a half a world away from Mohammed's homeland and is dated 68 years after Mohammed's death. Mohammed spread Islam throughout the Arabian Peninsula (622–632). The Rashidun Caliphate (632–661) expanded Islam into Egypt and the Middle East to Afghanistan and Pakistan. The Umayyad Caliphate (661–750) expanded Islam into Western North Africa and Iberia. According to Dr. Fell, Muslims were in Nevada by the year 700.[52] If the Umayyad Caliphate's expansion into Western North Africa and Spain were the lands from which Muslims launched their voyages to the Americas, then they were exceedingly expedient in doing so to have arrived in present-day Nevada by the year 700 AD. Dr. Fell's assertion has not been backed up by other, independent researches. Not even the history of ships or sailing has shown that Arabs could have crossed the Atlantic Ocean at this early date. Moreover, no historical written records have been found.

Dr. Fell provides a list of words that occur in the Abenaki/Micmac language which he claims are the same or similar to Arabic words. Yet, some of them are the same in

French and English starting in the seventeenth century and in the wars of 1724-1725. They have become concentrated nowadays at Saint François-du-Lac, Quebec. Their population is about 10,000.

[51] *Saga America*, pp. 400-404.

[52] *Saga America*, p. xiv.

Ptolemaic Greek, as well.[53] Thus, they might not have originated with the Arabic language, which crystallized as a language in the 7th century. Although no specific date of settlement is recorded, anthropologists generally consider that the Abenaki/Micmac Indians had already existed on the Eastern coast of North America by the time of Jesus Christ. Whether or not there was any contact with Arabic may be a moot point, because words can enter a language in many ways. More corroborative research is necessary. Nevertheless, Dr. Fell's word list is given below.

## Mariners and Navigation

| English | Abenaki/Micmac | Arabic |
|---|---|---|
| coastal seas | sobagwa | sobagwa |
| magnetic compass | el-ugwech | al-hukk |
| plumb, level | el-amkadu | a-immam |
| mast, rigging | el-dukadegw | al-daqal |
| sail, spread sail | siba- | sabih |
| cordage | pelum | barin |
| journey afar | aksit | aqsa |
| wind, weather | awan | ahwa |

## Astronomy and Meteorology

| | | |
|---|---|---|
| dew | nebiskat | naba saqt |
| sunrise | sposw | asbah |
| immediate | nitta | nitaij |
| by night | niboiwa | nabiha |
| star | alakws | alaq (twinkling) |
| constellation | kulokawechk | el-kaukab |

---

[53] http://dnaconsultants.com/_blog/DNA_Consultants_Blog/tag/Cajuns/, retrieved on 23.01.2012.

| falling rain | soglon | seqlaba |
| rainbow | managwon | mantaqa (girdle) (used for zodiac) |
| tomorrow | saba | sabah |

## Justice and Administration

| false statement | kabawa | kabwa (false step) |
| punishment | kalama- | kalal |
| insolent, malicious | majigo | majin |
| authority, king | malki- | malk |
| king | el-Agawit | el-Agelid (Libya) |
| master | al-susit | al-ustethj |

## Medical and Anatomical

| affliction | kalama- | kalal |
| coitus | lamo- | l'am |
| ill | madadmalso | madad+mall |
| orgasm | lawa | lau'a |
| adolescent | kiabes | kabr |
| nose | kiatam | kiatam |
| adolescent girl | kwet | qatauta |
| libido | kaza-l'mo | qassa (yearn for) + l'am (coitus) |
| youth | na-kabet | na+kabr |
| sneeze, cough | nakwhomo | nakam |

## Household and Clothing

| belt | taktek (pima tkak) | tikak |
| waist-cloth | nesunk | naazala-aniq |
| drink, water | nipi, naba | naba (spring) |
| to hold, handle | lum | lams |
| to thread | napa | nafad |

Complementing this supposed early settlement of America, the Basques, mariners from the Iberian Atlantic coast, settled in Pennsylvania; Libyan and Egyptian sailors settled in the Mississippi River Valley from the Gulf of Mexico as far north as Iowa and the Dakotas, as well as along the Arkansas River and Cimarron River. The Norse and Basques reached as far north as the Saint Lawrence Gulf and introduced much of their vocabulary into the language of the Algonquian Indians.[54] Several of the Amerindian tribes, according to Dr. Fell, speak dialects that can be traced back to the ancient languages of Phoenicia and North Africa, where the Tribe of Dan, which was a division of the Israelites, intermarried.[55]

To bolster the claim of a transatlantic transfer of language, Dr. Fell, in a lecture conducted at the *Proceedings of the Castleton Conference on Ancient Vermont*, October 14-15, 1977, presented the audience with a replica of an inscription

---

[54] A. J. B. Johnston, *Mathieu Da Costa and Early Canada: possibilities and probabilities*. Mathieu Da Costa is the first recorded free Black man who lived in Canada. Source: http://canadachannel.ca/HCO/index.php/Mathieu_Da_Costa_and_Early_Ca nada,_by_A._J._B._Johnston, retrieved on 19.01.2012.

[55] Howard Barraclough "Barry" Fell (emeritus of invertebrate zoology, Harvard University) *America B. C.: Ancient Settlers in the New World,* Quadrangle Books, New York: 1976; *Saga America*, Times Books, New York: 1980; and *Bronze Age America*, Little, Brown, Boston: 1982. For a discussion of some terms, jargons, and pidgins, consult Ives Goddard, *The Delaware Jargon* in *New Sweden in America*, edited by Carol E. Hoffecker et al., University of Delaware Press, Newark: 1995, pp. 137–149; John A. Holm, *Pidgins and Creoles*, Vol. 1: *Theory and Structure*, Cambridge Language Surveys, Cambridge University Press, Cambridge, U.K. & New York: 1988; Ives Goddard, ed., *Handbook of North American Indians*, Vol. 17: *Languages*, Smithsonian Institution, Washington, D.C.: 1996; and Bruce Trigger, ed., *Handbook of North American Indians*, Vol. 15: *Northeast*, Smithsonian Institution, Washington, D.C.: 1978.

that was found in a cave in central Texas. The University of Texas reported and cataloged it as a *sun sign*. Fell stated, "the Arabic inscription underneath, which says 'sun disc,' was reported as a black vermiform pictograph[56] – which tells its own story. Other examples of Old Arabic from New England are in Harvard University Museum." Dr. Fell then showed the audience an Algonkian manuscript that he had from the Cree Indians, which was written sometime between 1820 and 1850. Evidently, the manuscript was written by a child who was being directed by a priest who had learned the Cree language. Dr. Fell continued, "It says 'Manito saki,' 'God is Love' and the lower line says 'Kee-che-a-ya-ya,' the 'Great Spirit.' Show that (text) to an Arab who is learned in the ancient forms of his language and he will read it as 'M-N-T,' 'muntaj.' The next line is 'S-K,' 'saki,' 'God is Love,' or 'Allah is Love'; the next line 'Kee-che,' will bother him a bit; and the last one, 'a-ya-ya,' 'the Spirit,' 'Human Spirit.' So three of those four words are almost the same in Arabic, and their writing system is obviously Arabic. So here is another source of an American Indian alphabet, and some of the language, at least. That writing script is also used by the Ojibway Indians, and (showing a slide picture) that is what it would look like if the same thing was written in the script of Palmyra, in Syria, of about 200 A. D."[57]

---

[56] Resembling or having the long, thin, cylindrical shape of a worm; a worm-shaped pictograph.

[57] Fell, Barry. *Vermont's Ancient Sites and the Larger Picture of Trans-Atlantic Visitations to America, B. C.* in *Ancient Vermont, Proceedings of the Castleton Conference, Castleton State College*, October 14-15, 1977, edited by Warren L. Cook, published for Castleton State College by the Academy Books of Rutland, Vermont: 1978, pp. 70-84, specifically p. 81.

At this point, three matters deserve commentary. Firstly, 'S-K,' 'saki,' can mean that 'God is Love,' but it cannot mean that 'Allah is Love' because etymologists have shown that Allah is not the nomenclature for God. It is a nomenclature for a moon-god.[58] Secondly, Arabic applies to the language descendants of classical Arabic from the 6$^{th}$ century AD and crystallizing in the 7$^{th}$ century. Classical Arabic is also called Koranic Arabic and is considered a holy language by Muslims because the Koran was written in this language. Thirdly, the language of Palmyra, Syria in approximately 200 AD was Syriac, which developed from Old Aramaic in Assyria located in northern Mesopotamia. It was not Arabic. Therefore, there is not a foolproof connection from Arabic to Algonquin (Cree, Ojibway) via Palmyra, Syria in approximately 200 AD. These conflicts need to be resolved.

➢ Claim 2: Khashkhāsh ibn Sa`īd ibn Aswad, 899/933

Khashkhāsh ibn Sa`īd ibn Aswad (no dates) was born in Pechina, Andalusia, Islamic Iberia. The Muslim historian Abu al-Hasan 'Alī al-Mas'ūdī (871-957) wrote that Khashkhash Ibn Saeed Ibn Aswad, with a number of young men from the city of Córdoba, fitted ships and sailed into the Atlantic Ocean to search for new lands in 899. Upon his return Ibn Aswad reported that he had discovered *Ard Marjhoola*, the literal

---

B. C. in the title means Before Columbus, not Before Christ. The Cree Indians and the Ojibwe Indians belong to the Algonquian language group.

[58] Consult http://www.shiloahbooks.com/download/Muslim%20History, http://www.letusreason.org/islam6.htm; or http://www.bible.ca/islam/islam-allah-pre-islamic-origin.htmm, both retrieved on 24.01.2012.

translation of which is *unknown land*. He drew a world map calling these areas in the Atlantic Ocean *the unknown land*. As proof of this discovery, Ibn Aswad brought strange animals and plants. Present-day archaeologists and historians argue that Ibn Aswad may have found new lands in unknown regions of Africa. Nonetheless, his voyage gave rise to new expeditions into the Atlantic Ocean and perhaps resulted in the discovery of South America, with the possible establishment of colonies there in 933.[59] Abu al-Hasan 'Alī al-Mas'ūdī in his book *Muruj adh-dhahab wa maadin aljawhar* (956 AD) writes that Khashkhash Ibn Saeed Ibn Aswad, from Delba (Palos de la Frontera) sailed into the Atlantic Ocean in 889 and returned with a shipload of valuable treasures.[60] The 'Alī al-Mas'ūdī book provides the following description of the Ocean of Darkness and Fog, the Atlantic Ocean.

"In the Ocean of Fogs [the Atlantic] there are many curiosities which we have mentioned in detail in our Akhbar az-Zaman, on the basis of what we saw there, adventurers who penetrated it on the risk of their life, (sic) some returning back

---

[59] http://de.althistory.wikia.com/wiki/Ard_Marjhoola, retrieved on 24.01.2012.

[60] Khair, Tabish. *Other Routes: 1500 Years of African and Asian Travel Writing*, Signal Books, Oxford: 2006, p. 12. Two different translations of Ali al-Masudi's book are: *The Meadows of Gold and Mines of Gems* and *The Book of Golden Meadows*. Al-Masudi *Muruj Adh-Dhahab*, Vol. 1, p. 138. http://www.multilingualarchive.com/ma/enwiki/de/Khashkhash_Ibn_Saeed_Ibn_Aswad. Khashkhash Ibn Saeed Ibn Aswad was a Moorish admiral. It is only an unproved theory that Christopher Columbus had access to Al-Masudi's map at the Spanish court. The Mas'udi map is at http://cartographic-images.net/Cartographic_Images/212_Masudi.html, and was retrieved on 24.01.2012. Some sources give al-Mas'udi's birth year as 896.

safely, others perishing in the attempt. Thus a certain inhabitant of Cordoba, Khashkhash by name, assembled a group of young men, his co-citizens, and went on a voyage on this ocean. After a long time he returned back with booty. Every Spaniard knows this story."[61]

> ➤ Claim 3: Ibn Farrukh of Grenada, 999

Abu Bakr Ibn Umar Al Gutiyya recorded that another Muslim navigator Ibn Farrukh of Granada sailed from Kadesh into the Atlantic Ocean sometime in February of 999. He landed at Gando (Gran Canaria) of the Canary Islands and then continued westward until he reached two other islands. One of them he named Capraria, possibly after the island in the Tuscan Archipelago off Italy, Capraia, located 30 kilometers from the French Island of Corsica. It is volcaninc, like the Canary Islands. Ibn Farrukh named another island that he supposedly discovered Pluitana, the present-day nomenclatures of which are not known. It may have been another island in the Canary Island group. Ibn Farrukh returned to Spain in May of 999.[62]

---

[61] Hamidullah, Mohammad. *Muslim Discovery of America before Columbus*, in *Journal of the Muslim Students' Association of the United States and Canada*, 1968, 4, 2, pp. 7-9. Akhbar az-Zaman can be translated as *History of Time*, http://islam.wikia.com/wiki/Al-Masudi, retrieved on 24.01.2102, which also references the Arabic source Agha Hakim, Al-Mirza *Riyaadh Al-Ulama*, Vol. 2, p. 386 and Vol. 4 p. 175.

[62] Khai, Tabish. *Other Routes: 1500 Years of African and Asian Travel Writing,* Signal Books, Oxford: 2006, p. 12. Tabish Khai also references the Arabic source Al-Ameen, Sayed Mohsin. *Aayan Ash-Shia*, Vol. 7, p. 158 and Vol. 8, pp. 302-3. For purposes of authenticity, it is important that these

> Claim 4: North African Muslim Sailors in the 1100s

According to the famous Arab geographer Al Sharif al Idrisi (1097-1155), "A group of seafarers sailed into the Sea of Darkness and Fog (the Atlantic Ocean) from Lisbon in order to discover what was in it and to what extent were its limits. They were a party of eight and they took a boat that was loaded with supplies to last them for months. They sailed for eleven days till they reached turbulent waters with great waves and little light. They thought that they would perish so they turned their boat southward and traveled for twenty days. They finally reached an island that had people and cultivation but they were captured and chained for three days. On the fourth day a translator came speaking the Arabic language! He translated for the king and asked them about their mission. They informed him about themselves, then they were returned to their confinement. When the westerly wind began to blow, they were put in a canoe, blindfolded and brought to land after three days' sailing. They were left on the shore with their hands tied behind their backs. When the next day came, another tribe appeared freeing them and informing them that between them and their lands was a journey of two months."[63]

There are as many valid indications that the Caribbean peoples spoke some kind of language similar to Arabic as well as the possibility that they did not. Perhaps the tie-in is the

---

theories of Arab discoveries of the New World be further confirmed by archaeologists, epigraphers, and linguists.

[63] This statement is quoted from the *Geography of Al Idrisi*, http://www.oocities.org/mutmainaa/history/muslim_caribbean.html that was retrieved on 29.01.2012.

Kufic Arabic that Dr. Barry Fell claims to have been spoken and written in the Americas after 646 AD when some Libyan merchants arrived in the Americas,[64] or the arrival of Libyans even before 500 BC, when they spoke a language similar to the Phoenicians.[65]

## ➤ Claim 5: Muslim Sailors, 1178

There are two geographical Sung documents by two Chinese authors. The first, *Ling-wai tai-ta* was written by Zhōu Qù-Fēi in 1178. The second, *Chu-fan-chih* was written by Zhào Rŭ-Gùa in 1225.[66] In these documents both authors contend that Muslim sailors voyaged across great waters and eventually reached a place called Mu-Lan-Pi, which archaeological authorities associate with Spain. However, some other authorities, mainly Muslim, claim that Mu-Lan-Pi is some part of present-day California. These latter authorities thus claim that the Muslims show the earliest record of pre-Columbian trans-oceanic voyages from Eurasia to the shores of North America. The controversial point is that there are indications that the Sung document is not authentic and that identification of the region Mu-Lan-Pi as being on the western coast of North America is exceedingly doubtful. The very widely respected

---

[64] Fell, *America B. C. Ancient Settlers in the New World* pp. 239 ff; *Ancient Vermont*, p. 82.

[65] Fell, *America B. C. Ancient Settlers in the New World*, pp. 174-191.

[66] Li, Hui-lin. *Mu-lan-p'i: A Case for Pre-Columbian Transatlantic Travel by Arab Ships*, in the *Harvard Journal of Asiatic Studies*, Harvard-Yenching Institute, 1960-1961, 23, pp. 114–126.

historian Joseph Needham does not rule out this possibility, yet he is very doubtful that the sailing quality of Arab ships would have survived a return trip to Europe, particularly since they did not have knowledge of the currents and the prevailing Atlantic winds over the distant Atlantic Ocean. The Portuguese sailors supposedly discovered how to use these prevaling currents and winds five centuries after the so-called discovery of North America by the Muslim sailors.[67] From 711 to 1249 Portugal (Al-Garb Al-Andalus [the land west of Al-Andalus]) was under Moorish control. It is very unlikely that it took Portuguese sailors five hundred years to discover what the Moors knew of the prevailing Atlantic currents and winds.

> ➢ Claim 6: Sheikh Zayn Eddine Ali Ben Fadhel Al-Mazandarani, 1291

There are many internet sites which claim "the journey of Shaikh Zayn Eddine Ali Ben Fadhel Al-Mazandarani across the Atlantic has been well-documented." (sic) It is claimed that during the reign of the Marinid King Abu-Yacoub Sidi Youssef (1286-1307) the sheikh sailed to Green Island in the Caribbean Sea in the year 1291. Particularly on Islamic internet sites the phrase *well documented* means that statements are often repeated. They rely on each other for their documentation.[68]

---

[67] Joseph Needham, Joseph and & Colin A. Ronan, Colin A. *The Shorter Science and Civilisation in China*, Cambridge University Press, Cambridge: 1986, p. 120.

[68] Some interesting examples are: http://www.bostani.com/Discovered; http://www.whyMohammed.com/es/Contents.aspx?AID=4626; http://www.imamreza.net/eng/imamreza.php?id=6683htm;

## ➤ Claim 7: Abu Bakar I and Mansa Musa, 1311-1312

Bata Manding Bory was crowned Mansa Abu Bakar I in 1310. He was interested in the sea to the west of Mali. According to an account given by Mansa Musa I, Mali sent two expeditions into the Atlantic Ocean. This king's goal was to find out how what defined the western boundary of the Malian Empire. Abu Bakar I left Mansa Musa as regent of the empire, and departed in 1311 on the second expedition with 4,000 pirogues (long flat boats, not ships) that were equipped with sails and oars. He probably landed in Recife, Brazil. Mansa Musa claims that one of the boats returned to Mali. There is skepticism among modern historians that both voyages had success. However, there are both Malian written accounts and Malian oral tradition accounts of these voyages.[69] Such sources are considered to be valid documentation of these happenings and of contact with South America.

Many Islamic internet sources state that Mansa Musa gave a narration of the voyages when he was in Mecca making his famous hajj pilgrimage in 1324. Mansa Musa reported that

---

http://www.beforebc.de/Related.Subjects/Queen.Califia.and.California/Afric ansPredateColumbus-TheAbundantEvidence.html, all retrieved on 30.01.2012.

[69] http://news.bbc.co.uk/2/hi/africa/1068950.stm retrieved on 29.01.2012.
According to Dr. Youssef Mroueh's article *Pre-Columbian Muslims in the Americas* at http://sunnah.org/history/precolmb.htm, the Muslim historian Chihab ad-Dine Abul-l-Abbas Ahmad ben Fadhl al-Umari (1300-1384) described in detail the geographical explorations beyond the sea of fog and darkness of Mali's sultans in his famous book *Massaalik al-absaar fi mamaalik al-amsaar* (*The pathways of sights in the provinces of kingdoms*). Al-Asfahani, Ar-Raghib, *Adharea Ila Makarim Ash-Shia*,Vol.16, p. 343, and Cauvet, Giles. *Les Berbers de L'Amerique*, Paris 1912, pp. 100-101.

for the first voyage, "Abu Bakar equipped 2000 ships filled with men and the same number equipped with gold, water, and provisions, enough to last them for years ... they departed and a long time passed before anyone came back. Then one ship returned and we asked the captain what news they brought. The captain replied to Mansa Musa, 'Yes, O Sultan, we traveled for a long time until there appeared in the open sea a river with a powerful current ... the other ships went on ahead, but when they reached that place, they did not return and no more was seen of them ... . As for me, I went about at once and did not enter the river.' Abu Bakar left me (Mansa Musa) to deputize for him and embarked on the Atlantic Ocean with his men. That was the last we saw of him and all those who were with him. And so, I became king in my own right."[70]

For some Muslim and Arab scholars who are intent on proving that Muslims and therefore Islam were pre-Columbian discoverers of America, this is ample evidence that African Muslims from the Kingdom of Mali and other parts of West Africa (Mandinka) actually arrived in the Gulf of Mexico, the great river being identified by such so-called scholars as the Mississippi River that served as an access to the middle of North America, thus facilitating contact with the indigenous natives. Their claims are further corroborated by the research accomplished by the historian and linguist, Leo Weiner, who already in 1920 wrote that Christopher Columbus knew of the Mandinka settlements and presence in the New World. Leo Weiner further claims that West African Muslims had spread

---

[70] http://niger1.com/?tag=sundiata-keita, retrieved on 29.01.2012.
http://niger1.com/?tag=abu-bakari-ii, retrieved on 29.01.2012.

throughout the Caribbean, into Central, South and North America, even as far north as Canada. According to him, West African Muslims had traded and intermarried with the Iroquois and Algonquin Indians.[71] Yet, this does not mean that Muslims discovered America.

There is botanical evidence that Africans were in some manner acquainted with the New World. Professor M. D. W. Jeffreys of Witwatersrand University in South Africa has done extensive study of corn that was original to the inhabitants of South America, but is not at all endemic to Africa. He mentions studies of the pollen statistics of at least ten varieties of maize. His conclusion is that the South American variety of maize was introduced to the West Coast of Africa long before Columbus discovered America. His deduction is that African traders had contact with South American peoples before the age of discovery.[72] However, saying that these African traders were Muslims as Islamists do, and as Professor Jeffreys does not, is exaggerating the matter of discovery out of all proportion. Yet if the Islamists repeat it often enough, even without documentation, people will eventually believe it as fact and the history books on the Age of Discovery will be rewritten in favor of Islam. Allah-Hubal and the self-proclaimed prophet Mohammed will hug each other. In joy the Kaaba will spin in a circle, bore a hole in the ground, and hit oil!

---

[71] Wiener, Leo. *Africa and the Discovery of America*, Philadelphia: 1920, Vol. 2, pp. 365-6. This information is questionable.

[72] Jeffreys, M. D. W. *Pre-Columbian Maize North of the Old World Equator*, in *Cahiers d'études africaines*, 1969, Volume 9, Numéro 33, pp. 146-149.

> ## Claim 8: The Chinese Admiral Zheng He, 1421

The eighth claim/exposition that a Muslim discovered America is by Rowan Gavin Paton Menzies, a retired British submarine commander, who writes in his book *1421: The Year China Discovered the World*, that the fleet of the Chinese Admiral, Zheng He, arrived on the west coast of America and thus became the first to discover America seventy-one years before Christopher Columbus sighted land in the New World.[73]

Zheng He's original name was Ma He.[74] He was a young boy when the Chinese army officer Zhu Di campaigned against the Mongol Empire forces that occupied the mountainous province of Yuan in southwestern China. In 1382, Zhu Di was ordered to destroy the city of Kunming, located to the southwest of the Cloud Mountains, which was the only remaining Mongol stronghold. After the city was burned the Chinese butchered the adults and castrated the young boys who had not reached puberty. Many were conscripted into the Imperial Army. One of these boys was Ma He. Zhu Di took him into his household and changed his name to Zheng He. Many of the Mongols had adopted the Muslim faith and Zheng He was no different. Some accounts claim that Zheng He was "over two meters tall, weighed over one hundred kilos and had a stride like that of a tiger."[75] Zheng He was a feared soldier and

---

[73] Menzies, Gavin. *1421: The Year China Discovered America*, William Morrow, New York: 2003. There is another independent source at http://www.chinesediscoveramerica.com/, retrieved on 30.01.2012.

[74] The following account can be found in Menzies, pp. 46-74.

[75] Hoobler, Dorothy and Thomas. *Images Across the Ages: Chinese Portraits*, Raintree Publishers, Austin Texas: 1993.

an exceedingly devout Muslim. Zheng He eventually became Zhu Di's advisor. As the Prince of Yen, Zhu Di located himself in the Mongol capital Ta-tu and renamed it Beijing. In the struggle for the throne of China, Zhu Di eventually won out, seized the Dragon Throne, and named himself emperor, taking the dynastic title Yong Le, the third Ming Emperor. Zheng He became Grand Eunuch. Within a year Zheng He was appointed Commander-in-Chief of the largest Chinese fleet ever.

After consolidating the empire against the threats of the Mongol Tamerlane, having pacified Manchuria, and having brought Korea and Japan into the Chinese system of paying tribute, the emperor ordered Zheng He to set sail and explore the regions of Asia and the Middle East. Zheng He embarked on 5 March 1421. Menzies makes documented claims that although Zheng He did not personally make landfall in the Americas, his fleets did circumnavigate the world, possibly four times between 1421 and 1426, and they did land in North America, explored the following regions and established some settlements: the Caribbean, the Floridas, the Carolinas, the Virginias, New England (Massachusetts, Boston), New York, Mississippi, Upper Arizona, New Mexico, Texas Oklahoma, Arkansas, Colorado, California, Oregon, and British Columbia.[76]

This author's conclusion is that these statements do not support claims that Muslims, even some historical Chinese persons believing in Islamic dogma, discovered the Americas. There is no factual basis.

---

[76] Menzies, Appendix I, pp. 493-595.

> ➤ Claim 9: Rodrigo de Triana or Rodrigo de Lepe, 1492

Supposedly, after the return to Spain, Rodrigo de Triana or Rodrigo de Lepe, made his way to Africa and became a Muslim convert. Whether this was done out of spite, or to save himself from being killed as a non-believer, is open to debate.[77] What is known is the fact that Rodrigo de Triana, or Rodrigo de Lepe, the lookout on the ship *La Pinta*, was the first white person to see the Americas. Christopher Columbus did not give him any recognition for being the first Christian to see the American land. The captain of the *Pinta*, Martín Alonso Pinzón verified the sighting of land and signaled such to the other two ships.

It must be stated that neither the Arabs nor the Chinese ever laid claim to the new lands. As far as the Chinese are concerned, their reasoning in the history of discovery is that they were not interested in claiming these new lands at the time that the Chinese Muslim Zeng He made the discoveries. China was interested in discovery and exploration for the sake of trade. However, these voyages were the proof of the value of their historical inventions and development of scientific instruments used in navigation.

Both of these theories (Muslim and Chinese discoveries) and so-called new historical data must be corroborated by independent, academic, and archaeological experts. Otherwise the claims are only historical curiosities. The prevailing Muslim logic is that the Muslims did not have to

---

[77] http://www.multilingualarchive.com/ma/enwiki/de/Rodrigo_de_Triana, http://www.glencoe.com/qe/qe98columbus.php?qi=3990, both retrieved on 31.01.2012.

lay claims to these lands. The fact that Allah and Mohammed guided them spiritually on their voyages was enough argumentation that the lands now rightly belong to Islam, for the goal was "to expand the influence, seek new trade routes and of course expand the message of Islam (by encouraging) some brave of them to cross an area that (was) still considered to be dark in the maps (as) they were then."[78]

Muslim-Islamic sources like to claim that "historians have confirmed that during the golden days of the Muslim nation, Muslim ships were plying the Atlantic Ocean, which was then known as the Sea of Injustice, and they were heading west."[79] The problem with this statement is that "the golden days of the Muslim nation" never existed. "Muslim conquests (always) produced, instead of a golden age of science and learning, a bloodbath and an interminable war of attrition."[80] Furthermore, the concept of the nation is diametrically opposed to the Islamic concept of the umma, the world community of Islam.

---

[78]     http://mozadded1924.wordpress.com/2011/12/01/muslim-exploreres-over-the-past-untill-the-u-s-instead-of-colombus/, retrieved on 31.01.2102. http://edughoni.blogspot.com/2011/08/muslim-sailors-first-discovered.html, retrieved on 31.01.2012.

[79]     http://www.pkviews.com/forum/showthread.php/706-Does-America-Have-Muslim-Roots-SUPPRESSED-HISTORY, retrieved on 31.01.2012. http://www.mathaba.net/news/?x=66517, retrieved on 31.01.2012. http://destituterebel.instablogs.com/entry/does-america-have-muslim-roots/, retrieved on 31.01.2012.

[80] O'Neill, p. 116.

There are reports from Islamic sources that on his first voyage to the New World, Christopher Columbus recorded in his papers that while his ship was near Gibara on the northeast coast of Cuba on Monday, October 21, 1492, "he saw a mosque on top of a beautiful mountain." Google the quotation and the reader will receive 704,000 hits including repetitions. However, there are no archaeological excavations and no proof that a mosque was on top of a mountain on Gibara, located near Cuba. What Columbus saw was a land area with a mountain in its geological formation that resembled a minaret. "Now that the Arabs have become Castro's sponsors, too, perhaps they should mount an expedition to find the remains of the mosque that Columbus spotted atop a mountain in Gibara."[81]

After landing on Haiti during the second voyage, the indigenous people presented Columbus with a spear which they said came from black people of a land far across the ocean. The spears were tipped with a yellow metal that the natives called *guanin*, Columbus brought some of these spearheads back to Spain where they were analyzed. It was found that they consisted of 18 parts gold (56.25%), 6 parts silver (18.75%), and 8 parts copper (25%). It turns out that this is the same ratio that the people of Guinea used in their spears. Arabs claim that the word *guanin* comes from the Arab word *ghinaa*, which means wealth.[82] "In Susu, the language spoken by the coastal Susu ethnic group, the word *guinè* means *woman*. When a

---

[81]   http://reviewofcuban-americanblogs.blogspot.com/2008/10/columbus-saw-mosque-in-cuba-now-its.html, retrieved on 19.02.2012.

[82] Thacher, John Boyd. *Christopher Columbus*, New York: 1950, p. 380.

group of Europeans arrived on the coast, they met some women washing clothes in an estuary. The women indicated to the men that they were women. The Europeans misunderstood and thought the women were referring to a geographic area; they subsequently used the word *Guinea* to describe coastal West Africa. The truth of the matter is that the Arab word comes from the West African word.[83] There is no Arabic-Islamic origin of the word *guanin* or *ghinaa*.

In 1498, on his third voyage to the new world, Columbus landed in Trinidad. Later, he sighted the South American continent, where some of his crew went ashore and found natives using colorful handkerchiefs of symmetrically woven cotton. Columbus noticed that these handkerchiefs resembled the hair-dresses and loin cloths of Guinea in their colors, style, and function. He referred to them as Almayzars. Almayzar is an Arabic word for *wrapper*, *cover*, *apron* and/or *skirting* which was the cloth the Moors (Spanish or North African Muslims) imported from West Africa (Guinea) into Morocco, Spain, and Portugal. During this voyage, Columbus was surprised that the married women wore cotton panties (bragas) and he wondered where these natives learned their modesty. Hernando Cortes, Spanish conqueror, described the dress of the Indian women as *long veils* and the dress of Indian men as "breechcloths painted in the style of Moorish draperies." Ferdinand Columbus noted the similarity of the children's hammocks to those found in North Africa. He also called the native cotton garments "breechcloths of the same

---

[83] http://www.everyculture.com/Ge-It/Guinea.html was retrieved on 19.02.2012.

design and cloth as the shawls worn by the Moorish women of Granada."[84]

Mauricio Obregon claims that two of Columbus' ship's captains were Muslim: Martin Alonso Pinzon, captain of the *Pinta*, and his brother Vicente Yanez Pinzon, captain of the *Nina*. Moreover, he states that the Pinzon family had family ties to Abuzayan Mohammed III (1362-1366), the Sultan of the Marinid Dynasty (1196-1465). However if they were true Muslims, they would have had to have Arabic names. These are not documented by Mauricio Obregon.[85]

## Alternative Theories and the Validity of Muslim Claims

The only confirmed colonization of North America that is not a theory, but is a fact, is the settlement of L'Anse aux Meadows on the northern tip of Newfoundland, Canada. This settlement may be in relation to the *Vineland Sagas* of the Nordic peoples that tell of settlements to the west of Greenland by the Viking Leif Erikson. There are also archaeological finds on Baffin Island which have been dated after the finds at L'Anse aux Meadows.

There are as many alternative theories to the pre-Columbian discovery of America/the Americas as there are Muslim claims. Eight such alternative theories merit mention.

---

[84] Thacher, p. 380.

[85] Obregon, Mauricio. *The Columbus Papers, The Barcelona Letter of 1493, The Landfall Controversy, and the Indian Guides*, McMillan Co., New York: 1991, passim.

The reader can easily google them with the addition "and the discovery of America." The theories are:

- ➤ Peruvian mummies were embalmed with a resin from the Araucaria conifer that is related to the *monkey puzzle tree* found only in Oceania and perhaps New Guinea. The resins have been dated approximately 1200 BC.

- ➤ The Irish Monk Saint Brendan.

- ➤ The Mormon Story and the Izapa Stela 5.

- ➤ The Japanese and the Zuni Indians of New Mexico.

- ➤ Henry Sinclair, Earl of Orkney, which is very questionable.

- ➤ Traces of coca and tobacco (nicotine) have been found in Egyptian mummies. Since coca and tobacco are New World plants, the theorists maintain that there must have been some connection between parts of Africa and South America. The evidence is not 100 percent archaeologically conclusive.

- ➤ The Polynesian peoples may have had contact with indigenous peoples of South America, for example present-day Chile and even Peru.

- ➤ Roman coins have been found in New England in places that were supposedly settled before the American Colonies existed. Moreover, Roman chili peppers, which existed only in the New World, have been found in St. Botulf, Lund, Sweden.

The internet abounds with Islamic sites claiming that Muslims were in the New World before the major European countries made claims to the lands. Moreover, they quote each other without documenting what they quote. Thus, they give the reader the impression that their research is independent. Because another Islamic site will advance the same *facts*, the reader is subconsciously led to the conclusion that since the *facts* of one site are corroborated independently by the *facts* of another site, the Muslim discovery of the New World must be true! This is the basic method of creeping Islamists with the intent to change the development of history in their favor. The attentive reader is reminded of the deception within the concept of al-taqiyya, i.e., anything goes as long as it supports the advancement of Islam.

There must be absolute, scientific, conclusive evidence researched by linguists, archaeologists, and social historians in order to differentiate historical *facts* from Islamic claims of *facts*. It is one matter to claim that Africans (Arabs?) were in America before Columbus. It is another matter to claim that Muslims, and therefore, Islam, were in America, thus providing pillars on which the expansion of a dogma can be constructed, as if it were Allah's and Mohammed's will. That is truly a re-writing of history, phenakism, and an absurd wish!

# CHAPTER FOUR

## Muslims in America 1500-1800

### Arab Nautical Inventions and Maps

The previous chapter has recorded that there was definitely some African contact with the pre-Columbian Americas. To say that there was Arab contact is questionable. To contend that at that time there was Islamic contact is stretching the facts too far. A logical conclusion is that had there been straightforward attempts to spread Islam in the pre-Columbian era, there would undoubtedly have been archaeological discoveries of mosques, minarets, and even writings from the Koran. However, contrary to what Islamic sources would like to contend, such proofs are non-existent. Therefore, the pro-Islam formulations remain that *Muslims (or Islam) discovered America, Muslims (or Islam) discovered the New World,* or that *the New World would not have been discovered had it not been for Muslims and their navigational skills and their invention of navigational instruments and maps.*

#### The Magnetic Compass

As far as the last statement is concerned, Muslim seafarers did not invent any navigational instruments anew. The seafaring, pirating Arabs, particularly the Muslims, but not the Arab traders, did know how to use the magnetic compass. However, it is accepted historical fact that the ancient Chinese invented the *magnetic compass* and began to use it for navigation from the 9<sup>th</sup> century on into the 11<sup>th</sup> century.[86] Europeans and Arabs came into contact with the nautical compass as a result of contact with the Chinese.[87]

## The Kamal

The Arab seafarers, particularly on their pirate raids in the Mediterranean Sea used an instrument called the *kamal* in celestial navigation, whereby they measured the altitudes, and latitudes of the stars. Yet the first *kamal* was an instrument invented by the Polynesians.[88]

## The Quadrant

Another instrument supposedly developed by Arab Muslims is the *quadrant*. The truth behind this invention is that the *quadrant* is nothing more than a refinement of the *astrolabe*, which was invented in 150 BC by the Greek genius Hipparchus, who was an astrologer, astronomer, geographer, mathematician, and the founder of trigonometry.

These instruments were exceedingly important in navigation, particularly when used in conjunction with maps, the so-called papers of Islamic geography, which were maps based on Hellenistic geography. The most notable developers from the 8<sup>th</sup> to the 12<sup>th</sup> centuries were Al-Khwārizmī, Abū Zayd

---

[86] The Chinese had known the properties of magnetism since the 4<sup>th</sup> century BC. Temple, Robert. *The genius of China: 3,000 years of science, discovery & invention*, 3rd ed., Andre Deutsch, London: 2007, pp. 162–166.

[87] Temple, pp. 162-166.

[88] http://www.celestialnavigation.net/instruments.html was retrieved on 01.02.2012.

al-Balkhī, Abu Rayhan Biruni, and Muhammad al-Idrisi. Yet, this does not mean that the maps available to explorers during Columbus' time and thereafter were based on maps of Arabic origin, which if available, were mostly copies with updated facts. The notable Ottoman Turkish map scholars are Mahmud al-Kashgari and Piri Re'is.[89] Some of the most important maps available to both pre-and post-Columbian seafarers are:

## The World Map of Eratosthenes

This map is non-Arabic in origin. "Eratosthenes (276-194 BC) drew an improved world map, incorporating information from the campaigns of Alexander the Great and his successors. Asia became wider, reflecting the new understanding of the actual size of the continent. Eratosthenes was also the first geographer to incorporate parallels and meridians within his cartographic depictions."[90]

## The World Map of Ptolemy

This map is non-Arabic in origin. "Ptolemy was custodian of the library at Alexandria, which contained the greatest manuscript collection of ancient times, and it was there that he consulted the archaic source documents that enabled him to compile his own map. Acceptance of the possibility that the original version of at least one of the charts he referred to could have been made around 10,000 BC helps us to explain why he shows glaciers, characteristic of that exact epoch, together with

---

[89] Tibbetts, Gerald R. *The Beginnings of a Cartographic Tradition*, in: John Brian Harley, David Woodward, *Cartography in the Traditional Islamic and South Asian Societies*, Chicago: 1992, pp. 90-107.

[90] http://en.wikipedia.org/wiki/Early_world_maps, retrieved on 19.02.2012.

'lakes ... suggesting the shapes of present-day lakes, and streams very much suggesting glacial streams ... flowing from the glaciers into the lakes.'"[91]

## The Dulcert Portolano Map of 1339

This map is non-Arabic in origin. "The so-called Dulcert Portolano focuses on Europe and North Africa. Here latitude is perfect across huge distances and the total longitude of the Mediterranean and Black Seas is correct to within half a degree. ... (T)he maker of the original source from which the Dulcert Portolano was copied had, 'achieved highly scientific accuracy in finding the ratio of latitude to longitude. He could only have done this if he had precise information on the relative longitudes of a great many places scattered all the way from Galway in Ireland to the eastern bend of the Don in Russia.'"[92]

## The Portolano Map of Iehudi Ibn ben Zara of 1487

Although Ibn ben Zara was an Arab, the map is not of Arabic origin. "The 'Portolano' of Iehudi Ibn Ben Zara, drawn in the year 1487 (is) a chart of Europe and North Africa (that) may have been based on a source even earlier than Ptolemy's, for it seems to show glaciers much farther south than Sweden (roughly on the same latitude as England in fact) and to depict

---

[91] http://www.bibliotecapleyades.net/egipto/fingerprintgods/fingerprintgods 00.htm, retrieved on 19.02.2012.

[92] http://www.bibliotecapleyades.net/egipto/fingerprintgods/fingerprintgods 00.htm, retrieved on 19.02.2012.

the Mediterranean, Adriatic and Aegean Seas as they might have looked before the melting of the European ice-cap."[93]

## The Hamy-King Chart of 1502-1504

"The Hamy-King Chart of 1502 was found to be based partly on Ptolemaic and partly on Portolano traditions, with recently discovered lands added by an early explorer, thought to be Amerigo Vespucci. The European section seems to be based on the most accurate of the Portolano charts. This world map provides evidence of numerous and extensive geological changes since the first prototypes of its original local maps were drawn. It is interesting to note that in placing the center of the Portolano chart in the Indian Ocean, the cartographer made it possible to construct a world map embracing all of Europe, Asia, Africa, and the Americas as well. It is a much broader design than found on the Piri Re'is map."[94] This map is not of Arabic origin.

## The Piri Re'is Map of 1513

"In his day, Piri Re'is was a well-known figure; his historical identity is firmly established. An admiral in the navy of the Ottoman Turks, he was involved, often on the winning side, in numerous sea battles around the mid-sixteenth century. He was, in addition, considered an expert on the lands of the Mediterranean, and was the author of a famous sailing book, the *Kitabi Bahriye*, which provided a comprehensive

---

[93] http://www.bibliotecapleyades.net/egipto/fingerprintgods/fingerprintgods 00.htm, retrieved on 19.02.2012.

[94] http://members.tripod.com/~Glove_r/Hapgood.html, retrieved on 19.02.2012.

description of the coasts, harbours, currents, shallows, landing places, bays and straits of the Aegean and Mediterranean Seas. Despite this illustrious career, he fell afoul of his masters and was beheaded in 1554 or 1555."[95] The source maps Piri Re'is used to draw up his 1513 map were in all probability lodged originally in the Imperial Library at Constantinople, to which the admiral is known to have enjoyed privileged access. Those sources (which may have been transferred or copied from even more ancient centers of learning) no longer exist, or, at any rate, have not been found. It was, however, in the library of the old Imperial Palace at Constantinople that the Piri Re'is Map was rediscovered, painted on a gazelle skin and rolled up on a dusty shelf, as recently as 1929. The Piri Re'is map is based on pre-Islamic sources.

## The Mercator Map of 1538

This map is non-Arabic in origin. It is a map of the world that was the first ever to show America stretching from north to south.[96]

## The Ptolemaeus Basilae Map of 1540

This cartographic work is non-Arabic in origin. It is a reproduction of the World Map of Ptolemy with updated changes that was published in Basel, Switzerland in 1540.

---

[95] http://www.dreamscape.com/morgana/larissa2.htm was retrieved on 19.02.2012.

[96] http://www.mostlymaps.com/mapmakers/gerardus-mercator was retrieved on 19.02.2012.

## The Hadji Ahmed World Map of 1559

Although Hadji Ahmed was an Arab, he had no access to contemporary maps and charts of the Americas and so was stuck with simply copying some mysterious mappamundi in his possession.[97] Therefore, this map is not of Arabic origin.

# Slavery

Slavery in the history of humankind is when a person is in bondage to a master or household as an instrument of forced labor, as well as a method of production in which bonded persons are forced to work for nothing, while receiving their own sustenance and shelter. Christianity as a religious code has always been on the side of humanity. One of the most important aspects of this humanity is the Christian stance against slavery. Indeed, Christianity was instrumental in abolishing the entire, evil establishment of slavery, particularly the slavery of the Roman Empire. According to H. F. Stewart, "The effect of the Church upon the Empire may be summed up in one word 'freedom'"[98] Of course, the Church was morally correct in following the gospel of the New Testament, for God tells His servants, "So long as you did it (slavery) to these, the least of my brethren, you did it to me."[99] In fact, the concept of

---

[97] http://unmyst3.blogspot.com/2011/03/hadji-ahmed-map.html, retrieved on 19.02.2012.

[98] Stewart, H. F. *Thoughts and Ideas of the Period* in *The Cambridge Medieval History: The Christian Empire*, Vol. I, Cambridge University Press, Cambridge: 1936, p. 596.

[99] Read *The Gospel According to St. Mark*, 25:31-46.

human rights in the Western World that emerged in the Enlightenment is rooted deeply in the Judeo-Christian thinkers, precisely in as much as the core is that all human beings are created in God's image. Human rights are a divine, moral, and legal concept. The fact that God, in Christianity and in Judaism, holds persons accountable for their behavior to the lowest members of society means that God places the lowliest of humans on a level with the highest stationed persons in a society. In the slavery of the Roman Empire and those empires before it, male slaves were a source of labor, women and the youth were a source of sexual pleasure for their owners.

From the very beginning, the Christian Church gave free persons and bonded persons the sacraments. "Under the Christian emperors this tendency, in spite of relapses at certain points, became daily more marked, and ended, in the sixth century, in Justinian's very liberal legislation.[100] Although the civil law on slavery still lagged behind the demands of Christianity, nevertheless very great progress had been made."[101] However, in the Western Empire the abolition of slavery was abruptly stopped by the barbarian invasions. Edward Gibbon in *The Decline and Fall of the Roman Empire* writes that slavery "which had been almost suppressed by the peaceful sovereignty of Rome, was revived and multiplied by the perpetual hostilities of the independent Barbarians."[102]

---

[100] Wallon, H. A. *Histoire de l'esclavage dans l'antiquité, 3 Vols.,* Paris 1879, Vol. III, pp. ii and x.

[101] St. Jerome writes in his *Epistle* "The laws of Caesar are one thing, the laws of Christ another." *Epistle* lxxvii.

[102] Gibbon, Edward. *The Decline and Fall ...,* Chapter 38.

Gibbon also notes that the reaction of the Church was relatively swift. It redeemed slaves, it legislated on behalf of slaves in its church councils, and it set myriad examples of humane treatment of slaves.[103] The result of the activity of the Church was that by the ninth century the Christian Church had ended slavery in Europe. "… slavery ended in medieval Europe only because the church extended its sacraments to all slaves and then managed to impose a ban on the enslavement of Christians (and Jews). Within the context of medieval Europe, that prohibition was effectively a rule of universal abolition."[104]

Justinian I (482-565), Byzantine Roman Emperor from 527, restored imperial rule throughout Italy, Northern Africa, and parts of Spain in the middle of the sixth century. A most significant development was the codification of Roman law in *Codex Justinianus* and the commentary thereto titled *Institutiones*, where we read, "Slavery is an institution of the law of nations against nature, subjugating one man to the dominion of another … (and) … the law of nations is common to the whole human race; for nations to have settled certain things for themselves as occasions and human life required. For instance, wars arose and then captivity and slavery followed, which are contrary to the law of nature; for by the law of nature all men from the beginning were born free."[105]

---

[103] Gibbon, pp. 393-397; Lesne, Emile. *Histoire de la propriété ecclésiastique en France*, Vol. I, Facultés Catholiques, Lille: 1938, pp. 357-369.

[104] Stark, Rodney. *The Victory of Reason*, Random House, New York: 2005, p. 28.

[105] *Institutiones Iustiniani*, Title III, Book I, paragraph 2.

In Islam there is no prohibition of slavery. The obvious reason for this fact is that Mohammed himself was a slaver. Mohammed used the women at his right hand, a euphemism for female salves as sex objects. Indeed, there is not one verse in the Koran that says slavery is evil and must not be exercised. There are no sanctions and there are no penalties, either in the Koran or in the hadiths. Slavery has been an integral element of Islam since its inception by Mohammed. There are many suras in the Koran that justify and sanction slavery. There are more than two dozen suras in the Koran that concern the fact that slavery is legal. They are: 2:178, 4:3, 4:24, 4:92, 5:89, 8:69, 8:71, 12:29-30, 16:71, 16:75, 23:1-6, 24:31-33, 33:50-52, 58:3, 29-30, 90:13.

In the year 711 or perhaps as early as 630, the Muslim armies crossed the Straits of Gibraltar and by 730/731 they had reached the banks of the Loire River in France. The Muslim concept of war is based entirely on the suras of the Koran. War does not distinguish between the participants and non-participants. War exists for the Islamists to extinguish the non-believers.

For Muslims it is legitimate that the Muslims should live off the non-believers. The spoils of war are divinely sanctioned by Mohammed, and above all, by the Koran. Thus began the piracy, banditry, destruction, and slavery of conquered lands and peoples that lasted until Charles Martel (686-741) defeated the Muslims at the Battle of Tours in October 732, the two possible dates being the 10th or the 17th of the month. Between their expansion from after Mohammed's death in 632 to 732 and their final expulsion from Spain in

1492 with the completion of the *Reconquista*, the Muslims pillaged, burned, looted, enslaved, and freebooted. Crete became the center of Muslim slave trade until the Byzantine Emperor Nikephorus II Phokas (912-969, ruled from 963) recaptured and freed the island in about 956. Nevertheless, in their entire seven to eight hundred years of despotism, Islam and the Muslims left behind nothing but death. "Segregated in special quarters, (the subdued) had to wear discriminatory clothing. Subjected to heavy taxes, the Christian peasantry formed a servile class attached to the Arab domains; many abandoned their land and fled to the towns. Harsh reprisals with mutilations and crucifixions would sanction the Mozarab (Christian *dhimmis*) calls for help from the Christian kings. Moreover, if one *dhimmi* (subdued non-believer) harmed a Muslim, the whole community would lose its status of protection, leaving it open to pillage, enslavement, and arbitrary killing."[106] This was typical of the non-existent Muslim golden age and toleration. That golden age and the Muslim claims of their being tolerant are only myths.

The Muslims made Spain the center of European slave trading.[107] It was also in Spain that Muslims established the first inquisitions to investigate the loyalty of those who had converted to Islam. During the Islamic occupation of western lands many insurrections were punished by massacres and

---

[106] Ye'or, Bat and Bostom, Andrew. *Andalusian Myth, Eurabian Reality*, at http://www.jihadwatch.org/2004/04/andalusian-myth-eurabian-reality-print.html, retrieved on 02.02.2012.

[107] Ye'or, Bat and Bostom, Andrew. *Andalusian Myth, Eurabian Reality* at http://www.jihadwatch.org/2004/04/andalusian-myth-eurabian-reality-print.html, retrieved on 02.02.2012.

according to the Koran 5:33, by crucifixion. These facts alone characterize the misnomers *religion of peace* and the so-called *Muslim golden age.* The *Reconquista* freed the Iberian Peninsula from the ravages of Islamization.

The proof shows that Christianity is diametrically opposed to Islamic dogma and customs. Islam supported slavery, even insisted that it was divine and legitimate in the eyes of Allah, according to the Koran 4:24. Robert Spencer notes that "The Qur'an says that the followers of Muhammad are 'ruthless to the unbelievers but merciful to one another' (48:29) and that the unbelievers are the 'worst of created beings' (98:6). One may exercise the Golden Rule in relation to a fellow Muslim, but according to the laws of Islam, the same courtesy is not to be extended to unbelievers. That is one principal reason why the primary source of slaves in the Islamic world has been non-Muslims, whether Jews, Christians, Hindus, or pagans. Most slaves were non-Muslims who had been captured in jihad warfare."[108]

It was Mohammed personally who dictated that the principle booty of conquering the enemy non-believers was female slaves, who were to be under the right hand of the Muslim conqueror. Moreover, Mohammed gave his divine permission to marry at least four women. (Koran 4:3) Mohammed also divinely decreed that a man could divorce his wife by saying three times, *I divorce thee.* Nothing has changed in Islam. Nothing changes in Islam. Nothing will change in Islam. Change is contrary to what is the will of Allah-Hubal because Mohammed says that it is so.

---

[108] Spencer, Robert. *Religion of Peace,* p. 95.

# Muslims and Slavery in the American Colonies

Let us return to slavery, particularly in the American Colonies. The fact behind the fact of Colonial settlement is that black slaves from Africa were part of the original settlers. Whether or not they were Muslims or Arabs may be a moot point when we recall that slavery was re-instituted by the immoral Muslim conquerors of the Mediterranean regions. Nevertheless, already in 1619, one year before the Puritan Pilgrim Fathers landed at the bay of Plimoth, Massachusetts,[109] a Dutch man-of-war landed at the settlement of Jamestown in Virginia with "twenty black (slaves) of undetermined origin and status that the captain turned over to the Colonists in exchange for food and other necessities."[110] The terminological status of those African blacks on the Dutch man-of-war is ambiguous. There is no indication that they were to be brought to America as slaves. It could mean that some were considered to be slave material and some not. It would also mean that some had a definite social status in their homeland in Africa. Nevertheless, as enslaved persons, they had no important input into the politics and the establishment of an American Colonial society. They were present to work and be exploited, just as the Muslims had done with their slaves. For Muslims, "slave-trading and slave-raiding were perfectly legitimate occupations

---

[109] Plimoth (Plymouth) is *Patuxet* in the Algonquin language of the Massachusetts Indian tribe. *Patuxet* was the name of a Massachusetts tribal village on/near the site of the Plymouth settlement. The Massachusetts told the first colonists that the meaning of the word *Patuxet* is *at the little (water) fall*.

[110] *Ebony Pictorial History of Black America*, Vol. I, *African Past to Civil War*, Johnson Publishing Company, Inc., Chicago: 1971, p. 60.

89

that kept women (after their men were beheaded and their children used for pedophile purposes), in a state of abject subjugation."[111]

## Selected Examples of Muslims in America

### Estevanico

When a 300-member Spanish conquistador expedition explored the American southwest, particularly Arizona in 1539, some Spanish who wanted to settle there were accompanied by an Arab Muslim from Azamor, Morocco. His name was Istafan, the slave of the Spanish explorer Andrès Dorantes de Carranza, who brought him on an expedition to Florida in 1528. He accompanied the Spanish on a five thousand mile expedition across the American southwest, an expedition that took the lives of 296 men. Previously, Istafan had been on a Spanish expedition in Florida under the leadership of Panfilo de Narvaez in 1527. After violent encounters with the Native Americans, after experiencing a series of destructive hurricanes, and after having been left stranded by other Spanish explorers who sailed away on their main ship, somewhere between 250 to 300 men hastily built five rafts and left the Florida coast hoping to arrive in Mexico. Two of the rafts landed near present-day Galveston Island, Texas. The leader of the expedition, Panfilo Narvaez, did not survive. Only 15 men of the 80 who had landed on Galveston Island survived the coming winter. In the spring they traveled west and explored the Rio Grande River. By the year 1533, only Estevanico (his

---

[111] O'Neill, p. 8.

90

Spanish name), Andrès Dorantes de Carranza, Cabeza de Vaca, and Alonso Castillo Maldonado had survived. Some Indians captured them and enslaved them for a period of time. Indians of other tribes helped them to gain freedom and continue their journey. Finally, in 1536 or 1538 they reached Mexico City and were received by the Viceroy Antonio de Mendoza. They were the first non-natives to travel in this area of southwestern North America.

Carranza sold Istafan to the Viceroy. In 1539, the Viceroy sent him on an expedition under the leadership of the Franciscan Fray Marcos de Niza. Their goal was to find the fabled seven cities of Cíbola. Some Zuni Indians killed Istafan as he entered their pueblo, supposedly in the city of Cíbola, somewhere in present-day Arizona or New Mexico. If not the first, Istafan is considered to be among the first Muslims on American soil.[112]

### Norsereddin

A second, early Muslim in North America is a man named Norsereddin (also Nassereddin(e), Nasruddin). He was an Egyptian who settled in the Hudson River Valley in the Catskill Mountains of New York in the 1550s. He was not a slave. He claimed to be an Egyptian prince, but was not able to prove it. He fell in love with the local Mohawk princess Lotowana (Sparkling Water). However, she married an Indian brave of her choice who was also amenable to her tribe. The

---

[112] Kennedy, Brent. *Islamic Horizons* November/December 1994, pp. 24-27, in *Early Contact of Muslims in America* at http://obit.staff.umm.ac.id/files/2011/01/Lec-10.pptx; http://www.enchanted learning.com/explorers/page/e/estevanico.shtml, retrieved on 02.03.2012.

Islamic internet sites and pro-Islamic writings that this author researched stops with this statement of love and rejection. One site even claims that they probably married.[113] The truth behind Norsereddin's claim to fame is that he killed Princess Lotowana who had refused to marry him. The facts are related by Frederick L. Beers, in his *History of Greene County, New York: with biographical sketches of its prominent men.* They are summarized as follows:

Lotowana was a beautiful Mohawk princess whose hand was sought by a large number of Indian braves. Norsereddin tried to persuade her to marry him, but she and her father, the local Mohawk Indian chief Shandaken, refused. Both of them agreed that she marry one of her own and a man that she loved. Therefore, they had insulted Norsereddin's honor.

After Norsereddin had told his story to a Dutchman over some beer in a tavern (but surely Muslims do not drink alcohol?), the Dutchman egged him on into a wager that if he again courted the Indian princess and persuaded her to marry him, the Dutchman would give Norsereddin 1000 gold crowns. Norsereddin began the courtship anew. The attempt was blocked by Shandaken, who told Norsereddin that he could marry other beautiful women of the tribe. Norsereddin attacked Shandaken. He was chased out of the Indian camp. Norsereddin's honor had again been insulted. On the day of

---

[113] This conclusion is added to by an unfounded insinuation that the American Revolution was affected by the Muslim world, whatever that is, or whatever that was at the time. UMEA is United Muslims of America. http://www.umanet.org/cms.cfm?fuseaction=articles.viewThisArticle&articleID=263&pageID=159, retrieved on 31.01.2012.

Lotowana's wedding, Norsereddin returned to the Indian camp, made superficial apologies, and asked that Princess Lotowana accept a wedding gift as a sign that he was no longer jealous and had no ill will. Princess Lotowana took the handsomely decorated wooden box, drew aside the cover, and at that moment a spring apparatus snapped out of the box and drove a dart that had been poisoned with snake venom into her hand. The venom was so strong that Princess Lotowana died in the presence of her husband and father within minutes. In the commotion, Norsereddin had escaped to the woods.

Shandaken immediately sent twenty braves to capture Norsereddin. They overtook him on the Kalkberg, dragged him back to where Shandaken and the husband were mourning over Princess Lotowana's murder. The Indians had gathered on the top of a cliff overlooking the Catskills at Ontiora. They heaped a pile of branches and wood on the top of the cliff within a few feet of the edge. They tied Norsereddin to the woodpile, torched it, and danced with shouts of exultation while he burned to death. Princess Lotowana was buried by the mourning tribe. Norsereddin's ashes were left to be blown away by the wind. On the day of his revenge, Shandaken left the area and never returned to Ontiora.

Frederick L. Beers writes that Norsereddin "had little to recommend him to anyone, either in possessions or character, (for he was) haughty, morose, unprincipled, cruel, and dissipated." He possessed an invincible determination to accomplish his evil purpose.

Of course, the killing of Lotowana was justified under the Koranic dogma because Princess Lotowana had insulted

Norsereddin 's honor. Perhaps this was the first Islamic honor killing in America. This is only a small incident of Islamic revenge. It is one example of an early Muslim killing. Apparently, no one cares about a (savage) Mohawk princess, who probably refused to become an Islamic convert anyway. Yet, the question must be raised: What is there in Islam's and Mohammed's dogma that says a woman must be killed because she insults a man's honor by refusing to marry him? Norsereddine is honored by Islamic historians as the first permanent Arab Muslim settler in New York.[114]

## The Melungeons

In 1586, the English pirate Sir Francis Drake captured 400 prisoners held by the Spanish and Portuguese in Brazil. Among them were 300 Moorish and Turkish galley slaves who had been taken by the Spanish and Portuguese in the Mediterranean Sea battles with the Muslim kingdoms in North Africa. When Drake finally landed at Roanoke Island, North Carolina he encountered some stranded English settlers who pleaded with him to take them back to England. Drake left at least 200 of the Moors, Turks, West Africans, some Portuguese soldiers, and a few South American Indians on the island.

Out of this group emerged the Melungeons. *Melun-can* in Turkish means *one whose soul is a born loser*. By 1600 these prisoners left behind on Roanoke Island, the first Melungeons, had resettled in the southern Appalachian valleys. When English and Scotch-Irish settlers came into the area, they forced

---

[114] Beers, Frederick L. (J. B. Beers & Co.). *History of Greene County, New York: with biographical sketches of its prominent men*, Hope Farm Press, Cornwallville, N.Y.: 1969, reprinted from the 1884 edition, pp. 19-22.

the Melungeons westward into the mountains of North Carolina, Tennessee, Kentucky, and Virginia.

The Melungeons were the first people, apart from Native Americans, to penetrate so deeply into the Appalachian region. The principal family names of the Melungeons of Virginia and Tennessee are Adams, Adkins, Bell, Bolen, Collins, Denham, Fields, Freeman, Gann, Gibson, Goins, Gorvens, Graham, Lawson, Maloney, Mullins, Melons, Noel, Piniore, Sexton, and Wright.[115] The Melungeon families came to be operators of silver mines in the Straight Creek area in the Cumberland Plateau near Pineville, Kentucky. In 1654 some of the English settlers from Jamestown explored the surrounding region and came upon a colony of bearded Moors who wore European clothing. The Moors were evidently the Melungeons.

The Melungeons minted silver coins in the area for their own use. By the time Kentucky joined the Union the independent and secretive life of the Melungeons came to an end. When Jamestown, Virginia was settled, the neighboring Indians told the English settlers that within a week's walk there were "people like you" who had short hair and lived in log houses. Today most Melungeons have been assimilated into the American culture.

## Anthony Jan Janszoon van Haarlem (1570-1641)

Jan Janszoon van Haarlem was the first President and Admiral (1619-1627) of the Corsair Republic history knows as Salé. He was the Governor of Oualidia from 1640-1641. He

---

[115] Gilbert, William Harlen. *Surviving Indian Groups of the Eastern United States: Annual Report Smithsonian Institution*, Library of Congress: 1948.

was one of the most vicious of the 17<sup>th</sup> century Barbary pirates known as the Salé Rovers. Born in Haarlem, Netherlands, by the year 1600 Jan Janszoon had become a seaman. He sailed to Spain, and while in Cartagena, Spain, he apparently converted to Islam. He was captured by the Barbary pirates in 1618 and taken to Algiers. There he reasserted his conversion to Islam, most likely to save his life. He pirated with the corsair Sulayman Rais (Slemen Reis, originally De Veenboer, a Dutchman who had also converted to Islam). Records of Jan Janszoon van Haarlem and his scions are scarce after the year 1641. His fourth son Anthony Janszoon van Haarlem (sometimes Salee), who grew up in Morocco and married there, became one of the original settlers of New Amsterdam (New York City). There he purchased plots of land in Brooklyn, on Long Island, and on Manhattan Island, where he bought a farm in 1638. Historians are sure that his wealth was provided by his Islamic pirate father.

Anthony Jan Janszoon van Haarlem became involved with numerous legal disputes with the Church of Holland because they did not observe Islamic law. Maintaining that a Muslim answers only to Allah, he refused court orders to leave New Netherlands. Eventually, he became a successful businessman and a large landowner. Islamic historians are proud of him and his refusal to observe the religious rules of the Church of Holland and the civic law of New Netherlands, which were not sharia law. Anthony Jan Janszoon van Haarlem is considered the first European Muslim to build the first settlement in New Utrecht, present-day Brooklyn, New York.

## Moors and Turks[116]

In 1639, the first black Moor birth was recorded on the Delmarva Peninsula near present-day Wilmington, Delaware. Moors and Turks were not considered to be slaves because during the 17th century their home countries were in friendship with the king of England. By 1684, Moors arrived in Delaware and South New Jersey. Their ships were marooned off the coasts. Many Muslims were absorbed by Indian tribes. Most likely the Native Americans were friendly enough to keep them from starving, to welcome them into their tribes because they had similar skin features, and because they presented no serious threat to the existence of the Native Americans. The following Native American tribes have been found to have descendants of Muslim Moors:[117] Alibamu (Alabama); Anasazi; Apaches; Arab Indians of Summit, Schoharie County, New York; Arawak; Arikana; Black Indians of the Schuylkill River, New York; Blackfoot; Cherokees; Clappers of New York; Creeks; Hassanamisco Nipmug of Massachusetts; Kickapoo; Laster Tribe, Perquimans County, Hertford, North Carolina; Lenapi; Mahigans; Makkahs; Mecca Indians (Meccans); Mohanets; Mohegans; Nanticokes; and Seminoles.

Yet even in the days of the early American Colonies northern Europe was not safe from Muslim piracy and

---

[116] Weslager, Clinton Alfred. *Forgotten Moors* in *The Nanticoke Indians*, University of Delaware Press, Newark: 1983 and by the same author *Delaware's Forgotten Folk, The Story of the Moors & Nanticokes*, University of Pennsylvania Press, Philadelphia: 1943.

[117] Gilbert, William Harlen. *Surviving Indian Groups of the Eastern United States: Annual Report Smithsonian Institution*, Library of Congress: 1948. passim.

terrorism. As an example, between 1609 and 1616 England lost 466 merchant vessels to the Barbary pirates. In 1627, Muslim pirates from As-Sali, Morocco, in the Barbary Coast attacked Baltimore, County Cork, Ireland and held it for 68 days.[118] The captured villagers were taken away to live a life of slavery in North Africa. Some were turned into galley slaves. Some women and forced eunuchs spent their lives in harems. In the three years from 1677 to 1680, the English lost 160 ships. The captured sailors were held for ransom or turned into slaves. Some Muslims from As-Sali, Morocco, married Irish indentured servants who came to the American Colonies.

### Ayub Sulaiman ibn Diallo

In the listing of documented Muslims in America we next encounter Ayub Sulaiman ibn Diallo, who was enslaved in 1730 or 1731 by Muslims in the region of the Gambia River in Bundu, now the eastern part of present-day Senegal. Transported on a slave ship to Annapolis, Maryland, he was sold to a local tobacco plantation owner. He received the English name comparable to his Arab name: Job Ben Solomon, meaning Job the son of Solomon. Job ran away, was captured and returned to his owner. As a child he had learned to read and write Arabic and had memorized the Koran. He was fortunate enough to meet the founder of Georgia, James Oglethorpe, who eventually purchased his bond and took Job to England, where he even met the English royal family. While in England, he

---

[118] Wilson, Peter Lamborn. *Pirate Utopias: Moorish Corsairs & European Renegadoes*, Autonomedia, New York: 1996, passim and Chisholm, Hugh, ed. Barbary Pirates in *Encyclopædia Britannica*, 11th ed., Cambridge University Press, Cambridge: 1911, passim.

translated Arabic coins for the British Museum and drew a map of West Africa with the place names in Arabic. In 1734, he was set free and took part in a fact-finding mission for the British Royal African Company, the goal of which was to increase trade with regions of West Africa. By 1735, he had returned to his village, found his family in good health and stayed there. According to one account, he died in his home village in 1773.[119]

In Islamic history, Ayub Sulaiman ibn Diallo is praised as a kind of living martyr because he kept faith with Islam throughout his years as a slave and never swerved from the so-called *true faith*. The fact behind the fact is that his slave owners allowed him to practice his beliefs and never threatened to kill him if he did not convert to Christianity, which is quite the contrary to that which happened to Christians and Jews who became slaves under the Muslims and the Moors, Muslims from North Africa.

### Salim the Algerian

A fourth slave person sold into slavery after having been captured by a Spanish man-of-war and who is often presented by Islamic Internet sites as a true Muslim, is Salim the Algerian. He was born into a Muslim royal family (contradiction in terms?) in Constantinople. After having been captured by the Spaniards, who had learned the slave trade from the Moors in Spain, Salim was sold to the French in New Orleans, Louisiana Territory. The fact that he was not a black

---

[119] Curtis, Edward E. *Muslims in America A Short History*, Oxford University Press, Oxford: 2009, pp. 1-5.

African enabled him to escape enslavement and to live among some Indians. Salim ended up in rags and half-starved in Virginia sometime in the 1770s. As a youth in Africa, Salim was taught Greek and when he was able to communicate in English, people learned that he could speak Greek. He was given a copy of the New Testament in Greek. Several Congressmen befriended him. He converted to Christianity and returned to his homeland to preach the Gospel of Jesus Christ. In his homeland he was treated as an apostate – there is so much brotherly love in Islam – and as a result he journeyed back to America. He met Thomas Jefferson and attended the opening of the first Congress. He developed insanity as a result of the trip to his homeland. This lasted for a number of years but he was able to recover. There are conflicting reports of his death. Some sources say that he died in an insane asylum, or that he died a Christian at the home of Congressman Robert Page (1765-1840, Federalist Party Representative in Congress 1799-1801). Another source says that he renounced his Christianity and converted back to Islam before his death. This last possibility is hailed by Muslims as a possible reason why he regained his sanity.[120]

## The Wahhab Brothers

There are a number of Islamic internet sites that also list the Wahhab brothers, whose first names are unknown, as important Islamic settlers in North Carolina. Sometime in the

---

[120] *Graham's Illustrated Magazine*, 1857, pp. 433-437 at http://books.google.de/books?id=ranPAAAAMAAJ&printsec=frontcover& hl=de#v=onepage&q&f=false, retrieved on 03.02.2012. See also http://www.muslimsinamerica.org/index2.php?option=com_content&do_pd f=1&id=15, retrieved on 03.02.2012.

1770s, perhaps even in 1770, they were shipwrecked off the North Carolina coast. According to the scant reports, the Wahhab brothers, who were not slaves, settled in North Carolina, married and started a farm or a tobacco plantation. There is no certain proof that they kept their Islamic faith. Since they married into Christian families, they most likely gave up their Islamic dogma. Today the name is spelled Wahab. The present-day Wahab family own a famous hotel chain in North Carolina. The first hotel was the *Wahab Village Hotel*, built in the late 1930s. The hotel operates today under the name *Blackwood Hotel*.[121] There is also the Wahab Public Law Library in Virginia Beach, Virginia, named after the Honorable Robert S. Wahab, Jr., another descendant of the Wahhab Brothers.[122]

## Assessment

The reader should understand that the short biographies of the Muslims presented above are symbolical of the types of Muslims, the conditions under which they came to the American Colonies, and the conclusions that can be gathered from their presence in Colonial America.

Some Islamic historical internet sites are proud to point out that none of the persons above attempted to spread Islam in

---

[121] A history of the Sahibs of Ocracoke Island, North Carolina is at http://circanceast.beaufortccc.edu/BCCC/articles/Spring%201984/PDF/Story3.pdf, retrieved on 03.02.2012.

[122]http://www.vbgov.com/government/departments/libraries/research/lawlibrary/pages/wahab-public-law-library.aspx, retrieved on 03-02-2012.

their new (slave) surroundings. They were proud of their heritage and preserved their own beliefs by rigidly following the dogma of Islam. At the same time, it must be said that although these persons did not actively attempt to spread Islam, the fact that they kept an allegiance to their dogma was a silent method of spreading Islamic tradition and dogma by example.

When many slaves came to the American Colonies it was immediately apparent that they could speak Arabic. Of course, this was not unusual. They had learned it as children. There were many clandestine Arabic schools in the slave quarters of the Caribbean and South America where many African heritage slaves were held in bondage before they came to the American Colonies.[123]

Although a slave, Istafan of Azamor, Morocco, is praised as a Muslim explorer whose explorations give present-day Muslims a certain pride that one of their own is credited with establishing knowledge of the American south and southwest. As such, Istafan of Azamor, Morocco presents a starting point as a substantial, historical foothold for those who argue that Muslims and Islam contributed to the discovery and exploration of America and therefore, should receive proper acknowledgement. Moreover, it underscores the Islamic logic that Americans must learn that the United States of America must become an Islamic country because a Muslim set foot in the Southwest of America. The same logic applies to Mexico because Istafan of Azamor, Morocco set foot in Mexico, a

---

[123] Madden, Robert. *Twelve Months in Jamaica*, Carey Lea and Blanchard, Philadelphia: 1835. See http://afifichestclinic.ning.com/profiles/blogs/a-collection-of-islamic, retrieved on 03.02.2012.

colony of Spain, a country that had formerly belonged to Islam. Where Islam sets its cancerous tentacles, it is there to stay.

Norsereddine the murderer, who killed a native Indian princess, is presented as that type of Muslim who avenges his being insulted by committing an honor killing. The attention that is given to him is not that of a base murderer, but that of a Muslim who has to regain his honor because a woman refuses to marry him. For a Muslim man this is the insult of insults. It has always been a principle of Allah's via Mohammed that killing an infidel, male or female, is not considered as murder, since it is Allah's will. The reader must also understand that the killing of any Native American was condoned by the Colonists.

Ayub Sulaiman ibn Diallo symbolizes the Muslim who never resigns his faith and becomes an apostate. He is regarded as the type of Muslim who, regardless of all trials and tribulations will never forsake Allah and his so-called Islamic holy traditions.

Salim the Algerian represents the Muslim who through his education and intellect is able to achieve recognition in the upper circles of society in Colonial America. At the same time, present-day Islamic historians allude to the fact and strongly point out that should a Muslim renounce his/her faith, it is very likely that that person will end up becoming insane. The worst crime for a Muslim is to renounce Islam and to embrace Judaism or Christianity. Allah of course, via Mohammed ordered that apostates be killed. It was law in the eighteenth century and it is law now. Allah's words via Mohammed words are: "One who changes his faith is to be killed."[124] At the same time, because Salim the Algerian returned to Islam, the claim is that he undertook al-taqiyya to save his life.

On page 30 of *The Bill of Legal Punishments*, by scholars of the Al-Azhar University in Cairo, there is this explanatory note: "The ordained penalty for apostasy is based on the Sunnah. The Prophet, peace be on him, said, 'One who changes his faith is to be killed' (al Bukhari). It is also narrated by Al Dar Qutni that when a woman called Umm-Marwan had renounced Islam, the Prophet ordered that if she failed to repent she should be put to death. The rightly guided Caliphs continued this practice. It is fully known that Abu-Bakr the truthful fought against those who had deserted from the religion of Islam and killed many. The Gracious Companions were of the same view, and a consensus emerged on this issue."

The death penalty for apostates is also recorded in

➢ Sahih of Muslim, Vol. I, p. 267 (interpretation of Nawawi).

➢ Shafi'i, *The Ordinances of the Qur'an*, part 2, p. 46.

➢ Ibn Hazm, part 11, Vol. 8, p. 377 and restated on p. 400.

➢ The Sheikh Shaltute in *Islam: a Dogma and a Law*, p. 322.

➢ Dr. Afifi 'Abdul-Fattah, in *The Spirit of the Islamic Religion*, p. 408.

It is obvious that the ordainment of death for apostates is well documented and unquestionably ascribed to Mohammed.

---

[124] http://www.bibletopics.com/biblestudy/96a.htm, retrieved on 15, 03.2012.

It is also well known that the Sahih of al-Bukhari has recorded in part 9, p. 18 that: "The apostate has to be killed based on Allah's saying in the Qur'an: 'And whosoever of you turns from his religion and dies disbelieving...'" (The Koran, The Cow: 217). Before the killing takes place, a former Muslim will be examined for insanity. Muslims are not allowed to accept the situation that a believer in Islam could renounce the dogma.[125]

The Wahhab Brothers symbolize those Muslims who came to the American Colonies as free persons, their goal being to start their lives anew in the free, New World. There is no indication that they continued their Islamic beliefs. Indeed, the present-day descendants who spell their name Wahab have never said that they were Muslims or that their ancestors were Muslims. Yet, they must have been Muslims, since the name comes from the 18th century Muslim dogmatist Muhammad ibn Abd al-Wahhab (1703–1792), who came from Najd, Saudi Arabia. It is Ibn Abdul Al-Wahhab who advocated that Islam must be purged of impurities and innovations. The dominant form of Islam in Saudi Arabia today is Wahhabism, and the King of Saudi Arabia leads the forefront in purging Islam and spreading Wahhabism Islam throughout the world.[126]

By the 1790s, Moors from Spain had settled in South Carolina and Florida. The South Carolina legislature passed The Moors Sundry Act of 1790. It granted special status to the

---

[125] http://allaboutmuhammad.com/islamic-jurisprudence.html, retrieved on 05.02.2012.

[126] http://www.pbs.org/wgbh/pages/frontline/shows/saudi/analyses/wahhabism.html, retrieved on 05.02.2012.

subjects of the Sultan of Morocco and recognized the Moors as white people with the responsibility of jury duty. The Moors in South Carolina and Florida were not subject to the laws governing slaves and slavery.[127] The descendants of the Moors in Florida are certainly the tri-racial isolated Melungeons of Gulf and Calhoun Counties, also known as the *Florida Melungeons.*

It is most probable that the mixed-race families later named *Melungeons* originated in the Chesapeake Bay region during the 17th century with the so-called Atlantic Creoles, who were descendants of marriages and/or co-habitations of freed slaves (often of mixed race) and indentured servants who came from English, Northern European, and West African stock. It is accepted fact that some Atlantic Creoles were Hispanic or Latinos. Their ancestors had been paternal Portuguese or Spanish explorers and settlers in the New World who had mixed with African women either in African ports or with African slaves who had been brought to the Portuguese and Spanish colonies in the Americas. It is not uncommon that their family names are Chavez, Francisco, or Rodriguez. Intermarriages took place with indigenous whites, mostly English. They took on the English names and themselves owned slaves. Some Atlantic Creoles also intermarried or copulated with Native Americans, although to a far lesser extent. This was probably the first American sociological melting pot.

---

[127] Stevens, Michael and Allen, Christine *State Records of South Carolina. Journals of the House of Representatives*, 1789-90, University of South Carolina Press: 1984, pp. 364 ff.

# CHAPTER FIVE

# Islam and America 1800-2000

## Belligerent Engagements with Muslim Pirates

The young American Republic was not in an atmosphere of political isolation after the Revolutionary War with the establishment of the United States of America, and its emergence on the world scene. Everyday life in Colonial America had changed little from that of 1700. Yet, between 1800 and 1900, with the advent of the industrial revolution, transformations in world economies, international trade, and advances in ship building, the United States of America was destined to emerge as a world power. Naturally there were two main Islamic regions of the earth that would be adversaries of the emerging nation.

### The Barbary Wars[128]

The first of these Islamic regions is the Barbary Coast: countries of North Africa that stretch from the western border of Egypt to the Atlantic Ocean. The small, autonomous kingdoms under Ottoman rule that existed at the time of the Barbary Wars are Morocco, Algeria, Tunis, and Tripolitania. The nomenclature Barbary is the English corruption of Berbers, the people who lived in North Africa. When the Arab Muslims

---

[128] A thorough presentation of the importance of the Barbary Wars for the United States of America is Lambert, Frank. *The Barbary Wars American Independence in the Atlantic World*, Hill and Wang, New York: 2005.

conquered the regions they called the people Barbarians, from the Latin *barbaria* and Byzantine Greek βαρβαρία, meaning *land of barbarians*, a term that the Muslims borrowed to describe non-Islamic lands. Berber lands also included non-coastal regions, deep into the continent.[129]

During the seventeenth and eighteenth centuries, pirates from these kingdoms harassed merchant shipping in the Mediterranean and nearby Atlantic Ocean, selling their booty and enslaving or ransoming the prisoners.

The Muslims in North Africa possessed tens of thousands of slaves, many of them Christian, throughout the one thousand years beginning in approximately 707, when all of North Africa came under their control. The most feared of the pirate kingdoms were those located on the Barbary Coast. The Barbary pirates knew the open Atlantic Ocean well. Throughout a thousand years they plied the Mediterranean Sea and Atlantic Ocean searching for European ships to pillage and plunder. They were capable of sailing as far north and west as Iceland (where they went ashore and captured 800 slaves during one incident) and as far west as Newfoundland, Canada, sometimes pillaging more than 40 vessels at one time. By the 1630s, Algiers held 32,000 white Christian slaves, 2000 of them women. Even Miguel de Cervantes Saavedra, the author of *Don Quixote,* was enslaved in the Algerian Caliphate in the late 1500s. The Algerian Muslims thought that he was an

---

[129] *Encyclopaedia Britannica, Micropaedia*, William Benton, Chicago: 1974, Vol. 1, p. 806; and London, Joshua E. *Victory in Tripoli: How America's War with the Barbary Pirates Established the U.S. Navy and Shaped a Nation*, John Wiley & Sons, Inc., New Jersey: 2005.

important Spaniard and required a ransom of 500 gold escudos. Cervantes remained in Algerian captivity for five years.[130]

The British navy could have wiped out the pirates, destroying them completely. However, Great Britain allowed the Barbary pirates to remain a threat to those countries that were its maritime rivals. Great Britain purchased protection for its ships with an annual tribute.

Until the American Revolutionary War the British tribute arrangement protected American colonial shipping. However, after the war for independence was won, the Barbary pirates began raiding American shipping, causing substantial losses. Supported by the British, Algiers declared war on the United States of America in July 1785. Algiers captured an "'infinite number' of American vessels, including one carrying Benjamin Franklin home from France."[131] There were debates in the new Congress concerning the piracy. Yet, Congress was not willed to invest in the necessary funds for men and material to combat the Barbary pirates.

On June 28, 1786, the United States of America made one of its most important diplomatic mistakes. It signed a treaty with Morocco that guaranteed payment of an annual tribute. Throughout the next ten years, more treaties were made with the other Barbary kingdoms, some holding legality until the defeat of the Barbary pirate kingdoms in 1815.

---

[130] http://www.faithfreedom.org/Articles/SStephan/islamic_slavery.htm, retrieved on 08.02.2012.

[131] Allison, Robert J. *The Crescent Obscured The United States and the Muslim World 1776-1815*, Oxford University Press: 1995, p. 3.

There were two Barbary Wars between the United States and the Barbary countries of Northwest Africa. The first was from 1801-1805 and is called the Tripolitan War or the Barbary Coast War (Tripoli and Algiers). In 1801, the Pasha of Tripoli demanded more tribute money. The United States refused. On May 14, 1801, President Thomas Jefferson, who had always been against the tribute payments to any Barbary pirate kingdom, sent American warships to the Mediterranean. Under Commander Edward Preble, warring action began in 1803.

In February 1804, Lt. Stephen Decatur recaptured and destroyed the lost American ship *Philadelphia*, a frigate that Tripolitania had captured a few months before in late 1803. The American ships blockaded Tripoli. A peace treaty stipulating that there would be no tribute payments was signed on June 4, 1805. A quasi-peaceful period covered the next seven years. Sensing an opportunity to punish American shipping and the possibility of receiving tribute, Hadji Ali ben Khrelil, the Dey of Algiers, declared war on the United States in the War of 1812, thinking that the United States would not be strong enough to force his hand and combat him.

The long-term result of the Dey's action was the Second Barbary War of 1815, also known as the Algerine or Algerian War (Tripoli, Tunis, Algeria). On May 10, 1815, under the command of Captain Decatur, the United States sent a marine expedition to counter the Algerine kingdom. Captain Decatur promptly captured two enemy ships, and a treaty that guaranteed the future security of American vessels without payment of tribute with Algeria was signed on June 30, 1815.

The war was brought to a final conclusion with the assistance of the United Kingdom and the Netherlands. Further conclusive treaties were signed with Tunis and Tripolitania, and American ships suffered no further attacks. For the United States of America the days of paying tribute to the pirate states ended. Islamic piracy, which had been rampant in the 16th to 18th centuries was stopped in the Mediterranean Sea and regions of the Atlantic Ocean.

Although United States shipping was no longer attacked and America no longer had to pay any future tributes, the Barbary pirate slave trade continued sporadically up until the dawn of the 20th century. The trade was abolished only when military and economic pressures were instituted by the European colonial powers, namely France and Great Britain, with some assistance from the United States military.

European and American slaves were the mainstay of the Barbary Coast economies. European countries paid tribute in exchange for the halting of pirate attacks on their coasts and shipping. Many times those enslaved were set free for high ransoms. If ransoms were not forthcoming, the Muslims enjoyed the benefits of unpaid labor and sales of slaves in their markets. The bottom line was that Christian nations had to fight and be victorious or pay the Muslim ransom.

### The Depiction by Royall Tyler

Already in 1797, the American poet, dramatist, novelist and jurist Royall Tyler finished his research and published a novel, *The Algerine Captive, or, the Life and Adventures of Doctor Updike Underhill, Six Years a Prisoner Among the*

*Algerines*. The source of the story is true-fiction-quasi-auto-biography of Tyler's time that is based on the true-life experiences of Doctor Underhill, a New Englander with common sense, yet at the same time with prejudice and narrow mind, who is captured by the Algerines.[132] *The Algerine Captive* is a novel that presents the atmosphere of the Barbary Wars and the roots of the conflict into the decade of the 1780s. A major subject of the book is slavery. Tyler formidably, morally, and justly attacks the institution of slavery against the backdrop of the United States conflict with the Barbary states (Morocco, Algeria, Tunis, and Tripolitania) whose ships were pirating both the Mediterranean Sea and the African side of the Atlantic Ocean.

Tyler pictures in realistic and painful detail the terrors occurring aboard slave ships. His motive is to ridicule the pseudo-pre-romantic and biblically-oriented justifications of slavery and to attack the inhuman brutality of the immoral slave trade.

With the subject matter of slavery as his literary *raison d'être*, Tyler unfolds his uncanny ability to catch and express the major currents of his time. Thomas Jefferson and a few

---

[132] It seems that the Algerine adventure theme was quite well known in the early 1790s. Tanselle, Thomas in *Royall Tyler*, Harvard University Press, Cambridge, Massachusetts: 1967, pp. 142-143 lists fourteen works (twelve books, one play and one poem) by American and European authors concerning the Barbary Coast beginning with the year 1735. Oscar George Theodore Sonneck in *A Bibliography of Early Secular Music* lists the following item on page 12: "*ALGERINE CAPTIVE. Song by Raynor Taylor. Made part of his folio ... entirely new,' which was to be performed at Philadelphia, on February 1, 1794." This is three years before Tyler's publication of his *The Algerine Captive*.

other men with vision had grasped that slavery would be the great, divisive, moral issue of the coming century, and all of these political soothsayers, particularly Jefferson, terribly feared the issue of slavery would be the source of a future civil war between the states. Tyler's selection and treatment of the slavery issue illustrates with what instinct he was able to understand, present, and make a decision on the moral climate of his time. Tyler uses the reflections of his picaresque hero, Updike Underhill, an American doctor returning after seven years of captivity in the hands of the Algerine pirates, as a device to deliver his message on the slavery issue.

On 18 July 1788, Doctor Updike Underhill sets sail for the coast of Africa on the ship *Sympathy*. His responsibility is to make sure that the slaves being transported from Africa to America are in good health. An epidemic breaks out on the ship and Doctor Underhill advises that the slaves be set on land so that they can recover. While they are recuperating, the slave ship abandons them and they are subsequently captured by the Algerine pirate ship *Rover* and taken to Algiers. This is the situation at the end of the first volume.

Volume II of *The Algerine Captive* is a picaresque framework as far as it is concerned with Algeria's costuming, customs, economy, festivals, funerals, geography, government, history, language, law, marriage, military, taxes, urban development in Algiers, Mahomet's life, religion, Islamic sermons, sects, and the torture of slaves. One of the most popular tortures was the *bastinado*, during which the torturer struck the soles of the slave's feet at least one hundred times with a wooden truncheon. Slaves were executed for trying to escape, burned at the stake, or impaled on huge iron hooks or large wooden poles shoved up the rectum and extruding out of the slave's neck. One of the Muslim's favorite methods of dealing with runaway slaves or those who insulted Islam, Mohammed, or the Muslim ruler was public crucifixion. In their own minds the beys, deys and bashaws of the Barbary States were only doing Allah's and Mohammed's will.[133]

Doctor Underhill attempts to assist a slave who is undergoing a whipping and he ends up in a stone quarry. Tyler uses the situation to expound on freedom in America. In chapter 37, Doctor Underhill and the slaves accompanying him on a ship seized by Tunis are finally freed by a Portuguese ship. On 3 May 1795, after seven years in captivity, Doctor Updike Underhill finally arrives at Chesapeake Bay via Portugal and England, purchases a horse, and rides home for a reunion with his family.

The foremost political statement in *The Algerine Captive* is that allowing slavery to exist anywhere in the world is an insult to free America. The importance and high value of a free government is appreciated only when those who philosophize against it have experienced slavery.

What America can learn from the Barbary Wars is that when conducting relationships with Islamic states, they will

---

[133] A Bey is a Turkish title comparable to the Arabic *emir*, meaning *prince*. A Dey is the title of the rulers of the Regency of Algiers and the Regency of Tripoli under the Ottoman Empire from 1671 to 1830, when they were conquered and set free from Ottoman control. A bashaw is a pasha, which is equivalent to the title lord in English. *White Slaves, African Masters* at http://www.faithfreedom.org/Articles/SStephan/islamic_slavery.htm, which was retrieved on 06.02.2012.

understand only the total engagement of military might. Islamic regimes are dictatorial. They look upon diplomacy as a weakness. Such regimes are ready to make peace agreements only if it allows them time, however long, to regroup their forces. It is a good idea, when having relations with Islamic states, to follow the maxim *if you want peace, prepare to fight for it.*[134]

## Muslim Pirates in Sumatra

The second region where America had belligerent contact with Islam was Sumatra. The country had been a source of pepper since the Age of Discovery. In 1831, an American merchant vessel, the *Friendship* under Captain Charles Endicott, arrived in Kuala Batee to load a cargo of pepper. On February 7, 1831, while Captain Endicott and some men were ashore to purchase pepper, three small sailing vessels attacked the *Friendship*. The Muslims murdered the first officer, two crew members, and plundered the cargo. Captain Endicott and the survivors escaped to a friendlier port. There they enlisted assistance of other merchant vessel captains and returned to Kuala Batee to repossess their ship. After this successful undertaking, Captain Endicott eventually reached his home port of Salem, Massachusetts. Immediately a public outcry took place against the massacre.

The most feared terrorists in the Pacific were the Islamic pirates operating in the Straits of Melaka. In his third State of the Nation speech in December 1831, President

---

[134] Vegetius [Flavius Vegetius] (flourished. c.375) in the prologue to *De Rei Militari*, III, opined "Let him who desires peace prepare for war." at http://www.pvv.ntnu.no/~madsb/home/war/vegetius/.

Andrew Jackson recounted that a piratical threat was underway in the East Indies that involved the plunder of American merchant vessels taking part in the pepper trade of Sumatra. President Jackson was convinced that "A daring outrage having been committed in those seas by the plunder of one of our merchant-men engaged in the pepper trade at a port in Sumatra, and the piratical perpetrators belonging to tribes in such a state of society that the usual course of proceedings between civilized nations could not be pursued, I forthwith dispatched a frigate with orders to require immediate satisfaction for the injury and indemnity to the sufferers."[135]

President Andrew Jackson (1767-1845; President 1829-1837) sent forth the *USS Potomac*, a frigate under the command of Commodore John Downes, to punish the Muslim pirate natives for their treachery against the American merchant vessel *Friendship* in Sumatra in 1831.[136] Upon arriving at Kuala Batee on February 5, 1832, Commodore Downes disguised the *USS Potomac* as a Danish merchant vessel to guarantee an element of surprise. He also sent a reconnaissance party to bring back information about Kuala Batee. Downs equipped some of the ship's boats with light cannon and ordered a contingent of 282 Marines into the boats for an assault. They burned the Malay vessels in Kuala Batee's harbor, and their assault of the forts was supported by cannon fire from the *Potomac*. The American Marines had modern rifles that more than outperformed the Malayan matchlock guns. In the attack,

---

[135] http://www.let.rug.nl/usa/P/aj7/speeches/ajson3.htm, retrieved on 15.03.2012.

[136] http://www.sabrizain.org/malaya/potomac.htm, retrieved on 11.02.2012.

one Malay Raja and 150 of his soldiers were killed. Two Americans died in the battle. When Kuala Batee fell, the Americans looted, pillaged, and plundered the town, killing many of its inhabitants. Commodore Downes gave orders to his men to board ship. He bombarded the remaining fort, killing approximately 300 inhabitants. The leaders of Kuala Batee eventually agreed to surrender. Commodore Downes informed the surviving Rajas that should they attack American ships in the future, the same fate would befall them. The Rajas from nearby states sent their emissaries to obtain a truce. A treaty settlement was never signed. Commodore Downes departed and completed his scheduled circumnavigation of the globe.

In 1838, during the first year of the presidency of Martin van Buren (1782-1862; President 1837-1841) the Malaysians massacred the crew of another American merchant ship, *Eclipse*. This news reached the commander of the East India Squadron, Commodore George C. Read, who was riding the bounding main off the coast of Ceylon. Immediately he set sail with the frigates *Columbia* and *John Adams*. The *Columbia* had 500 men and 50 cannons. The *John Adams* had 220 men and 30 cannons. On January 1, 1839, they fired on Kuala Batee and destroyed it. They then set out for Mukie and destroyed that locality. This second Sumatran expedition had the result that the Malays never again plundered American merchant ships.[137]

---

[137] Meacham, Jon. *American lion: Andrew Jackson in the White House*, Random House New York: 2008, and Murrell, William Meacham. *Cruise Of The Frigate Columbia Around The World Under The Command Of Commodore George C. Read*, Benjamin B. Mussey, Boston, Mass.: 1840.

The dispatched chastisement vessels to demand retribution and put a stop to the piracy were successful in their efforts. Finally, in 1838, with the assistance of the British ship HMS Diana, the piracy of the Sumatra Islamists in the Strait of Melaka and in the East Indies was thwarted.

Other confrontations with Muslim pirates were averted when the first legal, commercial activity with a Muslim country was undertaken in 1839. Sayyid Sa'id, the ruler of Oman, understanding the naval might of the United States Navy and thinking it better that Oman be on friendly terms with the United States of America, sent a commercial representative to New York on his ship *Sultana*. In the Muslim psyche this year signals the beginning of friendly relations with the United States of America. Muslim historians claim that this friendly relationship with the America continues to this very day.[138] The claim is a double-edged sword: friendly relations on the one hand, jihad attacks by Islamists on the other hand.

## Slavery and Movements

The numbers of Muslim slaves in the American Colonies were in the thousands. By the year 1800 there were at least 500,000 Africans in the United States of America, up to 30 percent of the males and up to 15 percent of the females being Muslims. At least 200,000 came from Islamic controlled regions of Africa.[139] It is estimated that more than 30 percent of

---

[138] Eilts, Herman Fredrick. *The visit of Ahmad bin Na'aman to the U.S. in the Year 1840,* Embassy of Oman: 1962.

[139] Curtis, Edward E. *Muslims in America: A Short History,* Oxford University Press, Oxford: 2009, pp. 1-23; and Koszegi, Michael; Melton, J.

118

the circa 10 million enslaved by the conquering Arab Muslims in Africa who arrived in the American Colonies, Mexico, Cuba, and South America were Muslims. The records indicate that they were determined in their resistance to their being slaves; yet they were not resistant to others being slaves.[140] Muslims made an effort to observe their dogma, passing their beliefs on in their own core families. Islam was an important element in the social strata of Colonial America. There were numerous occurrences of polygamy among Muslim slaves and Muslim freemen in America in the eighteenth century and on into the nineteenth century. In many instances Muslims did not abide by the American heritage customs and they did not obey civil laws. They saw no need to do so because their highest law was the Koran and the hadiths. Muslims were literate and good organizers, ready to command other slaves.

# Randomly Selected Examples of Muslims in America During the Nineteenth Century.

## Sidi Soliman Mellimelli and an *Iftar* Dinner?

On December 9, 1805, President Thomas Jefferson received a temporary envoy from Tunisia, Sidi Soliman Mellimelli. He was sent to the United States by his sultan in hopes to deliver a declaration of war and to obtain restitution

---

Gordon. *Islam in North America: A Sourcebook*, Garland Publishers, New York: 1992, pp. 26–27.

[140] Hill, Samuel S. and Lippy, Charles H. Charles Reagan Wilson *Encyclopedia of religion in the South,* Mercer University Press, Macon, Georgia: 2005, p. 394.

for captured Tunisian vessels. Jefferson was interested in talking to the ambassador about the piracy being conducted against American merchant ships by Tunisia, but beyond that was not interested in Islam. It was the Islamic fasting month of Ramadan and the temporary envoy said that he could not come to dinner during the day. Jefferson was polite and delayed the dinner a few hours to sunset. There was no special menu. President Jefferson changed the time of the dinner from the usual 3:30 pm to sunset. This dinner was referred to by Barack Hussein Obama at the Iftar Dinner in the White House in 2010. Attempting to rewrite American history, Obama stated, "Ramadan is a reminder that Islam has always been a part of America. The first Muslim ambassador (who actually was not an ambassador) to the United States, from Tunisia, was hosted by President Jefferson, who arranged a sunset dinner for his guest because it was Ramadan – making it the first known iftar at the White House, more than 200 years ago." The truth is that Jefferson never referred to the dinner as an *iftar dinner*. After this presentation of social etiquette on Jefferson's part, there were no more *iftar dinners* at the White House until William Jefferson Clinton and Hillary Clinton began hosting similar affairs in 1996, followed by George W. Bush after the Islamic attack on the World Trade Center in New York City on September 11, 2001. These *iftar dinners* and the statement that Al-Qaida had hijacked a great religion (Islam) are two of the greatest *faux pas* in American diplomacy and politics that President George W. Bush made during his presidency.

Islam has not always been a part of America, at least not as a positive contributor to American history. Barack Hussein Obama is oblivious to the fact that during the era of the Barbary

Wars Presidents John Adams (1735-1826; President 1797-1801), Thomas Jefferson (1743-1826; President 1801-1809), James Madison (1751-1836; President 1809-1817), and James Monroe (1758-1831; President 1817-1825) did have knowledge of the secrets of Islam and an understanding of Muslim evil behavior. Particularly between 1805 and 1815, these presidents wanted nothing more than to make the Atlantic Ocean and the Mediterranean Sea safe for American and European merchant shipping and to put an end to the piracy, the capturing of vessels, the enslavement of the crews and the payment of ransom to the vicious, evil Muslim leaders of the Barbary kingdoms.

Already in 1786, President Jefferson had learned about the behavior of the Barbary pirates. In that year Jefferson, then the American ambassador to France, and John Adams, then the American ambassador to Britain, met in London with Sidi Haji Abdul Rahman Adja, the Tripolitan ambassador to Britain. Jefferson and Adams asked the ambassador why the Barbary kingdoms were always pirating and calling for ransom of captured crews. The ambassador gave Jefferson the answer that Muslim rulers have an inherent right to show such aggression because Allah in the Koran via Mohammed commands them to do so, for they are fighting against infidels who according to Allah, the Koran, and Mohammed have no rights.[141]

---

[141] A very good summation of the Tunisian ambassador's visit is at http://www.monticello.org/site/research-and-collections/tunisian-envoy, retrieved on 12.02.2012 and the information found at http://wn.com/Islam_in_America_Thomas_Jefferson%27s_Quran, retrieved on 14.03.2012. See also http://www.jihadwatch.org/2011/08/obama-spreads-false-claim-that-thomas-jefferson-hosted-first-ramadan-iftar-dinner-at-white-house.html, retrieved on 14.03.2012.

121

The opinions of John Quincy Adams (1767-1848; President 1825-1829) serve as being representative of the knowledge American politicians had about Muslim envoys and Islam. "The precept of the Koran (sic) is, perpetual war against all who deny that Mahomet is the prophet of God. The vanquished may purchase their lives, by the payment of tribute; the victorious may be appeased by a false and delusive promise of peace; and the faithful follower of the prophet, may submit to the imperious necessities of defeat: but the command to propagate the Moslem creed by the sword is always obligatory, when it can be made effective. The commands of the prophet may be performed alike by fraud or by force. ... Adopting from the new Revelation of Jesus the faith and hope of immortal life, and of future retribution, he humbled it to the dust, by adapting all the rewards and sanctions of his religion to the gratification of the sexual passion. He poisoned the sources of human felicity at the fountain, by degrading the condition of the female sex and the allowance of polygamy; and he declared undistinguishing and exterminating war, as a part of his religion, against all the rest of mankind. THE ESSENCE OF HIS DOCTRINE WAS VIOLENCE AND LUST: TO EXALT THE BRUTAL OVER THE SPIRITUAL PART OF HUMAN NATURE."[142]

This view of Islam was the truth accepted truth by American presidents in the early Republic. It has started to

---

[142] *The American Annual Register for 1827-28-29*, E. and G. W. Blunt, New York, 1830, p. 269. The emphasis is in the original source. In the quotation John Quincy Adama does not capitalize the word prophet, which, of course, refers to Mohammed.

change under Barack Hussein Obama's rewriting of history in a backdating atmosphere of *nunc pro tunc* (now for then).

Barack Hussein Obama will never admit the fact that the real truth is that Muslims and Islam have always been a threat to the United States of America. From the very first year after the American Revolutionary War, the United States of America have been confronted with Islamic terrorism or threats thereof. Yet, Barack Hussein Obama will always refer to historical Muslims and their supposed and so-called, but unfounded contributions to the American cultural heritage.

### Mamout Yarrow[143]

In a book entitled *A Chorographical and Statistical Description of the District of Columbia* by David Warden (Paris: 1816) we find the first narrative mention of Mamout Yarrow, who was born in Guinea into one of the nomadic tribes that speak Fulani. He was fluent in Arabic and Fulani. Moreover, the name Yaro is common in that language today. He and his sister came to the American Colonies (in 1750?) as slaves when Yarrow was ca. 14 years old. Yarrow was bought by and worked for Brooke Beall, who gave him slave work. Shortly before he was set free, Yarrow made bricks for the Beall house in Georgetown. Mr. Beall promised to free Yarrow when the work was done. However, Mr. Brooke Beall died before the house was completed. Consequently, his wife Margaret freed Yarrow in 1796. In freedom, Yarrow worked tirelessly and managed to save 100 dollars, which he gave to a

---

[143] http://www.ishof.org/black_history/pdf/mamoutYarrow.pdf, retrieved on 08.02.2012 and Austin, Allan D. *African Muslims in Antebellum America Transatlantic Stories and Spiritual Struggles*, Routledge, New York: 1997.

merchant for safekeeping and possible investment. The merchant died and the money was lost. Yarrow began to save more money, ultimately attaining another 100 dollars. He gave the money to another merchant with the same result. The merchant died before Yarrow could reap any investment. A third attempt at saving money resulted in the sum of 200 dollars. On the advice of a friend, who explained the operation of a bank, Yarrow purchased shares in the Bank of Columbia (the Georgetown Bank). The Columbia Bank became the second chartered bank in 1817, with headquarters in Philadelphia, Pennsylvania. With the interest from his shares Yarrow was able to purchase a house and live comfortably.

Although he could speak only broken English, Yarrow liked conversation. A specimen of his speech has been preserved: "Olda massa been tink he got all de work out of a Yaro bone. He tell a Yaro, go free Yaro; you been work nuff for me, go work for you now . . . Yaro work a soon – a late – a hot – a cold. Sometime he sweat – sometime he blow a finger."

When Charles Wilson Peale did Yarrow's portrait 1818, he noted in his diary, "I heard of a Negro who is living in Georgetown said to be 140 years of age ... He is comfortable in his Situation having Bank stock and lives in his own house ... . I propose to make a portrait of him should I have the opportunity. ... I spend [spent] the whole day & not only painted a good likeness of him, but also the drapery & background. ... Yarrow owns a House & lotts (sic) and is known by most of the Inhabitants of Georgetown & particularly by the Boys who are often teasing him which he takes in good humour. It appears to me that the good temper of the [m]an has contributed considerably to longevity. Yarrow has been noted for sobriety & a chearfull (sic) conduct, he professes to be a mahometan (sic), and is often seen & heard in the Streets singing Praises to God – and conversing with him he said man is no good unless his religion comes from the heart ... . The acquaintance of him often banter him about eating Bacon and drinking Whiskey – but Yarrow says it is no good to eat Hog – & drink whiskey is very bad. I retouched his Portrait the morning after his first setting to mark what rinkles (sic) & lines to characterize (sic) better his Portrait."

It was claimed that Yarrow was 134 or 140 years old. At the time of the portrait he was in his eighties. Yarrow had told Peale that he didn't drink whiskey. Another source says that "Yarrow fired a gun on (each) Christmas morning as a signal for his 'dram,' ... which ... presumably meant alcohol. In the *Gettysburg Compiler*, February 12, 1823, one can read Yarrow's obituary: "Died – at Georgetown, on the 19th ultimo, negro Yarrow, aged (according to his account) 136 years. He was interred in the corner of his garden, the spot where he usually resorted to pray . . . it is known to all that knew him, that he was industrious, honest, and moral – in the early part of his life he met with several losses by loaning money, which he never got, but he persevered in industry and economy, and accumulated some Bank stock and a house and lot, on which he lived comfortably in his old age – Yarrow was never known to eat of swine, nor drink ardent spirits."

Yarrow signed his documents in Arabic, family name first, which translated into *Mahmoud Yaro, God Willing*.

Yarrow had enough money to loan to a merchant so that he could buy a "two story brick dwelling and store house with extensive back buildings, situated on the west side" of present-day Wisconsin Avenue in Georgetown. Yarrow had a son named Aquilla who died at Harper's Ferry in 1832. Located near Harper's Ferry is a road named *Yarrowsburg Road.* Yarrowsburg was a collection of small houses at an intersection. Yarrowsburg was named after the family and forefathers of Polly Yarrow, who was over100 years old when she died. Records show that she was the wife of Yarrow's son Aquilla.

Islamic sites honor Yarrow because he overcame slavery and never gave up his Islam, which helped him win personal respect and respect for the religion. His historical importance is that Islamists can claim that he gave an early village the name of Yarrowsburg, the nomenclature of which, the Islamists claim, has its roots in Arabic and Islam. (See the explanations of the various towns named Yarrowsburg in Chapter Seven.)

### Omar Ibn Said[144]

One of the most famous African-Muslim auto-biographies is that written by Omar Ibn Said in 1839 while he was still a slave. He recalls his education in Africa, his ability to read, write, and speak Arabic, his knowledge of the Koran, his being taken as a prisoner of war in Africa and his life as a slave in America. Although it is interesting that he closes his

---

[144] http://docsouth.unc.edu/nc/omarsaid/omarsaid.html, retrieved on 08.02.2012

autobiography by stating that he is no longer a Muslim, Omar Ibn Said is often held in high esteem for the simple fact that he did not forget his Muslim ancestry and culture. Perhaps Omar Ibn Said was doing nothing more than executing al-taqiyya and saying that he was no longer a Muslim when in actuality he was still one, because he was born into a Muslim family. Once a Muslim, always a Muslim, or one must be killed because of apostasy.

### Abdu-l-Rahman Ibrahim Ibn Sori[145]

Abdu-I-Rahman Ibrahim Ibn Sori, a West African prince was a slave in the United States for 40 years. Of the Fulbe tribe, he was born in Timbo in 1762. At the age of twelve, he left his village to study in Timbuktu, Mali. As a leader of one of his father's army divisions, Ibrahim was ambushed, captured, enslaved, shipped to America, and finally sold to Thomas Foster in Natchez, Mississippi in 1728. Having knowledge of how to grow cotton which he had learned in his homeland, Ibrahim became the overseer of the Foster plantation. He married a slave named Isabella and they had five sons and four daughters.

One day while selling produce at the local market, he accidentally met Dr. John Cox, an Irish surgeon whom Ibrahim had met and had befriended in Timbo. Dr. Cox tried to purchase Ibrahim from Mr. Foster, but the latter adamantly refused, because Ibrahim was indispensable for the continuous profits of the cotton plantation.

---

[145] http://www.pbs.org/programs/prince-among-slaves/ was retrieved on 08.02.2012.

In 1826, Abdul-I-Rahman Ibrahim Sori wrote a letter in Arabic to his relatives in Africa. A local newspaperman, Andrew Marschalk, who was originally from New York, sent a copy of the letter to Senator Thomas Reed (1787-1829, served 1826-1827; 1828-1829) of Missouri in Washington, who forwarded it to the United States Consulate in Morocco. The Sultan of Morocco, Moulay Sharif Abderrahmane (Abd-er-Rahman) (1778–1859; sultan from 1822 to 1859), read the letter and recognizing that Ibrahim was a prince, requested that President John Quincy Adams (1767-1848; President 1825-1829) and Secretary of State Henry Clay (1777-1852, Secretary of State 1825-1829) free Abd al-Rahman Ibrahim. In 1828, Thomas Foster freed Ibrahim, without payment, but stipulated that Ibrahim had to return to Africa and was not to live as a free man in America.

About a year before leaving the United States of America, Ibrahim and his wife Isabella journeyed to various states and Washington, D. C., made personal appearances, asked for the support of the press, and collected private donations so that they could buy back the members of his family still under enslavement in Mississippi. In the course of ten months, they had raised only half of the funds that they needed to free their children. With this money they went to Monrovia, Liberia. Four months later Ibrahim contacted a fever and died at the age of 67. He never saw his children. The Mississippi plantation owner Thomas Foster died the same year. The plantation was divided amongst his heirs throughout Mississippi. With the breakup of the plantation it was possible for two sons and their families to travel to Monrovia where they were joined their mother. The other children stayed in

Mississippi. Abdul Rahman's descendants still live in Monrovia and the United States. In 2006, Abdul-Rahman's descendants gathered for a family reunion at Foster's Field.

Abdul Rahman wrote two autobiographies. His portrait hangs in the Library of Congress. In 1977, Terry Alford documented the life of Ibn Sori in *The Prince Among Slaves*, the first full portrayal of his life, pieced together from recorded memories and historical documents. Islamic sources honor Abdul-Rahman as an example of a Muslim who never gave up his belief and his homeland.

### Hadji Ali[146]

In 1856, the United States Army Cavalry engaged Hadji Ali (1828-1902), later known as Philip Tedro, also Teadrow, an Ottoman subject of Jordanian heritage, to experiment with camels in Arizona and to find out to what extent they could be used as service animals for the United States Army. For the experiment 75 camels and six camel handlers were brought to America. When the American Civil War broke out the experiment was stopped. Five of the camel handlers returned to their country of origin. Hadji Ali remained in the United States. Some of the camels were obtained by circuses and zoos, but most of them were released into the Arizona wilderness. They

---

[146] *Report of the Secretary of War, communicating, in compliance with a resolution of the Senate of February 2, 1857, information respecting the purchase of camels for the purposes of military transportation.* United States. War Dept., Davis, Jefferson, 1808-1889, Colombari, F., Wayne, Henry C. tr. (Henry Constantine), 1815-1883; retrieved on 15.03.2012 from http://quod.lib.umich.edu/cgi/t/text/text-idx?c=moa&cc=moa&view=text& rgn=main&idno=AGX7642.0001.001; http://www.outwestnewspaper.com/ camels.html that was retrieved on 16.03.2012.

became the terror of livestock and wild animals. In 1880 Ali, also called by the nickname Hi Jolly, became an American citizen. He changed his name to Philip Tedro (Teadrow) upon marrying Gertrudis Serna in Tucson, Arizona. They had two children. In 1885, during the Geronimo campaign, Philip Tedro was rehired by the US Army. He worked as a packer under Brigadier General George Crook (1828-1890). Philip Tedro remained in Arizona as a prospector in the region of the Colorado River. He lived in Quartzsite, Arizona, where he died in 1902. There is a monument dedicated to him on his grave in the Quartzsite Cemetery.

## A Non-Miracle of Saving the Koran from Burning

On the morning of April 4, 1865, during the American Civil War, federal troops advanced to the campus of the University of Alabama. Their orders were to destroy the university. André Delofre, the custodian of the Rotundra Library and a professor of French and Spanish pleaded with the commanding officer, Colonel Thomas F. Johnston of the Second Michigan Cavalry, to spare the valuable library. Colonel Johnston sent a message to Brigadier General John T. Croxton (1837-1874) located in Tuscaloosa, Alabama, who was the commander of the federal forces. Brigadier General Croxton sent the following message to the officer at the library, "My orders leave me no discretion. My orders are to destroy all public buildings." It is related that before the destruction took place, Colonel Johnston told André Deloffre, and Dr. William S. Wyman, professor of Latin and Greek he would save one book as a sign and remembrance of this occasion. It is part of the mythic fabric of the University of Alabama that the salvaged book was *The Koran: Commonly Called The Alcoran Of Mohammed*, English translation published in Philadelphia in 1853. The saving of the book is mere hearsay.[147] There is no documented substantiation. Islamic sites claim that the "well-chosen volume was a rare copy of the Qur'an", as if it had been the will of Allah, whereby, if the incident is more than hearsay, it was only matter of luck that the book was chosen. However, these websites insinuate that it was a sign from Allah that the Koran be spared destruction.

## The Blyden Bloop

Edward Wilmot Blyden (1832-1912) was a well-known Americo-Liberian diplomat, educator, minister, orator, politician, scholar, sociologist, and writer. Blyden is known today as the father of Pan-Africanism, a movement that has as its goal the unifying of all African peoples into one African community. In his *Christianity, Islam and the Negro Race* (1887), Blyden promoted the anti-Christian philosophy that Islam was more unifying and fulfilling for Africans than Christianity ever was or ever would become. Therein lies his bloop. Christianity is based on love. Islam is based on hate for everything that is not Islam. Blyden argued that because Christianity was introduced into Africa by European colonizers, it was bad and demoralizing. (Evidently, Blyden forgot that Christianity was also introduced into Africa by the Romans in the few hundred years after the Resurrection of Christ. The Copts introduced Christianity into the eastern regions of North Africa.) On the other hand, in his eyes Islam had more

---

[147] http://www.alabamaheritage.com/vault/UAburning.htm, retrieved on 16.03.2012.

authenticity for Africa. The failure in his logic is that totalitarian Islam was introduced into Africa by colonizing and dictatorial Islamists emulating Mohammed. Edward Wilmot Blyden failed to comprehend the evilness in the latter with the freedom in the former.

Nonetheless, in 1889, Edward Wilmot Blyden began a series of trips along the American eastern seaboard and into the American south. He gave lectures on Islam. In one of the speeches before the Colonization Society of Chicago, Blyden lectured the audience on the reasons Africans chose Islam instead of Christianity. He maintained that "the Qur'an protected the black man from self-depreciation in the presence of Arabs or Europeans".[148] The first problem with this quotation is that it is written as if Blyden said this, but it may be from some Islamic site owner who wants to infer that Blyden said the quotation. The second problem is that the quotation is repeated by at least ten Islamic internet sites without any documentation. One cannot find the quotation anywhere other than on these sites. The third problem with the quotation is that it contradicts what Edward Wilmot Blyden says about Christianity and Islam in other places, particularly his *The Elements of Permanent Influence* (1890). The fourth problem is that the opposite, that Christianity protected the black man from self-deprecation in the presence of Arabs or Europeans holds equally true. Blyden's position, if he ever stated it as such, may have been a convincing argument at the time to those who knew nothing about the system of slavery and death imposed

---

[148] http://www.jihadwatch.org/2006/01/fitzgerald-take-a-tour-of-dawanet. html, retrieved on 18.03.2012.

by the Arab Muslims on black Africans who would not convert to Islam. There is no sura in the Koran saying that Allah and Mohammed protect one against self-depreciation. Indeed, if the only recourse one has is either to convert to Islam or be killed for being an unbeliever, then self-depreciation is not a question. Remaining alive is.

## Two Presidents and Their Standpoints

The evil, willful killing of persons of different faiths other than the dogma of Islam did not go unnoticed by two American presidents in the second half of the nineteenth century. Even in 1880 the United States of America knew that the persecution of non-Muslims, the so-called unbelievers, was taking place in Islamic countries, specifically in this case Morocco. Islam was not then and it is not now a peaceful religion.

In his Fourth Annual Message to Congress of December 6, 1880, President Rutherford B. Hayes (1822-1893; President 1877-1881) reported that the government of the United States had signed a convention placing emphasis on Islamic Moroccan persecution of peoples other than the Muslims and that such persecution must be stopped. President Hayes stated that, "At the invitation of the Spanish government, a conference has recently been held at the city of Madrid to consider the subject of protection by foreign powers of native Moors in the Empire of Morocco. The minister of the United States in Spain was directed to take part in the deliberations of this conference, the result of which is a convention signed on behalf of all the powers represented. The instrument will be laid before the Senate for its consideration. The Government of the United

States has also lost no opportunity to urge upon that of the Emperor of Morocco the necessity, in accordance with the humane and enlightened spirit of the age, of *putting an end to the persecutions, which have been so prevalent in that country, of persons of a faith other than the Moslem, and especially of the Hebrew residents of Morocco.*"[149]

In his annual report to Congress on the massacres of Armenian Christians in 1895, President Grover Cleveland (1837-1908; President 1885-1889 and 1893-1897) stated,

"Occurrences in Turkey have continued to excite concern. *The reported massacres of Christians in Armenia and the development there and in other districts of a spirit of fanatic hostility to Christian influences* naturally excited apprehension for the safety of the devoted men and women who, as dependents of the foreign missionary societies in the United States, reside in Turkey under the guaranty of law and usage and in the legitimate performance of their educational and religious mission. No efforts have been spared in their behalf, and their protection in person and property has been earnestly and vigorously enforced by every means within our power."

"I regret, however, that an attempt on our part to obtain better information concerning the true condition of affairs in the disturbed quarter of the Ottoman Empire ... was thwarted by the objections of the Turkish Government ... concerning

---

[149]http://www.presidency.ucsb.edu/ws/index.php?pid=29521&st=moslem&stl=#axzz1mAc1ie7R, retrieved on 12.03.2012. The italic emphasis is by the present author.

interference with ... religious freedom of the non-Mussulman subjects of the Sultan ... ."

To secure the situation, President Cleveland had sent "naval vessels which are now in the vicinity of the disturbed localities (in order to) acquire a measure of familiarity with the condition of affairs and will enable us to take suitable steps for the protection of any interests of our countrymen within reach of our ships that might be found imperiled." Thereupon the Ottoman government issued guarantees that "institutions maintained and administered by (American) countrymen shall be secured in the enjoyment of all rights and that our citizens throughout the Empire shall be protected." However, in spite of these guarantees, it was necessary to provide American ships to those "obliged to flee, and we have the promise of other powers which have ships in the neighborhood that our citizens as well as theirs will be received and protected on board those ships. On the demand of our minister orders have been issued by the Sultan that Turkish soldiers shall guard and escort to the coast American refugees."

President Cleveland went on to say that America was an agent "of the Christian world (to ensure that) conduct of Turkish government as will restrain fanatical brutality, and if this fails (the) duty is to so interfere as to insure against such dreadful occurrences in Turkey as have lately shocked civilization. ... ."[150]

One year later in the annual message to Congress President Cleveland reported the following:

---

[150] http://www.presidency.ucsb.edu/ws/index.php?pid=29536#axzz1pSt BOxw6, emphasis by the present author. Retrieved on 18.03.2012.

"… it would afford me satisfaction if I could assure the Congress that the disturbed condition in Asiatic Turkey had during the past year assumed a less hideous and bloody aspect, and that, either as a consequence of the awakening of the Turkish Government to the demands of humane civilization, or as the result of decisive action on the part of the great nations having the right by treaty to interfere for the protection of those exposed to the rage of mad bigotry and cruel fanaticism, the shocking features of the situation had been mitigated. Instead, however, of welcoming a softened disposition or protective intervention, *we have been afflicted by continued and not unfrequent reports of the wanton destruction of homes and the bloody butchery of men, women, and children, made martyrs to their profession of Christian faith.*"

"While none of our citizens in Turkey have thus far been killed or wounded, though often in the midst of dreadful scenes of danger, their safety in the future is by no means assured. Our Government at home and our minister at Constantinople have left nothing undone to protect our missionaries in Ottoman territory, who constitute nearly all the individuals residing there who have a right to claim our protection on the score of American citizenship. Our efforts in this direction will not be relaxed; but the deep feeling and sympathy that have been aroused among our people ought not to so far blind their reason and judgment as to lead them to demand impossible things. *The outbreaks of the blind fury which lead to murder and pillage in Turkey occur suddenly and without notice, and an attempt on our part to force such a hostile presence there as might be effective for prevention or protection would* not only *be resisted by the Ottoman*

*Government,* but would be regarded as an interruption of their plans by the great nations who assert their exclusive right to intervene in their own time and method for the security of life and property in Turkey."

"Several naval vessels are stationed in the Mediterranean as a measure of caution and to furnish all possible relief and refuge in case of emergency."

"We have made claims against the Turkish Government for the pillage and destruction of missionary property at Harpoot and Marash during uprisings at those places. Thus far the validity of these demands has not been admitted, though our minister, prior to such outrages and in anticipation of danger, demanded protection for the persons and property of our missionary citizens in the localities mentioned and notwithstanding that strong evidence exists of actual complicity of Turkish soldiers in the work of destruction and robbery."

"The facts as they now appear do not permit us to doubt the justice of these claims, and nothing will be omitted to bring about their prompt settlement."

*"A number of Armenian refugees having arrived at our ports, an order has lately been obtained from the Turkish Government permitting the wives and children of such refugees to join them here.* It is hoped that hereafter no obstacle will be interposed to prevent the escape of all those who seek to avoid the perils which threaten them in Turkish dominions."

...

"I do not believe that the present somber prospect in Turkey will be long permitted to offend the sight of

Christendom. *It so mars the humane and enlightened civilization that belongs to the close of the nineteenth century that it seems hardly possible that the earnest demand of good people throughout the Christian world for its corrective treatment will remain unanswered.*"[151]

## The First American Convert to Islam

Against the backdrop of American politicians in Congress knowing about the wanton Islamic massacre of Armenians because they were Christians, the American Islamic Propaganda Movement was founded in 1893 by Mohammed Alexander Russell Webb, the first white American convert to Islam. The movement's purpose was "to spread the light of Islam in America"[152] in the interests of American Islamic propaganda, as stated in the first issue of the *Moslem World*, May 12, 1893, the organ of the movement. On September 20 and 21 of that year Webb delivered two lectures that have become mainstay arguments concerning the pure advantages that Islam has to offer to the world. The lectures are: *The spirit of Islam* and *The Influence of Islam on Social Conditions.*

Before his conversion to Islam, Alexander Russell Webb was the United States ambassador to the Philippines. He was born into a Presbyterian family. However, he found this way of living too restraining and dull. He started his study of religions with Buddhism, which according to him was lacking

---

[151] http://www.presidency.ucsb.edu/ws/index.php?pid=29537#ixzz1pSwv 44go. Emphasis in italics is by the present author. Retrieved on 18.03.2012.

[152] Campo, Juan E. *Encyclopedia of Islam*, Facts on File, New York: 2009, p 708.

in substance. Webb then began to study Islam. A year after being introduced to Islam by the self-acclaimed messiah of Islam, Mirza Ghulam Ahmad (1835-1908) of Qadian, India in 1887, the same year President Grover Cleveland appointed him as Counsel Representative to the Philippines, Alexander Russell Webb formally declared himself to be a Muslim. In 1888, he formally took the oath to be a Muslim, which is nothing more than a one-time honest recitation of the Shahadah, which in Arabic is *lā ilāha ílá l-Lāh, Muḥammad rasūlu l-Lāh, There is no god but Allah, and Muhammad is the messenger of Allah.* This is all that is required to become a jihadist and kill innocent non-believers. Evidently, Alexander Russell Webb found solace and meaning for mankind in the Koran's 169 war suras against non-believers. It is not known if Mohammed Alexander Russell Webb ever killed anyone due to a person's refusal to convert to Islam. However, he certainly did not propagandize against Mohammed's call to kill innocent non-believers.

After his conversion, the Turkish Sultan Abdul Hamid II appointed Mohammed Alexander Russell Webb the Honorary Turkish Consul in New York City.

*Islam in America and Other Writings* by Muhammad Alexander Russell Webb is a new collection of his works.[153] From the book's description we read that "Webb was one of the first converts to Islam in America. He opened one of the first Islamic reading rooms, published numerous pamphlets on Islam, edited the first American Islamic journal and newspaper,

---

[153] Webb, Muhammad Alexander Russell. *Islam in America and Other Writings,* Magribine Press, Chicago: 2006.

and served as Turkish emissary to the United States. His writing presents a philosophic, thoughtful Islam that can appeal to both the scholar and the common man and shows that Islam is the answer to the social ills of this nation." The last propaganda sentence is interesting because it undercuts the role of the *Constitution for the United States of America*, which is not the source of America's social ills, but the true solution to them, as long as big government observes the laws of the *Constitution*.

Many Islamic internet sites and historians regard Muhammad Alexander Russell Webb as the first American convert to Islam and the first to begin the organizational impetus for Islam in the United States of America.

# CHAPTER SIX

# Muslims in America Organize

## Organization and Islamic Propaganda

Beginning in 1908, immigrants from the Ottoman Empire, mainly Albanians (Christians), Turks (Muslims), and Kurds (Muslims) came to the United States of America for reasons of commerce and being able to earn a living in a free society. Another reason the Albanians immigrated was because the *Constitution for the United States of America* guarantees freedom from religious persecution. The Ottoman Empire conquered the Middle East and North Africa, receiving its impetus and justification from the Koran and Mohammed. It was made into a secular nation by Mustafa Kemal Atatürk, founder and first President of the Republic of Turkey after World War I and after the Ottoman Empire had conducted genocide on the Armenians living inside and on the borders to the Ottoman Empire. Today the Ottoman Empire is the Republic of Turkey. Officially, Turkey is a democratic, secular, unitary, constitutional republic. In reality, it is a centralized state rooted in Islam.

### Moorish Science Temple of America

In 1913, Timothy Drew (Noble Drew Ali) was commissioned by the Sultan of Morocco to convert American Blacks to the Islamic beliefs and to teach Islam to African Americans. Noble Drew Ali's work resulted in the first major conversions of African-Americans to Islam and the founding in Newark, New Jersey of the Moorish Science Temple of America. Drawing inspiration from Buddhism, Christianity, Freemasonry, Gnosticism, and Taoism, Noble Drew Ali presented his organization as a sect of Islam, labeling it Islamism and the adherents Moslems, to distinguish his movement from the traditional Islam and Muslims. Noble Drew Ali moved the organization to Chicago, Illinois in 1925, contending that the American midwest was "closer to Islam."[154] In 1926 he registered Temple Number 9. Today the Moorish Science Temple claims that they have 260 temples nationwide.

Many Islamic sources claim that the first American mosque (*masjid*) in the twentieth century was built by Moslems from Albania in Biddeford, Maine in 1915. An entry in *The Encyclopedia of American Religious History*.[155] However, this source relies on other Islamic sources which reiterate the statement that "The first mosque in America was probably build (sic) by Albanian Muslims in 1915 in Maine," including the improper grammar.[156] Some sources claim that the first mosque was built in Ross, North Dakota.[157] These assertions are

---

[154] Wilson, Peter Lamborn. *Sacred Drift: Essays on the Margins of Islam*, City Lights Books, San Francisco: 1993, p. 29.

[155] Queen, Edward L., Prothero, Stephen, and Shattuck Jr., Gardiner H. *The Encyclopedia of American Religious History*. Facts on File, New York: 1996.

[156] http://www.muslimsinamerica.org/index.php?option=com_content&task =view&id=17&Itemid=28; http://www.amp.ghazali.net/html/mosques_in_ us.html; both retrieved on 20.03.2012.

[157] voanews.com at http://www.voanews.com/english/archive/2005-10/2005-10-20-voa14.cfm?CFID=432813&CFTOKEN=38573615 as well

important to Islamists because they claim that such locations are documentary evidence that the regions belong to Islam. Within less than one hundred years, 1209 mosques have been built throughout America.[158]

In 1919, the Albanian Moslems built a second mosque in Connecticut. As long ago as 1926, a mosque was built in Brooklyn, New York by Polish-speaking Tatar Muslims. This was followed four years later by the building of the first mosque in Pittsburgh, Pennsylvania. In 1935, the Lebanese in Cedar Rapids, Iowa, opened their mosque.[159]

This author places emphasis on the fact that a mosque is not a church in the Christian sense of church. Neither is a mosque a house of assembly to pray to God, which is the Hebrew sense. A church is a symbol of the body of Christ. A synagogue is an assembly hall for the worshipping of Yahweh. A modern synagogue often has additional facilities like a day care center, a catering hall, kosher kitchen, religious school, library, and a smaller chapel for daily services. A mosque is a place to offer prayers to Allah-Hubal. It can serve as a center to settle disputes, to spread information, and to educate in the goals of Islam. A mosque is also used to incite hatred against

---

as http://30mosques.com/archive2010/2010/09/day-22-ross-north-dakota-a-leap-in-time/, retrieved on 20.03.2012.

[158] http://www.amp.ghazali.net/html/mosques_in_us.html, retrieved on 20.03.2012.

[159] http://www.familysecuritymatters.org/publications/id.9606,css.print/pub_detail.asp and https://islamquotes.org/?p=d&d=v&k=1711, retrieved on 20.03.2012.

non-believers. Thus, it is also a symbol of creeping sharia and the Islamic goal of destroying the Republic that is the United States of America.

In a screening of "2,300 mosques and Islamic centers and schools" throughout the United States of America, approximately "80 percent of the groups exhibit a high level of sharia-compliance and jihadi threat, including ultra-orthodox worship in which women are separated from men in the prayer hall and must enter the mosque from a separate, usually back, entrance; and are required to wear hijabs."

In mosques (and elsewhere) imams propagate the following doctrines:

➢ Women are inferior to men and can be beaten for disobedience.

➢ Non-Muslims, particularly Jews, are infidels and inferior to Muslims.

➢ Jihad or support of jihad is not only a Muslim's duty, but the noblest way, and suicide bombers and other so-called "martyrs" are worthy of the highest praise.

➢ An Islamic caliphate should one day encompass the United States of America.

➢ Financial support for jihad.

➢ Mosque bookstores sell books, CDs, and DVDs promoting jihad and glorifying martyrdom.[160]

---

[160] http://www.familysecuritymatters.org/publications/id.9606,css.print/pub _detail.asp, retrieved on 20.03.2012. This is also the source of the quote.

## The Red Crescent

Because Muslims have a penchant, indeed a psychological proneness, for being insulted when they see a cross or hear the word cross, they established The Red Crescent in Detroit in 1920. The red half moon is the Islamic counterpart to the International Red Cross. The Muslims had to do this because the cross is a symbol of Christianity, the religion of the non-believers. Muslims cannot be assisted in time of need by non-believers because according to the Koran and Mohammed they are impure.

The oldest and longest-running Muslim magazine *Muslim Sunrise* began publication in 1921. It was founded by Dr. Mufti Muhammad Sadiq, the first missionary of the Ahmadiyya (Messiah) Muslim Community to arrive in America. The goal in 1921 and now is that *MUSLIM SUNRISE* seeks to open discussions on Islam and topics relating to religion in general. It places emphasis on Islam's role in a global society. It presents solutions to national and international problems that have an Islamic perspective.[161]

## Universal Islamic Society

Under the motto *One God, One Imam, One Destiny* the Universal Islamic Society was established in Detroit, Michigan, in 1926 by Dues Muhammad Ali, the so-called mentor of Marcus Garvey, a Jamaican political leader and avid proponent of the early Black nationalism and Pan-Africanism movements.

---

[161] http://www.muslimsunrise.com/index.php?option=com_content&task=view&id=134&Itemid=1, retrieved on 10.02.2012.

## Nation of Islam (NOI)

The Nation of Islam publishes *Mohammed Speaks*, which within a year of its introduction became America's largest minority weekly publication. At its zenith the publication had 800,000 readers. After undergoing two name changes – *Bilalian News* and *A.M. Journal* – it is now entitled *The Muslim Journal*.

Wallace Ford (Fard Muhammad) founded the Nation of Islam in Detroit, Michigan in 1933. The Nation of Islam considers Fard Muhammad to be **the** mahdi, a redeemer of Islam as prophesied by the Koran and Mohammed. The mahdi will rule for 7 or 9 or 19 years before Judgment Day, (*yawm al-qiyamah, the Day of Resurrection*). The mahdi will rule with Jesus. The mahdi will exterminate injustice, wrongdoing, and tyranny.[162] There is only one mahdi. Yet, in organizations that ascribe to the Ahmadiyya (messiah) doctrine, there are many.

The purpose of the Nation of Islam is to provide for better economic conditions, encourage spiritual, mental, and social relationships, teach black pride and the principles of Islam to Black African Americans in the United States, and improve the spiritual, mental, social, and economic condition of African Americans in the United States.[163]

Many Islamic sources state that Fard Mohammed disappeared in June 1934, suggesting a resurrection and

---

[162] Momen, Moojan. *An introduction to Shi'i Islam*, Yale University Press New Haven, Connecticut: 1985, pp. 166-168.

[163] http://topics.nytimes.com/topics/reference/timestopics/organizations/n/nation_of_islam/index.html, retrieved on 10.02.2102.

ascension into heaven. Some sources contend that his successor Elijah Muhammad killed him while Elijah Muhammad says that he is on the Mother Plane, a UFO designed to take important Muslims from this earth.[164]

Elijah Muhammad established mosques and called them Temples. The schools were named Muhammad University of Islam Schools. In 1960 the Nation of Islam University of Islam Schools received its first publicity in the American media. The focus of these University of Islam Schools is that Blacks should develop their own self-help programs. The schools are diametrically opposed to the White establishment.

Elijah Mohammed turned the Nation of Islam into an international business with very large real estate holdings in the United States and foreign countries, namely Canada, France, the United Kingdom, and Trinidad and Tobago.

The Southern Poverty Law Center, a non-profit civil-rights organization which claims to fight hate, racism, bigotry, and social injustice, contends that the Nation of Islam has a "bizarre theology of innate black superiority over whites ... and the deeply racist, anti-Semitic and anti-gay rhetoric of its leaders, including top minister Louis Farrakhan, have earned the NOI a prominent position in the ranks of organized hate."[165]

---

[164] Turner, Richard Brent. *Islam in the African-American Experience*, Indiana University Press, Bloomington, Indiana: 2003, p. 167.

[165] http://www.splcenter.org/get-informed/intelligence-files/groups/nation-of-islam, retrieved on 10.02.2012. The Southern Poverty Law Center claims that mainstream Muslims, whoever they are, do not share the hate, racism, and bigotry of the Nation of Islam.

The known leaders of the Nation of Islam have been Elijah Muhammad, Malcolm X (murdered by members of the Nation of Islam), Muhammad Ali, and Louis Farrakhan. In 1965 the murder of Malcolm X (Al-Haj Malik al-Shabazz) shocked the Muslim world. Elijah Muhammad was quoted as saying, "Malcolm X got just what he preached."[166] Muslims consider Al-Haj Malik al-Shabazz to be one of the most important Muslims in American and Muslim history. They call him a dedicated fighter for justice and equality for all oppressed people who followed in the footsteps of Mohammed. What Muslim sources do not mention is the fact that Al-Haj Malik al-Shabazz was murdered by Talmadge Hayer (Thomas Hagan), Norman 3X Butler, Thomas 15X Johnson, all members of the Nation of Islam. Norman 3X Butler, present name Abdul Aziz, was paroled in 1985 and became the head of the Nation of Islam Harlem mosque. Thomas 15X Johnson changed his name to Khalil Islam and converted to Sunni Islam. He was released in 1987 and died in 2009. Talmadge Hayer is now Mujahid Halim. He received parole in 2010.

Elijah Muhammad, the leader of the Nation of Islam, died on February 25, 1975 after years of vitriolic attacks against the United States of America and inciting violence. He was succeeded by his son Warith Deen Mohammed, an African-American Muslim spiritual leader, reformer, educator, civil rights advocate, interfaith activist, and international goodwill ambassador, who directed the Nation of Islam towards a wider, global concept of Islam. Warith Deen

---

[166] Evanz, Karl. *The Judas Factor: The Plot to Kill Malcolm X*, Thunder's Mouth Press, New York: 1992, p. 301.

Mohammed disbanded the original Nation of Islam in 1976 and turned it into the World Community of Al-Islam in the West, later the American Society of Muslims.[167] Louis Farrakhan rebuilt the Nation of Islam in 1977.[168]

In 1952 the United States of America officially recognized Islam as a legitimate religion as a result of Muslims in the Armed Forces suing the federal government to allow them to be identified as Muslims with the religion Islam.

## Hanafi Muslim Movement

In 1958 Ernest Timothy McGee (Hamas Abdul Khaalis) established the Hanafi Muslim Movement in New York. This emerged out of the Hanafi Madh-Hab Center from 1947. Initially, the Hanafi Muslim Movement dedicated itself to the study and teaching of Hanafi Islamic law, founded in Baghdad in the 8th century by Abu al-Hanafa. In the 1950s and 1960s it was considered the least fundamentalist of Islamic law interpretations. In 1977, Khaalis with some of his followers went to Washington, D.C. occupied three buildings, took hostages, and killed one person. Khaalis is now serving a 41-120-year prison sentence in Washington, D.C. One of the more famous members of Khaalis' Hanafi Muslim Movement is Kareem Abdul-Jabbar, the famous basketball player.[169] On Wednesday, January 18, 2012, Secretary of State Hillary

---

[167] *Wall Street Journal*, Vol. CIV, NO. 6, Friday, July 9, 1999.

[168] Lincoln, C. Eric. *The Black Muslims in America*, Third Edition, Eerdmans Publishing Company, Grand Rapids, Michigan: 1994, p. 265.

[169] http://www.sage-ereference.com/abstract/terrorism/n185.xml, retrieved on 11.02.2102.

Rodham Clinton named Kareem Abdul-Jabbar as a United States global Cultural Ambassador.[170]

## Dar-al-Islam Movement

The State Street Masjid was founded in New York City in 1962 by Sheik Dawood Ahmed Faisal. The Dar-al-Islam Movement was born out of the State Street Masjid. The legal terminology in Islam Dār al-Islām دار الإسلام, House of Islam as opposed to the House of War, the non-believers, describes areas or regions that are under the control of Islam. This is the basis of erecting a state within a state so that the former legal, constitutional state can be exterminated from within.

## Muslim Student Union

The Muslim Student Union organization, the precursor of the Islamic Society of North America was established in 1963. It is an umbrella organization with affiliated chapters at various campuses across the North American continent. The organization's goal is to provide financial and counseling assistance to Muslim students studying in the United States and Canada. The Muslim Students Association of the United States and Canada is also known as MSA National.

The examples of Islamic organizing in America sketched above were complemented by violent actions conducted against the United States and American citizens at a number of places and times throughout the world. No freedom-loving country in the West seemed to care.

---

[170]    http://creepingsharia.wordpress.com/2012/01/19/clinton-announces-kareem-abdul-jabbar-as-cultural-ambassador/, retrieved on 11.02.2012.

150

# The Continued Islamic Organizing is Interspersed With Jihad Terrorist Attacks

The first significant jihad terrorist attack in the United States of America was the assassination of Robert F. Kennedy, the Democratic Party's presidential hopeful for the 1968 presidential elections. He was murdered on 4-5 June 1968 in the Ambassador Hotel, Los Angeles, California by the Palestinian immigrant Sirhan Bishara Sirhan (1944), most likely because Robert F. Kennedy was pro-Israel and not pro-Palestine and pro-Palestinian Liberation Organization (PLO).

On February 23, 1970, PLO terrorists opened fire on a busload of Christian pilgrims in Haloul, West Bank, Israel. They killed one American, Barbara Ertle of Michigan, and wounded two others.

On September 14, 1970, the PFLP (Popular Front for the Liberation of Palestine) hijacked a TWA flight to Amman. Four Americans were injured.

On May 30, 1972, the Ben Gurion Airport, Israel was attacked. The Islamic terrorists killed 26 and wounded 78 United States citizens from Puerto Rico.

On September 5, 1972, Palestinian Islamic terrorists seized 11 athletes in the Olympic Village in Munich, Germany. They took 9 hostages. David Berger from Cleveland, Ohio was killed. German security agents killed five terrorists.

On January 1, 1977, F. E. Melov, the United States Ambassador to Lebanon, and Robert O. Waring, the United States economic counselor, were kidnapped and later killed by Islamic terrorists in Beirut.

On March 11, 1978, Gail Rubin, a niece of United States Senator Abraham Ribicoff, was among 38 people shot to death by Islamic terrorists on a beach near Tel Aviv, Israel.

During October-November 1979, Iran, with the initial support of President James Earl Carter, voluntarily underwent a religious and political upheaval. On November 4, a group of Iranian Muslim students attacked and seized the American Embassy in Tehran. They took 66 American diplomats hostage; 13 were quickly freed, but 53 were held until their release on January 20, 1981 – 444 days. During Ronald Reagan's campaign for the Presidency of the United States of America, he sent a special envoy to Iran with the message that if he became president, the first political activity he would undertake would be to invade Iran and cause the Khomeini government to be deposed, even if it meant the loss of the American hostages in Iranian hands.

One of Iran's Islamist terrorist leaders of the time is the current president of Iran, Dr. Mahmoud Ahmadinejad. According to the internationally recognized principles and rules of international law, the occupation of the American Embassy in Tehran was an attack on American soil. An attack on any American embassy is an attack on American soil. This assault held the United States of America hostage. Islamists attacked the United States of America. America was not searching for an enemy. The results of this breach of international law have been established confrontations by the Islamic side vis-à-vis the West for the past 30-plus years.

When President James Earl Carter chose to conduct a clandestine raid in Iran in order to free the captured American diplomats and personnel held hostage in the embassy, the mission ended in a debacle for the United States, with the Iranian Muslim terrorists claiming that Allah wanted it so. For the Iranian Muslims it was a sign from Allah to continue the attacks on America and its allies whenever the time seemed right. Allah was on their side. For the politics of the United States of America, the ill-fated rescue mission became a symbol of America's inability to deal with Muslim terrorists, particularly that type of terrorism coming out of a dogmatic, Islamic fundamentalism, regardless of the country in which it resides. President Ronald Reagan stopped kowtowing to Islamic terrorist politics. The William Jefferson Clinton administration reversed the Reagan policy and began kowtowing to Islam and Muslims, the first sign being the beginning of the iftar dinners at the White House in 1996.

After the seizure of the American Embassy in Tehran by Islamic terrorists, it did not take long for attacks against Americans to increase. They were kidnapped and murdered throughout the Middle East and at other American embassies. These were continued violations of international law; no European country protested; and the United Nations undertook nothing, not even hearings to put an end to these internationally illegal activities or, at the least, a condemnation of these Islamic terrorist activities. The Muslim terrorists by this time were certainly convinced that the West was unable to react to their *Allah-sanctioned* power as it came via Mohammed and the Koran, the foundation of their *modus operandi*.

In 1982, the Islamic Society of North America (ISNA) was founded. Its 46 million dollar headquarters funded by

Muslim Brotherhood leader Youssef Nada and the Emir of Qatar is in Plainfield, Indiana.[171] In 2008, it claimed 400,000 members. The organization is an umbrella institution for a number of Muslim organizations. Among them are the American Muslim Scientists and Engineers (AMSE), American Muslim Social Scientists (AMSS), the North American Islamic Trust (NAIT), the Foundation of International Development (FID), the Islamic Medical Association (IMA), the Islamic Teaching Center (ITC), the Muslim Community Association (MCA), the Muslim Student Association (MSA), the Muslim Youth of North America (MYNA) and the Canadian Islamic Trust (CIT; NAIT's counterpart in Canada).[172]

The origin of ISNA is the Muslim Student Organization of January 1963. ISNA aims "to be an exemplary and unifying Islamic organization in North America that contributes to the betterment of the Muslim community and society at large." [173] ISNA certifies food services and products making sure that they are *halal*, permissible under Islamic law. ISNA provides marriage certificates to couples who have performed the Islamic ceremony and who have a marriage license.

In Beirut, Lebanon on April 18, 1983, Islamic terrorists attacked the United States Embassy compound in a large vehicle loaded with high explosives. It was driven into the US

---

[171] http://www.washingtonpost.com/ac2/wp-dyn/A128232004Sep10?Language=printer, retrieved on 11.02.2012.

[172] Glassé, Cyril. *The new encyclopedia of Islam*, Rowman & Littlefield, Lanham, Maryland: 2008, p. 251.

[173] http://www.isna.net/ISNAHQ/pages/Mission--Vision.aspx, retrieved on 10.02.2012 and http://www.isna.net/, retrieved on 11.02.2012.

Embassy, and 83 people were killed. A total of 120 people were injured. Again, the United States of America was attacked and other countries as well, because some of those killed were not American citizens. Yet, the European Community and the United Nations refused to take a stand.

On October 23, 1983, another truck loaded with high explosives, 2,500 pounds of TNT, was driven through the gate of the United States Marine Corps Headquarters in Beirut, Lebanon. The result of this Muslim-Islamic terrorist attack: 241 Marines dead, 82 seriously injured. At the same time, another suicide attack truck smashed into the French compound in Beirut and killed 58 French paratroopers. The simultaneous suicide attacks were acts sanctioned by Allah, according to Islamic terrorist doctrine.

In December 1983, another vehicle loaded with explosives smashed into the United States Embassy compound in Kuwait. The attack killed five people and injured 80. It was another Islamist terrorist attack on United States soil and a warning to Western European nations.

In September of 1984, there was another attack on the United States Embassy in Beirut. Two American service members were killed and 23 employees, as well as 21 American and British diplomats were injured. There were more than 50 Lebanese citizens injured. These were all warnings to America and to European governments that Allah, via Islamic Muslim terrorists, as they claimed, would seek revenge on the enemies of Islam wherever they were to be found.

In August 1985, a Volkswagen was driven into the main gate of the Rhine-Main United States Air Force Base in

Germany. It was loaded with explosives and the attack killed 22. It was an attack on German-American soil.

The Soviet Union is not a Western democratic country. Nevertheless, it must be mentioned how the Soviet Government handled a Muslim terrorist situation on September 30, 1985. On that day, four Soviet diplomats were kidnapped by Islamic terrorists in Lebanon. They killed one diplomat, but let the other three go and unharmed after a relative of the Islamic terrorist group leader was kidnapped and killed by the Soviet secret police (the KGB).[174]

On October 7, 1985 the cruise ship the *Achille Lauro*, on a cruise in the Mediterranean Sea was commandeered by terrorist sympathizers with the Islamist goals. They took 700 people hostage for three days. They chose as their victim a disabled Jewish-American in a wheelchair, executing Leon Klinghofer by throwing him into the Mediterranean Sea. It was an attack in European waters and Europe did nothing in response.

On April 2, 1986, Islamic terrorists and their sympathizers began bombing civilian airliners: TWA Flight 840 on March 30 from Rome to Athens was bombed, killing four Americans.

On May 27, 1986, Dr. Isma'il R. Al-Faruqi, the founder of the American Moslem Social Scientists and the International Institute of Islamic Thought and his wife were murdered. He and his wife authored many books, among them the highly

---

[174] It seems that this is the type of communication Islamic terrorists understand.

regarded *Cultural Atlas of Islam*. Many Islamic internet sites (too numerous to be listed[175]) state that the murder was predicted by the President of the Jewish Defense League in New York's *Village Voice* one week before the murder, wherein it was reported that "within a week an outspoken Palestinian professor will be eliminated."[176] The intent is suggestive and the suggestion is intentional. The murderer was Joseph Louis Young (Yusuf Ali) a member of the Muslim Students' Association. He claimed that Al-Faruqi had homosexual relations with his Malaysian co-students at Temple University. Yusuf Ali stated that he murdered Dr. and Mrs. Al-Faruqi on the instigation of Ghulam Nabi Fai, who was at that time the President of the Muslim Students' Association. Ghulam Nabi Fai became the president of the International Institute of Islamic Thought, the organization founded by Dr. and Mrs. Al-Faruqi. Presently Ghulam Nabi Fai is under house arrest for spying for Pakistan.[177]

On September 5, 1986, a Pan Am Boeing 747 en route to New York via Frankfurt was hijacked by Palestinian Islamic terrorists with 379 passengers on board, including 89 Americans. The Islamic terrorists killed 22 and wounded 127.

---

[175] Three examples are http://issuu.com/hazratamin/docs/mycrjul08, http://www.almoltaqa.ps/english/showthread.php?t=6604, http://www.zeriyt.com/islam-in-the-united-states-albanians-t15098.0.html, retrieved on 11.02.2012.

[176] http://www.carolmoore.net/sfm/jdl.html, retrieved on 11.02.2012.

[177] See http://www.theatlantic.com/international/archive/2011/10/the-man-behind-pakistani-spy-agencys-plot-to-influence-washington/246000/, which was retrieved on 11.02.2012.

Beginning in Chicago in 1987, a series of Muslim alarm networks were implemented to warn Muslims of discrimination against Muslims and to mobilize them to take action against such discrimination. This concept led to the establishment of the Council on American Islamic Relations (CAIR). Some of the threats that CAIR and Muslims see against them are the existence of crosses, the celebration and the nomenclature of Christmas, the location of a bar or restaurant near a mosque, particularly when the mosque was built or used after the bar or restaurant had already been in business for some years.

CAIR is the largest Muslim civil liberties association. Its goal is "to enhance understanding of Islam, encourage dialogue, protect civil liberties, empower American Muslims, and build coalitions that promote justice and mutual understanding."[178] That is a public propaganda surface goal only. CAIR is only one of the 100 front organizations of the Muslim Brotherhood in America and it is one of the largest. In the role of a front organization, its real goal is the Islamization of the United States of America.[179] In 2007, CAIR was named by the FBI as an unindicted co-conspirator with the Palestinian terrorist organization HAMAS.

On December 21, 1988 Pan Am Flight 103, a Boeing 747 from London to New York, was blown up over Lockerbie, Scotland. All 259 passengers and 11 persons on the ground were killed. Among the passengers were 35 Syracuse

---

[178] http://sun.cair.com/AboutUs/VisionMissionCorePrinciples.aspx, which was retrieved on 11.02.2012.

[179] Gaubatz, David P. and Sperry, Paul. *Muslim Mafia*, WND Books, New York: 2009, information throughout the complete book.

University students and many United States military service personnel who were flying home for the Christmas holidays.

In 1990, the American Muslim Council sponsored the first Muslims Against Apartheid solidarity conference to rally support for anti-apartheid groups in South Africa.

In 1991 Siraj Wahhaj (Jeffrey Kearse) an African-American convert to Islam and imam of the Al-Taqwa mosque in Brooklyn, New York became the first Muslim to give the invocation prayer at the opening of the House of Representatives. Siraj Wahhaj is also the leader of the Muslim Alliance in North America (MANA). In 1992, Warith Deen Mohammed gave the invocation in the Senate.

In 1992, ten Muslim organizations created the Bosnia Task Force in support of Bosnia, the only existing Islamic country in Europe. In 1993, in cooperation with the National Organization of Women, they organized demonstrations in 100 American cities against the rape of women in Bosnia.

On January 25, 1993, a Pakistani Islamic terrorist entered the Central Intelligence Agency (CIA) Headquarters in Langley, Virginia, and killed two CIA agents, Frank Darling and Bennett Lansing. He wounded three others.

In February of 1993, a group of Islamic terrorists were arrested after they had planted and detonated explosives in a van in the underground parking garage of the World Trade Center, New York City. The rented van that they used was packed with explosives. The Islamic terrorists killed six innocent people and injured over 1,042. This was another act of war against the United States of America and indirectly against all of the countries who had citizens from their countries working at the World Trade Center. The six killed and over 1,042 injured were not singled out by the Islamic terrorists. The goal was to destroy the World Trade Center, one of the pillars of trade in a free world that is not Islamic.

The Islamic Shura Council formed out of the Bosnia Task Force in 1994. *Shura* in Arabic means *consultation*. Muslims maintain that *shura* is Allah- and Mohammed-ordained democracy because all decisions are made as a result of consultation. Yet, the shura consultation councils are not formal, legally accepted forms of national government. Moreover, Mohammed did consult with his followers, especially when many disagreed with him. As a result of the consultations, some were murdered. At the same time, as documented by the hadiths that were written down long after Mohammed died in 632 AD, Mohammed made statements that there was no need for *shura* because Allah had already told him what to do. The Shura Council still proclaims, "We, members of the Shura Council, declare gender equality to be an intrinsic part of the Islamic faith. As Muslims, we affirm our conviction that the Muslim woman is worthy of respect and dignity, that as a legal individual, spiritual being, social person, responsible agent, free citizen, and servant of God, she holds fundamentally equal rights to exercise her abilities and talents in all areas of human activity. Furthermore, we insist that these rights are embedded within the Qur'an and six objectives of Shari'a—the protection and promotion of religion (*al-din*), life (*al-nafs*), mind (*al-'aql*), family (*al-nasl*), wealth (*al-mal*), and dignity

160

(*al-'ird*)."[180] This position is contradicted by the Koran in a number of verses and by Mohammed in the hadiths. Contradiction can always occur via abrogation, a later verse or command ruling out a former verse or command, while the former still holds validity.

In April 1995, Timothy McVeigh and Terry Nichols bombed the Alfred P. Murrah Building in Oklahoma City. It was reported on December 11, 2011 that the present Attorney General of the United States was the person responsible for the 168 deaths resulting from the bombings.[181] The present Attorney General of the United States, Eric Holder, had authorized the FBI to provide the explosives to McVeigh and Nichols in conjunction with a Clinton Administration undercover operation named PATCON, an acronym for "Patriot Conspiracy." Patriotic militias were/are seedbeds of anti-Islam movements. "PATCON was designed to infiltrate and incite... militia[s] and evangelical Christians to violence so that the Department of Justice could crush them."[182]

In November 1995, a car bomb exploded at the United States military complex in Riyadh, Saudi Arabia. It killed seven people, five of them United States military personnel. This was

---

[180] http://www.wisemuslimwomen.org/about/shuracouncil/, retrieved on 11.02.2012.

[181] http://www.coachisright.com/ag-eric-holder-responsible-for-168-deaths-in-1995-oklahoma-city-bombing%E2%80%A6and-more/ was retrieved on 11.02.2012.

[182] http://sipseystreetirregulars.blogspot.com/2012/02/jesse-trentadue-talks-to-lew-rockwell.html, http://sipseystreetirregulars.blogspot.com/, retrieved on 11.02.2012.

another act of war against America committed in an Arab country.

On June 25, 1996, a truck bomb exploded at the United States military compound in Dhahran, Saudi Arabia. The Khobar Towers, a United States Air Force barracks, was destroyed. There were 19 killed and over 500 injured, including 240 Americans.

In 1996 the first iftar dinner, a dinner breaking the fasting of the day during the Islamic month of Ramadan, was held on Capitol Hill. A Ramadan Eid (festivity) was held in the White House by the Clintons in 1996. Since 1996, the United States Department of State has held an annual iftar dinner for selected community leaders, ambassadors, and representatives from most Muslim countries. President George W. Bush held eight iftar dinners. Barack Hussein Obama has held four iftar dinners.[183]

On August 7, 1998, there were two simultaneous, precision-planned bombing attacks on the United States Embassies in Kenya and Tanzania. Although the United States possessed intelligence that the attacks were forthcoming, and that the attacks had been planned by Osama Bin Laden, the Clinton Administration decided not to take any pre-emptive action because it might be construed as an act of war on Somalia, the originating country of the intelligence information. It would be bad propaganda for peaceful American diplomacy. For the Islamic terrorists it was another demonstration that Allah-Hubal was on their side. In Nairobi,

---

[183] http://www.csmonitor.com/USA/Politics/2011/0810/President-Obama, retrieved on 11.02.2012.

Kenya 292 people were killed, including 12 Americans. In Tanzania 320 people died and 5,086 were injured. All of this human destruction against the non-believers took place within one hour. The United States of America did respond with cruise missiles aimed at targets that were singled out based on inadequate information. It turned out that the targets that the United States exploded with their cruise missiles were the wrong ones and the world was in an uproar. The United States of America had attacked a Muslim country. This was an act of war!

The Islamic terrorists understood the mistake to be another indication that Allah-Hubal was on their side. The above information, as well as that to follow below, confirms the double-edged strategy of Islam: organize and at the same terrorize! Indeed, the Muslim Brotherhood, the Islamic organization that is behind the manifold Islamic groups in the United States of America, is adamant in its philosophy that the destruction of the American Republic is dependent on a double-edged strategy. This is in accord with the teachings of the Egyptian author, educator, Islamist, and Islam theorist Sayyid Qutb (1906-1966) (also Said, Syed, Seyyid, Sayid, or Sayed, as well as Koteb, Qutub, Kotb, or Kutb). He was the de facto leader of the Egyptian Brotherhood in the 1950s and 1960s. He more than strongly disapproved of the culture and traditions of the United States of America, which he regarded as amounting to nothing more than an obsession with materialism, sex, and violence. It is Sayyid Qutb who formed the ideas of Islamists and groups such as Al Qaeda. One can read his philosophy in his books *Social Justice* (English translation 1953) and his manifesto *Milestones*, published in English in 1991. However, as was the case with Adolf Hitler's *Mein Kampf*, the Western democratic republics have not bothered to examine Qutb's anti-freedom philosophy. In reality, Sayyid Qutb was an Islamic Adolf Hitler.

# CHAPTER SEVEN

# A Case of Cultural Jihad
# and Geographical Taqiyya

## Cultural Legislative Jihad

There is a proposed legislative bill in the United States Senate that was introduced on October 25, 2011 and again in 2012 as follows:[184]

"A Bill For An Act Entitled: Sundry Free Moors Act of 2012 an Act to deter violations of the treaty, civil and political rights of 'Any' Moor living within the Territorial Borders of the United States and recognition of Moors native to America as an indigenous group to protect and preserve for Moors their inherent right of freedom to believe, express, and exercise the traditional religions of the Moor, including but not limited to access to sites, use and possession of sacred objects, and the freedom to worship through ceremonial and traditional rites."

In the Senate:

10-25-2011

---

[184]    http://www.scribd.com/doc/71994512/Sundry-Free-Moors-Act-2012, retrieved on 21.03.2012.

"Whereas the Murakish Caliphate of America Corporation for its subsidiary corporate body politics and all Moors native to or living in the Several States, territories of outlying possessions governed by the United States introduce the following bill, which was referred to the Committee on Foreign Relations and the United States Commission on International Religious Freedom."

_____ Proposal

Seeking Resolution by the US Senate of the following article is proposed as federal law under the jurisdiction of the United States of America, enforceable by Executive action."

"Be it enacted by the Senate and House of Representatives of the United States of America in Congress assembled."

This legislative proposal is a typical example of cultural jihad and an attempt to impose and make Islamic sharia law legal in the United States of America. Everything that the proposed legislation contains is already guaranteed by the *Constitution for the United States of America*, except for sharia law, which is easily camouflaged by the phrasing "freedom to believe, express, and exercise the traditional religions of the Moor". Sharia law is part of the belief, exercise, and tradition of all Muslims. Should this legislation become federal law, the Moors would have the legal right to apply sharia law to their

166

communities and Moorish American citizens, thus eclipsing the federal laws of the *Constitution* and subordinate laws. The sharia would become the law of the land for those professing the faith of the American Moors. The goal of creeping sharia would eventually have been achieved: the eclipse and destruction of the *Constitution for the United States of America.*

The legislative proposal is 63 pages long. Among other matters, the legislation would have special regulations concerning

- social security account numbers for Moors,

- the status of wives in a marriage, i.e., recognition of a domestic partnership as constituting a marriage,

- crimes directed against Moors only,

- the Moors as the true discoverers of America five centuries before Christopher Columbus, (COMMENT: Remember: Where a Muslim sets his feet, that land must become Islamic forever.)

- outlawing situations that the Moors would define as neo-slavery, i. e., requests for identification papers, the issuing of fines as examples of discrimination,

- the imprisonment of Moors in relation to the number of whites imprisoned,

- recognition of a fictitious Moorish Republic,

- the institutionalization of the United Nations Declaration on the Rights of Indigenous Peoples, Resolution 61/295, 13 September 2007.

- the right of Moors regarding their self-determination,

- recognition of all historical (international) apologies and declarations to the Moors,

- recognition that Moorish treaty rights take precedence (are supreme) over federal and state law when there is a conflict,

- the formation of a Bureau of Moorish Affairs as an independent federal agency "that promotes the health and welfare of Moorish peoples", as well as "Congressional approval for a Federal Executive agency called the United States Bureau of Moorish Affairs to interface with state and federal municipalities and promote the welfare of Moors native to America." and "Assignment of a (sic) Agency Location Code (ALC) and OCC approval of a foreign bank for Transitional Council." (section 609) (COMMENT: It must be noted that the latter provision could be used for money laundering.)

- Recognition that the "Murakesh Caliphate of America Corporation is a Moorish Corporate Body Politic whose fundamental Divine Constitution and By Laws is (sic) based entirely upon the Islamic code; or an Islamic Corporation composed of Moors, or Moorish Body Politic, or Moorish Body Corporate wholly owned by the non US citizen Moors of the Murakesh Caliphate." (section 707).

Succinctly, the intent is to receive from the federal government protected, special status because the Sundry Moors do not consider themselves to be legal citizens of the United States of America. Only the passage of this legislative proposal would guarantee their Islamic beliefs, their true citizenship, and the obedience to Islamic law.

In bolstering their argument that the Moors in America deserve this legislation, there are statements on pages 15 and 16 *proving* that the Moors in America are an integral part of American indigenous history. The following is stated on page 15, at section 206: "Iroquois, Algonquin, Anasazi, Hohokam, Apache, Arawak, Arikana, Chavin, Cherokee, Cree, Hupa, Hopi, Makkah, Mohawk, Naca, Zulu, Zuni ... derive from Arabic root origins." Herewith is a prime example of cultural al-taqiyya. It is all a lie with a purpose. The source that is given is "Precolumbian Muslims in the Americas's (sic) by Dr. Youssef A. Mroueh."[185] (See Appendix II.) Dr. Mroueh's article *Muslims in America Before Columbus*,[186] is cross-referenced by a plethora of Islamic Internet sites eager to prove that Muslims were in America long before Columbus. One receives 1,440,000 internet hits (including repetitions) when googling *pre-columbian Muslims in America*. Dr. Mroueh's assertions are not worth the paper on which they are printed. Although the reader may be inclined to think that the following documented

---

[185] Dr. Youssef A. Mroueh wrote the article in 1996 celebrating the 1000th anniversary of the Islamic discovery of America. The article is at http://sunnah.org/history/precolmb.htm, retrieved on 21.03.2012.

[186] http://www.cyberistan.org/islamic/mamerica.html, which was retrieved on 30.01.2012.

research is pedantic, it is too important not to be undertaken and to be relegated to a place in an appendix to this book.

Without citing any documentary evidence, Dr. Mroueh continues, "A careful study of the names of the native Indian tribes revealed that many names are derived from Arab and Islamic roots and origins, ..." The list that the *Sundry Free Moors Act of 2012* has on page 15 and the list by Dr. Mroueh are exposed as a lie by this author as follows:

- Anasazi. The name of these Indians comes from the Navajo word *Anaasází*, meaning *Ancient Ones* or *Ancient Enemy*.[187] There is no Arabic-Islamic origin or connection.

- Apache. This word come from the Zuni Indian word *ʔa·paču* meaning *Navajos* or from the Yavapai Indian word *ʔpačə* meaning *enemy*.[188] There is no Arabic-Islamic origin or connection.

- Arawak. From *aru*, the Lucayan (the original inhabitants of the Bahamas) word for *cassava flour*.[189] There is no Arabic-Islamic origin or connection.

- Arikana, This is a misspelling. It should be Arikara Indians, also Sahnish. They are located in North Dakota.[190] The name

---

[187] http://hewit.unco.edu/DOHIST/puebloan/begin.htm, retrieved on 17.02.2012

[188] http://www.mce.k12tn.net/indians/reports2/apache.htm, retrieved on 17.02.2012. Respective entry in Newman, Stanley. *Zuni dictionary*, Indiana University Bloomington: 1958.

[189] http://en.wikipedia.org/wiki/Arawak_peoples, retrieved on 17.02.2012.

[190] http://www.mhanation.com/main/history/history_arikara.html, retrieved on 18.02.2012.

170

is believed to mean *horns*, due to their ancient custom of wearing two upright bones in their hair. The name also could mean *elk people or corn eaters*.[191] The Arikara have neither an Arabic-Islamic origin nor connection. Arikana Indians do not exist.

- <u>Chavin</u>. The Chavín civilization existed in the northern Andean highlands of Peru from 900 BC to 200 BC.[192] There is no Arabic-Islamic connection or origin.

- <u>Cherokee</u>. The Cherokee refer to themselves as *Tsalagi*or *Aniyvwiyai*, or *Tsalagi* which means *principal people*. The Iroquois, who were based in New York, called the Cherokee *Oyata'ge'ronoñ*, the *inhabitants of the cave country*. The name could come from the Choctaw word *Cha-la-kee*, which means *those who live in the mountain*, or Choctaw *Chi-luk-ik-bi*, meaning *those who live in the cave county*.[193] The simplest origin of the name is the Anglicization of their name *Tsalagi*. The Cherokee have neither an Arabic-Islamic origin nor connection.

- <u>Cree</u>. The Algonkian-language exonym *Kiristino*, used for tribes inhabiting the Hudson Bay Region.[194] The name Cree

---

[191] Waldman, Carl. *Encyclopedia of Native American Tribes*, Checkmark Books, New York: 2009, p. 26f.

[192] http://en.wikipedia.org/wiki/Chav%C3%ADn_culture, retrieved on 18.02.2012.

[193] http://www.accessgenealogy.com/native/tribes/cherokee/cherohist.htm, retrieved on 18.02.2012.

[194] http://en.wikipedia.org/wiki/Cree, retrieved on 18.02.2012.

comes from this source. The Cree have neither an Arab-Islamic origin nor connection.

- Hohokam. The term Hohokam is borrowed from the Akimel O'odham. It defines an archaeological culture that existed from approximately the first century AD to the 15th century AD.[195] Hohokam has neither an Arab-Islamic origin nor connection.

- Hupa. The Hupa people migrated from the south into northern California around 1000 AD. They came from the Puebloan cultures in New Mexico.[196] The Hupa have neither an Arab-Islamic origin nor connection.

- Makkah. There is no Makkah Indian tribe. The spelling seems to have been intentionally changed from Makah to Makkah to connect to the city in Saudi Arabia. The name was given to them by a neighboring tribe and means *generous ones.* The Makah tribe's name in their own language is *Qwiqwidicciat,* which means *people of the point.*[197] There is no connection whatsoever between the Makah Indians and Makkah and thus there is no Arabic-Islamic root.[198]

- Mahigan. Mahigan Native Americans do not exist. The term is probably a misspelling of Mahican or Mohegan. Mahican

---

[195] http://en.wikipedia.org/wiki/Hohokam, retrieved on 18.02.2012.

[196] Pritzker, Barry M. *A Native American Encyclopedia: History, Culture, and Peoples.* Oxford University Press, Oxford: 2000, p. 126-127. http://en.wikipedia.org/wiki/Hopi, retrieved on 18.02.2012.

[197] http://www.bigorrin.org/makah_kids.htm, retrieved on 17.02. 2012.

[198] http://www.makah.com/; http://www.historyofmecca.com/, retrieved on 17.02.2012.

is derived from their name *Muhhekanneuw,* or *Muh-he-con-ne-ok,* meaning *people of the waters that are never still.* Mohegan comes from *Maingan,* meaning *wolf.* Both tribes are referred to as Mohican. They lived in the northern Hudson River Valley. The Mahican/Mohegan tribes have neither an Arab-Islamic origin nor connection.[199]

- Mohawk. The name Mohawk is from the Algonquian language and not the Iroquoian. It means *eaters of men.* Although they spoke Iroquois, the Algonquin tribes gave them their name because they practiced communal cannibalism so that they could absorb the strength of their enemies. Their homeland was upper New York.[200] The Mohawk Native Americans have neither an Arab-Islamic origin nor connection.

- Nazca. The Nazca (Nasca) culture flourished from 100 AD to 800 AD in and near the dry coast of Southern Peru in the river valleys of the Rio Grande de Nazca drainage and the Ica Valley.[201] The meaning of Nazca is *I am born* or *I am being born.*[202] The Nazca Americans have neither an Arab-Islamic origin nor connection.

- Zulu. There is no Zulu Indian tribe, either in North America or in South America, Zulus are found in South Africa. They

---

[199] Pritzker, p. 147. http://en.wikipedia.org/wiki/Mahican, retrieved on 18.02.2012.

[200] Pritzker, p. 170.

[201] http://en.wikipedia.org/wiki/Nazca_culture, retrieved on 18.02.2012.

[202] http://www.world-mysteries.com/mpl 1_2.htm, retrieved on 18.02.2012.

came from the present-day Cameroon sometime in the second millennium BC. [203] The name means *heaven*. Thus, the Zulus are *the people of heaven*.[204] The Zulus have neither an Arab-Islamic origin nor connection.

- <u>Zuni</u>. The Zuni live in western New Mexico and eastern Arizona. They are descendants of the Hopi Native Americans. The name comes from the language, which is called *Shiwi'ma* (*shiwi* (Zuni) + -*'ma* = *Zuni way*)[205] In the Zuni tribe the mother (female) serves as the basis of society, which is contrary to all Islamic societies.[206] The Zuni have neither an Arab-Islamic origin nor connection.

Dr. Mroueh's documentation of Muslim-Arabic Indian names resulting from: "A careful study of the names of the native Indian tribes revealed that many names are derived from Arab and Islamic roots and origins, ..." has no validity. There is no truthful fact behind his allegations. It is all creeping al-taqiyya. Dr. Mroueh is a liar.

On page 16 in section 206 of *The Sundry Moors Act of 2012* one reads, "There are more than 500 names of places, villages, streets, towns, cities, lakes, rivers, etc … in the United States in which their names are derived from African, Islamic, and Arabic words. Places like Mecca, Indiana; Morocco,

---

[203] http://de.wikipedia.org/wiki/Zulu_%28Volk%29, which was retrieved on 18.02.2012.

[204] http://www.babynames.com/name/ZULU, retrieved on 18.02.2012.

[205] http://en.wikipedia.org/wiki/Zuni_language, retrieved on 18.02.2012.

[206] Taylor, Colin F. editor. *The Native Americans The Indigenous People of North America*, Smithmark, New York: 1991, p. 45.

Indiana; Medina, NY; Medina, OH; Medina, TX; Toledo, OH; Mahomet, IL; Mahomet, Texas; Yarrowsburg, MD; Islamorada, FL, and Tallahassee, FL are found throughout America. There are at least two cities in Illinois named after Nubian Cities: Argo and Dongola, Illinois. Other cities with Islamic and African root names are Allakaket, Alakanuk, and Soloman, Alaska; Ali Chuk, Ali Molina, Ali Oidak, Arizona; Cushman, Arkansas; Alameda, and Malcolm X Square, California; Abeyta, and Medina Plaza, Colorado; Liberia Historical, Connecticut; Medulla, and Sallee Heights, Florida; Mecca Historical, Tallulah Falls, and Zaidee, Georgia; Aliamanu, and Maili, Hawaii; Hagerstown, Samaria, and Syria, Indiana; Cairo Junction, Egypt Shores, Egyptian Hills, Egyptian Acres, Hagarstown, Media, Medinah, and Shabbona, Illinois; Mingo, Ollie, Palestine Historical, Sabula, Salem, Tama, Makee, and Malak, Iowa; Assaria, Kansas; Gamaliel, Kentucky; Jordan Hill, and Tallulah, Louisiana; Hagerstown, and Yarrowsburg, Maryland; Egypt Beach, Massachusetts; Almira, Hagar Township, and Zilwaukee, Michigan; Amiret, Amor, Isanti, Mesaba, Kanaranzi, Quamba, and Suomi, Minnesota; Egypt Hill, and Itta Bena, Mississippi; Ameera Historical, Ebo, Egypt Grove, Egypt Mills, Sabula, and Yarrow, Missouri; Madrid, Nebraska; Alhambra Historical, New Mexico; Cairo Junction, Hague, Nunda, Salem, Salamanc, and Unadilla, New York; Babylon Historical, Nevada; Amenia, North Dakota; Ashtabula, Damascus Historical, Kalida, Sabina, and Toledo, Ohio; Damascus Heights, Jordan Creek, Jordan Valley, and South Lebanon, Oregon; Aliquippa, Egypt Corners, Egypt Mills, Jordan Valley, and Media, Pennsylvania; Jordan Village, Utah; Bagdad Historical, Cairo Bend, Isham, Palestine

Historical, and Zu Zu, Texas; Ahmedabad, Egypt Bend Estates, and Jordan Springs, Virginia; Bagdad Junction, Illahee, Shuwah, and Yarrow Point, Washington; Algeria Historical, Egypt Historical, Jordan Run, and Jumbo, West Virginia; Medina Junction and Mecan, Wisconsin; and Holy Islamville, South Carolina."

These place names are also taken from Dr. Mroueh's 1996 article referenced above. If the reader googles *There are more than 500 names of places (villages, towns, cities, mountains, lakes, rivers, etc.) in USA (484) and Canada (81) which are derived from Islamic and Arabic roots,* there will be approximately 14,100 hits, including repetitions. The information on these sites will be the same. Self-appointed Islamic *historians* (?) in the twenty-first century are still propagandizing a list of place names of streets, villages, towns, cities, lakes, and rivers that they contend are derived from Arabic and Islamic words or are possible derivations thereof.[207]

---

[207] It is likely that the listing originated with one or two sites, most probably Dr. Youssef Mroueh's *Pre-Columbian Muslims in the Americas* at http://sunnah.org/history/precolmb.htm, discussed above, or one of the sites listed in this footnote. The reader must be exceedingly cautious in accepting the writings of Islamic sites that are attempting to creep their versions and stories of American settlement into American history. This author advises not to believe one iota of their ranting. They are not true and they are not documented. Essentially, the information is crap! The information is lies! http://www.muslimsinamerica.org/index2.php?option=com_content&do_pd f=1&id=14;
http://spiritualchange.blogsome.com/2010/12/18/muslim-contacts-with-american-indians-before-columbus/;
http://rupeenews.com/usa/california-was-named-after-calif-haronia-caliph-haroon-rashid-al-hambra-was-also-from-muslim-spainmore-than-500-american-town-have-muslim-origins/;

This internet address will give you the listing: http://www.muslimsinamerica.org/index2.php?option=com_co ntent&do_pdf=1&id=14. They are essentially the same as in the addresses in footnote number 207.

These places are listed below with the correct meanings and their origins. The reader will be surprised concerning the inaccuracy of the Islamic *historians* and the Islamic internet sites. The names are in quasi-alphabetical order followed by the state. The footnote is where the reader can find the true answers.

1. Abeyta, and Medina Plaza, Colorado

Abeyta can mean *a gay*, or *homosexual young boy*. Abeyta has roots from the Basque Country or Euskal Herria, Spain. There it means *a person who dwells near a hard wood tree or a pine tree.* [208] The origin is not Arab-Islamic.

Medina comes from Aramaic *mədintā, mədinā*, the language that Jesus spoke. It means *jurisdiction, district,*

---

http://www.middle-east-studies.net/?p=2755;
http://sunnah.org/history/precolmb.htm;
http://www.al-huda.com/Article_13of42.htm;
http://muslimwiki.com/mw/index.php/Islamic_place_names_in_America;
http://www.witness-pioneer.org/vil/Articles/politics/muslims_in_the_americas_before_columbus. htm;
http://www.imamreza.net/eng/imamreza.php?id=3932;
http://www.iol.ie/~afifi/BICNews/Personal/personal1.htm.
http://www.wafin.com/articles/23/index.phtml; all retrieved on 14.02.2012.

[208] http://www.definition-of.net/abeyta; http://wiki.name.com/en/Abeyta, retrieved on 14.02.2012.

*from dān, to judge, administer.* [209] Thus its origin is not Arabic-Islamic, although Arabic translates it into English as meaning *the city of the prophet.* At least these cities in Colorado are not closed. Medina and Mecca, Saudi Arabia are so friendly that the cities are off limits to non-believers. Medina is the second holiest city and the burial place of Mohammed. Although now Arabic, the city's history is not Arabic. It is Assyrian and Hebrew, dating back to the period between the 6th century BC and the 2nd century AD. [210]

## 2. Ahmedabad, Egypt Bend Estates, Jordan Springs, Virginia

Although founded by Mongols, the origin of the name Ahmedabad is Persian and means *founded by Ahmed.* Its origin is not Arabic-Islamic. [211]

Egypt and Jordan existed centuries before the Arabs, Mohammed, and Islam. Egypt most likely derives from the Coptic *Gebtu*, modern *Qift.* [212] It is not Arabic-Islamic.

Jordan derives from the Hebrew and the Canaanite root for *descend (into the Dead Sea.)* [213] Jordan is not of Arabic-Islamic origin.

---

[209] http://www.answers.com/topic/medina-1, retrieved on 14.02.2012.

[210] http://www.livius.org/ct-cz/cyrus_I/babylon02.html#Chronicle%20of%20Nabonidus, retrieved on 18.02.2012.

[211] http://de.wikipedia.org/wiki/Ahmedabad; retrieved on 14.02.2012. http://en.wikipedia.org/wiki/List_of_country-name_etymologies, retrieved on 14.02.2012.

[212] http://en.wikipedia.org/wiki/List_of_country-name_etymologies that was retrieved on 14.02.2012.

## 3. Bagdad Junction, Illahee, Shuwah, Yarrow Point, Washington

Although founded by the Abbasid Kalif al-Mansur, Bagdad comes from the Persian and means *gift from God* (not from Allah), or *gift from the great king*.[214] Its origin is not Arabic-Islamic.

Illahee means *land*. It comes from the Native American Chinook language.[215] Its origin is not Arabic-Islamic.

Shuwah is Hebrew and means salvation or *I am he who saves*.[216] Its origin is not Arabic-Islamic.

Yarrow is an "*ubiquitous strong-scented mat-forming Eurasian herb of wasteland, hedgerow or pasture having narrow serrate leaves and small usually white florets; widely naturalized in North America*." Its origin is Old English *gearwe* and perhaps from Proto-Germanic *ȝarwō*. As a boy's name, it can connote *rough stream*.[217] Its origin is not Arabic-Islamic.

---

[213] http://en.wikipedia.org/wiki/List_of_country-name_etymologies, which was retrieved on 14.02.2012

[214] http://de.wikipedia.org/wiki/Bagdad;;http://yahuwah-is.net/, retrieved on 14.02.2012.

[215] http://www.websters-online-dictionary.org/Chinook/illahee, retrieved on 14.02.2012.

[216] http://www.yahuwah-is.net/Files/yahuwshua.html, which was retrieved on 14.02.2012.

[217] http://www.onenesspentecostal.com/nameofgod.htm was retrieved on 14.02.2012.

If Yarrow is the Anglicized writing of the name Yaro in the Fulani language of Guinea (See Mamout Yarrow in Chapter Five) then this source is not of Arabic-Islamic origin either. Traditionally, the Fulani are a nomadic, pastoral community making their livelihoods herding cattle, goats, and sheep. They are located in the populating grasslands between the towns throughout West Africa. The Fulani have existed as a nomadic people in Western Africa for over 1000 years. They became mostly Muslims in the transition from the 18th to the 19th centuries. Therefore the regions which they inhabit have been Muslim, Arabic-Islam for no more than 200-plus years. *Yaro* in Hausa-Fulani means *It's a boy*. The name also occurs as a first name in India Kurdish where it means *loved one*. [218] This use is not related to Arabic or Islamic origins.

### 4.   Alameda, and Malcolm X Square, California

The history of *Alameda* originates with the *Spanish* language.[219] The name _Alameda_ in Spanish means *from the poplar tree*. The name does not have an Arabic-Islamic origin.

Malcolm X derives from Malcolm Little, an American Muslim, but the name has nothing to do with Islam or

---

[218]   http://www.humnet.ucla.edu/aflang/Hausa/Language/dialectframe.html and   http://www.baby-vornamen.de/Jungen/Y/Ya/Yaro/,   retrieved   on 14.02.2012.

[219]   http://www.meaning-of-names.com/spanish-names/alameda.asp,   which was retrieved on 14.02.2012.

Arabic. He called himself Malcolm X because he descended from slaves and was not sure what his last name was. Malcolm means *a devotee of Saint Columba*. It is of Scottish and Gaelic origin.[220] Malcolm X does not have Arabic-Islamic roots.

5. Algeria (Historical), Egypt (Historical), Jordan Run, Jumbo, West Virginia

Algeria possibly comes from the Berber Ldzayer in reference to Ziri ibn-Manad, who founded the Zirid Dynasty. In the Berber language *ziri* means *moonlight*. The Berber languages have been in existence for over 2,200 years.[221] Algeria does not have Arabic-Islamic origins.

For Egypt, see number 2. For Jordan, see number 2.

Jumbo got its name from Jumbo the elephant of P. T. Barnum's Circus fame. "In 1882 P.T. Barnum brought Jumbo the huge elephant over from England for his circus. Jumbo became synonymous with anything big and exciting. Since making money in new mines was usually about convincing others they could make money, new strikes were heavily promoted and an exciting or memorable name was important. Anyway, that's ... how Jumbo got its

---

[220] http://www.thinkbabynames.com/meaning/1/Malcolm was retrieved on 14.02.2012.

[221] http://en.wikipedia.org/wiki/List_of_country-name_etymologies, which was retrieved on 14.02.2012.

name."[222] Jumbo is likely a variation of one or two Swahili words: *jambo*, which means *hello* or *jumbe*, which means *chief*.[223] It has come to mean *huge, large*. Jumbo has no Arabic-Islamic roots.

## 6. Alhambra (Historical), New Mexico

Alhambra is a fortress and palace. Although partly constructed by the Moors in Granada, the term is not of Arabic-Islamic origin. It is Spanish and means *the red one*.[224] Its origin is not Arabic-Islamic.

## 7. Ali Chuk, Ali-Molina, Ali Oidak, Arizona

*Ali-Chuk* means *small clearing*. The word comes from O'odham, an Uto-Aztecan *language* of southern Arizona and northern Sonora.[225] It has no Arabic-Islamic roots.

---

[222] http://washoevalley.org/wv/wv%20history.htm#Jumbo_Grade, retrieved on 14.02.2012.

[223] http://en.wikipedia.org/wiki/Jumbo, retrieved on 14.02.2012.

[224] http://en.wikipedia.org/wiki/Alhambra was retrieved on 14.02.2012.

[225] http://www.nps.gov/sagu/forteachers/upload/Unit%208%20-%20Water %20in%20the%20Desert.pdf, which was retrieved on 14.02.2012. http://books.google.de/books?id=9lCM_c35aJAC&pg=PA277&lpg=PA277 &dq=meaning+of+AliChuk&source=bl&ots=tF5qtLSW19&sig=WpsQNhm xyG0cOwKVxSIZkmNeoMc&hl=de&sa=X&ei=hk06T5e4BMXMtAbtm_T OBg&sqi=2&ved=0CCAQ6AEwAA#v=onepage&q=meaning%20of%20Al i-Chuk&f=false, retrieved on 14.02.2012.

Ali-Molina means *little Magdalena* in O'odham which was taken from Spanish Magdalena.[226]

Ali Oidak means *little field* in O'odham.[227] These places in Arizona do not have Arabic-Islamic origins.

## 8. Aliquippa, Egypt Corners, Egypt Mills, Media, Pennsylvania.

Aliquippa is said to mean *hat*. It was the title of a female leader of the Seneca (Mohawk, Delaware) Indians. The word is from the Algonquin language.[228]

For Egypt, see number 2.

Media may derive from the Medes of the Median Empire in an area known as Media. They came into the area at the end of the second millennium BC. They were Persians, not Arabs. Media may also have its name from the

---

http://books.google.de/books?id=5XfxzCm1qa4C&pg=PA32&dq=%22Ali-Molina%22&hl=de&sa=X&ei=yk86T5r4As3Nswbpg92nBg&ved=0CEcQ6AEwBA#v=onepage&q=%22Ali-Molina%22&f=false was retrieved on 14.02.2012.

[226] http://en.wikipedia.org/wiki/O%27odham_language, retrieved on 14.02.2012.

[227] http://books.google.de/books?id=5XfxzCm1qa4C&pg=PA32&lpg=PA32&dq=little+field+in+O%27odham&source=bl&ots=ZSeuk3hios&sig=FM86WvfZmHmNlggv5L-MN5brsak&hl=de&sa=X&ei=tNRIT-OXDoLl4QTehKXhDg&ved=0CCUQ6AEwAA#v=onepage&q=little%20field%20in%20O%27odham&f=false, retrieved on 14.02.2012.

[228] http://www.bchistory.org/beavercounty/BeaverCountyTopical/NativeAmerican/IndianNamesinBCMA97.html; and the internet link http://www.answers.com/topic/aliquippa, retrieved on 14.02.2012.

fact that the town is located somewhat in the middle of Baltimore County, Pennsylvania.[229] What is certain is that it does not have an Arabic-Islamic origin or any historical connection.

For Jordan, see number 2.

9. Allakaket, Alakanuk, and Soloman, Alaska

Allakaket is a Koyukuk Indian name meaning *mouth of the Alatna River*.[230]

Alakanuk, is a Yup'ik word meaning *wrong way* or *mistake village*.[231]

Solomon is derived from the Hebrew *Shelomoh* and means *peace*.[232] Definitely, the names do not have any Arabic-Islamic origin or connection.

10. Almira, Hagar Township, and Zilwaukee, Michigan

Almira means *queen* or *princess*. It comes from Amira, Persian for *queen* or *princess*.[233]

---

[229] http://en.wikipedia.org/wiki/Media,_Pennsylvania; and the internet link http://en.wikipedia.org/wiki/Medes, retrieved on 14.02.2012.

[230] http://www.uaf.edu/anla/collections/search/files/KO972J-PN-04/f.08 VillageProf.pdf, retrieved on 14.02.2012.

[231] http://en.wikipedia.org/wiki/Alakanuk,_Alaska, retrieved on 14.02.2012.

[232] http://www.abarim-publications.com/Meaning/Solomon.html#.TzpWElH z7mc, retrieved on 14.02.2012.

[233] http://de.wikipedia.org/wiki/Amira, retrieved on 14.02.2012.

Hagar comes from the Hebrew. Hagar was an Egyptian handmaiden of Sarah, the first wife of Abraham. Hagar became Abraham's second wife. Although mentioned in the Koran and misappropriated for Islam's purposes by Mohammed, Hagar was born in approximately 2000 BC, 2,600 years before Mohammed. Hagar means *stranger.*[234]

Zilwaukee is a corruption of Milwaukee. Zilwaukee has no meaning.[235] Hagar, Almira, and Zilwaukee have no Arabic-Islamic origin.


11. Ameera (Historical), Ebo, Egypt Grove, Egypt Mills, Sabula, Yarrow, Missouri

Ameera is Hebrew and means *top of the tree*, as well as *princess.* [236]

Ebo means *Tuesday born* and is of African (Ghanaian) origin.[237] Neither Ameera nor Ebo have Arabic-Islamic origins.

---

[234] http://en.wikipedia.org/wiki/Hagar, retrieved on 14.02.2012.

[235] http://books.google.de/books?id=T5d5wS7so14C&pg=PA81&lpg=PA81 &dq=meaning+of+Zilwaukee&source=bl&ots=VcJhvYSqzw&sig=nPInI2y 03CdlN6my_pRMg9m4uf8&hl=de&sa=X&ei=OVc6T5i9HcPOsgbI0KjzBg &ved=0CCIQ6AEwAA#v=onepage&q=Zilwaukee&f=false, retrieved on 14.02.2012.

[236] http://babynames.fortunebaby.com/meaning_of_the_name_ameera.html, retrieved on 14.02.2012.

[237] http://babynamesworld.parentsconnect.com/meaning_of_Ebo.html was retrieved on 14.02.2012.

"In 1846 the settlers of <u>Sabula</u> decided to find a name no one else could claim. Because of its sandy soil, William Hubble looked up sand in the dictionary and found the Latin word for sand to be *Sabulum* ... but (it) did not please some of the ladies in town. At a tea party, one of the ladies suggested that *Sabula* was easier to say and sounded more elegant. Her suggestion was adopted and so named was Sabula."[238]

For <u>Egypt</u>, see number 2.

For <u>Yarrow</u>, see number 3.


## 12. <u>Amenia, North Dakota</u>

<u>Amenia</u> definitely comes from Latin, *amoena*, meaning *pleasant to the eye*. <u>Amenia</u> can also mean *the absence or cessation of menstruation*.[239] It is also known as *amenorrhea*. However, Amenia may be a misspelling of Armenia. The complete etymology Armenia is unknown. We can trace it backwards into history from the Latinized Greek *Arменía*, meaning *Land of the Armenioi*, to Old Persian *Armina*, perhaps a continuation of the Assyrian *Armânum*, or a variant of the *Urmani* or *Urmenu*, known as the *Armens*, or a continuation of the Biblical *Minni* and Assyrian *Minnai*, which corresponds to the *Mannai*, indicating the meaning of *the mountainous region of the*

---

[238] http://www.islandcityharbor.com/History/index.htm was retrieved on 14.02.2012.

[239] http://www.medterms.com/script/main/art.asp?articlekey=6992 was retrieved on 14.02.2012.

*Minni*. It could also come from *\*Armnaia*, meaning *inhabitant of Arme or Urme*. A possible ultimate root is the Proto-Indo-European root *\*ar-* (*assemble, create*). An Armenian tradition traces the name to an eponymous ancestor Aram, sometimes equated with Arame, the earliest known king of Urartu.[240] What is certain is that Amenia and Armenia have no Arabic-Islamic origin.

### 13. Amiret, Amor, Isanti, Mesaba, Kanaranzi, Quamba, and Suomi, Minnesota

Amiret was named after Amiretta Sykes, the wife of a local railroad president, M. K. Sykes. Amiretta is Spanish and means *little princess*.[241] See also number 10.

Amor was named after the Roman god of love and means *love*.[242]

Isanti was named after a Minnesota Indian tribe of the same name.[243]

Mesaba is a spelling of Mesabi of the Ojibwe Indians and Chippewa Indians. In their cultures, Missabe is an

---

[240] For people who know Latin, the source is obvious. Evidently, Dr. Mroueh has no knowledge of Latin.

[241] http://www.epodunk.com/cgi-bin/genInfo.php?locIndex=20806 was retrieved on 14.02.2012.

[242] Those who know Latin are obvious of this fact.

[243] http://www.epodunk.com/cgi-bin/genInfo.php?locIndex=21144 was retrieved on 14.02.2012.

*immense giant and a cannibal.* The Missabe Mountain Range is where this giant lives.[244]

Kanaranzi is a Dakota Indian word that means *where the Kansas Indians were killed.*[245]

Quamba is a Minnesotan Indian word meaning *mudhole.*[246]

Suomi gets its name from the Finnish settlers who gave the place the name of their country, Suomi (Finland, *land of the fens).*[247] Not one of the localities has an Arabic-Islamic origin. There are absolutely no Arabic-Islamic historical connections.


## 14. Argo, Illinois

Argo comes from the Greek Argos meaning *bright.* Argo has no Arabic-Islamic origin.[248]

---

[244] http://www.archive.org/stream/minnesotageogra00uphagoog/minnesota geogra00uphagoog_djvu.txt, retrieved on 14.02.2012.

[245] http://en.wikipedia.org/wiki/Kanaranzi,_Minnesota was retrieved on 14.02.2012.

[246] http://en.wikipedia.org/wiki/Quamba,_Minnesota, which was retrieved on 14.02.2012.

[247] http://en.wikipedia.org/wiki/List_of_country-name_etymologies, which was retrieved on 14.02.2012.

[248] Every person who knows Greek is aware of this fact.

## 15. Ashtabula, Damascus (Historical), Kalida, Sabina, and Toledo, Ohio

Ashtabula comes from the Algonkin Indian language *Hash-tah-buh-lah*, meaning *river of many fish*.[249]

As far back as the 15th century BC, Damascus appears in a geographical list of Thutmose III as *T-m-ś-q*, the origin of which is uncertain. However it appears to be pre-Semitic. It occurs as *Dimašqa* in Akkadian, *T-ms-ḵw* in Egyptian, *Dammaśq* in Old Aramaic and *Dammeśeq* in Biblical Hebrew. Generally, it means a *well-watered place*.[250]

Kalida comes from a local Indian language and means *beautiful*.[251]

Sabine is the original Latin word and means *of the tribe of the Sabines*.[252]

As a boy's name, Toledo means *informal*. *Toledo* derives from the Roman outpost in Spain that they named *Toletum*. The locality was already a Celtic-Iberian town before the Romans conquered it in 192 BC. The word *Toletum* may refer to the fact that the region was always famous for metal work. *Tole (tôle)* is the French for sheet

---

[249] http://en.wikipedia.org/wiki/Ashtabula_River, retrieved on 14.02.2012.

[250] http://en.wikipedia.org/wiki/Damascus, retrieved on 14.02.2012.

[251] http://userpages.bright.net/~kcc/kalida/history.htm was retrieved on 14.02.2012.

[252] http://de.wikipedia.org/wiki/Sabina, retrieved on 14.02.2012.

metal.[253] The names in the listing have no Arabic-Islamic origins.

## 16. Assaria, Kansas

Assaria comes from Assyria. Assarian coins were common in the second century AD, four hundred years before the appearance of Mohammed. The word is Aramaic.[254] It has no Arabic-Islamic origin.

## 17. Babylon (Historical), Nevada

Babylon has Sumerian, Acadian, and Babylonian roots. It means *Gate of God* (not Gate of Allah). The name has been in existence since the second millennium BC.[255] It has no Arabic-Islamic origins.

## 18. Bagdad Historical, Cairo Bend, Isham, Palestine (Historical), and Zu Zu, Texas

For Bagdad refer to number 3. The meaning of Cairo is *victorious one.*[256] Although the new city of Cairo was

---

[253] http://de.wikipedia.org/wiki/Toledo, retrieved on 14.02.2012.

[254] See number 27.

[255] http://en.wikipedia.org/wiki/Babylon, retrieved on 14.02.2012.

[256] Hawass, Zahi A.; Brock, Lyla Pinch *Egyptology at the Dawn of the Twenty-First Century: Archaeology* (2nd ed.). Cairo: American University in Cairo (2003), http://pioneercity.com/history.html, retrieved on 14.02.2012.

founded by caliph Omar ibn al-Khattāb in 969, its historical roots go back to the pre-Islamic times of the 4th century AD.

Isham, Texas was named after Reverend Washington Marion Isham, the town's founder. The name Isham is a Celtic river-name (meaning *water*) plus Old English *hām* or *hamm* that exists in Northants, England, spelled *Ysham* in 974 and *Isham* in 1086. It is a homestead or promontory by the River Ise.[257] There is no word Isham of Arabic-Islamic origin. The word Isham does not exist in Arabic.

Palestine, Texas was named after Palestine, Illinois, which received its name from the French explorer Jean Lamotte, who first viewed the region 1678. "He gave it the name Palestine, as it reminded him of the promised land of milk and honey, as written in the scriptures." Palestine is a "conventional name, among others, used to describe the geographic region between the Mediterranean Sea and the Jordan River, and various adjoining lands." It was never an independent country. Palestine comes from *Peleset*, the Sea Peoples who invaded Egypt during the reign of Ramses III. Palestine means *rolling or migratory*.[258] It has no Arab-Islamic origin. It has always been known as the Land of Israel!

---

[257] http://www.ishamcemetery.org/, retrieved on 20.02.2012, A. D. MILLS. "Isham." A Dictionary of British Place-Names. 2003, retrieved on February 20, 2012 from Encyclopedia.com: http://www.encyclopedia.com/doc/1O40-Isham.html.

[258] http://www.palestinefacts.org/pf early_palestine_name_origin.php, and http://en.wikipedia.org/wiki/Palestine, retrieved on 14.02.2012.

Zu Zu or Zuzu is a short form of Susannah, which comes from the Czech Susan, meaning *lily*. Zuzu can also be Slavic, meaning *lily*.[259] There is no such place as Zu Zu, Texas. The name has no Arabic-Islamic origin. The origin is Greek.

19. Cairo Junction, Egypt Shores, Egyptian Hills, Egyptian Acres, Hagarstown, Media, Medinah, and Shabbona, Illinois

For Cairo see number 18.

For Egypt and Egyptian see number 2.

For Hagarstown see number 10.

The name Media, Illinois "originated from the fact that the town is situated halfway between Chicago, IL and Kansas City, MO on the Santa Fe Railroad."[260]

Medinah, Illinois gets its name from the Medinah Country Club. In the 1920s, a group of members of the city of Chicago's Medinah Temple … (affiliated with the Shriners, the Free Masons who originated in Western England and Scotland in the 15th and 17th centuries respectively. This organization established rules for masters of the trade of masonry.) The Free Masons moved into the area, then known as Meacham (for the Meacham, Lawrence and Rosenwinkel families). The reason why some of the

---

[259] http://www.biblical-baby-names.com/meaning-of-zuzu.html, and http; www.parenting.com/baby-names/girls/Zuzu, retrieved on 20.02.2012.

[260] http://en.wikipedia.org/wiki/Media,_Illinois, retrieved on 14.02.2012.

temples have nomenclature from some Arabic places is that "(i)n 1870, there were several thousand Masons in Manhattan, many of whom lunched at the Knickerbocker Cottage at a special table on the second floor. There, the idea of a new fraternity for Masons stressing fun and fellowship was discussed. Walter M. Fleming, M.D., and William J. Florence took the idea seriously enough to act upon it. Florence, a world-renowned actor, while on tour in Marseilles, was invited to a party given by an Arabian diplomat. The entertainment was something in the nature of an elaborately staged musical comedy. At its conclusion, the guests became members of a secret society. Florence took copious notes and drawings at his initial viewing and on two other occasions, once in Algiers and once in Cairo. When he returned to New York in 1870, he showed his material to Fleming. Fleming took the ideas supplied by Florence and converted them into what would become the Ancient Arabic Order of the Nobles of the Mystic Shrine (A.A.O.N.M.S.). Fleming created the ritual, emblem, and costumes. Florence and Fleming were initiated on August 13, 1870, and initiated 11 other men on June 16, 1871. The group adopted a Middle Eastern theme (due to the architecture) and soon established Temples meeting in Mosques (though the term Temple has now generally been replaced by Shrine Auditorium or Shrine Center because temples were never used for the observance of Islamic rituals). The first Temple established was Mecca Temple (now known as Mecca Shriners), established at the New York City, Masonic Hall on September 26, 1872. Fleming was the first Potentate." Other than the use of these terms as nomenclatures, Medinah, a corruption of Medina has nothing to do with Arabian or Islamic roots. As a matter of fact, Medina itself is of pre-Arabic origin. [261] (See number 1.)

Shabbona gets its name from the Potawatomi Indian chief Shabbona.[262] The name Shabbona is from either the Ottawa Indian language word *Zhaabne* or the Potawatomi Indian language word *Zhabné*. In both languages the meaning is *indomitable* or *hardy*. It came to mean *built strong like a bear* or *built like a bear*. Shabbona has no Arabic-Islamic origin.

## 20. Cairo Junction, Hague, Nunda, Salem, Salamanc, and Unadilla, New York

For Cairo see number 18.

Hague, New York was named after the city Hague in Holland in 1803. Hague is a Dutch word meaning *woods* or *hedge*.[263]

Nunda, New York. In the Seneca language, Nunda relates to hills and a popular translation is *Where the valley meets the hills*. The name is from *Nunda-wa-ono*, a Seneca

---

[261] http://en.wikipedia.org/wiki/Medinah,_Illinois; and the Internet link http://en.wikipedia.org/wiki/Masonic_manuscripts, retrieved on 14.02.2012.

[262] http://en.wikipedia.org/wiki/Shabbona and http://en.wikipedia.org/wiki/ Shabbona, Illinois, both retrieved on 14.02.2012.

[263] http://en.wikipedia.org/wiki/Hague,_New_York, which was retrieved on 14.02.2012.

Indian tribe that once lived in the beautiful hills and valleys along the Genesee River and Keshequa Stream within the Township of Nunda.[264]

Salem, New York. In the Book of Psalms (76:2) we read that the biblical town Salem was renamed Jerusalem. The name Salem probably had something to do with "a Ugaritic god, but transliterated this name neatly concurs with the Hebrew word (*shalem*) meaning *to be complete, sound.* The similar derivative (*shalem*) means *perfect, whole, full.* Another derivative is (*shalom*) meaning *peace.*"[265]

Salamanca, New York. The name of the city comes from a major investor in a local railroad (Don José de Salamanca y Mayol, Marquis of Salamanca, in Spain, which gets its name from a famous Greek historian named Salamntica who lived in the town.[266]

Unadilla, New York. The name comes from the Iroquois language meaning *meeting place.*[267]

None of these places in New York have Arabic-Islamic origins.

---

[264] http://www.nundahistory.org/shorthistory.html, retrieved on 14.02.2012.

[265] http://www.abarim-publications.com/Meaning/Salem.html#.T0YxPHlGTmc, retrieved on 14.02.2012.

[266] http://www.spanish-town-guides.com/Salamanca_History.htm, retrieved on 14.02.2012.

[267] http://en.wikipedia.org/wiki/Unadilla %28town%29,_New_York was retrieved on 14.02.2012.

## 21. Cushman, Arkansas

Cushman is a person who made and sold *cuish* (*thigh Armor*).[268] It has no Arabic-Islamic origin. The ancient Kingdom of Kush, located in northeastern Africa, comprised the large areas within present-day Egypt, Sudan and South Sudan. The kingdom had no relationship to an Arabic-Islamic origin.

## 22. Damascus Heights, Jordan Creek, Jordan Valley, and South Lebanon, Oregon

For Damascus see number 15.

For Jordan, see number 2.

"The name Lebanon comes from the Semitic root *lbn*, meaning *white*, likely a reference to the snow-capped Mount Lebanon. Upon his arrival in Lebanon around 47 BC, Julius Caesar proclaimed *Lub Na'an*, meaning *White-Land* in Semitic. Occurrences of the name have been found in texts from the library of Ebla, Syriam that date to the third millennium BC, nearly 70 times in the Hebrew Bible, and three of the twelve tablets of the Epic of Gilgamesh (perhaps as early as 2100 BC). The name is recorded in Ancient Egyptian as *Rmnn*, where R stood for Canaanite L."[269] The name Lebanon has no Arabic-Islamic origin.

---

[268] http://surnames.meaning-of-names.com/Cushman/, which was retrieved on 14.02.2012.

[269] http://en.wikipedia.org/wiki/Lebanon, retrieved on 14.02.2012.

## 23. Dongola, Illinois

Dongola is also Dunqulah. In Old Nubian it is Tungul. The city was the capital of the Christian kingdom of Makurra. Dongola is located in present-day Sudan. The region was Christian until the Muslims invaded and ravaged Nubia in the 14th century. Thereafter Nubia and the Sudan became Muslim. In Old Nubian Tungul was the place name of Old Dongola as well as the name or title of the King of Old Dongola. There is no specific meaning of Tungul. Yet, from related words in Old Nubian, like *tungil* and *tungur*, which were used to designate the bow weapon, we can deduce that Tungul has something to do with the bow. As Dr. Julie Anderson notes "Historically the Nubians were referred to as 'the pupil-smiters' due to their great prowess with the bow." This means that they were able to hit the eyes of their opponents at a formidable distance. There is a tanning process named after the Dongola sheep in the Sudan. The leather is tanned with gambier, alum, and salt. Because Dongola or Tungul was a pre-Arabic settlement and comes from the Old Nubian language, there is no Arabic-Islamic origin or association.[270]

## 24. Egypt Beach, Massachusetts

For Egypt, see Number 2.

## 25. Egypt Hill, and Itta Bena, Mississippi

---

[270] Armbruster, C. H. *Dongolese Nubian. A Lexicon*, Cambridge University Press, Cambridge: 1965, p. 206. The author is indebted to Dr. Julie Anderson, Assistant Keeper (Curator), Department of Ancient Egypt and Sudan, The British Museum for this information.

For Egypt, see number 2.

Itta Bena comes from the Choctaw phrase *iti bina*, meaning *forest camp*.[271] Neither Egypt nor *Itta Bene* have Arabic-Islamic origins.

## 26. Gamaliel, Kentucky

*Gamaliel* or Gamliel is Hebrew-Aramaic and means *God looks out for me*.[272] It has no Arabic-Islamic origin.

## 27. Hagerstown, Maryland

For Hagarstown, see number 10. Hagerstown comes from the Hebrew. Town is, of course, English and means *village*.[273]

## 28. Hagerstown, Samaria, and Syria, Indiana

For Hagarstown, see number 10.

Samaria was the capital of the Kingdom of Israel in the 9$^{th}$ and 8$^{th}$ centuries BC. Samaria comes from *Shomron* and literally means a *watch-mountain* or a *watch-tower*.[274]

---

[271] http://en.wikipedia.org/wiki/Itta_Bena, retrieved on 14.02.2012.

[272] http://de.wikipedia.org/wiki/Gamaliel, retrieved on 14.02.2012.

[273] http://en.wikipedia.org/wiki/Hagar; http://en.wikipedia.org/wiki/Assyria; http://www.abarim-publications.com/Meaning/Asshur.html#.TzuIxFHz7mc, retrieved on 14.02.2012.

Syria may mean *reasoning*, or *straight ahead*. Indications are that it is associated with the Semitic Akkadian Kingdom Assyria from the 25th or early 24th century BC to 608 BC. Its root is Hebrew because Syria goes back to Assyria which goes back to Asshur, the Biblical name for Assyria, where the descendants of Asshur, a son of Shem, son of Noah (Genesis 10:22) settled.[275] Hagerstown, Samaria, and Syria have no Arabic-Islamic origins.

29. Holy Islamville, South Carolina

Holy means *something, or someone preserved, intact which cannot be transgressed or violated.* The Proto-Germanic word root is **Haila₃ás*.

Islam means *voluntary submission to Allah.* It is interesting that in Islam if you do not voluntarily submit to Allah and the dogma of Mohammed, you can be killed, or you will have to pay a special tax, which may not save your life. The word Islām is a verbal noun derived from *s-l-m*, which means *submission*. Its true roots are Aramaic *Š-L-M and Hebrew Š-L-M*, which mean *Shin-Lamedh-Mem*, the letters of their respective alphabets. They also exist in Arabic. However, Arabic developed much later than Aramaic and Hebrew. They go back to the 8th century

---

[274] http://en.wikipedia.org/wiki/Samaria_%28ancient_city%29, retrieved on 14.02.2012.

[275] http://www.abarim-publications.com/Meaning/Asshur.html; http://en.wikipedia.org/wiki/Assyria, retrieved on 14.02.2012.

BC.[276] Therefore, etymologically speaking, Islam as a word does not have an Arabic origin.

Holy Islamville was founded as a Muslim village in South Carolina, by El-Sheikh Syed Mubarik Ali Shah Gilani, in 1983. Evidently the sheikh does not know anything about etymology. Certainly the sheikh does not know anything about the origin of the word Islam.

### 30. Islamorada, Tallahassee, Florida

"The name Islamorada, (Isla morada) means *purple island*, designated by the early Spanish explorers in the area. The English pronunciation is *aisle-a-more-AH-dah*.[277] The name has no Arabic-Islamic origin.

"The name Tallahassee is a Muskogean Indian word often translated as *old fields*. This likely stems from the Creek (later called Seminole) Indians who migrated from Georgia and Alabama to this region in the late 18th and early 19th centuries. Upon arrival, they found large areas of cleared land previously occupied by the Apalachee tribe. Earlier, the Mississippian Indians built mounds near Lake Jackson around AD 1200, which survive today in the Lake Jackson Archaeological State Park."[278]

---

[276] http://en.wikipedia.org/wiki/S-L-M, retrieved on 14.02.2012.

[277] http://en.wikipedia.org/wiki/Islamorada,_Florida, which was retrieved on 14.02.2012.

[278] http://en.wikipedia.org/wiki/Tallahassee,_Florida, retrieved 14.02.2012.

## 31. Jordan Hill, and Tallulah, Louisiana

For Jordan, see number 2.

"Tallulah got its name in an unusual way. When the railroad was expanding in the area, a widow who owned a large plantation became friendly with the contractor and persuaded him to change the route of the railroad to run through her plantation. After the railroad was built, she had nothing else to do with him. Feeling rejected, he named the water stop for an old girlfriend named Tallulah, instead of the plantation owner." Tallulah is a Gaelic name meaning *abundance, lady,* or *princess.*[279]

## 32. Liberia (Historical), Connecticut

Liberia means the *country of the free.* It was colonized by emancipated slaves from America. Its word root is Latin *libertas,* from the Indo-European word root *leudh*[-2], meaning *to mount up, to grow,* which emerged in Latin as *liber.* The exact semantic transition and development is obscure. The fact is that it has no Arabic-Islamic origin.[280]

## 33. Madrid, Nebraska

Legend has it that Ocno Bianor, the son of King Tyrrhenius of Tuscany and Mantua, founded *Metragirta* or *Mantua Carpetana.* Another legend says that the original name of the city was *Ursaria,* which means *the land of*

---

[279] http://en.wikipedia.org/wiki/Tallulah,_Louisiana, retrieved 14.02.2012.

[280] http://www.sacklunch.net/placenames/L/Liberia.html; and the internet link http://en.wikipedia.org/wiki/Liberia, retrieved on 14.02.2012.

*bears* in Latin. There were a large number of bears that inhabited the nearby forests. The bear and the strawberry tree (*madroño* in Spanish) have been the emblem of the city since the Middle Ages.

"The most ancient recorded name of the city Magerit (for *Materit* or *Mageterit?*) comes from the name of a fortress built on the Manzanares River in the 9th century AD, and means *place of abundant water*. If the form is correct, it could be a Celtic place-name from *ritu- ford* (Old Welsh *rit*, Welsh *rhyd*, Old Breton *rit*, Old Northern French *roy*) and a first element that is not clearly identified, yet perhaps *mageto*, a derivation of *magos, field place* (Old Irish *mag, field*, Breton *ma, place*), or *matu*, meaning *bear*, which could explain the Latin translation *Ursalia*. Nevertheless, it is now commonly believed that the origin of the current name of the city comes from the 2nd century BC.

The Roman Empire established a settlement on the banks of the Manzanares River. The name of this first village was *Matrice*, a reference to the river that crossed through the settlement."[281] The second century is more than eight hundred years before the existence of Mohammed. Places named Madrid, regardless of where they are located, have an Ibero-Celtic origin and no other foundation. Madrid (Magerit) has no Arabic-Islamic origin and certainly it does not have any Arabic-Islamic meaning.

---

[281] http://en.wikipedia.org/wiki/Madrid, retrieved on 14.02.2012.

## 34. Mahomet, Illinois[282]

Mahomet has nothing to do with the Arabic-Islam name Mohammed. "The post office there was named by someone in the Post Office Department at Washington, D. C, without so far as we have ever been able to learn, consulting anyone here. The old Masonic Lodge records say: 'The name Mahomet was selected because the Masonic lodge in Middletown was known as Mahomet Lodge, U. D. Records show that the dispensation was granted January 23, 1856, by W. B. Herrick, then Grand Master of Illinois, to open a lodge of Masons at Middletown, Champaign County, Illinois, to be known as Mahomet Lodge, U. D. When the Indiana, Bloomington, and Western Railway (later called in jest the "I Better Walk Railroad") was built, T. M. Brown who was a member of the first Board of Directors, used his influence to have the station named Mahomet after the post office instead of Middletown. He afterwards laid out the Town of Mahomet between the old depot and the old town, and later the name of the township was changed to that of Mahomet. His reasons for desiring the change were that it was a short name, easily spelled and written and not common (there is no other river, mountain, lake or town in the world by the name of Mahomet), and it was a nuisance to have two different names for the town and post office.

The old Champaign County History states 'The name was changed from Middletown to Mahomet in 1871. Then next

---

[282]   http://zionsake.tripod.com/MuD-No_prophecies.html#D   and   the following  links:  http://en.wikipedia.org/wiki/Maili,_Hawaii,  retrieved  on 14.02.2012.

year, 1872, Mahomet became an incorporated village."[283] (See Number 34.)

Mahomet is a corruption of Mohammed, which is originally *machmad* in Hebrew. Thus Mohammed is not Arabic-Islamic in its origin. The Hebrew word *machmad* means *desirable thing*, but not desirable person. The name Mahomet and thus Mohammed come from the triconsonantal root of Ḥ-M-D. In Phonecian Ḥ-M-D in the verb form means *to love*, in the noun form *with strong desire, with strong covetousness*. In the Bible, *Song of Solomon* 5:15-16, Ḥ-M-D means *altogether lovely, desirable*. Ḥ-M-D is Semitic-Canaanite from the Phoenicians ca. 1550-300 BC. It was used to describe events and things, sometimes people. The original meaning changed when it was transferred into Arabic, where it came to mean *to give thanks to* and *to give praise*. In Arabic it can mean *one worthy of praise*. Perhaps Mohammed received this meaning of his name from Allah-Hubal. Specifically speaking, Ḥ-M-D does not relate in any way to Mohammed. It is not Arabic-Islamic in origin.[284]

## 35. Mahomet, Texas

See number 34.

---

[283] Purnell, Isabelle S. *History of Mahomet: Mahomet Methodist Church Centennial*, Mahomet Methodist Church, 1955, p. 36.

[284] http://en.wikipedia.org/wiki/Muhammad_%28name%29, retrieved on 18.02.2012.
http://www.youtube.com/watch?feature=player_embedded&v=n2uwtk6Isxk#!, retrieved on 18.02.2012.

## 36. Mecca (Historical), Tallulah Falls, and Zaidee, Georgia; Aliamanu, and Maili Hawaii

Mecca Historical, Georgia is a grove of cedar trees with no Arabic-Islamic roots! *Georgia Place-Names* does not list it. The terminology may mean a place that is a mecca for certain people. In this sense *mecca* means *any place visited by many people* for some reason. See number 37.

For Tallulah, see number 30.

Zaidee is a variant of Sarah and means *princess*. In the Old Testament Sarah is the wife of the patriarch Abraham. (Genesis 20:12). [285]

Aliamanu is a volcanic crater in Hawaii. It could be a variant of Ahuimanu, the name of a village in Hawaii. In Hawaiian it means *cluster of birds*.[286]

Mailu is a Hawaiian word meaning *pebbly*.[287] There is no Arabic-Islamic origin of these places.

## 37. Mecca, Indiana[288]

"The name Mecca was originally attributed to the city in Saudi Arabia that is a center to the Moslem faith.

---

[285] http://www.quickbabynames.com/meaning-of-Zaidee.html, retrieved on 14.02.2012.

[286] http://en.wikipedia.org/wiki/Salt_Lake,_Hawaii and the internet link http://en.wikipedia.org/wiki/Ahuimanu,_Hawaii, retrieved on 14.02.2012.

[287]http://www.citytowninfo.com/places/hawaii/maili; http://en.wikipedia.org /wiki/Maili,_Hawaii, which were retrieved on 14.02.2012.

[288] http://www.coveredbridges.com/index.php/poi_detail?poiID=46 was retrieved on 24.02.2012.

There are two stories about how <u>Mecca</u>, Indiana got its name. The first story is that an immigration of Syrian Moslems led to a settlement among the white sands and clay banks of the Big Raccoon River. The settlement became known as Little Arabia or Arabia. The Arabian Church and the Arabian Cemetery were located on top of the hill, south of the Philips Covered Bridge, also known as the Arabian Covered Bridge.

In a second story, *Arabians* was a name for second class citizens thought of as scoundrels and cattle thieves. In either case, the Arabians made trips to the larger town with a mill and stores that became known as pilgrimages. The name came from the expression, "There goes another caravan of Arabs on their way to Mecca!" Mecca comes from the ancient Arabic word *Bakkah* meaning *narrow* to describe the geological land formation where the city is located. In the Southern Arabian language the B and M were/are interchangeable. The term Mecca is of Arabic origin, but the meaning is not that of *Makkat al-Mukarramah*, pronounced *makka lmukarrama* or *makkat almukarrama*, which means *Mecca the Honored*, but is also loosely translated as *The Holy City of Mecca*. By at least the 4<sup>th</sup> century AD there were large numbers of pilgrims coming to Mecca to perform a ritual act of walking seven times (a)round a small square building known as the Kaaba (*Ka'ba*, Arabic for *cube*). They were performing a ritual to their moon-gods. The building was full of idols, which are the objects of worship. The Kaaba also includes a black stone, possibly in origin a meteorite, which the believers regard as a sacred present from the moon-god, also known as Hubal or Allah, or Allah-Hubal.[289] Since the pilgrimages were taking place more than two centuries before the birth of Mohammed, the word, although of Arabic origin, has no true Islamic root.

The strictly correct spelling is Mekkah, which in Arabic means *the honored*. It is the birthplace of Mohammed and the place where Mohammed dictated the Koran after claiming that Allah had sent an angel to him with the message. (The angel was Gabriel, perhaps because this was the only angel of which Mohammed knew.) Mekkah is the first of the holy cities in Saudi Arabia. "The Yemeni tribe of Khuzaa'h built the city of Mecca in the 4th century A.D. Yemeni pagan religious worship has left its fingerprints all over the temple in Mekkah thus showing that Abraham and Ishmael could not have built it."[290] Therefore, Mecca is of pagan Yemeni origin and has no Arabic-Islamic roots.


38. Medina Junction, Mecan, Wisconsin

For Medina see number 1.

Mecan may derive from *Mikana*, the Ojibwa word for *trail*.[291] It has no Arabic-Islamic roots.

---

[289] http://www.historyworld.net/wrldhis/PlainTextHistories.asp?historyid=aa51#ixzz1nPFl79eB, retrieved on 14.02.2012. Glassé, Cyril and Smith, Huston, *The New Encyclopedia of Islam*, pp. 302-304.

[290] http://religionresearchinstitute.org/mecca/construction.htm, retrieved on 18.02.2012.

[291] http://www.wiroots.org/wimarquette/marqplaces2c.html, retrieved on 25.02.2012. The author thanks Ms. Jean Bucknum for this link.

## 39. Medina, New York

For Medina, see number 1.


## 40. Medina, Ohio

For Medina, see number 1.


## 41. Medina, Texas

For Medina, see number 1.


## 42. Medulla, and Sallee Heights, Florida

Medulla. In *An Historical Gazetteer of Imperial Polk County* which is the county in which Medulla, Florida is situated, the entry for Medulla, Florida reads: "(the) (n)ame in Latin means *the prime of quintessence of anything.* ... Once applied to a large expanse S(outh) of Lakeland including the highlands, now generally thought of as a community between Pipkin and Shepherd Roads W(est) of Florida Ave." "(There is) a clipping of an article in *The Ledger* (Lakeland, FL) indicating the postmaster at Spring Hill changed the name to Medulla in 1881 after discovery of a large phosphate deposit. At the time, according to the article, phosphate was associated with bones (although phosphate in the Bone Valley area of Florida is primarily from guano). From the *Gazetteer*, Spring Hill was the area from Lake Hollingsworth south and west about six miles. First settlers were P. R. McCrary, wife, and six children about 1877. A store opened in 1878. The 1882 McNally map only shows Bartow and Spring Hill as the only towns, besides the towns that sprung up around area forts (Ft. Meade, Ft. Lonesome, Ft. Arbuckle, etc.). Aside from the above entry, the noun *medulla* also *means the marrow or pith."* The Latin word is *medulla,* most likely from *\*merulla,* influenced by *media,* meaning *middle (of the bone).* Its Indo-European word root is **smer-**[3], meaning *grease, fat.* "The name Medulla was first used when Lewis M. Ballard opened a post office there on January 14, 1881. Ballard moved his post office elsewhere in 1883, but a post office was subsequently re-established at Medulla on July 14, 1893. Two early phosphate companies had their plants and villages located south of Medulla. Nearest was the Standard Phosphate Company located at what would later be named Tancrede. This company was acquired by a French company, the Société Anonyme des Phosphates de Floride. In November 1913, it was acquired by another French company, the Société Franco-Americaine des Phosphates de Medulla. In February 1920, it was then acquired by the Southern Phosphate Corporation. South of Tancrede was the location of the Medulla Phosphate Company, established by C. G. Memminger in September 1907. The location of the plant and village was named Christina, after his only child. The mines were primarily located east of the plant, in the area now known as Christina. This company was acquired by the Phosphate Mining Company in January 1910."[292] Therefore, Medulla is not of Arabic-Islamic origin.

---

[292] The author thanks Mr. Varrick Nunez, Reference Supervisor, Lakeland Public Library, Lakeland, Florida for the email information concerning Medulla, Florida and Ms. Debbie Hamilton for providing the link http://www.flickr.com/photos/mikewoodfin/4607874292/in/photostream/.

<u>Sallee</u> is a variant spelling of Sarah, which is Hebrew for *princess*.[293] Sallee has no Arabic-Islamic origin.

### 43. <u>Mingo, Ollie, Palestine Historical, Sabula, Salem, Tama, Makee, and Malak, Iowa</u>

<u>Mingo</u> is named after the historic Iroquoian Mingo people.[294] There is no Arabic-Islamic root.

<u>Ollie</u> Around 1840, Ollie was called Fairview. A railroad depot there in 1881 was named to "honor Ollie Fye, the daughter of Margaret and William Fye, landowners in the area. Ollie was incorporated on March 1, 1892."[295] There is no Arabic-Islamic connection.

<u>Palestine</u> Historical, See number 18.

<u>Sabula</u> is named after the Latin word for sand, *Sabulum*, because there is a lot of sand in the area.[296] See number 11.

For <u>Salem</u>, see number 20.

---

[293] http://www.thinkbabynames.com/meaning/0/Sallee was retrieved on 14.02.2012.

[294] http://en.wikipedia.org/wiki/Mingo,_Iowa, retrieved on 14.02.2012.

[295] Savage, Tom; Horton, Loren N. *Dictionary of Iowa Place-Names*, University of Iowa Press: Iowa City: 2007, p. 170 and Dilts, Howard E. *From Ackley to Zwingle: The Origins of Iowa Place Names*, Iowa State University Press: Ames, Iowa: 1993, p. 144. The author thanks Ms. Janalyn Moss, University Librarian, University of Iowa, for the information.

[296] http://www.islandcityharbor.com/History/index.htm, retrieved on 14.02.2012.

Tama comes from Taimah, the chief of the 19th century Meskwaki Indians.[297] Makee "... is of Indian origin says Fulton in his *Red Men of Iowa*; while other authorities claim that it took its name from Allen Makee, a famous Indian trader and trapper who established a trading post within its limits at an early day."[298] It has no Arabic-Islamic root.

There is no Malak, Iowa. There is a Malaka Township, Iowa. The name has nothing to do with an Arabic-Islamic root. It appears that there is an intentional dropping off of the a-ending in order that the word becomes Malak, which in Arabic means *angel*.[299] However, even this word is not Arabic. The root is Hebrew *mlk* yielding *malak*, meaning *king*.[300]


## 44. Morocco, Indiana

Morocco comes from *Marruecos*, which is the Spanish pronunciation of the city of *Marrakesh* (more precisely

---

[297] http://en.wikipedia.org/wiki/Tama,_Iowa, retrieved on 14.02.2012.

[298] http://www.past2present.org/own/counties/Allamakee.htm, retrieved on 14.02.2012.

[299] http://www.thinkbabynames.com/meaning/1/Malak was retrieved on 17.02.2012. The author thanks email information from Shelley Arri for relative information concerning Malaka township.

[300] Seuren, Pieter A. M. *Western Linguistics, an historical introduction*, Blackwell, Oxford: 1998, p. 246. The author thanks Ms. Janalyn L. Moss, University Librarian, University of Iowa, for information that there is no locality named Malak, Iowa.

*Murakush*). Etymologists state that it is most likely derived from two Berber words *amur, (ta)murt* meaning *land or sanctuary*, and *akuc (akush)*, meaning *God*. Thus, *mur akush* means *land of God* or *sanctuary of God*.[301] It does not mean land of Allah or sanctuary of Allah. Morocco in medieval Latin is Morroch, which comes from the Berber language. As such, it has no Arabic-Islamic origin.

### 45. Toledo, Ohio

"The inhabitants of this ... settlement chose the name Toledo, ... but the reason for this choice is buried in a welter of legends. One recounts that Washington Irving, who was traveling in Spain at the time, suggested the name to his brother, a local resident; this explanation ignores the fact that Irving returned to the United States in 1832. Others award the honor to Two Stickney, son of the mayor, who quaintly numbered his sons and named his daughters after States. The most popular version attributes the naming to Willard J. Daniels, a merchant, who reportedly suggested Toledo because it 'is easy to pronounce, is pleasant in sound, and there is no other city of that name on the American continent.'"[302] See number 15.

### 46. Yarrowsburg, Maryland

See number 3.

---

[301]   http://en.wikipedia.org/wiki/List_of_country-name_etymologies   was retrieved on 14.02.2012.

[302] http://en.wikipedia.org/wiki/Toledo,_Ohio, retrieved on 14.02.2012.

There were attempts in the 1996 and thereafter to claim the One Thousand Year Anniversary of the Muslim (Islam) Discovery of America, a most-quoted call made by Dr. Youssef A. Mroueh. Dr. Mroueh is a radiation physicist, specializing in radiation control, industrial radiology, and ultrasonic waves. Dr. Mroueh was a member of the Preparatory Committee for International Festivals to celebrate the millennium of the Muslims' arrival to the Americas (996-1996). He wrote the article *Precolumbian Muslims in America* to celebrate this cause. Without valid documentation, Dr. Mroueh stated that there are numerous pieces of evidence that the Arab Muslims were the true discoverers of the New World and "the Ocean of Darkness and Fog." He lists places in America that have their origin in Arabic. He states "There are 565 names of places (villages, towns, cities, mountains, lakes, rivers,.. etc.) in (the) U.S.A. (484) and Canada (81) which derived from Islamic and Arabic roots. These places were originally named by the natives in pre-columbian periods. Some of these names carried holy meanings … ."[303] Dr. Mroueh does not offer any documentation in support of his claims. In addition to the above nomenclatures, Dr. Mroueh asserts the following localities have Arabic-Islamic word roots:

- Hazen, (North Dakota). Hazen is a variant of the English name Hayes, which means *hedged area*.[304] It has no Arab-Islam roots.

---

[303] Dr. Mroueh's article is at http://sunnah.org/history/precolmb.htm, notes 185 and 207.

[304] http://www.thinkbabynames.com/meaning/1/Hayes, retrieved on 18.02.2012.

- Mona, Jordan Village, Utah has nothing to do with Arabic-Islam. "Mona is on US-91 eight miles north of Nephi. The community was settled in 1852 with an early name of Clover Creek for the luxurious patches of wild clover growing in the area. The name was changed to Willow Creek, then Starr for an early settler. There is disagreement as to the origin of the name Mona, an Indian word meaning *beautiful* and a contraction of the Italian word *madonna*. The name has a comical meaning. It means *Manx, by the Mountains* whereby the word 'Manx' refers to the people from the Isle of Mann. Dr. Matthew McCune, a former surgeon in the British Army, is reported to be the one who suggested Mona, because it was the name of his former home on the Isle of Mann."[305]

Jordan Village has nothing to do with Arabic or Islam As noted above in Number 2, Jordan derives from the Hebrew and the Canaanite root for *descend* (*into the Dead Sea.*)

- Arva, (Ontario). Although the name Arva is used by Muslims and they misappropriate it by claiming that it is Arabic, anyone who knows Latin realizes that the name Arva has nothing to do with Arabic Islam. Arva is Latin and means *fertile, arable land.*

Based on the exposé of the true roots of the above historical, geographical and linguistic place names and those that Dr. Mroueh cited as reasons to call for a millennium celebration of the arrival of Muslims in America, we can conclude that the

---

[305] http://www.onlineutah.com/monahistory.shtml, retrieved on 17.02.2012.

whole listing was nothing more than the Muslim exercise of taqiyya, There was and there is no reason for an international call to celebrate any Muslim arrival in the Americas five centuries before Columbus, unless the goal is to rewrite history and to delude people into believing that the founded cities and places in America owe their existence to Muslims, Mohammed's dogma of world domination, and Islam. The fact that Dr. Mroueh issued such a call "to all Muslim nations and communities around the world" and the fact that he has been exposed as a liar means that there is absolutely no reason to believe in and call for an understanding of the Muslim communities and their false claims. The age-old adage surely applies: Show me a liar and I will show you a hypocrite.

## The Rationale Behind the Non-Violent Cultural Jihad and the Geographical Taqiyya

The reason that Islamic internet sites conduct such creeping, slimy Islamic claims is because they are intent on convincing unknowledgeable persons that wherever a Muslim set his foot, that land belongs to Islam. It does not matter when this happened.

There are three fundamental suras in the Koran that state the unequalled omnipotence of Islam over all other religions. It is thus accepted fact that Mohammed did realize that there would be other cultural groupings outside of his limited, knowable, physical, geographic location. To reiterate from Chapter Two, the pertinent verses are:

215

<u>Sura 9:33</u> *He it is Who hath sent His messenger with the guidance and the Religion of Truth, that He may cause it to prevail over all religion, however much the idolaters may be averse.*

<u>Sura 48:28</u> *He it is Who hath sent His messenger with the guidance and the religion of truth, that He may cause it to prevail over all religion. And Allah suffices as a Witness.*

<u>Sura 61:9</u> *He has sent His messenger with the guidance and the true religion, and will make it dominate all religions, in spite of the idol worshipers.*

Islamic scholars believe that these three suras are the prophecies that unflinchingly prove that Islam will become the only world power. According to Islam, the repetition underscores their truth. These suras have been used to spread Islamic violence repeatedly. The suras have also been used to lay claims to land that Islam never knew existed. As such, the Islamic logic of expansion is that whenever and wherever a Muslim appears in a foreign land, regardless of the historical age, it is only logical according to the Koran that that land must become Islamic, otherwise Allah would never have made it possible for that Muslim discoverer or explorer to be physically present in said new country. This viewpoint is so encompassing that it is retroactive to include all places where a Muslim was before there was Islam, for Islam maintains that only Islam is the complete and valid religion. Therefore, it encompasses all time and all places. With this Islamic logic as the raison d'être of historical discovery, scientific exploration, and land claiming, it is only obvious that all geographical landmasses of the world will eventually become dominated by Islam because Allah and Mohammed will it.

The rational for al-taqiyya, intentional lying and deception, is found in the following suras:

<u>Sura 16:106:</u> States the principle that there are circumstances that can "compel" a Muslim to tell a lie.

<u>Sura 3:28:</u> This sura tells Muslims that they can deceive with friendship – they are not to take those outside the faith as friends, unless it is to "guard themselves."

<u>Sura 9:3:</u> "... *Allah and His Messenger are free from liability to the idolaters... .*" The dissolution of oaths with the pagans who remained at Mecca following its capture. They did nothing wrong, but were evicted anyway.

<u>Sura 2:225:</u> "*Allah will not call you to account for thoughtlessness in your oaths, but for the intention in your hearts.*"

<u>Sura 66:2:</u> "*Allah has already ordained for you, (O men), the dissolution of your oath.*"

<u>Sura 3:54:</u> "*And they (the disbelievers) schemed, and Allah schemed (against them): and Allah is the best of schemers.*" The Arabic word used here for scheme (or plot) is *makara*, which literally means *deceit*. If Allah is deceitful toward unbelievers, then there is little basis for denying that Muslims are allowed to do the same.

217

<u>Sura 8:30:</u> "*And when those who disbelieved devised plans against you that they might confine you or slay you or drive you away; and they devised plans and Allah too had arranged a plan; and Allah is the best of planners.*"

<u>Sura 10:21:</u> "*And when We make people taste of mercy after an affliction touches them, they devise plans against Our communication. Say: Allah is quicker to plan; surely Our messengers write down what you plan.*"

The last two suras placed together are justification for lying and deceiving without quoting the previous suras. Taken collectively, all of the quoted suras are interpreted to mean that there are circumstances when a Muslim may be *compelled* to deceive others for a greater purpose as a servant of Allah-Hubal, Mohammed, and Islam.

You can trust a Muslim to be a Muslim. That is as far as trust vis à vis Muslims and Islam can go. Muslims will lie as much as necessary to gain domination and maintain that domination over the subdued!

# CHAPTER EIGHT

## Islamization and Jihad Continue in the Twenty-First Century

### The First Decade

Throughout the 1980s and 1990s, the Muslim community in America grew rapidly. The Islamization of America has continued. There are now many Muslims and Islamic ideologues who hold office as community council members, state legislative representatives, mayors of large cities, judges, teachers, doctors, and lawyers. Muslims are present in almost every profession. There are even pedophile Muslims, Muslim prostitutes, and Muslim sex traffickers in the United States.[306] Evidently, Muslims will do anything and everything for Allah-Hubal and Mohammed!

Historically, Muslim Americans have supported the Republican Party. The Muslim support for the Republicans may be due to the fact that the Republican Party was always the leader in American politics for the equality of races and

---

[306] Mattu, Ayesha and Nura, Maznovi. *Love InshAllah: The Secret Love Lives of American Muslim Women*, Soft Skull Press, Berkeley, California: 2012.
Consult also the site http://www.youtube.com/watch?v=FMh3IYfuwf4; http://atlasshrugs2000.typepad.com/atlas_shrugs/2012/02/muslim-gang-sex-trafficking-trial-in-tennessee-unusual-in-scope-30-on-trial.html, which were retrieved on 23.03.2012.

minorities. Nearly 80% of Muslims supported George W. Bush over Democratic candidate Al Gore in the 2000 presidential election. Muslim support declined sharply within four years. In 2004, half of the Muslim support went to the Democratic Party candidate John Kerry. In 2008, Barack Hussein Obama, one of their own, received 67% to 90% of the Muslim vote depending on the region.[307] While making their voices known through the vote, Muslims are continually active in public and surreptitious undertakings to change the United States of America from a democratic republic to an Islamic country in which sharia law is to replace the *Constitution for the United States of America.*

### Selected Incidences

Every day in every week in every month in every year there are innumerable undertakings that attempt to chip away at American tradition and culture. The following incidences of the Islamization of America and jihad against America are a random selection. Of course, it is not difficult to find such happenings. They occur almost daily. The news items below are presented in summary paragraphs with the sources footnoted. The only criteria were the surety that there were tie-ins to Islam and actions by jihadists and those sympathizing with the goal of Islam: the final domination of the world. The author has chosen to comment on the incidences of jihad and creeping Islamization.

---

[307]     http://www.reuters.com/article/2008/11/06/us-usa-election-muslims-idUSTRE4A57ZC20081106, retrieved on 18.03.2012.

## 2000

October 12. *Attack on the USS Cole.*

An American war ship, the USS Cole, was docked in the Arab port of Aden, Yemen for refuelling. A small boat craft came alongside the ship. It exploded and killed 17 United States Navy sailors and injured 39.

COMMENT: Attacking a United States war ship is an act of war. Yemen did not undertake any action against the Islamic terrorists, even though the governmental authorities at Aden knew that the harbor master of the port of Aden was Osama Bin Laden's brother-in-law. Of course, one cannot say that he was an accomplice. On the other hand, it is hard to believe that the small boat was able to come so near without some quasi-official support.

## 2001

September 11. *The World Trade Center, the Pentagon, a field in Pennsylvania.*

The next sequential Muslim terrorist acts of war were the attacks on the World Trade Center and the Pentagon. A total of 266 people lost their lives in the four planes involved, 2,602 people were killed on the ground, 343 fire fighters lost their lives, 184 people at the Pentagon were killed and 40 airplane passengers died on the crash of flight 93 near Shanksville, Pennsylvania, when the plane's passengers thwarted the terrorist attempt to fly the plane into the White House (or the US Capitol) and blow it up. There were almost 5,000 injured. Seven buildings in New York City collapsed, 23 were damaged and there was damage to four subway stations. On the same day, an Islamic terrorist attack on the embassy in Paris was foiled.

COMMENT: The Muslim terrorists planned their attack from secure positions as so-called student and foreign workers in Germany. Already in the latter part of the 1990s, their religious mentors and leaders from the Taliban regime in Afghanistan were cordially received in Germany and officially recognized as emissaries from a foreign country throughout the previous years by the leftist members of the German Green Party. (*Bündnis 90 – Die Grünen*) The Green Party functionaries, among them the later German Foreign Minister Joseph Fischer and the Green Party functionaries, Andrea Fischer and Petra Roth, had accepted the Taliban leaders' false diplomatic credentials thus disregarding the fact that the German Ministry of Foreign Affairs (*Auswärtiges Amt*) repeatedly stated that the Taliban leaders in Germany were not recognized members of a foreign government. The German Green Party even went so far as to insist that these Taliban leaders from Afghanistan possessed diplomatic immunity and were on a friendly religious visit to the Federal Republic of Germany. The German Green Party even helped these Taliban personages to collect money in mosques in Germany for *welfare* use in Afghanistan. This is to say that the righteous, peace-loving Green Party was an accomplice in collecting money for the religious charities of the moon-god-adoring Taliban who only pray the whole day and worship Allah-Hubal. In television and newspaper interviews this freedom-loving German political party – *Die Grünen* – hosted the Taliban religious leaders saying, *Wir sind liberal gegenüber religiöse und freiheitliebende Menschen die nichts anderes haben wollen als Frieden und die Freiheit Gott anzubeten.* (We are liberal to all religious and freedom-loving people who want nothing more than peace and the freedom to worship God.)[308]

As of this writing, there have been over 18,628 deadly Islamic terrorist attacks worldwide since 9/11.[309] There have been at least 45 attempts of Muslim terrorists to attack targets in the United States of America since 9/11.[310] Not even regarding such actions as terror, but rather as man-caused disasters, Barack Hussein Obama has caved in to Islamic supremacists and their apologists.

Barack Hussein Obama most recently ordered that the FBI investigate its counterterrorism training and purge "hundreds of bureau documents of instructional material about Muslims, some of which characterized them as prone to violence or terrorism. The bureau disclosed initial findings from its months-long review during a meeting at FBI

---

[308] The presentation in the above paragraph is based on the author's notes of the connection between the German Green Party and the Taliban representatives, but he neglected to note the documentation, believing that such facts of history would not be scrubbed from books or the internet. A search of periodicals and internet sites leads the author to the conclusion that reports of any relationship between the German Green Party and the Taliban in the1990s have been scrubbed. The reader is assured that the above presentation represents the actual relationship at the time.

[309] http://www.thereligionofpeace.com/, retrieved on 23.03.2012. There is a chronology of terrorist attacks and operations against the United States of America beginning in the year 1865 at http://www.sage-ereference.com/view/terrorism/pdfs/Reading_d10.pdf, which was retrieved on 23.03.2012.

[310] http://global-security-news.com/2011/09/16/40-terror-plots-foiled-since-911-combating-complacency-in-the-long-war-on-terror/ was retrieved on 23.03.2012.

headquarters on Wednesday with several Arab and Muslim advocacy groups, attended by Director Robert Mueller. So far, the inquiry has uncovered and purged over 700 pages of documentation from approximately 300 presentations given to agents since 9/11 – some of which were similar to briefings published by Danger Room last year describing 'mainstream' Muslims as 'violent.' And more disclosures may be forthcoming, as the FBI continues its inquiry and responds to Freedom of Information Act requests for the documents themselves."[311] This action is nothing more than Barack Hussein Obama kowtowing to the demands of Islamic organizations in the United States of America, particularly the Council on American Islamic Relations (CAIR).

## 2002

January 5. *Charles J. Bishop Bishra, mujahidin, crashes airplane into building, in Florida.*

"The suicide note found in Charles' pocket said: 'I have prepared this statement in regards to the acts I am about to commit. First of all, Osama bin Laden is absolutely justified in the terror he has caused on 9-11. He has brought a mighty nation to its knees! God blesses him and the others who helped make September 11th happen. The US will have to face the consequences for its horrific actions against the Palestinian people and Iraqis by its allegiance with the monstrous Israelis-- who want nothing short of world domination! You will pay-- God help you--and I will make you pay! There will be more

---

[311]     http://m.wired.com/dangerroom/2012/02/hundreds-fbi-documents-muslims/, retrieved on 23.03.2012.

coming! Al Qaeda and other organizations have met with me several times to discuss the option of me joining. I didn't. This is an operation done by me only. I had no other help, although, I am acting on their behalf. Osama bin Laden is planning on blowing up the Super Bowl with an antiquated nuclear bomb left over from the 1967 Israeli-Syrian war.'"

COMMENT: If he was not an official Al-Qaeda member, he was an unofficial mujahidin. These are exactly the idiots Islam wants and needs. They are present in Islam and outside of Islam. Furthermore, Charles J. Bishop committed suicide for Islam. Was he emulating Mohammed? There is documented evidence that Mohammed attempted suicide more than once in his life.[312]

May 22. *Patrick Gott, mujahidin, shoots at many, kills one in airport, New Orleans.*

"On May 22, 2002, Gott traveled to New Orleans with his mother and sister to put his niece, a recent high school graduate, on a plane to San Jose, Calif. As they dropped her off to catch her flight, Gott told the others he needed to use the restroom and went inside the airport building. With him he carried a copy of the Quran and a green duffel bag. Inside the bag was a 4-foot-long PVC tube wrapped in foam. In the tube was a 12-gauge shotgun, part of its barrel and stock sawed off. Gott propped the bag against a counter across from the Southwest Airlines ticket counter, removed the gun and fired, hitting Amy Michaelson, 45, a US Defense Department

---

[312] http://answering-islam.org/Silas/suicide.htm, retrieved on 10.04.2012.

employee. He tried to squeeze off a second blast but the gun jammed. As travelers ran for cover, Southwest employee Lenny Tully, aided by co-worker Ricardo Parris and customer Timothy Freeman, tackled Gott. Afterward, Gott, a heavy-set, 6-foot-1-inch man with long red hair, a beard and mustache, told investigators that he fired the gun because someone had made fun of his headdress earlier at a restaurant near the airport. His mother and sister, who had been there with him, remembered no such incident. Michaelson was shot in her chest and abdomen. She died four days later at Kenner Regional Medical Center."[313]

COMMENT: Jihadists are not interested in who kills Americans as long as they are killed.

July 4. *FBI: Gunman went to LA airport intending to kill.*

"LOS ANGELES — The heavily armed Egyptian immigrant who fatally shot two people at the ticket counter of Israel's national airline went to the Los Angeles airport to kill, the FBI said Friday. 'Why he did that is what we are still trying to determine,' FBI special agent Richard Garcia said. Hesham Mohamed Hadayet was the fourth person in line at the El Al counter when he opened fire, authorities said. He fired 10 or 11 bullets before he was fatally shot himself by an airline security guard, as hundreds of people dived for cover. Three other people were wounded, including a guard who was stabbed by Hadayet as he fought with the wounded gunman. A fourth bystander suffered heart trouble after the attack. In his pockets,

---

[313] http://www.freerepublic.com/focus/f-news/1440602/posts, retrieved on 23.03.2012.

authorities found an extra magazine for each gun, FBI spokesman Matt McLaughlin said. 'I think it's safe to say he planned to reload his guns and didn't get the chance to do it,' McLaughlin said. Hadayet was identified by tracing the weapons he used, a law enforcement source said, speaking on condition of anonymity. Hadayet had owned one of the guns 'for years' and purchased the other a couple of months ago, the source said. ... Israeli officials said they would consider the attack an act of terror unless it was proven otherwise. A source close to Israeli Foreign Minister Shimon Peres said Peres' granddaughter was in the terminal at the time of the attack. ... Abdul Zahav, a man who said he worked for Hadayet until he was fired two years ago, said Hadayet once told him he hated all Israelis. 'He kept all his anger inside him. So he can't hold it anymore, he can't hold it anymore,' Zahav said. ... Relatives said Hadayet was a Cairo-born accountant who ran a limousine company out of his Irvine apartment. Hassan Mostafa Mahfouz, who is married to Hadayet's aunt, said Hadayet had studied commerce at Ain Shams University in Cairo, and had worked as an accountant in a bank before he left for the United States in 1992. – Andrew Bridges."[314]

COMMENT: The mainstream media call such killings isolated incidents with no connection to jihad terror.[315] Hesham Mohamed Ali Hadayet targeted Jews at the Los Angeles Airport to conduct an act of terrorism against Israel. The US government claimed it was not an act of terror and that killing

---

[314] http://www.berkeleydailyplanet.com/issue/2002-07-06/full_text, which was retrieved on 23.03.2012.

[315] http://www.akdart.com/med14.html, retrieved on 23.03.2012.

Jews was not Hadayet's goal.[316] Imams praise such men of Allah and portray them as martyrs for Allah.

October 2 – 22. *John Mohammad, mujahidin, beltway sniper.*

A total of thirteen killings were committed by John Mohammed, born John Allen Williams. Another twelve killings have been attributed to him. He was a member of Louis Farrakhan's Nation of Islam for which he helped provide security for the *Million Man March* in 1995. Federal authorities said that "Muhammad admitted that he admired and modeled himself after Osama bin Laden and Al Qaeda, and approved of the September 11 attacks."[317]

COMMENT: There is an *Islam in America Timeline* from 1993 to 2012 at Atlas Shrugs.[318] There are many who are of the opinion that Muslims are insane for being Muslims.

## 2003

June 23. *Randall Ismail Royer is arrested as a terrorist.*

"Randall (Ismail) Royer, an American convert to Islam is indicted and arrested for his association with terrorism, specifically his having joined the Pakistani group *Lashkar-e-Taiba*, traveled to Pakistan, done propaganda work for it, and fired at Indian positions in Kashmir." The grand jury charges

---

[316] http://www.wnd.com/2002/07/14478/, retrieved on 23.03.2012.

[317] http://en.wikipedia.org/wiki/John_Allen_Muhammad was retrieved on 23.03.2012.

[318] http://atlasshrugs2000.typepad.com/atlas_shrugs/islam-in-america.html, retrieved on 23.03.2012.

that Royer "did unlawfully and knowingly begin, provide for, prepare a means for, and take part in a military expedition and enterprise to be carried on from the United States against the territory and dominion of India, a foreign state with whom the United States was at peace. ... Royer was working for the Council on American-Islamic Relations (CAIR), militant Islam's most aggressive political organization in North America, when he began training with *Lashkar-e-Taiba*. (He served there variously as a communications specialist and a civil rights coordinator ... .) CAIR now has a record of at least two former employees indicted and arrested in 2003 on terrorism charges; the other was Bassem Khafagi, CAIR's director of community relations before his arrest in January, 2012, as well a member of CAIR's advisory board, Siraj Wahhaj, was named as one of the 'unindicted persons who may be alleged as co-conspirator' in the attempt to blow up New York City monuments nearly a decade ago. So, CAIR not only apologizes for terrorism but is now implicitly accused of having more direct links to it."[319]

COMMENT: CAIR still has close connections to Washington, D. C. politicians. It constantly agitates for sharia law to supplant the *Constitution for the United States of America*.[320] That alone is reason enough for CAIR to be legally extinguished from the American public.

---

[319] http://www.danielpipes.org/blog/2003/06/cairs-legal-tribulations; June 23, 27, and May 2, 2010.http://www.danielpipes.org/blog/2003/06/cairs-legal-tribulations, retrieved on 24.03.2012.

[320] http://counterjihadreport.com/tag/islamist-lobbies/, retrieved on April 11, 2012.

## 2004

January 29. *Hezbollah is entering the United States through Mexico with the aid of Mexican officials.*

"Terence Jeffrey has been courageous and virtually alone in pointing out that Islamic radicals are entering the United States through Mexico. Now, he shows that a Hezbollah operative entered the country the same way. ... Politicians serious about preventing another Sept. 11 should listen to the leader of Hezbollah, and then read an indictment unsealed this month in Detroit. "Let the entire world hear me," said Sheik Hassan Nasrallah on Sept. 27, 2002. "Our hostility to the Great Satan is absolute." ... Now, turn to May 3, 2003. That's when FBI agents searched the Dearborn, Mich., residence of Mahmoud Kourani, a 32-year-old illegal alien from Lebanon. In a statement submitted last week in federal court, Assistant US Attorney Kenneth Chadwell revealed words the FBI found on audiotapes there: "You alone are the sun of my lands, Nasrallah! Nasrallah!/. . . your voice is nothing less than my jihad." "We offer to you Hezbollah, a pledge of loyalty," said a tape. " ... Rise for jihad! ... I offer you, Hezbollah, my blood in my hand." Kourani pleaded guilty to harboring an illegal alien. A judge sentenced him to six months. On Jan. 15, a second indictment was unsealed, charging Kourani with conspiracy to provide material support to Hezballah. "Kourani was a member, fighter, recruiter and fundraiser for Hezbollah," said the indictment. "Operating at first from Lebanon and later in the United States, Kourani was a dedicated member of Hezbollah who received specialized training in radical Shiite fundamentalism, weaponry, spy craft, and counterintelligence in Lebanon and Iran." "Kourani," Chadwell added in his statement, "is charged with conspiring with individuals at the highest levels of the terrorist organization, including one of his brothers who is the Hezbollah chief of military security for southern Lebanon." Kourani got to America, the prosecutors allege, with the help of a Mexican official. "On approximately Feb. 4, 2001, Kourani surreptitiously entered the United States by sneaking across the US/Mexico border in the trunk of a car," wrote Chadwell. "He reached Mexico by paying $3,000 used to bribe an official in the Mexican Consulate in Beirut, Lebanon, to give him a Mexican visa." ... In a sentencing memorandum in Kourani's alien-harboring case, Chadwell told the court Kourani's "offense of conviction was part of a continuing scheme to bring illegal aliens to the United States from Lebanon through Mexico. ..."[321]

COMMENT: If the United States of America cannot secure its borders against all aliens, poor, illegal, or whatever, how can the country be secure against Hezbollah. The United States cannot live in peace when its neighbors are part of the conspiracy against the United States. What is Hezbollah's battle cry? *Death to America.*

April 29. *CAIR has Terror Connections*

"The US Code Title 18, Part 1, Chapter 113B, Section 2339A says: "Whoever provides material support or resources or conceals or disguises the nature, location, source, or ownership of material support or resources, knowing or intending that they

---

[321]    http://www.jihadwatch.org/2004/01/hizballah-entering-us-through-mexico.html, retrieved on 24.03.2012.

are to be used in preparation for, or in carrying out [terrorist acts], or in preparation for, or in carrying out, the concealment or an escape from the commission of any such violation, or attempts or conspires to do such an act, shall be fined under this title, imprisoned not more than 15 years, or both, and, if the death of any person results, shall be imprisoned for any term of years or for life."

... In late 2001, CAIR appeared to be in violation of United States law, as in regards to the providing of material support to terrorists. In September of 2001, just following the worst terrorist attack ever suffered in modern history, CAIR placed on its website, under a picture of the World Trade Center in flames, a plea for donations. It read, "Donate to the NY/DC Emergency Relief Fund." Yet, when people clicked on the link, it did not take them to any NY/DC Emergency Relief Fund. No, it took them straight to the website of the Holy Land Foundation for Relief and Development, an Islamic 'charity' that was soon to be shut down by the United States for 'raising millions of dollars annually for HAMAS.' Later that month, on September 25, 2001, CAIR changed the link to explicitly ask persons to 'Donate through the Holy Land Foundation.' And in addition, CAIR added a new link to its site, soliciting persons to 'Donate through the Global Relief Foundation.' The Global Relief Foundation, like the Holy Land Foundation, was soon to be shut down by the US government on terrorism related charges. As stated by the Treasury Department, 'The Global Relief Foundation has connections to, has provided support for, and has provided assistance to Osama Bin Laden, the al-Qaeda Network, and other known terrorist groups." ... The question we now have to ask is, "Did CAIR know that these organizations existed as terrorist related entities, prior to CAIR removing the links?" Or, considering CAIR's connection to both offending organizations, the more appropriate question would be, "How did they not know?"

**"Mousa Abu Marzook - Grandfather of CAIR** The Holy Land Foundation for Relief and Development was founded by HAMAS leader Mousa Abu Marzook, a man who was deported by the United States to Jordan in 1997. Marzook, who may very well be, today, second in command of HAMAS, also founded, in 1981, CAIR's parent organization, the Islamic Association for Palestine. This is important, when considering the previous questions asked, but - - there is a much bigger connection to CAIR, with respect to the Holy Land Foundation."

**"Ghassan Elashi - CAIR Board Member** The Chairman of the Holy Land Foundation, before the group's closure, was Ghassan Elashi. Elashi, in December of 2002, was charged with 'selling computers and computer parts to Libya and Syria, both designated state sponsors of terrorism.'"

"Besides the Holy Land Foundation, Ghassan Elashi was also involved with CAIR. In fact, Elashi was one of the founding board members of CAIR's Texas chapter. What this means is that CAIR didn't just stick a link to the Holy Land Foundation on its website, but instead, CAIR was directly linked to the Holy Land Foundation itself!"

**"Rabih Haddad - CAIR Fundraiser** Rabih Haddad was a co-founder of the Global Relief Foundation. Before being deported by the United States to Lebanon in July of 2003, Haddad had held various positions with Global Relief, including that of

233

Executive Director and Public Relations Director. And like Ghassan Elashi, Haddad was also active in CAIR. According to the Quaker organization, the group that runs the large charitable foundation, the American Friends Service Committee, Haddad had served as a fundraiser for CAIR."

"Just as in the previous case, this shows that the Global Relief Foundation was not only a link on the CAIR website, but that CAIR was directly involved in the organization."

"Considering this evidence, it would be somewhat difficult for CAIR to deny any knowledge of the two pseudo-charities' nefarious involvements -- involvements that directly led to the murders of innocents abroad. This includes the December 2, 2001 suicide bombing of a bus in Haifa, Israel, murdering 15 and wounding 40 others... and the suicide bombing in an entertainment area in Jerusalem, which took the lives of 11 young people, just a day earlier. Both incidents occurred, while CAIR was soliciting funds for the terrorist charities on its site. If CAIR was indeed involved, under the Justice Department code stated earlier, it could result in life imprisonment for all implicated. But while it's hard for CAIR to run away from its connections to the Holy Land Foundation and the Global Relief Foundation, because of the connections, it's easy to understand why CAIR tried vigorously to defend and protect the groups."[322]

COMMENT: CAIR took the position that the shutting down of the Holy Land Relief Foundation was not only *unjust* but also *disturbing*. Unjust and disturbing to whom? To the Islamic jihad movement! Closing the Global Relief Foundation was

---

[322] http://archive.frontpagemag.com/readArticle.aspx?ARTID=13221 article by Joe Kaufman at FrontPage, retrieved on 24.03.2012.

racial profiling of a charitable organization. Racial profiling to whom? To the Islamic jihad movement. These basic standpoints on the part of CAIR indicate that CAIR was involved in the criminal conspiracy to raise funds for terrorist organizations that murder innocent non-believers is criminal. Yet CAIR was not indicted. It should have been and it should have been exterminated then and now!

September 29. *Legal suit brought against Boston on the mosque project.*

"A Roxbury resident filed suit yesterday against the city of Boston and a controversial new $22 million Islamic center in his neighborhood, arguing that Boston violated the separation of church and state when it cut a complex land deal with the center's developers. In a suit filed in Suffolk Superior Court, plaintiff James C. Policastro alleges two violations each of the state and federal constitutions: He claims the Boston Redevelopment Authority (BRA) accepted less than fair market value for the parcel of city land where the towering new mosque and community center are being built. The project is expected to yield the biggest Islamic institution in the Northeast. The BRA valued the parcel at $401,187.50. According to the suit, it took a cash payment of $175,000 from the center's developers, then made up the rest of the price tag by valuing at $272,663 a series of benefits the developers are granting Roxbury Community College. For example, the BRA assessed the value of a lecture series the Islamic Society of Boston plans to conduct at the college at $115,598. It assessed the value of an Islamic library of 5,000 volumes slated for the community college at $80,000. Policastro claims the valuations are 'substantially inflated,' and as a result the city is unconstitutionally subsidizing a religion - Islam."[323]

COMMENT: This article has all of the ingredients of creeping Islamization of America: claims of freedom of religion when Islam is not a religion, but a political dogma; using the government for illegal purposes; getting involved in the community by becoming a large donor to an educational institution; providing benefits for the community, which one day will be used to undermine the constitutional freedoms of the community; building the biggest Islamic institution in the Northeast as a symbol of supremacy over all that is America in the Northeast. The legal suit was dropped in 2007 and the Boston mosque officially opened on June 26, 2009, which proves that if evil creeps long enough it will achieve its goal. On June 13, the unfinished mosque in Roxbury flew the American flag upside down.[324] Islam is so tolerant!

## 2005

January 16. *Coptic Christians slain in Jersey City, New Jersey.*

Hossam Armanious, 47, his wife and two daughters were slain, stabbed, and mutilated to death. ... The police said that the motive was Islamic hate against (Coptic) Christians.[325]

---

[323] http://www.jihadwatch.org/2004/09/boston-suit-challenges-city-on-mosque-project.html, retrieved on 24.03.2012.

[324] http://www.moonbattery.com/archives/2007/06/boston-mosque-f.html, retrieved on 24.03.2012.

[325] http://www.jihadwatch.org/2005/01/new-jersey-an-islamic-murder-of-coptic-christians.html, retrieved on 24. 03.2012.

COMMENT: Islamists, particularly the Salafists, consider the Copts their enemies, named as such by Allah-Hubal, and Mohammed, with support from the Saudi Arabian King Abdullah and his Sunni Islam Wahhabites.

<u>January 18.</u> *Mob violence against speakers who denounce terrorism.*

"San Francisco, California police were braced for more violence Monday following yesterday's violent attack by Arabs and other anti-Zionists who charged into a crowd of 500 anti-terror protesters. Fists flew as the pro-Israel group gathered in Berkeley and heard speakers denounce terrorism. More than 200 anti-Israel demonstrators yelled taunts at the crowd until several of them tried to break up the anti-terror rally while waving Palestinian flags and covering their faces, posing as would-be Arab terrorists. *Two, four, six, eight, we are martyrs, we can't wait,* several of them chanted as they charged the crowd. Riot police separated the two sides after several fights broke out. One man was arrested for assault as 'emotions were high,' according to a police sergeant. Among the anti-Israeli crowd were many Arabs, including Cairo-born Essam Maghoub, who said, 'We are here to make sure these people are ashamed of themselves. [Israelis] stole our land, raped our women, destroyed our olive trees and destroyed our homes.' The rally featured the bombed-out bus number 19 that Arab suicide terrorists bombed in Jerusalem last year, killing 11 people and injuring 45. The same bus is to stand in San Francisco at a similar rally Monday afternoon, which is Martin Luther King Jr. holiday in the United States. 'They attempted to disrupt the rally through the same kinds of intimidation and indiscriminate violence that are the hallmarks of our 21st century scourge, global terrorism,' said David Meir-Levi who was the master-of-ceremonies at the Berkeley rally."[326]

COMMENT: The source of Israel stealing Arab land is Mohammed. Mohammed said to the Jews "The earth belongs to Allah and His apostle, and I want to expel you from this land (the Arabian Peninsula), so, if anyone owns property, he is permitted to sell it." (Hadith vol. 4:392) Of course, in the geographical concept of Muslims, the state of Israel belongs to the Arabian Peninsula.

April 14. *Former CAIR Member, Ghassan Elashi, along with two brothers, Bayan and Basman, are convicted in Dallas, Texas on 10 counts of terror charges, each count carrying a maximum of ten years imprisonment.*[327]

COMMENT: If one commits crimes for CAIR one goes to jail for CAIR, and for Allah-Hubal, and for Mohammed.

November 14. *Daniel Pipes writes an article about Muslim taxi drivers refusing to carry blind persons with guide dogs, as dogs are unclean for Muslims.*

COMMENT: The article has continuous updates to February 2, 2012.[328] Yet, Muslims engage in bestiality.[329]

---

[326] http://www.militantislammonitor.org/article/id/383 was retrieved on 23.03.2012.

[327] http://www.wnd.com/2005/04/29850/, retrieved on 23.03.2012.

[328] http://www.danielpipes.org/blog/2005/11/muslim-taxi-drivers-vs-seeing-eye-dogs, retrieved on 23.03.2012.

[329] http://wikiislam.net/wiki/Bestiality, retrieved on 03.03.2012.

<u>November 22.</u> *Houston, Texas-born Muslim Omar Abu Ali charged with plot to kill President Bush.*

There is a new generation of American homegrown radical Muslims. "A 23-year-old American born and educated Muslim Omar Abu Ali, was detained in Saudi Arabia for planning to kill President Bush. "The show of support which Ali received from Muslim organisations in America who protested his arrest as 'anti Muslim discrimination' and are campaigning for his release reveals the radical Islamist agenda of a fifth column of Muslim groups in America who are operating under the guise of civil rights organisations. Even more brazen is the fact that the head of the Muslim American Society, Mahdi Bray wrote a letter to President Bush demanding his would be assassin's release (and) that he 'return one of their native sons to the soil of the United States'".[330]

COMMENT: Planning the assassination of the President of the United States of America is not executing the plan. Therefore, Omar Abu Ali must be freed. The leftists also got into the propaganda for Omar Abu Ali.

## 2006

<u>March 14.</u> *KindHearts for Charitable Humanitarian Development*

"KindHearts for Charitable Humanitarian Development was incorporated as a 'Domestic/Non-Profit' in Toledo, Ohio, far from the city lights of GRF's Chicago surroundings. Hatem El-

---

[330] http://news.bbc.co.uk/2/hi/americas/4461642.stm was retrieved on 23.03.2012 and http://www.militantislammonitor.org/article/id/457 was retrieved on 23.03.2012.

Hady, a Toledo physician, became KindHearts' Chairman of the Board, and jihad Smaili, a Cleveland attorney (and Khaled's older brother), became KindHearts' legal counsel. jihad is also the Registered Agent for KindHearts U.S.A., which was incorporated in June of 2003. ... The focus of KindHearts was on assisting 'Palestinians,' both in Israel and in Lebanon. 'Orphan sponsorships, medical centers, housing projects, and other pleasant-sounding programs were advertised and showcased by the organization.'"[331]

COMMENT: KindHearts was a front organization to collect and launder money for the Hamas Terrorist Organization and the Islamic Resistance Organization. KindHearts, the Hamas charity with Al-Qaeda affiliations, is no longer operating, having been forbidden by the United States government under George W. Bush. All Islamic organizations of this type should be shut down permanently.

October 10. *No transportation of alcohol in taxis.*

The Minneapolis-St. Paul International Airport "has potentially major implications for the future of Islam in America. Starting about a decade ago, some Islamic taxi drivers serving the airport declared that they would not transport passengers visibly carrying alcohol — in transparent duty-free shopping bags, for example. This stance stemmed from their understanding of the Koran's ban on alcohol. A driver named Fuad Omar explained: 'This is our religion. We could be punished in the afterlife if we agree to [transport alcohol]. This is a Koran issue. This came from heaven.' ... Another driver,

---

[331] http://archive.frontpagemag.com/readArticle.aspx?ARTID=5236, which was retrieved on 31.03.2012.

Muhamed Mursal, echoed his words: 'It is forbidden in Islam to carry alcohol.' The issue emerged publicly in 2000. On one occasion, 16 drivers in a row refused a passenger with bottles of alcohol."[332]

COMMENT: Wine is praised in the Koran. (Sura 13:4). Wine is an aspect of heaven. (Sura 47:15). The Koran says that there is some goodness as well as some badness in intoxicants. (Sura: 2:219). Having found one of his followers Hamza in a state of drunkenness, Mohammed outlawed intoxicants in the Sahih Muslim, Book 023, Hadith 4962. After announcing the Sura 5:90, Muhammad ordered that anyone who violated his rules (not Allah-Hubal's rules) was to receive beatings. Alcohol is forbidden in Afghanistan, Bahrain, Bangladesh, Brunei, Iran, Kuwait, Libya, Malaysia, the Maldives, Morocco, Pakistan, Qatar, Saudi Arabia, Sudan, Tunisia, and the United Arab Emirates. Between 2005 and 2011 alcohol use increased by 25 percent in predominantly Muslim regions of the world, according to Euromonitor International.[333] Malaysia has a large Muslim majority. The World Health Organization ranks Malaysia tenth in world alcohol consumption.[334]

COMMENT: Perhaps a Muslim can bear the dogma only under the influence of alcohol.

---

[332] http://www.nysun.com/national/dont-bring-that-booze-into-my-taxi/41264/, retrieved on 31.03.2012.

[333] http://www.webcitation.org/query?url=http://www.ansamed.info/en/news/ME.XEF93985.html&date=2011-02-25, retrieved on 31.03.2012.

[334] http://www.medindia.net/news/Despite-Its-Muslim-Majority-WHO-Names-Malaysia-as-Worlds-10th-Largest-Alcohol-Consumer-85415-1.htm, retrieved on 31.03.2012.

<u>October 13</u>. *American citizens aid Hamas terror.*

"Ghassan Elashi, a founder of the Holy Land Foundation for Relief and Development and a member of the founding board of directors of the Texas branch of the Council on American-Islamic Relations, or CAIR, was sentenced to nearly seven years in prison for financial ties to a high-ranking terrorist and for making illegal computer exports to countries that back terrorism. … An Atlanta imam, Mohamed Shorbagi, pleaded guilty to providing material support to Hamas."[335]

COMMENT: Islam will use them for its evil purposes and then name them martyrs if they *die on duty* or they will become heroes of Allah-Hubal for their deeds.

<u>December 2</u>. *Muslims seek a prayer room at the Minneapolis-St. Paul International Airport.*

"Airport officials said Friday they will consider setting aside a private area for prayer and meditation at the request of imams concerned about the removal of six Muslim clerics from a US Airways flight last week. Steve Wareham, director of Minneapolis-St. Paul International Airport, said other airports have 'meditation rooms' used for prayers or by passengers who simply need quiet time. A group of Somali clerics met with airport officials Friday and said they would attract less attention if they had a private area for prayer. Devout Muslims pray five times daily, facing the holy city of Mecca. 'When we pray, we don't want a problem. We don't want what happened last week,' said Abdulrehman Hersi, an imam at Darul-Quba mosque in Minneapolis, referring to six clerics who were barred from a

---

[335] http://www.wnd.com/2006/10/38376/, retrieved on 31.03.2012.

242

US Airways flight in Minneapolis after drawing the concern of some passengers. Airports in Nashville, Tenn.; Columbus, Ohio; and Fort Lauderdale, Fla., all advertise meditation rooms. Fort Lauderdale's is billed as 'For travelers seeking a quiet time.' All note they are nonsectarian."[336]

COMMENT: It would be logical to have such *prayer rooms* monitored, considering the Islamic threat against the United States of America. Moreover, in Islamic countries having to pray at certain prayer times is not an obligation when people work, or are in situations that are inappropriate. If a Muslim is making an Eid prayer (the holiday that ends Ramadan), it is better that the prayer take place in an open area. Otherwise, the prayers can take place anywhere.[337]

## 2007

March 13. *Muslim workers at the department store chain Target refuse to handle pork.*

"'I showed up at the cash register with a frozen pepperoni pizza. She immediately called for help, and another employee rang up the pizza and placed it in the basket. I asked her if it was because she was Muslim, and she nodded her head." I can't even touch it,' she said."

COMMENT: No one is forcing the female Muslim to work as a cashier at Target. Furthermore, if she cannot touch pork, how do Muslims justify their concept of pork in their minds? If the

---

[336] See http://www.jihadwatch.org/2006/12/muslims-seek-prayer-room-at-airport.html, retrieved on 31.03.2012.

[337] http://www.islamhelpline.com/node/5780, retrieved on 31.03.2012.

concept is in their minds, it is in their physical body, even as a concept. Are Muslims, thus infested with the non-halal pork?[338]

March 17. *A Muslim immigrant rampages at Salt Lake City, Utah shopping mall, killing five Americans while shouting Allahu Akbar.*

COMMENT: The Salt Lake City Police denied that the murder was an act of jihad.[339]

March 21. *Muslims demand special prayer time.*

Fort Morgan, Colorado: The *Denver Post* argues that Muslims at the Cargill Meat Solutions plant are being discriminated against because they are denied prayer breaks.

COMMENT: Allowing such prayer time would cost the company greatly. It would mean shutting down the plant production line. Moreover, this author's personal experience in Islamic Turkey is that prayer times are not an obligation while people are at work, or are in situations that are inappropriate. Even in Islamic countries there are Muslims who do not strictly adhere to the sharia rules of behavior. At the same time, there are some who are so pious because they want to set a precedent for sharia law, particularly in non-Muslim countries.[340]

---

[338] http://www.jihadwatch.org/2007/03/minneapolis-some-muslim-workers-at-target-refuse-to-handle-pork.html, retrieved on 31.03.2012.

[339] See http://www.serbianna.com/news/2007/01377.shtml, retrieved on 31.03.2012.

[340] See http://marychristinalove.wordpress.com/muslims-in-the-workplace/, retrieved on 31.03.2012.

September 7. *Osama Bin Laden praises hijacker in a new video.*[341]

COMMENT: The video proves that Islam jihadists committed the 9/11 attacks. There was no George W. Bush conspiracy and there was no Jewish conspiracy.

September 8. *Message from a judge.*

Muhammad Taqi Usmani, a former sharia judge on Pakistan's Supreme Court, "argues that Muslims should live peacefully in countries ... where they have the freedom to practice (sic) Islam, only until they gain enough power to engage in battle." His logic is: "the question is whether aggressive battle is by itself commendable or not". "If it is, why should the Muslims stop simply because territorial expansion in these days is regarded as bad? And if it is not commendable, but deplorable, why did Islam not stop it in the past?" His answer is: "Even in those days ... aggressive jihads were waged ... because it was truly commendable for establishing the grandeur of the religion of Allah."[342]

COMMENT: This is nothing more than the logic of a person who has revered Allah-Hubal too long. In medical terms, such persons have a severe mental illness. The vernacular terminology is lunacy!

---

[341] www.airforcetimes.com/news/2007/09/ap_binladen_070911/, retrieved on 31.03.2012.

[342] http://www.jihadwatch.org/2007/09/our-followers-must-live-in-peace-until-strong-enough-to-wage-jihad.html, retrieved on 31.03.2012.

## 2008

<u>On February 23.</u> *Exposé on Islamic schools and mosques.*

WorldNetDaily reports that "an undercover survey of more than 100 mosques and Islamic schools in America has exposed widespread radicalism, including the alarming finding that 3 in 4 Islamic centers are hotbeds of anti-Western extremism."[343]

COMMENT: The mosques and schools are used in the same fashion as the madrasas in Pakistan. The imams preach hate and the children learn the Koran by memory and how *important* it is to be subservient to Islam.

<u>June 3.</u> *An American wanted to use methods of mass destruction in the US and Europe.*

"Christopher Paul, aka 'Abdul Malek', aka 'Paul Kenyatta Laws', a 44-year-old US citizen born in Columbus, Ohio, has pleaded guilty today to conspiring with others to use a weapon of mass destruction, namely explosive devices, against targets in Europe and the United States in violation of 18 USC, Section 2332a. ... In the early 1990s, Paul traveled to Pakistan and Afghanistan to join the mujahedeen. At an Al Qaeda training camp in Afghanistan, he received initial training in, among other things, the use of assault rifles, rocket-propelled grenades, and small unit tactics. After successfully completing this training, he joined al Qaeda and stayed at the *Beit ur Salam* guesthouse, which was exclusively for al Qaeda members. Having distinguished himself to Al Qaeda, Paul was then selected for and obtained advanced training in explosives,

---

[343] http://www.wnd.com/2008/02/57141/, retrieved on 31.03.2012.

climbing, and military history. Paul then fought in Afghanistan alongside other mujahedeen."[344]

COMMENT: He did it all for Allah-Hubal!

June 19. *Ohio men wanted to kill American soldiers.*

"Three Ohio men were convicted Friday of plotting to recruit and train terrorists to kill American soldiers in Iraq, a case put together with help from a former soldier who posed as a radical bent on violence. ... Mohammad Amawi, 28, Marwan El-Hindi, 45, and Wassim Mazloum, 27, face maximum sentences of life in prison. Prosecutors said the men were learning to shoot guns and make explosives while raising money to fund their plans to wage a holy war against US troops."[345]

COMMENT: The Islamic holy war has been going on continuously since 613, when Mohammed at the age of 43 began preaching it because Allah-Hubal told him to do so.

September 13. *Fired Somali workers' dispute leads to flyers urging **Behead those who insult Islam**.*

"Fired workers from JBS Swift & Co. stayed at home and observed the Ramadan fast with family and friends on Friday as Somali community leaders organized their constituents for possible legal action. Several organizations, including Somali Aid, the Colorado Muslim Council, the Colorado Immigrant Rights Coalition as well as faith and labor leaders, joined on

---

[344] http://www.justice.gov/opa/pr/2008/June/08-nsd-492.html, retrieved on 31.03.2012.

[345] http://www.militantislammonitor.org/article/id/3507, retrieved on 31.03.2012.

Friday in condemning the firing of more than 100 Somali workers on Tuesday for not showing up to work at the JBS Swift plant, according to a release. The Council on American Islamic Relations, a Saudi funded front group for Hamas and an unindicted co-conspirator in the Holyland Foundation Hamas funding trial, is involved in the negotiations between the Somali Muslim workers and JBS Swift."[346]

COMMENT: It appears that no Muslim is forced to work in such meat processing plants. The thought is near at hand that Muslims work at such meat processing plants in order to insinuate their creepy sharia in the local community.

September 30. *Muslim convert gets 35 years in plot to attack shopping mall during Christmas season.*

"A 24-year-old convert to Islam has been sentenced to 35 years in prison for plotting to set off hand grenades in a crowded shopping mall during the Christmas season. Derrick Shareef must serve 30 of those years — with five off for good behavior — unless he can get an appeals court to reduce the sentence. He was arrested in 2006 on charges of scheming to use weapons of mass destruction at the Cherryvale Mall in the northern Illinois city of Rockford. Federal Judge David Coar said Tuesday he didn't believe Shareef was evil. But he said people could have been severely hurt if federal agents hadn't broken up the plot."[347]

---

[346] http://www.militantislammonitor.org/article/id/3604, retrieved on 31.03.2012.

[347] http://middlesborodailynews.com/bookmark/1407025-Islam-convert-gets-35-years-in-plot-to-attack-mall, retrieved on 31.03.2012.

COMMENT: Islam and Christmas. Some Islamic scholars (?) contend that "Saying Merry Christmas is worse than fornication or killing someone."[348]

*October 6. Feds charge 14 in Missouri-based Hamas terror funding prosecution.*

"On Tuesday, a St. Louis grand jury handed down a federal indictment charging 14 operators of local convenience marts with a complex scheme to help finance the Palestinian terror group Hamas. Charges include bank fraud, racketeering conspiracy, and conspiracy to receive stolen goods. The conspirators are known collectively as the 'Hamed' group, named after lead plotter, Bassam H. 'Sam' Hamed who is 33. The plan originated 8 years ago, in 2000 when it was decided to fund the terror group, sometimes through the sale of contraband items, in the convenience stores and through a complex web of sales and re-sales from which funds were skimmed. It is estimated that a minimum of $250,000 and as much as $1.5 million was netted in the illegal operation."[349]

COMMENT: Convenience stores sell pork. Profits from pork sales are being used to fund Islamic terror. This is the epitome of Islamic evil, ludicrous actions.

*October 10. Muslims attack gay men in Washington, saying if the victims were in their country, they'd be stoned to death.*

---

[348] http://www.youtube.com/watch?feature=player_embedded&v=FFW3Z NC8sjw, retrieved on 23.03.2012.

[349] http://www.militantislammonitor.org/article/id/3673 was retrieved on 31.03.2012.

"Muslim attackers, 19-year-old Saad Elorch and 19-year-old Abdulgader Ruddad, are illegal aliens who have previous criminal convictions for drugs and assault and are wanted for deportation by Immigration and Customs Enforcement (ICE). And they're not just Muslim, they're religious Muslims, as evidenced by their mother's hijab-encrusted visage on the video. Oh, and not so religious that it didn't keep 'em from drinking alcohol and using the vodka bottle as part of the vicious attack. Prosecutors say 19-year-old Saad Elorch and 19-year-old Abdulgader Ruddad targeted and taunted their victims, then assaulted one of them because they are gay. In court on Wednesday, Elorch, the alleged ring leader, jumped up and begged the judge to let him go. But the judge in the case denied his request."[350]

COMMENT: It is common for jihadists to make themselves intoxicated with alcohol or high on drugs before they commit an act of violence against non-believers and gay persons. The intoxication or the high gives them courage to commit the act of violence. Furthermore, Allah is forgiving of them for using alcohol or drugs.

November 24. *One of the largest Islamic charities in the US guilty of funding terror.*

"The leaders of what was once the largest Muslim charity in the United States were found guilty on Monday of acting as a front for Palestinian militants in the largest terrorism financing prosecution in American history. It was a major victory in the White House's legal 'war on terror' and comes after a mistrial

---

[350] http://www.debbieschlussel.com/archives/2008/10/religion_of_tol_1. html, retrieved on 31.03.2012. The video is linked.

was declared last year in the case involving the now defunct Texas-based Holy Land Foundation, charged with funneling $12 million to Hamas."[351]

COMMENT: Hamas Funneled campaign contributions to Barack Hussein Obama in the 2008 presidential election. Hamas is full of charity and good will!

December 23. *Five Muslim extremists convicted in Fort Dix terror case*

"A New Jersey jury today convicted five Islamic radicals on charges of plotting to kill members of the U.S. military. The announcement was made by acting United States Attorney Ralph J. Marra, Jr. The convicted were Mohamad Ibrahim Shnewer, brothers Dritan Duka, Shain Duka and Eljvir Duka and Serdar Tatar on Count One of the seven-count Superseding Indictment that charged them with conspiracy to murder members of the U.S. military. The jury acquitted each of defendants of Count Two, which charged attempt to murder members of the U.S. military. Because of the severity of the charges the defendants face up to life in prison."[352]

COMMENT: The plot was only part of the 1,400-year-old Islamic holy war.

---

[351] http://www.telegraph.co.uk/news/worldnews/northamerica/usa/3515658/US-based-Muslim-charity-guilty-of-funding-terrorism.html, retrieved on 31.03.2012.

[352] http://www.militantislammonitor.org/article/id/3770, retrieved on 31.03.2012.

# 2009

January 22. *Chabad Lubavitch Headquarters threatened with attack by New York-based radical Muslim group.*

"The site www.revolutionmuslim.com, ... run by Yousef Al-Khattab, a New York City cab driver who operates the extremist Islamic anti-American Web site that features violent images on a daily basis ... threatened with this: From the Statue of Liberty, with an ax blade cutting through her side; to a video mocking the beheading of American journalist Daniel Pearl, entitled 'Daniel Pearl I am Happy Your Dead' (sic); or the latest speech from Sheikh Abdullah Faisal, an extremist Muslim cleric convicted in the UK and later deported for soliciting the murder of non-Muslims. The latest - a cartoon-like image depicting 770 Eastern Parkway, Lubavitch World Headquarters, as a target in retaliation for Israel's attacks on Gaza. Formerly known as Joseph Cohen, al-Khattab is an American-born Jew who converted to Islam after attending an Orthodox Rabbinical school, which he later described as a 'racist cult.' The 39-year-old New York taxi driver launched RevolutionMuslim.com with the mission of 'preserving Islamic culture, calling people to the oneness of G-d' and asking them to 'support the beloved Sheik Abdullah Faisal, who's preaching the religion of Islam and serving as a spiritual guide.'"[353]

COMMENT: Evidently, there are a large number of American Jews who are traitors to the United States and to Israel.

---

[353]http://www.militantislammonitor.org/article/id/3830; http://adamholland. blogspot.de/2010/05/alan-sabrosky-large-majority-of-us-jews.html, both of which were retrieved on 31.03.2012.

<u>March 21</u>. *Jordanian charged in bomb-threat to Jewish school.*

Chicago: "A postage stamp, a fingerprint and a Google search helped lead authorities to arrest a West Rogers Park man Friday on a charge he mailed a bomb threat to a Jewish school in late December. Forensic investigators matched a fingerprint from the letter's envelope to Mohammed Alkaramla, authorities said. During a search of Alkaramla's apartment last month, agents also found a book of postage stamps -- bearing a design of two swans forming a heart shape, the same design as the stamp on the bomb threat letter. That particular stamp hadn't been produced in more than a decade, and the book found in a dresser drawer was missing one stamp, charges say."[354]

COMMENT: This is the use of the United States Postal Service to conduct jihad.

<u>May 22</u>. *New York synagogue bomb plotters were intent on holy war.*

"Four men arrested after planting what they thought were explosives near two New York City synagogues were disappointed that the World Trade Center wasn't still around to attack, a federal prosecutor said Thursday as the men appeared in court for the first time. The suspects were arrested Wednesday night, shortly after planting a 37-pound mock explosive device in the trunk of a car outside the Riverdale Temple and two mock bombs in the backseat of a car outside the Riverdale Jewish Center, another synagogue a few blocks

---

[354] http://articles.chicagotribune.com/2009-03 21/news/0903200518_1_
bomb-threat-jewish-school-google-search, retrieved on 31.03.2012.

253

away, authorities said. Police blocked their escape with an 18-wheel truck, smashing their tinted Sport Utility Vehicle windows and apprehending the unarmed suspects. Authorities said the men also plotted to shoot down a military plane. James Cromitie, 55; David Williams, 28; Onta Williams, 32; and Laguerre Payen, all of Newburgh, were charged with conspiracy to use weapons of mass destruction within the United States and conspiracy to acquire and use anti-aircraft missiles. All the suspects except Payen appeared in federal court in White Plains on Thursday, their hands shackled to their waists, preventing them from raising their hands while swearing to tell the truth. Assistant U.S. Attorney Eric Snyder said the defendants were 'eager to bring death to Jews.' And he quoted one as saying: 'I would like to get a synagogue.' They were 'disappointed ... that the best target (the World Trade Center) was hit already,' he said, adding that the men were 'eager to bring death to Jews.' He also said Cromitie wanted to see what he did on TV and be able to say, 'I'm the one who did that.'"[355]

COMMENT: This is the utmost extreme of narcissism: violence for the purpose of achieving limelight and jihad.

June 1. *Muslim convert shoots two soldiers at a US Army Recruiting Center in Arkansas.*

"LITTLE ROCK, Ark. — A 23-year-old man upset about the wars in Iraq and Afghanistan opened fire from his truck at two soldiers standing outside a military recruiting station here on

---

[355] http://www.cbsnews.com/2100-201_162-5030167.html, retrieved on 31.03.2012.

Monday morning, killing one private and wounding another, the police said. Abdulhakim Mujahid Muhammad, 23, was escorted from the Little Rock police headquarters in Arkansas on Monday. Muhammad is the suspect in the killing of a soldier in a targeted attack on a military recruiting center, police said. The gunman, identified by the police as Abdulhakim Mujahid Muhammad of Little Rock, fled the scene and was arrested minutes later a short distance from the recruiting station, in a bustling suburban shopping center. The police confiscated a Russian-made SKS semiautomatic rifle, a .22-caliber rifle and a handgun from his black pickup truck."[356]

COMMENT: Another instance of the 1,400-year-old holy war of Islam.

June 6. *Muslim woman crashes memorial for Arkansas jihad victim, shouting, "Jesus was Muslim!"*

"An Islamic jihadist murders an American soldier on American soil, and a hijab-wearing Muslim woman shows up at a memorial rally for him, claiming Muslim victimization and proclaiming Islamic supremacist dogma – 'Jesus was Muslim!,' etc. -- and railing about how 'Jews' control the New York Times and Fox News."[357]

COMMENT: Mohammed claimed that Jesus would return as a Muslim and destroy all of the non-believers. (Koran 43:57-67)

---

[356] http://www.nytimes.com/2009/06/02/us/02recruit.html, retrieved on 31.03.2012.

[357] http://www.jihadwatch.org/2009/06/hijab-wearing-islamic-supremacist-woman-crashes-memorial-for-arkansas-jihad-victim-shouting-jesus-wa.html, retrieved on 31.03.2012.

<u>June 6</u>. *Muslim shoots Christian five times, after religious argument.*

A Muslim was in a bar in San Diego, California, "so he probably wasn't drinking apple juice, and so this has nothing to do with jihad, right? Maybe not. But when one comes from a culture of violent intransigence regarding religion, this kind of thing is going to happen. ... What started as an argument over religion at a bar escalated when one man shot another five times overnight, as the victim's sister watched in horror. Toni Simpson says she was waiting for her brother, Ernest McCullough, 29, in the 3800 block of Van Dyke Avenue at about 4:30 a.m. after a night of drinking at Nancy's Pub. She was listening to the pair argue over religion but never thought it would lead to what happened next. 'He pulled up his shirt and it looked like a knife and it was a gun. He pulled it out and shot him,' she said. Simpson says she was so shocked that she blacked out after the first two rounds were fired. When she came around she saw her brother covered in blood. 'I said 'he shot you?' And he said 'yeah, he shot me' and then he fell to the ground,' Simpson said. The victim, who is Christian, was taken to Scripps Mercy Hospital in serious condition but is expected to be okay. The suspect, who Simpson says was of Muslim faith, remains at large."[358]

COMMENT: Evidently, not all Muslims abhor alcohol.

---

[358] Address http://www.jihadwatch.org/2009/06/christian-and-muslim-get-in-religious-argument-in-bar-muslim-shoots-christian.html, retrieved on 31.03.2012.

<u>June 18.</u> *Arab Christian group told they cannot walk around and pass out literature during annual Arab International Festival.*

"ANN ARBOR, MI – For the last five years, Pastor George Saieg and scores of his volunteers have visited Dearborn, Michigan during its annual Dearborn Arab International Festival to pass out religious literature and discuss their Christian Faith. Pastor Saieg is a Sudanese Christian, and Founder and Director of the Arabic Christian Perspective (ACP), which ministers to Muslims. Dearborn happens to be one of the most densely populated Muslim communities in the United States. An estimated 30,000 of its 98,000 residents are Muslims. Even though there has never been a disruption of the public peace during this Christian ministry, last week Dearborn police officials told Pastor Saieg that he and his group are prohibited from freely traveling the public sidewalks to distribute their literature outside the festival. They must remain at a specific location."[359]

COMMENT: "The Thomas More Law Center, a national public interest law firm based in Ann Arbor, Michigan, and the Becker Law Firm based in Los Angeles, California, the general counsel for ACP, filed a federal lawsuit challenging the constitutionality of Dearborn's policy."

<u>June 30.</u> *Gay man harassed by angry stone-throwing Muslim youths in Minneapolis.*

---

[359]    http://islaminaction08.blogspot.de/2009/06/christians-oppressed-in-islamic.html, as well as the quotes in the COMMENT, retrieved on 31.03.2012.

"Cultures collided Sunday when a gay man was harassed by more than a dozen Somali youths while heading home after the Twin Cities GLBT Pride Festival. Shouting 'I hate gay people,' 'Fuck gay people,' and 'Gay is not the way,' the youths followed the man for several blocks. The entire incident was caught on video."

COMMENT: "My friend and I were leaving the Gay Pride Festival ... and came across a group of Somalian kids who asked my friend if he was gay. When he answered 'yes', they proceeded to harass him and me with verbal threats and even throwing rocks at my friend at one point."[360] Of course, Muslims can claim and do claim that recording their actions on video is a hate crime against them. There is a video of the incident.[361]

<u>July 6.</u> *A Muslim mob surrounds and attacks Christians in Michigan at the Arab International Festival in Dearborn, Michigan.*

"This is a video from this year's Arab International Festival taking place in the Islamic capital of the USA, Michigan. It was not enough that sharia loving Muslims were able to stop Christians from handing out Christian literature in the festival, so they also had to gang up and punch other law abiding

---

[360] http://minnesotaindependent.com/38101/cultures-collide-somali-youth-harass-gay-man-at-pride, retrieved on 31.03.2012.

[361] http://www.youtube.com/watch?v=TfW9inRkTpU&feature=player_em bedded, retrieved on 31.03.2012.

Christians. Things are starting to look like the UK here. Wake up guys, the enemy is in our backyard."[362]

COMMENT: There was a video of the Islamic attacks on YouTube. However, it has been scrubbed. Dearborn, Michigan, indeed, Michigan, is considered the Islamic capital of America. Out of a population of 98,000 in Dearborn, 30,000 are Muslim.[363]

<u>July 27.</u> *Christian coach canned after student converts - Muslim principal allegedly irate that wrestler left Islam to be baptized.*

"A high school hall-of-fame and Christian wrestling coach in Dearborn, Mich., claims he was muscled out of his long-tenured coaching job by the school's principal, a devout Muslim, because the administrator was furious over a student wrestler who had converted to Christianity from Islam. Gerald Marszalek has coached wrestling for 35 years at Dearborn Public Schools, amassing more than 450 wins and, in addition to being added to the Michigan High School Athletic Association Hall of Fame, was named 'Sportsman of the Year' by the All-American Athletic Association. Despite Marszalek's success, however, Principal Imad Fadlallah of Dearborn's Fordson High School ordered the administration not to renew the coach's contract, allegedly in retaliation over the student's conversion and to continue a campaign of flushing Christianity out of the school. Marszalek is suing both the principal and the

---

[362] See http://islaminaction08.blogspot.de/2009/07/michiganmuslim-mob-surrounds-and.html, retrieved on 31.03.2012.

[363] http://www.renewamerica.com/columns/zieve/070111, retrieved on 31.03.2012.

school in the US District Court of Eastern Michigan, seeking back pay, injunctive and declaratory relief, damages, and to be reinstated as coach of the wrestling team. ... According to the lawsuit, however, Marszalek's treatment by Fadlallah isn't isolated, but part of an intentional eradication of Christianity from the school. 'Fadlallah, since assuming duties as Fordson's principal in 2005, has systematically weeded out Christian teachers, coaches and employees and has terminated, demoted or reassigned them because of their Christian beliefs,' the lawsuit continues. 'Fadlallah has publicly stated he sees 'Dearborn Fordson High School as a Muslim school, both in students and faculty, and is working to that end.'"[364]

COMMENT: "We are getting a glimpse of what happens when Muslims who refuse to accept American values and principles gain political power in an American community," said Richard Thompson, president and chief counsel of the Thomas More Law Center, which is representing Marszalek. 'Failure to renew coach Marszalek's contract had nothing to do with wrestling and everything to do with religion.'"

September 24. *Muslim immigrant tries to car-bomb Dallas skyscraper, to make his dream of "violent jihad" a reality.*

"A Jordanian immigrant named Hosam Smadi was arrested for attempting to detonate what he thought was a car bomb in the parking lot of a 60-story skyscraper in Dallas, TX. On May 26, 2010, he pled guilty to one count of attempted use of a weapon

---

[364] http://www.wnd.com/2009/07/105227/, as well as the quotation in the COMMENT, retrieved on 31.03.2012.

of mass destruction. Smadi's apprehension resulted from an FBI operation including at least three undercover employees. The operation duped Smadi into believing he was planning an attack with Al Qaeda operatives. It ended with Smadi driving a truck he believed to contain a live bomb into the underground garage of 60-story Fountain Place in Dallas, TX. He used a cell phone to try and trigger the dud."[365]

COMMENT: Jihadists try not only to emulate Mohammed, but Osama bin Laden as well.

October 10. *Muslim threatens to blow up D. C. metro station.*

"WASHINGTON, D.C. – A man who was arrested in a security scare in Northwest D.C. on Tuesday night threatened to blow up the Friendship Heights Metro station, according to a criminal complaint in the case. ... Police say the man's name is Ahamed Ali, based on a driver license from Bangladesh. Witnesses and police say Ali had been hanging around Chevy Chase Pavilion for a couple of days, taking notes, making threats, and acting strangely. ... Investigators say Ali was overheard calling out: 'I'm not scared to die! I will kill you! I will blow people up and the Metro!'"[366]

COMMENT: Can one not call such persons mentally ill specifically because they are convinced of their calling to do the work of Mohammed and Allah-Hubal?

---

[365] http://www.fas.org/sgp/crs/terror/R41416.pdf, p. 48, retrieved on 31.03.2012.

[366] http://www.liveleak.com/view?i=dfb_1255153840 was retrieved on 31.03.2012.

<u>October 15, 22, and November 2.</u> *Decision to trust imam backfired on New York City police when he tipped off the suspects, putting lives at risk.*

"A Queens imam accused of tipping off a suspected al-Qaida operative pleaded not guilty today during his arraignment ... . Prosecutors say Afzali told alleged terror suspect Najibullah Zazi and his father the two were under surveillance and then lied to the FBI about it. Afzali has denied the charges. Zazi is being held without bond in the city. He is accused of planning to build homemade bombs to use in an attack on the city's mass transit system ... ."[367]

COMMENT: This is a typical situation of Muslim al-taqiyya.

<u>November 5.</u> *Muslim Major shouts 'Allahu Akbar' as he massacres 13 soldiers and injures 30 at Fort Hood, Texas.*

"News comes that the man responsible for the massacre of 13 US Army soldiers, Major Nidal Malik Hasan, was shouting 'Allahu Akbar' as he opened fire on the unsuspecting men and women: Soldiers who witnessed the shooting rampage at Fort Hood, Texas that left 13 people dead reported that the gunman shouted 'Allahu Akbar!' before opening fire, the base commander said Friday."[368]

---

[367]    http://www.jihadwatch.org/cgi-sys/cgiwrap/br0nc0s/managed-mt/mt-search.cgi?blog_id=1&tag=New%20York%2FColorado%20bomb%20plot &limit=20, retrieved on 31.03.2012.

[368]    http://theopinionator.typepad.com/my_weblog/2009/11/muslim-major-shouts-allahu-akbar-as-he-massacres-13-soldiers-injures-30.html, retrieved on 31.03.2012.

COMMENT: "The media and Muslim apologists continue to dance around the truth of the Ft. Hood massacre. Many are rushing to blame the military or Hasan's co-workers for his state of mind and subsequent murderous rampage. Lame excuses such as Hasan was supposedly 'harassed' by other military personnel don't hold water. Hasan was an officer - and anyone who has been in the military KNOWS that particularly officers do NOT get harassed. To do so would be the end of the offender's military career. An official report released by the Department of Defense soon after the attack, concludes that Hasan was over-worked and not accepted by his military comrades. Anwar al-Awlaki posted praise for Hasan for the shooting on his website, and encouraged other Muslims serving in the military to "follow in the footsteps of men like Nidal."[369]

COMMENT: As of this writing, Hasan Nidal Malik has still not been brought to trial. This is willful delay and non-observance of justice by the Barack Hussein Obama regime.

November 5, 10. *Muslim arrested after terrifying shoppers at a mall, as he shouts "Allah is power", "Islam is great" and other anti-Christian comments and tears a crucifix off a man's neck.*

Pleasanton, California. "Police arrested 22-year-old Hamid of Hayward Wednesday evening after he reportedly robbed a man and scared others at Stoneridge Shopping Center. According to reports, Hamid was yelling 'Allah is power' and 'Islam is great' while holding a pen in a fist over his head and witnesses said he had been shouting anti-Christian comments. Pleasanton Police Lt. Mike Elerick said the man was not provoked and didn't

---

[369] http://www.google.com/hostednews/ap/article/ALeqM5hDlRkRffov JlX8OT05h89h3zfgWwD9BS4ETO3, retrieved on 31.03.2012.

threaten violence, but he committed robbery when he grabbed and broke a crucifix off a man's neck."[370]

COMMENT: Islam and Crucifixes. Muslims are provoked by the cross because the cross symbolizes the crusades in the 11th, 12th, and 13th centuries with the aim of freeing the Holy Land from the Muslims. Yet, more important is that fact that the cross symbolizes the everlasting love of Christ for humankind. Mohammed never showed self-sacrificing love for fellow humans.

## 2010

February 13. *Fort Worth bomb scare, Muslim women and accomplice caught with pipe bombs in truck.*

FORT WORTH, Texas — "Southeast Loop 820 and East Rosedale Street in Fort Worth were reopened early Sunday morning after being shut down for five hours overnight. The Fort Worth bomb squad detonated four charges that were found in a pickup truck that spun out on a slick road during a police pursuit. Two people are in custody, and one of them — Kimberly Suzanne Al-Homsi — is well-known to police and federal agents. ... Al-Homsi was charged with evading arrest, two counts of terroristic threats, and also a prohibited weapons count. Both Kimberly Al-Homsi, ... and Yasinul Ansari remained in custody Sunday without bond due to federal holds. News 8 has learned that Al-Homsi has been under government surveillance and was on the federal 'no-fly' list after being involved in a road rage incident in December, 2005. At that

---

[370] http://www.pleasantonweekly.com/news/show_story.php?id=2916 was retrieved on 31.03.2012.

time, she held up an inert grenade and threatened another motorist. The Garland bomb squad found ammunition in her car. In an exclusive interview with News 8 in 2007, Al-Homsi said she disagreed with U.S. policy in the Middle East."[371]

COMMENT: There were no reports that Kimberly Al-Homsi, and Yasinul Ansari are active jihad Muslims, just that they are sympathizers!

June 24. *Dearborn Police Chief Ronald Haddad refuses to release Christians' cameras.*

In Dearborn, Christians were arrested for having a peaceful dialogue with Muslims. "The police claimed we were being disruptive. We invited them to view the video footage, which would prove our innocence. They refused, preferring to take us to jail when we had indisputable proof against the false charges. Police seized our cameras illegally, and have to this day refused to share the footage with us, footage that will completely exonerate us. Police Chief Ronald Haddad refuses to return our cameras, despite the fact that he knows we are innocent. He is responsible for the persecution and oppression of Christians in Dearborn. So guess who should be appointed to the Homeland Security Advisory Council? You guessed it: Dearborn Police Chief Ronald Haddad. ... Well, Christians have been persecuted by Muslims for centuries, so Haddad's not actually engaging the community in a new way. Perhaps he means that he's engaging the American community in a new way, e.g., by taking away the Constitutional rights of

---

[371] http://www.wfaa.com/news/local/Possible-terror-incident-in-Fort-Worth-84316367.html, retrieved on 31.03.2012.

Christians. But he needs to be clear about that. People might get the idea that he believes in American values."[372]

COMMENT: This is Islamic double subversive activity. Prohibit Christian activity on a local level and become an insurgent on a federal level.

July 5. *Bronx mosque forcing call to prayer on neighborhood "Imagine sunrise behind a minaret."*

"Imagine a bearded imam. Listen for his thunderous call to worship. Not in Baghdad or Tehran or Islamabad. In the Bronx. Neighbors of dissimilar backgrounds clashed at a Community Board 9 public hearing on Tuesday, October 20. Members of the Parkchester Jame Masjid (mosque) on Virginia Avenue near Parkchester want to use electronic amplification to perform 'adhan,' the Muslim call to prayer. The mosque would be the first in the Bronx to do so and has asked the police department for a sound permit. Some neighbors oppose the plan. The Bronx was home to 2,442 Bangladeshi Americans in 2000, a 320 percent increase from 1990. There are even more Bangladeshi Americans in the Bronx today. Most reside in Parkchester, Soundview, and Castle Hill. Community District 9 is 34 percent African American and 55 percent Hispanic American. 'I have no problem with them,' neighbor Ruben Rios, 75, asserted. 'But I hear their parties. People think Puerto Ricans play loud music. The [Muslims'] music is louder.' ...

---

[372] See http://www.answeringmuslims.com/2010/06/in-dearborn-we-were-arrested-for-having.html, retrieved on 31.03.2012.

The mosque has prospered without amplified adhan thus far... . Shahid is optimistic the mosque will get its amp."[373]

COMMENT: Call to prayer in the Koran! Call for sharia in the Bronx!

August 23. *Jihadist website vows to conduct suicide bombings in Florida to avenge church Koran burning.*

"Islamic radicals are seizing on protests against a planned Islamic community center near Manhattan's Ground Zero and anti-Muslim rhetoric elsewhere as a propaganda opportunity and are stepping up anti-U.S. chatter and threats on their websites. One jihadist site vowed to conduct suicide bombings in Florida to avenge a threatened Koran burning, while others predicted an increase in terrorist recruits as a result of such actions. 'By Allah, the wars are heated and you Americans are the ones who ... enflamed it,' says one such posting. 'By Allah you will be the first to taste its flames.'"[374]

COMMENT: The report originally appeared in the Wall Street Journal online. It has been scrubbed from the Internet.

September 15. *Molly Norris, artist behind 'Everybody Draw Mohammed Day' cartoon which resulted in death threats and global protests, goes into hiding.*

---

[373] http://atlasshrugs2000.typepad.com/atlas_shrugs/2010/07/nyc-mosque-forcing-muslim-call-to-prayer-on-neighborhood-.html, which was retrieved on 31.03.2012.

[374] http://online.wsj.com/article/SB10001424052748703589804575445844 1837725272.html, retrieved on 31.02.2012.

"So much for freedom of speech. At the urging of the FBI, Molly Norris, the Seattle-based illustrator and cartoonist whose satirical drawing marking 'Everybody Draw Mohammed Day' resulted in death threats, global protests and impassioned debate about religion and censorship, has been forced to change her name and abandon her former life as a result of her controversial cartoon. The news that Morris had, out of concerns for her safety, decided to go into hiding was first reported in the Seattle Weekly today, a paper where Norris' cartoons had regularly appeared. The gifted artist is alive and well, thankfully. But on the insistence of top security specialists at the FBI, she is, as they put it, 'going ghost': moving, changing her name, and essentially wiping away her identity. She will no longer be publishing cartoons in our paper or in City Arts magazine, where she has been a regular contributor. She is, in effect, being put into a witness-protection program -- except, as she notes, without the government picking up the tab. Norris originally posted her tongue-in-cheek cartoon announcing May 20 as 'Everybody Draw Mohammed Day' on her website, which no longer seems to be operating. It was dedicated to the creators of the Comedy Central animated television series 'South Park' after one of their episodes was censored for its portrayal of the Islamic prophet. As expected, Norris' creation touched a nerve, and her drawing soon became a viral hit on the internet, posted to a variety of high-profile websites and forwarded in countless e-mails. Soon her fictitious drawing morphed into an actual event as Facebook groups championing the idea popped up and started attracting fans. With media outlets covering the phenomenon, word of 'Everybody Draw Mohammed Day' spread across the globe, and the government of Pakistan announced it was suspending the use of Facebook to residents there. Norris seemed caught off guard by the whirlwind. She removed the original cartoon from her website, took pains to disassociate herself from an actual 'Everybody Draw Muhammad Day' and pleaded for tolerance. 'I did NOT 'declare' May 20 to be *Everybody Draw Mohammed Day*. … I never started a Facebook page; I never set up any place for people to send drawings to and I never received any drawings, … I apologize to people of Muslim faith and ask that this 'day be called off.' In June, despite her renunciation of the event spawned by her cartoon, Norris was placed on a hit list by Yemeni-American cleric Anwar al-Awlaki, an al-Qaida-linked figure who has been tied to the Fort Hood, Texas, massacre as well as the failed bombing in Times Square, … Shortly thereafter, the FBI contacted Norris. 'We're hoping the religious bigots go into full and immediate remission,' the Seattle Weekly said about Norris' need to go into hiding, 'and we wish her the best.'"[375]

COMMENT: One should never apologize for exercising freedom of speech!

October 15. *Naples pastor receives death threat at the Islamic Center of Southwest Florida.*

"A conservative Christian pastor, who hosts a television program and radio show, has reported he was threatened by a Muslim at the Islamic Center of Southwest Florida. According to Bill Keller of Naples, an individual at the center left a message for him, saying he was a 'bad man,' that he would

---

[375] Refer to http://www.aolnews.com/2010/09/15/molly-norris-artist-behind-everybody-draw-mohammad-day-cartoo/, retrieved on 31.03.2012.

269

'soon be finished' and threatened a 'jihad' on him. Keller ... said because he takes a hard line against controversial issues like abortion and homosexuality, he has received death threats in the past. However, he is especially concerned about this, he said, because the caller was so specific. 'I guess the specificity of this particular message, the location and all that, was more the issue,' Keller said. 'I certainly don't live my life in fear, but I'm not going to be foolish when there is the opportunity to report this to authorities. I'm sure our 'friends' on the Left in America would celebrate this threat - what better scenario than one of their Muslim co-conspirators for the overthrow of America to actually take out one of those evil Evangelicals!'"[376]

COMMENT: Every day Americans are reminded of the evil of Islam. There are suspicious packages left unattended. There are jihad terrorists plotting to bomb us. Muslims, via organizations like CAIR, sue Americans for hate crimes. American military Muslims kill their own soldiers. Muslims threaten to kill pastors. Islam is such a tolerant religion! There should be only American justice and no sharia law. The original internet page at News-Press that reported the threat has been scrubbed.

November 27. Violent jihad *are forbidden words.*

"If it's Monday, Tuesday, Wednesday, Thursday, Friday, Saturday, or Sunday, it's just another day in the life of a true believer in violent jihad. Yes: Violent jihad. Two words the current occupant of the White House won't say together and about which he remains in stubborn denial. Violent jihad. A

---

[376] http://holgerawakens.blogspot.de/2010/10/florida-pastor-receives-death-threat.html, retrieved on 30.03.2012.

fundamental tenet of legions and legions of Muslims worldwide — and untold numbers of homegrown and immigrant practitioners of the Religion of Perpetual Outrage here on American soil. ... Undercover agents in a sting operation arrested a Somali-born teenager just as he tried blowing up a van full of what he believed were explosives at a crowded Christmas tree lighting ceremony in Portland, federal authorities said. The bomb was a fake supplied by the agents and the public was never in danger, authorities said. Mohamed Osman Mohamud, 19, was arrested at 5:40 p.m. Friday just after he dialed a cell phone that he thought would set off the blast but instead brought federal agents and police swooping down on him. Yelling 'Allahu Akbar!' — Arabic for 'God is great!' — Mohamud tried to kick agents and police after he was taken into custody, according to prosecutors. 'The threat was very real,' said Arthur Balizan, special agent in charge of the FBI in Oregon. 'Our investigation shows that Mohamud was absolutely committed to carrying out an attack on a very grand scale.'"[377]

COMMENT: "Now we have a naturalized Son of Oregon, and former student at the publicly funded university in Corvallis to boot, who decided to become a Soldier of Allah and bring death en-masse to the city that protected its Muslim population from some appropriate scrutiny – and while they were at it, blindly ignored Islam's doctrine and history. How ironic, and utterly

---

[377]     http://michellemalkin.com/2010/11/27/just-another-bomb-plotting-jihadist-yelling-allahu-akbar/and the COMMENT below, retrieved on 31.03.2012. 'Allahu Akbar! The cry means Allah is the greatest of all (moon) gods.

stupid, that the City Fathers of Portland were so ignorant of what has been repeatedly and relentlessly thrown directly into our faces since 9/11. Now they, as well as other Sanctuary City governments, can either awaken to what we are really up against – or continue the blindfolded charade of pretending that Islam has nothing to do with violence or acts of mass terrorism. Any bets here? Think the President is going to help us along in opening our eyes? Think the Dept. of Homeland Security is going to step up to the plate and demand a halt to Muslim immigration into the United States? State Department? Repubs in the 2011 House of Representatives? That the suicidal insanity has persisted this long after 2001 is much more than disturbing. It makes one wonder how much longer can a civilization that refuses to face reality continue to exist?"[378]

COMMENT: There is a mug shot collection of jihadists sought by the FBI and other enforcement agencies.[379]

---

[378]    http://work949.wordpress.com/2010/11/28/michelle-malkins-jihadist-mugshot-collection-worthy-of-viewing-what-say-you-now-portland/, retrieved on 31.03.2012.

[379] http://s.michellemalkin.com/wp/wpcontent/uploads/2009/02/1aaaasaud.jpg, retrieved on 31.03.2012.

# CHAPTER NINE

## Willful Blindness Continues in the Twenty-First Century

### The Second Decade

*Willful Blindness* is the title of a bestselling book by Andrew C. McCarthy which describes the attitude of William Jefferson Clinton's administration vis-à-vis jihad and Clinton's refusal to recognize jihad as Islam's declaration of war on the United States of America with the first attack on the World Trade Center on February 26, 1993. President George W. Bush, although attempting to appease Muslims, understood that Islam via the organization Al Qaeda was conducting war against America. In one full propaganda sweep, Barack Hussein Obama by executive order proclaimed that there were no Islamic terrorists and therefore no Islamic terrorism.[380]

With the experience of a decade of active Islamization and jihad in the United States of America, a spectre is still haunting American society. It has two sides. Side one is the claim that Islam is peaceful and renounces violence. Side two is the acceleration of jihad activism while claiming that Islam observes the principles of human rights. Creeping Islam activities continue into the second decade of the 21st century.

---

[380] http://www.washingtonpost.com/wp-dyn/content/article/2009/03/24/AR2009032402818.html, retrieved on 30.03.2012.

## Selected Incidences

**2011**

<u>January 12</u>. *Muslim school told to stop intimidating ACLU witnesses.*

"Tarek ibn Ziyad Academy (TiZA), a publicly funded Minnesota charter school, twice has been ordered by a federal district court to stop intimidating witnesses while fighting an ACLU (American Civil Liberties Union) lawsuit alleging violations of the constitutional prohibition against government endorsement of religion. ... Minnesota's federal district court has twice ordered the school, which has campuses in the Minneapolis suburbs of Inver Grove Heights and Blaine, to stop intimidating witnesses in the case. ... Most recently, on Oct. 1, 2010, Judge Donovan Frank instructed the school not to enforce a 'secrecy clause' in the employee handbook that threatened legal action if employees testified about school operations. TiZA uses the clause '... as a sledgehammer to keep former employees quiet about what they saw at the school,' according to the ACLU. In Jan. 2010, the court forbade any witness intimidation by either party after a former TiZA parent and a former TiZA staff member complained the school threatened them with violence. ... The former staff member testified in an affidavit that TiZA executive director Asad Zaman told her, 'We could just kill you, yeah tell your husband we'll do his job for him.' In his own affidavit, Zaman said he didn't remember making the statement. On another front, three organizations not named in the lawsuit filed a motion in Sept. 2010 to remove Dorsey and Whitney, the law firm representing the ACLU, from the case. The Muslim American Society of

Minnesota, the MAS-MN Property Holding Corporation and the Minnesota Education Trust asserted 'Dorsey personnel had previously communicated with Zaman about entities involved in the litigation,' according to Kersten. The Minnesota ACLU filed suit against TiZA in January, 2009, alleging 'the operation and public funding of the Tarek ibn Ziyad Academy (TiZA) is unconstitutional as a violation of the Establishment Clause of the First Amendment to the US Constitution ... and that the leasing of space by Muslim organizations to TiZA and the resulting transfer of state funds intended for the support of charter schools to such Muslim organizations through excessive lease payments also violates the Establishment Clause.' TiZA uses government money to endorse a religion, in this case Islam,' Minnesota ACLU Executive Director Chuck Samuelson told WND. 'Money was being funneled to the mosque that owns the building' through rent payments. TiZA has 'permitted prayer to be posted prominently in the school's entryway, prayer sessions to be held during school hours, teacher-sanctioned religious material to be posted in classrooms, parent-led or volunteer-led prayer during class-time, and teacher participation in prayer activities.' ... TiZA executive director Asad Zaman stated, 'As an inspiration to our students, we have named our school after Tarek Ibn Ziyad, the Ummayad administrator of medieval Spain. Thirteen hundred years ago, serving in the multifaceted roles of activist, leader, explorer, teacher, administrator and peacemaker, he inspired his fellow citizens to the same striving for human greatness that we hope to instill in our students today.'"[381]

---

[381] http://www.wnd.com/2011/01/250597/, retrieved on 30.03.2012.

COMMENT: TiZA, a K-8 school, has about 500 pupils, many the children of immigrants. All pupils receive "tuition-free education." Charter schools have no legal rights to impose Islam on their teachers, student body or the parents. The school is named after Tarek Ibn Ziyad, who invaded Spain in 711. Under his conquest, Spain experienced nothing but death or subjugation to the dhimmi-jizya tax. Tarek Ibn Ziyad was supposedly a great orator and field marshal who burned his invasion ships to force his army to stay in Spain and fight. The interesting matter is that it is all legend. Charles F. Horne of City College of New York already in 1917 in *The Sacred Books and Early Literature of the East* observed,

"In al Maqqari's day (1577-1632) the older Arabic traditions of exact service had quite faded. The Moors had become poets and dreamers instead of scientists and critical historians. The very name of al Maqqari's history may be accepted as typifying its character. He called it *Breath of Perfumes*. (The full title hardly disproves Horne's point: *The Breath of Perfume from the Branch of Green Andalusia and Memorials of its Vizier Lisan ud-Din ibn ul-Khattib*.) Florid though he was, al Maqqari gave us one of the great battlefield speeches, an Arabic bookend to Shakespeare's St Crispin's Day monologue. He wrote: 'When Tariq had been informed of the approach of the enemy, he rose in the midst of his companions and, after having glorified God in the highest, he spoke to his soldiers thus:

'Oh my warriors, whither would you flee? Behind you is the sea, before you, the enemy. You have left now only the hope of your courage and your constancy. Remember that in this country you are more unfortunate than the orphan seated at the table of the avaricious master. Your enemy is before you, protected by an innumerable army; he has men in abundance, but you, as your only aid, have your own swords, and, as your only chance for life, such chance as you can snatch from the hands of your enemy. If the absolute want to which you are reduced is prolonged ever so little, if you delay to seize immediate success, your good fortune will vanish, and your enemies, whom your very presence has filled with fear, will take courage. Put far from you the disgrace from which you flee in dreams, and attack this monarch who has left his strongly fortified city to meet you. Here is a splendid opportunity to defeat him, if you will consent to expose yourselves freely to death. Do not believe that I desire to incite you to face dangers which I shall refuse to share with you. In the attack I myself will be in the fore, where the chance of life is always least.'

"The strange thing is that when al Maqqari wrote about this stratagem of burning the boats, it had also been ascribed to Hernando Cortes, the Spaniard who conquered the Aztecs, in 1519. But he didn't do it either. While he is believed to have sunk most of his ships or run them aground to deter any thoughts of mutiny or surrender, the idea that he torched them did not arise until later, perhaps because a chronicler misread *quebrando* (smashing) as *quemando* (burning). Furthermore, the ships, if he ever burned them, did not belong to Tarek Ibn Ziyad, but to the Caliph of Cueta."

"Arsonist or not, Tariq had subdued Hispania within about a year. Though the history is sketchy, it must have helped that the Visigoths were a minority and had alienated the masses, in particular by persecuting Jews and slaves." (Which is what the Moors continued to do!)

"British Arabist Sir Thomas Walker Arnold wrote in 1896, in *The Preaching of Islam*: '(I)t was probably in a great measure their tolerant attitude towards the Christian religion that facilitated their rapid acquisition of the country.' (Forced conversion came later.) The culminating moment came in either 711 or 712 at the Battle of Guadalete, location uncertain, and there King Roderick died. The Muslims' rule of Hispania, which they called Al-Andalus, would extend over almost eight centuries."

"But just as the politics of the Visigoths provided Tariq with his way into Al-Andalus, the politics of the Umayyads sent him on his way out. Amid squabbling over spoils and a difficult succession to the throne, Tariq was recalled to Damascus to provide his version of events. From there Tariq fades into the background. He died in 720.

"And then, nearer our time than his, he was resurrected by al Maqqari, and fine words were put in his mouth, and a dramatic action imputed to him that carried the power of metaphor – the burning of boats is a timeless expression of commitment, of fearlessness, of believing so much in something that we deny the possibility of failure. Fittingly, given the intellectual eruption that followed the Moorish conquest, in the afterlife of Tariq himself we see that the pen is, if not mightier than the sword, certainly more enduring."[382]

---

[382] http://en.alukah.net/Thoughts_Knowledge/0/412/; http://www.thenation al.ae/news/uae-news/tariq-ibn-ziyads-legacy-stands-as-a-reminder-to-reject-failure#full, retrieved on 31.03.2012.

Thus the TiZA school is named after a historical person based on non-proven legendary events that were written 900 years after they supposedly happened. This is another case of Muslims rewriting history to suit their needs.

_January 12._ *Maryland Muslim inmate hopes to Allah to 'Chop Off' Obama's head.*

"Prosecutors indicted on Tuesday a Maryland inmate who threatened a federal judge and sent a letter to President Obama, stating, 'I just hope Allah grants me the opportunity to be the one who chops off your head.' Willie Ray Bryant, 40, is reportedly serving a 40-year sentence for his role in a string of Maryland robberies. This week's indictment, filed in Maryland federal court, charges Bryant with mailing threatening communications and threats against the president. Prosecutors say Bryant mailed US District Judge William Quarles Jr. a letter on Sept. 11, 2010, 'containing a threat to injure him with a mailed explosive device.' Quarles is a judge on the Maryland federal court. A month later, Bryant mailed a threatening letter to Obama, according to the two-page indictment. Prosecutors say Bryant wrote: 'I just hope Allah grants me the opportunity to be the one who chops off your head,' 'die die die!!!' and 'If I ever get out I promise you I'm coming after you.'"[383]

COMMENT: One can have any opinion of Barack Hussein Obama. Surely, however, wanting to chop off a person's head for Allah-Hubal is a crime, at least in the still existing United States of America. Using the United States Postal Service to communicate the threat is also a crime.

---

[383] http://www.courthousenews.com/2011/01/12/33268.htm, retrieved on 31.03.2012.

<u>January 13.</u> *CAIR.*

"Any question about the Council on American-Islamic Relations' (CAIR) attitude toward law enforcement in terrorism investigations has been put to rest by the group's San Francisco chapter. 'Build a Wall of Resistance,' a poster announcing a Feb. 9 event published on the group's website says, 'Don't Talk to the FBI.' A dark, sinister FBI agent is shown lurking in front of people's homes as doors slam shut. ... CAIR's hostility toward law enforcement is long-standing, but the organization's rhetoric has increased since the FBI cut off formal communication with the group in 2008. That decision was based on exhibits admitted into evidence during a terror-financing trial in Dallas that showed CAIR founders were part of a Hamas-support network. ... CAIR petitioned the Texas court to be removed from a list of unindicted co-conspirators in that case. But the district judge refused, ruling there is 'ample evidence to establish the associations of CAIR' and others 'with Hamas.'"[384]

COMMENT: CAIR's goal, according to its founder, Omar M. Ahmad: "Islam isn't in America to be equal to any other faith but to become dominant. The Koran, the Muslim book of scripture, should be the highest authority in America, and Islam the only accepted religion on Earth."[385]

<u>March 22.</u> *$2.2 million fatwa on Terry Jones after Quran burning.*

---

[384]    http://www.liveleak.com/view?i=1ea_1294982297, retrieved on 31.03.2012.

[385]    http://www.anti-cair-net.org/AhmadStateScanned.pdf, retrieved on 31.03.2012.

"Terry Jones, the Florida evangelical pastor who threatened to hold a Quran burning last Sept. 11 only to back down in the face of international outrage, finally went ahead and burned one. And now there's a 2.2-million-dollar price on his head. Jones appointed himself 'judge' and presided over a trial hearing evidence and testimony against Islam's holy book. A 'jury' found the book guilty of crimes against humanity; promoting terrorist acts; raping, torturing and killing people 'whose only crime was not being of the Islamic faith.' Also, its treatment of women was found lacking."[386]

COMMENT: There are similarities in the Koran with Mohammed's opinions in the hadiths concerning women and persons who do not believe in Islam and what happens to them.

May 9. *Air steward tackles Yemeni passenger battering on cockpit, shouting 'Allahu Akbar' as plane comes in to land at San Francisco.*

"Rageit Almurisi sparked panic when he started yelling and banging on the cockpit door on American Airlines flight 1561 from Chicago, just ten minutes before it was due to land on Sunday night, according to police. ... The Yemeni man who was wrestled to the floor after pounding on the cockpit door of a plane approaching San Francisco may have mistaken it for the bathroom. Rageit Almurisi cannot speak English very well and could have misunderstood the signs inside the jet, his cousin claimed. The maths (sic) teacher, who was heard yelling 'Allahu Akbar' as he allegedly battered the door, had also only

---

[386]   http://blog.seattlepi.com/hottopics/2011/03/22/2-2-million-fatwa-on-terry-jones-after-quran-burning/, retrieved on 31.03.2012.

been on three planes in his life and would have been unfamiliar with the layout."[387]

COMMENT: This is surely the first instance of a Muslim shouting 'Allahu Akbar' before going to the restroom!

May 13. *Two Islamist extremists bent on killing Jews.*

"Two New Yorkers have been arrested after purchasing weapons, saying they wanted to blow up a Manhattan synagogue and attack the Empire State Building. Police commissioner Raymond Kelly said one man was a US citizen and the other a legal resident. Both are of North African descent. He said they purchased two Browning semi-automatic pistols, a Smith and Wesson handgun, ammunition and a hand grenade during an undercover sting operation. They were arrested immediately after the purchase. ... Officials described the pair as Islamist extremists bent on killing Jews, but said they were 'lone wolves' not connected to any formal group such as al-Qaeda. 'They did it for jihad,' District Attorney Cyrus Vance, the head prosecutor in the case, said. He was (sic) fed up with the way Muslims were being treated around the world. 'They're treating us like dogs,' Kelly quoted one defendant as saying. 'We will blow up the synagogue in Manhattan and take out the entire building,' Kelly quoted a suspect as saying. One 'also expressed interest in bombing the Empire State Building.' In an unusual move, the pair were (sic) being charged by New York state, not federal prosecutors. Vance said there were four

---

[387] Refer to http://www.dailymail.co.uk/news/article-1385083/Rageit-Almurisi-Family-defends-Yemeni-man-stormed-cockpit-San-Francisco-flight.html, retrieved on 31.03.2012.

counts under terrorism and hate crimes laws. The charges carry a potential penalty of life in prison."[388]

COMMENT: If a Muslim is afraid of dogs and keeps away from dogs, then how can they maintain that they are treated like dogs? Dogs receive exceptional treatment in Christian and Jewish families.

June 22. *Muslim Marine arrested for shooting at buildings.*

"Yonathan Melaku, 22, of Alexandria, Va., a naturalized US citizen from Ethiopia, was detained Friday after he was spotted carrying a suspicious backpack near the Pentagon. Melaku also had a notebook with the words 'al-Qaida' and 'Taliban Rules' written inside. ... The case had apparently gone cold. But after several months of no progress, federal authorities have now zeroed in on a suspect in last year's shootings at several military sites around the nation's capital. Their suspect: the 22-year-old Marine reservist arrested Friday after causing a terror scare near the Pentagon. Ballistics obtained at the suspect's home have been linked to evidence found at the scenes of the 2010 shootings, including the Marine Corps Museum in Triangle, Va., a vacant Marine recruiting station in Chantilly, Va., and the Pentagon itself, ... . Melaku was arrested early Friday morning at Arlington National Cemetery when the site was closed. He was carrying a backpack with what authorities initially thought might be explosives, and they found a notebook containing words and phrases such as 'Taliban,' 'Al Qaeda,' 'defeated coalition forces,' and 'mujahedeen.' The discoveries caused 'concerns about the public's safety,' the FBI

---

[388]    http://news.smh.com.au/breaking-news-world/two-arrested-in-nyc-synagogue-bomb-plot-20110513-1ekyf.html, retrieved on 31.03.2012.

283

said at the time, and shut down major highways for much of Friday."[389]

COMMENT: Yonathan Melaku is a bad, unsuccessful jihadist. He did not kill any non-believers. According to the Koran and the hadiths it is most likely that Yonathan Melaku will go to hell on Allah-Hubal judgment day.

July 3. *2011 Dearborn Arab Festival: "You're disrespecting our f\*\*\*ing religion... by being here, bitch!" Christian preacher harassed and bullied by Muslim mob.*

"Dearborn is caught in a spiral. A few years ago, peaceful Christian missionaries would quietly come to Dearborn to preach the Gospel. Then security started slapping Christians around, and police began throwing Christians in jail and trampling on the Constitution. This drew some of the more vocal, confrontational, anti-sharia Christian groups to the city (e.g., Terry Jones, Ruben Israel, etc.). But instead of showing the world how peaceful and loving Muslims are, Dearborn reacted with further hostility, even towards peaceful Christian preachers. This, of course, will draw even more anti-sharia groups to Dearborn in the future."[390]

COMMENT: There is a video, unless it has been scrubbed![391]

---

[389] http://www.thegatewaypundit.com/2011/06/marine-reservist-yonathan-melaku-arrested-in-connection-to-dc-military-building-shootings/, retrieved on 31.03.2012.

[390] http://www.answeringmuslims.com/2011/07/christian-preacher-harassed-and-bullied.html, retrieved on 31.03.2012.

[391] http://www.youtube.com/watch?feature=player_embedded&v=43INJy_cf3M, retrieved on 31.03.2012.

<u>October 8.</u> *Mosqueing the workplace: Hertz suspends 35 Muslim workers for abusing special prayer break times, refusing to clock out when praying.*

Pamela Geller says, "Here, yet again, is another glaring example of what I call in my book, *Stop the Islamization of America: A Practical Guide to the Resistance,* the mosqueing of the workplace: the imposing of Islamic law on the secular marketplace. No big media outlet will talk about the bigger picture, but one only needs to look at Europe to see the bleak future if this supremacism goes unchallenged. Demands for accommodation result in ... more demands. Take for example, the Heinz company. Heinz has bent over backward to accommodate these Muslim workers: they have prayer rooms, prayer, etc. They just don't want them leaving work to pray outside of scheduled break times. Mind you, they could easily pray before or after work, but no. This imposes Islam on everyone else. Now Muslim workers are suing Heinz, demanding to be allowed to say prayers in the workplace at the time of day specified by their religion. Is this any different? You'll notice, big companies are always targeted. Why? To set precedent. 'On the part of workers, they don't want to clock out despite being paid because, according to Thompson, they don't want to feel 'monitored' during their religious rituals.' So Hertz is giving them prayer breaks but stipulates that workers must clock out for them. But that's not enough to meet Muslim demands; if they clock out they're being 'monitored.' Beware, America, it's never enough. For years, Hertz-Rent-A-Car has employed dozens of Muslim workers to shuttle its vehicles back and forth between Sea-Tac Airport and its nearby corporate office. The workers, mostly Somali immigrants, earn relatively low pay--about $10 an hour and no benefits--but they insist on one thing: praying two or three times a day. Managers, however, were concerned that the prayer breaks would 'get out of hand,' according to Hertz spokesperson Rich Broome. So they warned employees that they better (sic) start clocking out when they pray. Many refused. So on Friday, the company indefinitely suspended approximately 35 workers."[392]

COMMENT: Pamela Geller's reporting needs no comment!

<u>October 9</u>. *Muslim accuses Wisconsin man of criticizing Islam, attacks him with tire iron.*

"A Wausau man was hospitalized Friday after he was attacked and beaten with a tire iron in what witnesses said was an argument over religion, according to police. The incident occurred shortly before 4 p.m. in the 600 block of Jefferson Street in Wausau. Two men began arguing, and a 47-year-old Wausau man was struck in the head with a tire iron, Wausau Police Lt. Matt Barnes said Friday night. Police had not released the identity of the victim Friday night. Barnes said the suspect knows the victim, but he could not comment Friday night on what provoked the argument. A witness told a Wausau Daily Herald reporter at the scene that he was sitting on the back porch of a home when the suspect pulled up in his vehicle, got out and accused the victim of criticizing his Islamic religion. The victim denied that he had been critical of Islam, but the suspect then grabbed a tire iron, hit the victim in the head and punched him before speeding off in his vehicle,

---

[392] http://atlasshrugs2000.typepad.com/atlas_shrugs/2011/10/mosqueing-the-workplace-hertz-suspends-34-muslim-workers-for-abusing-special-prayer-break-times-refu.html, retrieved on 31.03.2012.

witnesses said. A second witness, Bakonn Jackson, told the Daily Herald reporter she saw the entire incident, including the tire iron attack. Although police have a lead on the suspect's identity, he was not in custody Friday night and the incident still was under investigation, Barnes said."[393]

COMMENT: A tire iron becomes an instrument of sharia law!

December 19. *Prince Alwaleed bin Talal invests in Twitter.*

"Prince Alwaleed bin Talal, the Saudi billionaire, has acquired a $300m stake in the US microblogging service after buying shares from existing shareholders in a secondary offer, according to one person familiar with the arrangement. The deal will leave him in control of a stake of about 3 per cent (sic) in the site, based on the value of other recent private transactions. The Saudi investment – a joint arrangement between the prince and the Kingdom Holding Company that he controls – came after months of talks and was a 'strategic stake', Kingdom Holding said. Prince Alwaleed – a high-profile investor in technology and media shares including News Corp and Apple – said the deal showed his enthusiasm for 'promising, high-growth businesses with a global impact'. Twitter confirmed the investment but refused to comment on the implications of having a member of the Saudi ruling family among its shareholders"[394]

---

[393]    http://atlasshrugs2000.typepad.com/atlas_shrugs/2011/10/muslim-attacks-wisconsin-man-with-tire-iron-accusing-him-of-criticizing-his-islamic-religion.html, retrieved on 31.03.2012.

[394]   http://atlasshrugs2000.typepad.com/atlas_shrugs/2011/12/there-goes-the-nabe.html, retrieved on 31.03.2012.

COMMENT: The investment is not only an investment in 'promising, high-growth businesses with a global impact'. It is also a way to gain insights into anti-Islam tweeting and possible control of freedom of speech in tweeting. Prince Alwaleed bin Talal is the second largest shareholder of FOX News.[395]

<u>December 23.</u> *Hamas, Hezbollah and Al Qaeda flags fly at Occupy Movement demonstration.*

"I wrote in November here at Atlas that 'despite the criminal media's attempt to glamorize this vile and destructive Occupy movement, it will inevitably usher in the death of the left's chokehold on the American culture. Since the late sixties America has been held hostage by these tyrants. They have done everything to destroy all that is good and original and righteous in America. We will not go down with them. This is O-merica, where lawlessness, anarchy, antisemitism, rape, sexual attacks, the spread of deadly diseases, and now murder are sanctioned, even hailed.' And now add 'alliance with jihad murderers' to that list. **INSIDE OCCUPY D.C.** Bill Gertz Washington Times, December 21, People monitoring the Occupy D.C. movement tell Inside the Ring that the two encampments are fast becoming health hazards. Numerous protesters also recently were sickened with unusual respiratory illnesses. The major emerging problem for the leftists camped out in tents at McPherson Square and Freedom Plaza is rats. **The rodents appear to be moving into the area by the hundreds**, and their numbers are increasing daily. **The McPherson camp appears to be where more radical leftists**

---

[395] http://www.godlikeproductions.com/forum1/message1534398/pg1 was retrieved on 31.03.2012.

**are based.** An observer familiar with the McPherson camp said one distinctive smell coming from the park area is that of methamphetamine being smoked. **Among the flags being flown by some protesters are those from the Palestinian terrorist group Hamas, the Iranian-backed Hezbollah and al Qaeda.**"[396]

COMMENT: Are rats attracting rats?

December 19. *Crusades or jihad?*

Jay Rubenstein, Associate Professor of Medieval History, University of Tennessee, MacArthur Fellow, posts the following article at the Huffington Post: Crusade vs. jihad: Which Is Worse?[397]

COMMENT: Jay Rubenstein concludes that the crusades were much worse than jihad. Not only Muslims rewrite history![398]

December 19. *American Muslim clerics are raising money for Aafia Siddiqui, 'Lady Al Qaeda'.*

"Leading American Muslim clerics are raising money for Aafia Siddiqui, 'Lady Al Qaeda,' who was convicted of attempting to murder Americans in Afghanistan after she was found with plans for a 'mass casualty attack' in the United States, along

---

[396] See http://atlasshrugs2000.typepad.com/atlas_shrugs/2011/12/hamas-hizballah-and-al-qaeda-flags-at-obama-endorsed-occupy-dc.html, retrieved on 31.03.2013.

[397] http://www.huffingtonpost.com/jay-rubenstein/crusade-vs-jihad-was-one-_b_1146871.html, retrieved on 31.03.2012.

[398] http://midnightwatcher.wordpress.com/2012/04/23/education-in-america-textbooks-are-being-systematically-rewritten-to-include-lies-half-truths-and-misleading-narratives-to-promote-islamist-agenda/, retrieved on 31.03.2012.

with a list of New York landmarks. Aafia Siddiqui named Farha Ahmed as her legal counsel in a handwritten letter in October of 2010. Farha Ahmed was running for office in Texas. Farha Ahmed was leading the anti-Geller protests outside my Sugar Land, Texas Tea party event. Farha Ahmed, lawyer for chemical weapons jihadist Lady Al Qaeda, is trying to infiltrate the Republican party by running for office. Ahmed ran for Sugar Land City Council District 4 but was defeated, thanks to great Americans who alerted Texans to the subversive politician in their midst. Ahmed lied about her involvement in the Lady Al Qaeda case. Despite the craven quisling government officials like the DA, who wrote glowing letters to their constituents endorsing the stealth jihadist candidate Ahmed, and the fact that her terror-tied alliances were scrubbed from the web, she was defeated. But remember, the enemy never sleeps and never quits. So she will be back. Raising Money for 'Lady Al-Qaida'"

*IPT News* December 19, 2011 A Northeastern University Muslim chaplain, who also is a Roxbury, Mass. imam, hailed a terrorist convicted of attempting to murder Americans in Afghanistan as 'brave,' while painting the United States as an oppressive nation of infidels. 'They say that she took up a machine gun while they held her captive in the other room and was ready to attack her captives. What a brave woman she is,' Abdullah Faaruuq said at a Dec. 8 fundraiser for Aafia Siddiqui. Siddiqui, a Pakistani scientist also known as 'Lady al-Qaida,' is serving an 86-year prison sentence after being convicted of attempting to assault and murder American officers in Afghanistan. ... The fundraiser, 'In Support of our Sister, Dr. Aafia Siddiqui,' was held at the Islamic Center of

Worcester. Speakers repeatedly cast her prosecution and conviction as unjust. 'What a brave woman she continues to be, and how much her bravery and her faith and her belief warrant our support at this time,' said Faaruuq, an imam at Roxbury's Mosque for the Praising of Allah. 'It is said that we're trying to raise $30,000 tonight. I would say it's better that we've raised your awareness and raised your ire, as your anger against a government who would level the charges that they have against this woman and they say she is guilty. I would say she's only guilty of defending herself.' In addition to lauding Siddiqui's 'bravery,' Faaruuq also condemned American soldiers, the very people who defend America, as 'kafirs,' meaning infidels. 'And if my mother was in the same place,' he said, 'she would have took (sic) her West Indian machete and cut her way through those kafirs.' He repeated an unsubstantiated claim that Siddiqui was abused while in custody. Muslims around the world are 'cowering at the hand of the disbeliever,' Faaruuq said, 'and this one woman locked up deep down, possibly raped and abused, and they're saying that she was a terrorist, afraid of a 100-pound woman. And I say they call this the land of the free and the home of the brave. And I call it the land of the coward and the home of the slave.' The presiding judge who reviewed all the evidence saw things differently. US District Judge Richard M. Berman said 'significant incarceration' was called for because Siddiqui's acts were premeditated. In his sentencing, he also noted anti-American statements witnesses said were made by Siddiqui while firing on the soldiers, like 'I want to kill Americans' and 'Death to America.' It's not the first time Faaruuq has engaged in violent rhetoric while standing up for Siddiqui. Boston-based watchdog of radical Islamists

Charles Jacobs wrote in October that Faaruuq sees cases like Siddiqui's as part of an effort to target Muslims in America. Muslims should 'grab onto the gun and the sword, go out and do your job' in response, Faaruuq said. Faaruuq also is advocating for Tarek Mehanna, on trial in Boston for conspiring to support terrorists and to kill Americans in a foreign country. Also coming to Siddiqui's defense at the fundraiser was Imam Siraj Wahhaj of the Masjid Al-Taqwa mosque in Brooklyn, New York. Wahhaj has a history of defending convicted terrorists, listed as an unindicted co-conspirator and having served as a character witness for Omar Abdel-Rahman, the so-called 'blind sheik,' convicted of conspiring to bomb the World Trade Center in 1993. While acknowledging that he knew little about Siddiqui's case, Wahhaj provided a long explanation of the American judicial system and highlighted its perceived flaws. 'How many people do you think are wrongfully convicted in the United States every year? About 10,000 people, 10,000.' After suggesting that Siddiqui might be one of the 10,000, he pledged $500 to her cause. 'But I will tell you this. I studied the case a little bit. I think that she (sic) innocent. And I think at least there is grounds (sic), there's reasonable doubt. And by law, if there's reasonable doubt, you have to acquit.' The Muslim American Society also has supported Siddiqui, claiming her 'conviction is seriously flawed and her kidnapping and detention is a grave violation of human rights and international law.'"[399]

---

[399] http://atlasshrugs2000.typepad.com/atlas_shrugs/2011/12/raising-money-for-lady-al-qaida-i-want-to-kill-americans-and-death-to-america.html, retrieved on 31.03.2012.

COMMENT: Pamela Geller's reporting needs no commentary. It is truth as truth is!

<u>December 19.</u> *Muslims should be independent of the laws of economics.*

"In addition to being exempt from satirical cartoons, airline security procedures and human rights -- the chattering media classes in all their wisdom have decided that Muslims should also be exempt from the laws of economics. Forget welfare, Muslims are now entitled to media welfare. When normal religions want to put on a show promoting their religion, they build themselves a cable channel. Sadly Bridges TV, the Muslim cable channel dedicated to challenging stereotypes, hating Jews and promoting Islam ran into some trouble when its founder and president beheaded its co-founder, who also happened to be his wife. Muzzammil Hassan turned out not just to be the president and founder of Bridges TV, but also a member of the Muslim Club for Men, and is now challenging stereotypes about Islam at Clinton Correctional Facility. But TLC stepped into the breach to provide Americans with more of that programming challenging stereotypes about Islam that they never asked for. All-American Muslim was founded dedicated to the proposition that Muslims are just like the rest of us. They put on their Hijabs one head at a time just like the rest of us and promote wearing them more often than the Geico reptile comes on to sell insurance. After a media blitz for the launch of the series, the Americans, being the Islamophobic bastards that they are, turned the channel to watch something else. In Orwell's 1984, the television sets were always turned on and only leading party members were allowed to turn down the volume. Sadly for the left that kind of programming is beyond them, though if they could you can bet there would be an Al Gore, Chris Matthews or Stephen Colbert looking back at you through your television. While the left can't penalize viewers for choosing The Walking Dead over The Jersey Shore Goes jihad, they can penalize advertisers, as Lowe's Home Improvement is finding out. Muslim groups have decided to play their losing hand by going after the advertisers who jumped ship in search of television shows that have actual viewers. Mia Farrow and Russell Simmons have called for a boycott of Lowe's until the home improvement giant apologizes for not advertising on a Muslim show with bad ratings. Now that Lowe's has lost Mia Farrow's business it may have to listen, apologize and acknowledge that advertising on failing shows is a new civil right. Forget the four freedoms, there's now a whole raft of Muslim entitlements at the expense of everyone else's freedom. It's bad enough that you can't show a Muslim terrorist on television or in a movie without CAIR's thugs knocking on your door, but now you're obligated to fund Muslim television programs in the bargain. And don't we already have PBS for that? Fighting Muslim stereotypes is a worthwhile cause. And the best place to begin is with the bomb belt, the exploding shoes and the burning underpants. Americans don't question the patriotism of the people trying to kill them because of what's on prime time programming, but because of what's on the news. Judge Judy's famous catchphrase is, 'Don't pee on my leg and tell me it's raining.' The equivalent of that is 'Don't shoot me in the head while shouting Allah Akbar and tell me it's workplace violence.' Technically Major Hasan showing up on base and gunning down American soldiers was violence that took place at work. The same could be said of Muzzammil Hassan, aka Hassan Chop, who killed his wife on location at a cable channel dedicated to showing the moderate side of Islam. Or of the undocumented pilots who flew planes into the World Trade Center and the Pentagon in a truly regrettable incident of workplace violence that had nothing to do with Islam. But instead of changing their reality, Muslim advocates would rather ply us with fiction. The Arabian Nights began with the story of a feminist Muslim king who married virgins and then had them killed the next day and the woman who kept plying him with stories until he decided to spare her life. In the United States, Muslims are determined to play both Scheherazade and the King, telling us fanciful stories until they get around to chopping our heads off. And we're expected to keep retelling them to ourselves so we can go blindly into the abattoir when the time comes, and also to foot the bill. ... But is pandering to Muslim entitlement really the way to check terror? The West has already given Islam extensive and elaborate privileges, beginning with an unquestioned status, the censorship of any offending material and the constant sycophancy of elected officials. Now that we have also decided that Muslim television shows must remain on the air and must be paid for by American companies, no matter how poorly they perform, will Hassan chop and bomb less? Or will he bomb more?"[400]

COMMENT: Muslims are responsible for their own, weird behavior and beliefs. It may be nice that Barack Hussein

---

[400] Refer to http://sultanknish.blogspot.de/2011/12/unlimited-muslim-entitlement.html, retrieved on 31.03.2012.

Obama attends an eid dinner and that we know where the next mosque of the peaceful religion is located. It is also good to know that Muslims cause violence in the name of Allah-Hubal and Mohammed!

December 20. *Hezbollah laundering money from South American drug trafficking.*

"According to a report published by the *World News Tribune*, the Lebanon-based terrorist organization is using American banks and other financial institutions to process money earned from trafficking in South America. The complaint filed by the US Drug Enforcement Administration and the Department of Justice, charges Hezbollah with using the money to buy used cars in the US for transport to West Africa, where they are then sold, mostly in Benin. US Attorney Preet Bhara noted, 'It puts into start relief the nexus between narcotics trafficking and terrorism.' According to a British security source, Hezbollah also sets up straw companies in African and Arab countries which then sell vehicles and/or other goods. Hezbollah operatives also steal passports, which are then used to cover terrorists as they travel the world to raise money."[401]

COMMENT: There are no rules and observance of laws and ethics in spreading Islam. Why should there be? Islam has no ethics.

December 20. *UN praises non-interfaith Saudi Arabia for its interfaith initiative.*

---

[401]    http://atlasshrugs2000.typepad.com/atlas_shrugs/2011/12/hezballah-laundering-drug-money-in-us-banks-html, retrieved on 31.03.2012.

"The U.N. General Assembly on Monday adopted a resolution condemning the stereotyping, negative profiling and stigmatization of people based on their religion, and urging countries to take effective steps 'to address and combat such incidents.' ... The resolution, an initiative of the Organization of Islamic Cooperation (OIC), is based on one passed by the U.N.'s Human Rights Council in Geneva last spring. The State Department last week hosted a meeting to discuss ways of 'implementing' it. Every year since 1999 the OIC has steered through the U.N.'s human rights apparatus a resolution condemning the 'defamation of religion,' which for the bloc of 56 Muslim states covered incidents ranging from satirizing Mohammed in a newspaper cartoon to criticism of shari'a and post-9/11 security check profiling. Critics regard the measure as an attempt to outlaw valid and critical scrutiny of Islamic teachings, as some OIC states do through controversial blasphemy laws at home. Strongly opposed by mostly Western democracies, the divisive 'defamation' resolution received a dwindling number of votes each year, with the margin of success falling from 57 votes in 2007 to 19 in 2009 and just 12 last year. This year's text was a departure, in that it dropped the 'defamation' language and included a paragraph that reaffirms 'the positive role that the exercise of the right to freedom of opinion and expression and the full respect for the freedom to seek, receive and impart information can play in strengthening democracy and combating religious intolerance.' The nod to freedom of expression won the resolution the support of the US and other democracies, with the Obama administration and others hailing it as a breakthrough after years of acrimonious debate. Secretary of State Hillary Clinton took the opportunity of the State Department-hosted talks with foreign governments, the OIC and other international bodies last week to stress the importance of freedom of speech in the US. She argued that 'the best way to treat offensive speech is by people either ignoring it or combating it with good arguments and good speech that overwhelms it. ... Nonetheless, the resolution adopted in New York on Monday does contain elements that concern some free speech and religious freedom advocates. It calls on states 'to take effective measures to ensure that public functionaries in the conduct of their public duties do not discriminate against an individual on the basis of religion or belief.' Governments also are expected to make 'a strong effort to counter religious profiling, which is understood to be the invidious use of religion as a criterion in conducting questionings, searches and other law enforcement investigative procedures.' 'Effective measures' to counter cases of religious stereotyping and stigmatization include education, interfaith dialogue and 'training of government officials.' And in the worst cases, those of 'incitement to imminent violence' based on religion, the resolution calls on countries to implement 'measures to criminalize' such behavior. Also of note is the fact that the resolution singles out for praise only one interfaith initiative – and that initiative was established by Saudi Arabia, a leading OIC member-state with a long history of enforcing blasphemy laws."[402]

COMMENT: There is no interfaith atmosphere in Saudi Arabia. Islam has 'incitement to imminent violence' based on

---

[402] http://atlasshrugs2000.typepad.com/atlas_shrugs/2011/12/oic-driven-un-adopts-anti-free-speech-resolution-championed-by-obama-administration.html, retrieved on 31.03.2012.

religion (non-believers must be killed or pay special taxes) 'Measures to criminalize' such behavior are indeed necessary!

December 20. *Man convicted of plotting to kill US soldiers.*

"A Massachusetts man was convicted Tuesday, December 20, 2011 of conspiring to help al-Qaida and plotting to kill US soldiers in Iraq. Tarek Mehanna, 24, of Sudbury, faced four terror-related charges and three charges of lying to authorities. A federal jury found him guilty on all counts after deliberating for about 10 hours. Prosecutors said Mehanna and two friends conspired to travel to Yemen so they could receive training at a terrorism camp and eventually go on to Iraq to fight and kill US soldiers there. When the men were unable to find such a training camp, Mehanna returned home and began to see himself as part of the al-Qaida 'media wing,' translating materials promoting violent jihad and distributing them over the internet, prosecutors said. Mehanna, who was born in the US and raised in the Boston suburbs, will be sentenced April 12 and could be sent to prison for the rest of his life. His mother, Souad Mehanna, sobbed after the verdict was read and was consoled by her younger son, Tamer. Mehanna's lawyers also wept. Mehanna's father, Ahmed, a professor at the Massachusetts College of Pharmacy and Health Sciences, said he was stunned by the verdict. ... He said. 'It was political.'"[403]

COMMENT: Evidently, Tarek Mehanna's actions were humane.

---

[403] Refer to http://atlasshrugs2000.typepad.com/atlas_shrugs/2011/12/tarek-mehanna-guilty-devout-muslim-found-guilty-of-conspiring-against-us.html, retrieved on 30.03.2012.

December 21. *Americans will have swords at their necks.*

"Jordanian Sheik Nader Tamimi, Mufti of the Palestinian Liberation Army, to the West: We Will Restore the Caliphate and You Will Pay the Jizya 'or Else We Will Bring the Sword to Your Necks'"[404]

COMMENT: This is all part of the Palestinian *liberation* of Palestine. Liberation for what?

December 22. *Hijabs in ROTC*

"This is how they impose Islam in the public square. Chip, chip, chip. Anywhere Islamic law conflicts with American law, it is American law that must give way. And there is ..... no end to these accommodations (submissions). *...Defense department agrees to allow Muslim cadets to wear hijabs Orlando Sentinel December 22.* The Council on American-Islamic Relations (CAIR) announced today that the Department of Defense will begin allowing Muslim and Sikh students who wear an Islamic head scarf (hijab) or a turban to participate in the Junior Reserve Officers' Training Corps (JROTC). 'We welcome the fact that Muslim and Sikh students nationwide will now be able to participate fully in JROTC leadership activities while maintaining their religious beliefs and practices,' said CAIR National Executive Director Nihad Awad. In October, the Washington-based Muslim civil rights and advocacy organization wrote to Defense Secretary Leon Panetta after a 14-year-old Muslim student at Ravenwood High School in Brentwood, Tenn., was forced to transfer out of a JROTC class

---

[404]    http://atlasshrugs2000.typepad.com/atlas_shrugs/2011/12/palestinian-liberation-army-mufti-caliphate-will-return-and-west-will-pay-jizya-or-else-you-will-bri.html, retrieved on 31.03.2012.

when her commanding officers told her she could not wear hijab while marching in the September homecoming parade. CAIR requested constitutionally-protected religious accommodations for the girl and for future Muslim JROTC participants."[405]

COMMENT: They might as well be allowed to wear brown shirts and the left turning symbol of the sun in the crescent of the moon. There is no difference. Muslims are using constitutional freedoms to destroy the *Constitution*.

<u>December 23.</u> *Manhattan Children's Museum gets funding for 'Muslim Worlds' exhibit.*

"Whirling dervishes, mosaics and 1,001 tales will soon be coming to the Upper West Side, thanks to a $40,000 grant from the National Endowment of the Humanities. The Children's Museum of Manhattan says its future exhibition new 'Muslim Worlds' is the first show of its kind in the US geared toward a family audience. ... According to information provided by the controversial Council on American-Islamic Relations, 'Muslim Worlds' will have hands-on exhibits, performances and other events geared toward getting children involved with the thousands of years of cultural heritage that has come from the Muslim world. Besides hosting individual visitors, the Children's Museum will extend invitations for school groups including those from public schools. Although the museum promises to 'bring to life the similarities and differences of Muslim cultures,' John Jay College Sociology Professor

---

[405] See http://atlasshrugs2000.typepad.com/atlas_shrugs/2011/12/obama-defense-dept-allows-muslim-cadets-to-wear-hijabs-or-turbans-hamas-tied-cair-thrilled.html, retrieved on 31.03.2012.

Mucahit Bilici said that exhibits like this operate on the assumption that Muslim people are separate from American society. Visitors to the Children's Museum of Manhattan dance as part of a festival celebrating Muslim culture. 'I would say that the major problem with this project is that it treats Muslims as exclusively external people -- as foreigners,' he said. 'I'm sure that a significant percentage of their audience, like the kids who will visit that exhibition, will be Muslim. I wish that they would be aware of this and that they would frame it in a much more inclusive way.' Cyrus McGoldrick, the civil rights manager of the New York Council on American Islamic Relations, argues that the exhibit will do good things for the Muslim community. He said a lot of the civil rights violations that he investigates happen to Muslim kids who are mocked by their peers at school. The Children's Museum of Manhattan says its future exhibition new 'Muslim Worlds' is the first show of its kind in the US geared toward a family audience. But many detractors believe this is an example of liberal-left hypocrisy. 'Imagine a group of Methodists or Anabaptists holding an exhibition in a government-funded facility? Does anyone believe the politicians and the ACLU would allow such a show to be held in a city-financed facility with audiences being brought in by public school teachers? How long would that last?' asks political strategist and consultant Mike Baker. 'Tolerance is one thing,' says former NYPD Officer Edie Aquina, 'but why are we bending over backwards for the sake of political correctness. This group CAIR, for example, has repeatedly attacked the NYPD for trying to protect New Yorkers and Americans from radical Islamic terrorists. Will this Muslim World exhibition feature the role of Islam in the slaughter of 3,000 people on 9-11? Or the hate speech directed at Jews?"[406]

COMMENT: "Thousands of years of cultural heritage that has come from the Muslim world. Will the Children's Museum of Manhattan have exhibits on the hundreds of millions of victims of over a millennium of jihadi wars, land appropriations, cultural annihilations and enslavements? Will it have video on the over 18,000 Islamic jihad attacks since 911, each one done with the imprimatur of a Muslim cleric? Will it showcase the ongoing jihad against the Jews and Christians and Hindus and Sikhs? And 'Muslims in America"? I look forward to seeing the profiles of the 9/11 hijackers, explaining how they were motivated to kill by the quran (sic). That could be right next to the study center dedicated to expunging the quran (sic) of its violent teachings. There should also be exhibits dedicated to Muslim Major Nidal Malik Hasan, showing how Islam drove him to murder 13 people at Fort Hood and led another Muslim, "moderate" Naser Abdo, to try to imitate him. There should also be exhibits all about Khalid Aldawsari, the jihad murder plotter in Lubbock, Texas; Muhammad Hussain, the jihad bomb plotter in Baltimore; Mohamed Mohamud, the jihad Christmas tree lighting ceremony bomb plotter in Portland; Faisal Shahzad, the failed Times Square jihad car bomber; Abdulhakim Mujahid Muhammad, the Little Rock, Arkansas jihad murderer; Naveed Haq, the cold-blooded jihad killer at the Jewish Community Center in Seattle; Mohammed Reza Taheri-Azar, the jihad attempted murderer in Chapel Hill,

---

[406] http://atlasshrugs2000.typepad.com/atlas_shrugs/2011/12/nyc-taxpayer-funded-childrens-museum-to-hold-muslim-program-.html, retrieved on 31.03.2012.

North Carolina; Umar Farouk Abdulmutallab, the Christmas balls bomber in the airplane over Detroit; and all the rest. There could be more exhibits dedicated to the stealth jihad -- to exposing, for example, grifter Gamal, radical Rauf and Daisy the Con, and their sinister and deceptive Ground Zero Mosque project, and all the Islamic supremacist initiatives to assert Islamic law over American law all over the country. And it could also explain why security is so tight at synagogues right now. All this could serve as a warning to non-Muslims to be resolute in defense of freedom against jihad. But you and I know this exhibit will showcase none of that. Instead, it will be another Hamas-tied CAIR attempt to portray Muslims as the victims of 'Islamophobia.' At the taxpayers' expense."[407]

COMMENT: Visit the museum to see America's Enemy Number One!

<u>December 23.</u> *More faked hate.*

"Hamas-tied CAIR was unavailable for comment ... too busy planting more imaginary 'islamophobia' stories in the lapdog servile press. HuffPo trumpets anti-Muslim hate crime that wasn't. Robert Spencer at jihadwatch (sic). In order to deflect attention away from jihad activity and try to portray Muslims as victims, so as to shame non-Muslims into not investigating or even being suspicious of further jihad activity, Hamas-linked CAIR and other Muslims have not hesitated to fabricate 'hate crimes.' CAIR and other groups like it *want* and *need* hate crimes against Muslims, because they can use them for political

---

[407] http://atlasshrugs2000.typepad.com/atlas_shrugs/2011/12/nyc-taxpayer-funded-childrens-museum-to-hold-muslim-program-.html, retrieved on 31.03.2012.

points and as weapons to intimidate people into remaining silent about the jihad threat. Also, so avid are some Muslims to discredit me and obscure the truths I tell that they were even prepared to blame me for a murder in New Jersey that turned out to be a love triangle that the killer tried to frame as an anti-Muslim hate crime. Impervious to shame, the Anti-Muslim Hate Crime industry keeps churning out spurious product. In this case it was a HuffPo Leftist pseudo-journalist who was trumpeting the fake hate crime: 'Another Huffington Post Hate Crime Fizzles (Aisha Khan Found Safe),' by David Wood at Answering Muslims, December 22: [...] In a recent Huffington Post article about Islamophobia and the Lowe's controversy, Daniel Tutt drew his readers' attention to two vicious hate crimes against Muslims -- clear proof that Islamophobia is rampant and spreading: In the background of this grassroots work, two tragic events have taken place, which reveal the real world 'human impact' of Islamophobia. In Kansas City, a young Muslim college student, Aisha Khan has gone missing after complaining to her family of a drunken man harassing her. In Houston, Texas a Muslim man named Yaqub Bham was severely beaten in what family members are calling a hate crime. These events show the urgency of the problem at hand. What evidence did Tutt have to support his claims? A Muslim student went missing after a drunken man harassed her. Tutt sees this as clear proof that Khan was abducted by anti-Muslim bigots (probably those who regularly visit jihad Watch (sic) and Atlas Shrugs). And a Muslim man's family is calling an attack a 'hate crime.' Tutt doesn't bother questioning his assessment at all. Now for the reality check. Aisha Khan wasn't abducted at all. ABC News reported this morning: Aisha Khan, the 19-

year-old Kansas college student missing for nearly a week has been found safe and unharmed, according to ABC News' Kansas City affiliate KMBC. Overland Park Police Officer Brian Schnavel said that Khan was not abducted or held against her will, according to KMBC. Schnavel said no criminal act occurred. Will Tutt apologize for falsely accusing Americans of a hate crime against a Muslim girl? We can only hope. Hope all you like, David, but 'journalists' like Tutt have no sense of accountability or responsibility. They behave this way all the time, and *never* backtrack or apologize. As for Tutt's other example of Islamophobia, the evidence isn't in yet. However, based on the reports so far, the man who committed the attack seems to be insane."[408]

COMMENT: There are insane pseudo-reporters, insane criminals, and there are insane Muslims!

December 29. *Where is free speech?*

"Hamas-tied CAIR has been calling for some time for BNI (Bare Naked Islam) to be shut down because of comments. Wordpress (the blog platform) responded by shutting down BNI in late November and then reinstating it; now it has been shut down again, and the Hamas-linked nazi group CAIR is doing a victory dance. They're claiming credit, although details are sketchy: the BNI publisher says Wordpress hasn't given her any explanation for suspending the site, and that she has been monitoring comments closely since November 26, when the site was first shut down. This is how BNI's publisher explained

---

[408] See http://atlasshrugs2000.typepad.com/atlas_shrugs/2011/12/puffho-trumpets-another-anti-muslim-hate-crime-that-wasnt.html, retrieved on 31.03.2012.

what happened in an email to me: I allowed them to delete ALL comments prior to 11/26 and they did. After that I was very careful to delete anything that could be deemed a threat. In CAIR's press release today they mentioned the comments from the other post all of which were deleted immediately. There were no new comments that they listed today. But ... they did mention my close involvement with the All American Muslim/Lowe's Buycott campaign. I had about 12 or 14 different posts on that so I think the ratings dive for AAM was what made them threaten WP with a lawsuit. I am just assuming as WP didn't say this. That any rational freedom lover would listen to the enemies of free speech at Hamas-tied CAIR is beyond the pale. Across the web, I have seen calls for a holocaust II, killing Jews, killing conservatives, killing Blacks, etc. I have been called a neo-kikess while being libeled, smeared and defamed. And Hamas-tied CAIR itself is a libel machine. Calls for my death and execution have been posted to youtube, twitter and other websites. The death threats and calls for genocide are daily."

"Just recently there was this comment: xxxsampsonxxxX has made a comment on Pamela Geller: **THIS BITCH SHOULD GET SHOT. I H8 HER.** The blood libel against Israel organ trafficking in Haiti was started in the notoriously anti-Jewish Huffington Post comment section. Anti-Semitism is raging in the pages of the NY Times, Time magazine, LA Times, etc. Nothing was ever said or done -- that's free speech. I condemn all calls for killing and genocide. I don't know what was said at Bare Naked Islam. Some of what I see I would not host or post on Atlas. But I don't CAIR. The difference between an exchange of ideas and an exchange of blows is self-evident. If I

307

had a blog on wordpress, I would pull it. I would. Because it's only a matter of time until something you say doesn't meet with the Muslim Brotherhood guidelines. The fundamental principle of free speech is the protection of all speech, not just speech we like. Because who decides what's good and what's forbidden? The Hamas-tied thugs and enemies of free speech at CAIR? *I disapprove of what you say, but I will defend to the death your right to say it – Voltaire.*"[409]

COMMENT: Has free speech in the United States come to mean that it is free speech when and only when a group or individual political leader dictates what free speech is?

December 30. *Muslims are the real victims of 9/11.*

"*All-American Muslim* stoops to a new low. The Hizb'Allah imam wasn't enough. The coerced conversion and banishment of the dog wasn't enough. Now they're going to school and admonish us about how Muslims were the real victims of 9/11. TV show on Muslims takes on Sept. 11 attacks. … A television show about members of a Muslim community in Michigan is focusing what may be its second-to-last episode almost entirely on the conflicted feelings that its featured participants have about marking anniversaries of the Sept. 11 terrorist attacks. Why might it be the second-to-last episode? Was it the media controversy? Or perhaps the boring story line? The coerced conversion to Islam? The banishment of the newly converted husband's dog? Or perhaps it was the Hezb'Allah-supporting (the same Hezb'Allah killing our CIA agents in Lebanon and Iran) Husham Alhusayni -- the main spiritual leader of the

---

[409] http://atlasshrugs2000.typepad.com/atlas_shrugs/2011/12/bni-shut-down-again-hamas-tied-cair-does-victory-dance.html, retrieved on 31.03.2012.

Karbala Center in Dearborn, who is featured in *All-American Muslim*. In the program, Hezbo-linked Alhusayni is seen presiding over marriages within Muslim families in Dearborn.[410] ... The episode of TLC's 'All-American Muslim' airs Sunday (10 p.m. EST). The series attracted attention earlier this month when a conservative Christian group called on advertisers to boycott the series, calling it 'propaganda that riskily hides the Islamic agenda's clear and present danger to American liberties and traditional values.' I do not recall such a media uproar over Media Matters and other Soros orgs' boycott of Beck. Or Rush. Or any program boycott. There was never such a media storm over the calls to boycott Israel products or for the divestment from Israel. Two companies, the Lowe's home improvement chain and travel planning website Kayak.com, announced they were pulling ads. TLC hasn't said how many companies responded to the Florida Family Association's call to stop sponsoring the show. The controversy prompted a backlash of people protesting against Lowe's. Some new advertisers have signed on since then, TLC General Manager Amy Winter said Thursday. Filming for the reality TV series took place during commemorations for the 10th anniversary of the attacks. Both TLC and the show's characters, Muslims living in and around Dearborn, a suburb of Detroit at the heart of one of the largest Arab-American populations outside the Middle East, wanted to address the topic, Winter said. 'I'm very proud of it,' she said. 'What you'll see in there is a community with a range of emotions that they express over

---

[410] For the complete, true background information read http://atlasshrugs2000.typepad.com/atlas shrugs/2011/12/the-shocking-truth-about-lowes-and-all-american-muslim.html, retrieved on 31.03.2012.

what was probably one of the most pivotal moments in our nation's history.' Mike Jaafar, a deputy sheriff who participated in a Sept. 11 memorial service at Tiger Stadium in Detroit, helped law enforcement prepare for any problems related to the anniversary. He choked up when recalling how police officers in New York City were killed as they tried to rescue people at the World Trade Center. 'You think about your guys who work for you, going into a building and not coming home,' he said. Nawal Auode was a high school sophomore on Sept. 11, 2001, when her mother called to say she was picking her up at school. Her mother found out about the attacks as she was passing out flyers to advertise a day care center and a man spit at her and ordered her off his porch. 'It was the first time I realized that people looked at me as less American,' said Suehaila Amen. 'As a person who was born and raised in this country, it was very difficult.' If the Islamic community had been honest and patriotic after 9/11, instead of claiming to be the real victims and denying the key role that the quran's (sic) teachings of violence had in 9/11, Americans would be a lot less suspicious of them. Auode said she dreads the anniversary of the attacks because of a sense that members of her community have to defend themselves for something they had nothing to do with. That's at the root of the biggest conflict in Sunday's episode. One woman talks about how important it was to attend a Sept. 11 commemoration, but her adult-age children didn't want to go. One man, Bilal Amen, traveled to New York City to visit the Sept. 11 memorial because, he said, 'I want to see the place that changed my life.' Changed *his* life. What about the lives of all the people who were killed, and their families? Another woman, Nina Bazzy, spoke angrily about the Sept. 11 terrorists

310

and said they weren't real Muslims because 'a real Muslim would not do anything like that.' She said Osama bin Laden made life difficult for many Muslims in the United States. 'He ruined it for us,' Bazzy said. 'He ruined it for our kids. He made us scared in our own homes.' 'He ruined it for us.' For the Muslims. Not a word about how he ruined it for the 3,000 who were killed, or for their families. And 'he made us scared in our own homes'? Of whom? Who is breaking into Muslims' homes? This is pure victimhood fantasy. No one is bothering innocent Muslims in the US. 'All-American Muslim' ends its eight-episode first season on Jan. 8. Its ratings are considered disappointing for TLC, and the attention caused by this month's controversy didn't improve them. Based on ratings alone, a second season would be considered unlikely. Working in its favor is TLC's pride in a series that spotlights communities that many viewers aren't familiar with. Also working in its favor is that Islamic supremacists all over the country will charge TLC with 'Islamophobia' if the show is canceled."[411]

COMMENT: The Koran says in its 169 war suras that you are not a Muslim until you do commit acts of violence and killings of non-believers. What has caused some Muslims in America to believe the way they do is the fact that they do not know their own Koran and what it teaches. If one asks them about the war suras or the suras against women, they will claim that they are non-existent, at best only guidelines that were in effect during Mohammed's day, but not now in the modern world. It is a two-

---

[411]   http://atlasshrugs2000.typepad.com/atlas_shrugs/2011/12/all-american-muslim-dawah-show-to-highlight-how-911-hurt-muslims.html, retrieved on 31.03.2012. TLC is a television network that reports on life's realities.

pronged strategy: denial and rationalization for the past and taqiyya application in the present.

## 2012

January 6. *Michael Coren and family threatened by Muslim!*

"Michael Coren is host of 'The Arena' on the Sun News Network. Unlike most other talk show hosts, Coren discusses Islam in a critical manner. Not surprisingly, Muslims are upset, offering the standard 'Don't say Islam is violent or we'll kill you' irony so familiar to those of us who dare speak about Islam, the Qur'an, and Muhammad.[412]

COMMENT: The report is supported with a video, unless it has been scrubbed.[413]

January 10. *Islamic extremist shoots at businesses in Alabama City to lure police officers, engages them in a shootout.*

"It's only Tuesday but this has already been a banner week for American jihadists. First, we had the arrest of Sami Osmakac, a Kosovo-born Islamist and U.S. citizen who authorities say was plotting terrorist attacks against targets in Tampa. Then we learned of the arrest of Islamic convert Craig Baxham, a Maryland resident and former U.S. Army soldier (trained in intelligence and cryptology, no less) who traveled to Africa in an attempt join up with the Al Qaeda-linked terror group Al Shabaab in Somalia. Now comes the curious case of 21-year-

---

[412] http://atlasshrugs2000.typepad.com/atlas_shrugs/2012/01/michael-coren-family-threatened-by-muslim.html, retrieved on 31.03.2012.

[413] http://www.youtube.com/watch?feature=player_embedded&v=X4mbTL0d4fs, retrieved on 31.03.2012.

old Luis Ibarra-Hernandez, who says he was just trying to draw attention to Islam when he opened fire on police in Alabama. Here's more, from the Gadsden Times:

A man thought to be an Islamic extremist is believed to have shot the windows out of at least two businesses in Alabama City early Sunday to lure police officers to the area and engage them in a shootout. Luis Ibarra-Hernandez, 21, from Albertville, was charged today with attempted murder, according to a news release from the Gadsden Police Department. 'After the man was taken into custody, he reported that he knew he must do something extreme to draw attention to Islam and himself, so he planned to shoot police officers,' Gadsden Police Capt. Regina May said. Gadsden police officers responded to alarm calls for glass breakage after doors were shot out about 1:30 a.m. Sunday at AutoZone and Rainbow Food Mart near the intersection of 27th Street and West Meighan Boulevard. While investigating the broken doors and determining they were shot out, officers heard gunfire and spotted a man near the old CVS building. The man knew he had been seen and ran toward the Cathedral of Praise church parking lot, then started firing rounds at the officers. The man continued to run through several blocks and at one point was in the Dwight Baptist Church parking lot. Shots were fired over about six blocks, and at least eight officers were shot at, before officers talked the man into dropping his weapon. ...

The three above-mentioned cases represent the future of jihad in America. Small-scale. Low-tech. Inexpensive. Self-starters who may not have any links to overseas terror groups and are often radicalized online. And notice also the non-traditional profiles of the three alleged jihadis: one white, one African-American and one Hispanic."[414]

COMMENT: This is the strategy of Islam in America: chip away at the culture one small step at a time, regardless of the nationalities of those doing the chipping.

January 10. *Terror suspect arrested over 'bomb plot' in Florida, caught on camera assaulting Christian protesters and threatening viewers to convert to Islam 'before it is too late'.*

"Moment terror suspect, 25, arrested over 'bomb plot' in Florida was caught on camera brawling with Christian protesters. A Muslim accused of plotting to bomb locations in the U.S. has apparently been identified as the same man assaulting Christian protesters in a video posted online.[415] Sami Osmakac, 25, an immigrant from Kosovo, was said to have been planning an attack in Tampa, Florida using a car bomb, machine guns and other explosives. Kosovo? Doesn't he know that all the Muslims there are moderate and peaceful, and love America? The message from Abdul Samia, believed to be one of Osmakac's aliases, warns viewers to convert to Islam 'before it is too late.'"[416]

---

[414]    http://blogs.cbn.com/stakelbeckonterror/archive/2012/01/10/alabama-muslim-opens-fire-on-police-wanted-to-draw-attention.aspx, retrieved on 31.03.2012.

[415]http://www.youtube.com/watch?feature=player_embedded&v=yJvGGuLr Vzo, retrieved on 31.03.2012.

[416]    http://www.jihadwatch.org/2012/01/florida-jihad-suspect-brawled-with-christians-warned-on-youtube-to-convert-to-islam-before-it-is-too.html, retrieved on 31.03.2012.

COMMENT: The original reports from the Daily Mail have been scrubbed from the internet.[417]

January 24. *Muslim football players arrested.*

DEARBORN HEIGHTS — "A figurative beat down turned literal beating has led to the felony arrests of a group of local high school football players. Police arrested four Star International Academy seniors Wednesday on aggravated assault charges stemming from an altercation in the team's last game of the season. The players -- Mohamed Ahmed, Fanar Al-Alsady, Hadee Attia and Ali Bajjey, all age 17 -- are accused of gang-beating Lutheran Westland's quarterback as time expired in Lutheran's 47-6 drubbing of Star on Oct. 21. ... Lutheran's quarterback was set to take a knee to run out the clock. Before the snap, referees told both teams to refrain from contact, police said. After the snap, however, the four arrested Star players burst through the line and allegedly manhandled Lutheran's quarterback. Police said they ripped off his helmet, threw him to the ground and punched and kicked him repeatedly. The incident came to an end after coaches, players and refs stepped in and broke it up. Police took a statement from a referee who said he heard a Star player say to hit the referees after being directed not to hit the other team. According to published reports, Lutheran's quarterback suffered a concussion from the beating."[418]

---

[417] http://www.dailymail.co.uk/news/article-2084551/Sami-Osmakac-Terror-suspect-caught-camera-brawling-Christian-protesters.html, retrieved on 31.03.2012.

[418] http://www.pressandguide.com/articles/2012/01/14/news/doc4f10672d3e47d004412938.txt, retrieved on 31.03.2012.

COMMENT: MSNBC stated that Hamas-CAIR contends, "that the allegations are not true. CAIR said there is new video showing the incident was 'greatly exaggerated' and that the players were targeted because they were Arab-American. 'We believe that from the very beginning that (sic), if these young men may have been of a different ethnicity, of a different religion, different skin color, that Dearborn Heights police officer most likely would not have been so aggressive in the means in which he carried out his investigation,' said CAIR Executive Director Dawud Walid."

The MSNBC report about Hamas-CAIR's position has been scrubbed from the Internet. Furthermore, this author deems Pamela Geller's comments noteworthy. *It appears that the contention is that Muslims can beat up anybody they want, but if they are charged, it is Islamophobia. One can only imagine the nationwide crackdown on infidels if four Christian football players attacked a Muslim quarterback (and then alleged Jesusophobia). I'm not sure what motivated these Muslim players to rip off a quarterback's helmet and beat him senseless, but if their lawyer is claiming that their arrests were racially motivated (Islamophobia, of course), then I will say that the attacks themselves were racially motivated (Christianophobia). Could you imagine the media uproar if four Christian players had given a Muslim quarterback a concussion?*[419]

---

[419] See http://atlasshrugs2000.typepad.com/atlas_shrugs/2012/01/muslim-football-players-in-dearborn-heights-arrested-for-assault-on-christian-quarterback-.html, retrieved on 31.03.2012.

February 3. *CAIR pressures West Point.*

"The US Military Academy at West Point is going forward with a scheduled prayer breakfast next week, despite the controversy over the originally scheduled keynote speaker. As previously reported on OneNewsnow, Lt. Gen. Jerry Boykin (USA-Ret.) decided to withdraw from speaking at the prayer breakfast after the Council on American-Islamic Relations (CAIR) and several left-wing groups pressured the Academy to disinvite him from the event. They claimed that allowing the former Army special operations commander to speak would be disrespectful to Muslim cadets. Now the Academy has announced a West Point chaplain will be the keynote speaker. Boykin says the majority of the leadership in the US is unwilling to confront the reality of what CAIR and other radical Islamic groups are doing. 'So instead, they reach out to these people and they give them a lot of credibility. I think the bottom line is that the [country's] leadership is afraid of them,' he suggests. 'I think they're afraid of terrorism. I think they're afraid to take them on because of the liberal media. The media is going to support the enemy. That's the bottom line -- the *mainstream* media is.' That is why the former intelligence officer says people of faith must be willing to take a stand. 'Organizations like the Council on American-Islamic Relations and these atheist groups are going to be doing exactly what the homosexual lobby has done in America. They're going to be gaining strength to the point that they dominate the dialogue in America on ... our social and spiritual matters,' he warns. And Boykin assures that he will not be deterred from telling the

317

truth about the dangers of sharia law and what organizations like the Muslim Brotherhood are doing in America."[420]

COMMENT: If you make people fear you enough, they will do what you want them to do. The same holds true for organizations. If the military cadets who are Muslims would be suffering disrespect by the speaker who was a commanding general, then that logic will be used by Muslim soldiers to refuse to take orders from non-Muslim officers. Muslims, regardless of their being military or government officials, or not, obey the Koran and the teachings of Mohammed only. If they do not obey the Koran and the teachings of Mohammed, they are not Muslims.

On February 3. *Sharia law in Philadelphia.*[421]

The Philadelphia City Council passed a resolution welcoming sharia law in the city and in Pennsylvania.

COMMENT: Philadelphia is the *City of Brotherly Love.* Once there is acceptance of sharia law in Philadelphia or anywhere else in America, the smallest town or the largest city, there is no longer love for humanity's brothers and sisters, unless they are all Muslims. It is a proven fact of history. There are approximately 285,950 Jews living in Philadelphia who live under American law. There are approximately 30,000 Muslims living in Philadelphia who want to live under sharia law. sharia law says that it is the duty of Muslims to kill Jews and other

---

[420] See http://www.onenewsnow.com/Culture/Default.aspx?id=1528354, retrieved on 31.03.2012.

[421] See http://creepingsharia.wordpress.com/2012/02/03/philadelphia-city-council-passes-bill-oking-sharia-law/, retrieved on 24.03.2012.

non-believers. Sharia law is the highest law in Islam and takes precedence over the *Constitution for the United States of America*.[422] Muslim participation in interfaith activities in any city is only a ruse, a deception to placate non-Muslims. Although imams have issued fatwas against terrorists, this must also be regarded as a deceptive tactic of al-taqiyya.[423] There is no need to issue fatwas. There are laws in the United States of America against terrorist activities. Issuing fatwas is another method of undermining the American legal system.

February 4. *Freedom of speech threatened.*

"Paul Marshall, a religious liberty expert, says that attempts to "export" Islamic anti-blasphemy laws to the West could pose a threat to freedom of speech in the US. Marshall, senior fellow at the Hudson Institute's Center for Religious Freedom, said that many governments deliberately manipulate alleged instances of blasphemy by provoking popular outrage, enabling them to advance 'particular policy goals.' Marshall made his remarks Feb. 3 at Hillsdale College's Allan P. Kirby, Jr. Center for Constitutional Studies and Citizenship in Washington, D.C. He argued that blasphemy codes in the Muslim world are used to stifle religious minorities, as well as Muslim reformers who support religious liberty, freedom of speech and democracy. In the US, Marshall observed, courts generally uphold the First Amendment's free speech protections. But he said that America is still threatened by blasphemy laws, and cited efforts by the

---

[422] Refer to http://pluralism.org/reports/view/75http://en.wikipedia.org/wiki/American_Jews, retrieved on 31.03.2012.

[423] http://www.islamicity.com/forum/printer_friendly_posts.asp?TID=16191, retrieved on 31.03.2012.

Organisation of Islamic Cooperation to promote international laws that ban insults to Islam, through the United Nations. Marshall also cautioned against a growing tendency towards 'extra-legal intimidation,' which involves private individuals pre-emptively censoring themselves -- often under the guise of religious sensitivity -- because they realize that it is 'too dangerous' to insult Islam. To illustrate the effectiveness of this intimidation, he gave multiple examples of books, newspapers and television shows that refused to publish content that could be deemed offensive to Islam, although they chose to carry similar material that mocked Christianity and other religions. He also recounted the 2010 story of Molly Norris, a Seattle cartoonist, who called for an 'Everybody Draw Mohammed Day' in response to such self-censorship. She received death threats for the suggestion and, under the advice of the FBI, changed her name and went into hiding. Marshall also warned of the potential for government policies that seek to restrict speech. He observed that the Obama administration has vocalized a commitment to fighting 'negative stereotypes of Islam,' although it has not done the same for other religions. Secretary of State Hillary Clinton, he noted, invited the Organisation of Islamic Cooperation to a meeting in Washington, D.C. to discuss how the US could carry out this commitment. According to Marshall, the December 2011 meeting featured presentations on how America should fix its treatment of Muslims. It was also suggested that the US should learn from countries in the organization which use the death penalty to fight blasphemy within their borders, he said. Although Clinton claimed to be simply pursuing tolerance, Marshall said it was concerning that she was partnering with an organization that has been aggressively lobbying to restrict free speech through legal controls. He urged the Obama administration to end this partnership and instead promote the idea that 'in open, boisterous, free societies' all religions will likely be subject to criticism. The American founders considered freedom of speech to be critical, Marshall concluded, adding that 'their example is always needed, but never more so than in a time such as this.'"[424]

COMMENT: More should be done on how Muslims can fix their evil treatment of non-Muslims and American freedoms.

February 5. *Have your schools been indoctrinated with whitewashed Islamic propaganda yet?*

"If you are new to this website (barenakedislam), you might not know there is a destructive propaganda war being waged in our nation's classrooms. More and more, we are seeing extensive lessons on Islam in the public schools, extolling the virtues of Islamic misogyny and waxing poetic about sharia. One of the worst ideas is inviting Muslim leaders and/or clerics into the schools in the interest of multicultural 'tolerance' and 'awareness.' Religious studies are generally unwelcome in public schools, with the exception of the study of Islam. Perhaps there are people in the education system who think that a broader understanding of Islam will make it easier to understand barbaric acts of mass murder, such as we saw on September 11, 2001. But there is another more likely goal:

---

[424] http://www.catholicnewsagency.com/news/us-free-speech-faces-islamic-blasphemy-law-pressure-analyst-says/ Washington D.C., Feb 4, 2012 / 07:05 am (CNA), retrieved on 31.03.2012.

making all religions morally equivalent, so that no specific religion is considered superior to any other."[425]

COMMENT: Saudi Arabia has invested millions of dollars to rewrite American history books and books on world history in favor of Islam. It would be Sisyphean work to make Islam morally equivalent with any religion.

February 7. *The Islamic Circle of North America uses a billboard as kickoff for Islamic propaganda, accompanied by a video calling "Let's share the beauty of shariah with our American bretheren."*

"A billboard is the kickoff of a national propaganda campaign funded by the Islamic Circle of North America (ICNA), a Muslim Brotherhood organization, to con the American people. The premise of the campaign is an insult to every freedom loving non-Muslims and Muslim of conscience. The idea is that opposition to the oppressive, racist and misogynist sharia law is supposedly an infringement on the first amendment protection of religious freedom. The only reason why anyone wants to restrict sharia is because of its political and supremacist aspects, and denial of free speech and equality of rights of all before the law. How can anyone oppose the anti-sharia laws that seek to prevent foreign laws from undermining fundamental constitutional liberties? We now have groups that have come to this country with a ready-made model of society and government they believe to be superior to what we have

---

[425] See http://barenakedislam.com/2012/02/05/have-your-schools-been-indoctrinated-with-whitewashed-islamic-propaganda-yet/, retrieved on 31.03.2012.

here, and are working to institute it. Jewish law is voluntary. Canon law is voluntary."[426]

COMMENT: Sharia law is all about submission and anti-individual freedom. sharia asserts authority over non-Muslims and is also political in nature.

- In sharia, a woman's testimony is half that of a man's (Koran 2:282),

- The Koran endorses wife-beating (Koran 4:34),

- There are double standards in women's ability to get out of a marriage,[427]

- The sharia mandates the death penalty for apostasy (Sahih Bukhari 4:52:260),

- The sharia mandates the subjugation of non-Muslims, and more. (Koran 9:5; 5:51 and other Suras).[428]

The ICNA presentation is a complete whitewash. ICNA is a Muslim Brotherhood group, according to a captured internal document of the Brotherhood. Muslim Brotherhood groups in America are trying to norm sharia, mainstream sharia. The Muslim Brotherhood group ICNA needs to lie to Americans about sharia and advance a false narrative about the most extreme and radical ideology on the face of the earth. ... They don't want Americans to know the truth that the gendercide of

---

[426] See http://atlasshrugs2000.typepad.com/atlas_shrugs/2012/02/sionafdi-counters-muslim-brotherhoods-icna-ad-campaign-to-mainstream-shariah.html, retrieved on 31.03.2012.

[427] See http://wikiislam.net/wiki/Qur%27an,_Hadith_and_Scholars:Women, for further information.

[428] Consult http://wikiislam.net for further information.

honor killings, the clitorectomies, the stonings, and the 1,400 years of cultural annihilations and enslavements are all sharia-mandated.[429]

February 8. *Tax dollars being used for religious purposes.*

"What happened to the separation of mosque and state? Why are infidel taxpayer dollars (jizya) being used for a religious purpose (financial or not)? Further, it's a ruse. They are charging interest on these loans, but repackaging them sans the term interest. Puhleeze. This is more adherence to Islamic supremacism, imposing Islam on the secular marketplace. The cost of interest is factored into the loan, so how can that be an interest-free loan? What rubbish. In any case, a lawsuit should be filed immediately against the use of taxpayer dollars for religious purposes. Every taxpayer in Minneapolis has standing. Let's sue. Don't miss our event at CPAC, Islamic Law in America, 3:30 pm, February 10th, in the McKinley room at the Marriot Wardman Park in Washington, DC."

"**Minneapolis helps Muslim businesses follow sharia** MN Daily (hat tip Jack) **Loans that collect interest are considered by some to be sinful under sharia law.** Owner Abdi Adem makes a transaction Monday morning at Afrik Grocery and Halal Meat on Cedar Avenue. Adem was able to expand his business through the city of Minneapolis' Alternative Financing Program. In 2005, Afrik Grocery and Halal Meat on Cedar Avenue needed to expand. Owner Abdi Adem, who operates his business under sharia law, needed to find a loan that funded

---

[429] See http://atlasshrugs2000.typepad.com/atlas_shrugs/2012/02/sionafdi-counters-muslim-brotherhoods-icna-ad-campaign-to-mainstream-shariah.html, retrieved on 31.03.2012.

the expansion and complied with his religious beliefs. Finding the loan was easier than he expected. Since December 2006, the city of Minneapolis, in partnership with the African Development Center, has given out 54 loans in a way that is compliant with Islamic law by using a fixed rate in place of a variable interest rate, which some considered sinful. Instead of charging interest, the city and the ADC estimate how long it will take the business to pay off the loan and totals what the interest would be. That amount is added as a lump sum to the total cost of the loan. "It feels like, looks like and acts like a loan, but it's just a different way of looking at it," said Hussein Samatar, executive director of the ADC. Abdulwahid Qalinle, an adjunct associate professor of Islamic law at the University of Minnesota, said interest rates can be considered sinful under sharia law. "Islam has specific guidelines where people can acquire wealth and how to spend their wealth," Qalinle said. Through the Alternative Financing Program, small lenders — usually the ADC — will offer a loan and the city will match it up to $50,000. Business owners will then pay back the lender and the city. The loans can be used for buying equipment or making renovations. Becky Shaw, an economic development specialist with the city, said most loans are around $5,000 to $10,000 and are paid off within three years. Shaw added that although the loans are targeted toward Muslims, any business owner can apply for a similar loan with an interest rate that has a similar effect as the sharia law loans. The city also offers a handful of other business assistance programs. Of the 54 loans the city and the ADC has given, only one has gone into default. According to a 2009 report from the Small Business Administration, the national default rates are around 12 percent." "This really, truly has been one of the phenomenal success stories of Minneapolis," Samatar said. Through the loan, Adem borrowed $42,000 and was able to move his business down the street, expand his halal meat section and purchase new equipment, which he said helped attract new customers. Adem paid off his loan in 2009. "I benefited very much from the loan. The customers liked the new store and we liked it," said Adem. Although he has no immediate plans to expand his business, Adem said it's nice to know the loans are available to him. "I don't want to go to the bank and get charged for interest," he said. "If I need more funds, I can use [the program] again, not now, but if I need it I can go and get it."

COMMENT: The mosque is the state and the state is the mosque.

February 7. *Emboldened and brazen – Hamas and CAIR are on the march and organizing support for 'Lady Al Qaeda' in America. The era of the I-want-to-kill-Americans female Islamic terrorist is at hand!*

"On Friday, February 10th, an appeals hearing will be held regarding Aafia Siddiqui at the Daniel Patrick Moynihan U.S. Courthouse, 500 Pearl Street, New York, NY, 9th Floor Ceremonial Courtroom. We encourage supporters of Aafia to be present at the courthouse. The hearing will be held at 10:00AM. Please mark your calendars and spread the word! 'Lady Al Qaeda' was convicted of attempting to murder Americans in Afghanistan after she was found with plans for a

326

'mass casualty attack' in the United States, along with a list of New York landmarks."[430]

COMMENT: Mohammed said that women should be beaten, unless, of course they beat and want to kill others for Islam!

*February 17. Jihadist failed. A devout Muslim homicide bomber targeted the US Capitol Building, synagogues, and military installations in the cause of Islam.*

"A 29-year-old Moroccan man, Amine El Khalifi of Alexandria, Virginia, was arrested near the United States Capitol and taken into custody. He had an inoperable gun and inert explosives in his possession. He thought he was detonating an explosive vest that was loaded with fake explosives. Undercover FBI agents had been observing him for about a year. Amine El Khalifi, who came to the United States when he was sixteen, had overstayed his visa for many years."[431] ... "Amine El Khalifi prayed at the Dar al-Hirjah mosque in Northern Virginia where several of the September 11 terrorists prayed. Again, Pamela Geller analyzed the situation and its threat to America succinctly and truly as follows: 'We have had more cases like this in the past two years then we had in all the years prior up to 911. And what is Obama's response? Disarm the FBI, disarm the military, ban 'jihad' from the lexicon. Obama invites the universal caliphate

---

[430] http://atlasshrugs2000.typepad.com/atlas_shrugs/2012/02/hamas-cair-organizing-support-for-lady-al-qaeda-hearing-i-want-to-kill-americans.html, retrieved on 31.03.2012.

[431] http://www.jihadwatch.org/2012/02/would-be-capitol-jihad-bomber-wanted-to-target-synagogue-military-gathering-place.html, retrieved on 23.03.2012.

organization, the OIC (Organization of Islamic Cooperation), to Washington, DC *behind closed doors* to talk about imposing bans on free speech in submission to the blasphemy laws under the sharia. In the past year alone, at least 20 people have been arrested in the United States on terrorism-related charges, according to the Senate Select Committee on Intelligence. But the NY Times says there is no jihad threat. ... This jihadist [Amine El Khalifi] has been living in the US for twelve years, but FOX and the rest of the US media refers to this devout Muslim as Moroccan (as if Morocco had anything to do with this act of war). The press does not dare say 'Muslim', even though these Muslim soldiers scream 'allahu akbar' and go jihad in the cause of Islam. No, in the UK, the enemedia and political quislings use the word 'Asian' for Muslim. In France, they use 'youth.' In Denmark, Sweden and Germany, they use 'immigrant' for Muslim (even if the jihadists are second or third generation). In many European countries, 'immigrant youth.' In the US, the media use country of origin or nationality in place of Muslim. In Israel, they use 'Arab.' Lipstick on a savage. It is jihad in the cause of Islam. Period. ... The thwarted homicide bombing marked at least the 45th publicly known attempted Islamic terrorist attack against the United States since 9/11, and is the sixth such attack targeting Washington, D.C."[432]

COMMENT: Such items never reach national headlines because the mainstream media is in *Gleichschaltung* with the Obama regime and Islam in America.

---

[432]     http://atlasshrugs2000.typepad.com/atlas_shrugs/2012/02/what-the-headline-isnt.html, retrieved on 23.03.2012.

February 23. *The creeping of Islam in America continues and threatens American high schoolers.*

James Harper, a senior at Grand Junction High School in Grand Junction, Colorado refused to sing a song in the school choir praising Allah. He received death threats and decided to quit school, rather than be attacked.[433]

COMMENT: Allah-Hubal and Mohammed are dictating what high schoolers must sing, although music is condemned in Islam. "From among the artful machinations and entrapments of Allah's enemy [Satan], with which he has snared those possessing little good sense, knowledge and deen [faith], and by which he has stalked the hearts of the false and ignorant people, there is the listening to whistling, wailing, handclapping and song to the accompaniment of forbidden [musical] instruments. Such things block the Quraan (sic) from people's hearts and make them devoted to sin and disobedience. For song [to musical accompaniment] is the Quraan (sic) of Ash-Shaytaan (Satan). It is a dense veil and barrier, preventing nearness to Ar-Rahmaaan! By way of such song, Satan deceives vain souls, making it appear pleasing to them through his cunning appeal to their vanities. He insidiously whispers false, specious arguments suggesting the 'goodness' in song. These arguments are accepted, and as a result, the Quraan (sic) becomes an object of neglect and abandonment."[434] (This is a fitting result.)

---

[433] http://www.thegatewaypundit.com/2012/02/colorado-high-school-choir-forced-to-praise-allah/, retrieved on 23.02.2012.

[434] http://wikiislam.net/wiki/Music_and_Singing:_Wisdom_Behind_Its_Prohibition_by_the_Shari%27ah, retrieved on 31.03.2012.

<u>February 23</u>. *Muslim admits attacking "Zombie Muhammed" atheist, corrupt Muslim Judge dismisses case, calls the atheist names, lectures him on Islam and tells him he would be killed in a Muslim country.*

"In October (2011) *The Blaze* reported on the now-infamous Zombie Muhammed, who was attacked by an irate Muslim man over what he believed was the unspeakable act of dishonoring his prophet. Zombie Muhammed, along with his counterpart, Zombie Pope, were costumes worn by Atheists during a Halloween parade last year. The assault was captured on video and the Muslim man admitted to his crime, saying that he did not know mocking Muhammed was actually legal in the US Charges, of course, were filed. Seems like a clear-cut case in favor of the victim, no? Think again. The court case in the assault has since come to trial and was dismissed by the presiding judge, who is reportedly Muslim as well. The judge refused to allow the video as evidence, stating, 'All that aside I've got here basically. I don't want to say he said she said but I've got two sides of the story that are in conflict with each other.' He added, … 'he [the plaintiff] has not proven to me beyond a reasonable doubt that this defendant is guilty of harassment, therefore I am going to dismiss the charge.' To add insult to injury, the defendant also testified that his 9 year old son was present, and the man said he felt he needed to show his young son that he was willing to fight for his Prophet. The case went to trial, and as circumstances would dictate, Judge Mark Martin is also a Muslim. What transpired next was surreal. The Judge not only ruled in favor of the defendant, but called Mr. Perce a name and told him that if he were in a Muslim country, he'd be put to death. … Judge Martin's comments included the

330

following: 'Having had the benefit of having spent over 2 and a half years in predominantly Muslim countries I think I know a little bit about the faith of Islam. In fact I have a copy of the Koran here and I challenge you sir to show me where it says in the Koran that Mohammad arose and walked among the dead. I think you misinterpreted things. Before you start mocking someone else's religion you may want to find out a little bit more about it (sic) makes you look like a dufus and Mr. (defendant) is correct. In many Arabic speaking countries something like this is definitely against the law there. In their society in fact it can be punishable by death and it frequently is in their society.' Judge Martin then offered a lesson in Islam — as a religion *and* a culture: 'Islam is not just a religion, it's their culture, their culture. It's their very essence their very being. They pray five times a day towards Mecca to be a good Muslim, before you die you have to make a pilgrimage to Mecca unless you are otherwise told you can not (sic) because you are too ill, too elderly, whatever but you must make the attempt. Their greetings wa-laikum as-Salâm – may god be with you.' ... Judge Martin presses further, showing what seems to be little regard for the First Amendment: 'Then what you have done is you have completely trashed their essence, their being. They find it very very very offensive. I'm a Muslim, I find it offensive. But you have that right, but you're way outside your boundaries or first amendment rights. This is what, and I said I spent half my years altogether living in other countries. When we go to other countries it's not uncommon for people to refer to us as 'ugly Americans.' This is why we are referred to as ugly Americans, because we are so concerned about our own rights we don't care about other people's rights

331

as long as we get our say but we don't care about the other people's say.'[435]

COMMENT: Judge Martin's position that the case rests on *I don't want to say he said she said but I've got two sides of the story that are in conflict with each other* is inexcusable. There is a video tape and a statement by a police officer that there was an assault on Mr. Perce, but the judge refused to allow these two items as evidence. A video commentary of the trial is also available.[436] There is a great fallacy in Judge Martin's statement that *we are so concerned about our own rights we don't care about other people's rights as long as we get our say but we don't care about the other people's say.* If the United States of America and the *Constitution for the United States of America* really *do not care about the other people's say*, then there is no logical and valid reason for the inclusion of the First Amendment by the Founding Fathers. Judge Martin should take courses in constitutional law and logic! Does the fact that Judge Martin is a Muslim and an American citizen and an American judge mean that Americans are triple ugly? Evidently, his judge examination – a four-week course for the position of a magisterial judgeship in Pennsylvania did not include any information about the *Constitution* or the First Amendment. In fact Judge Mark W. Martin never graduated from law school. Being a Muslim was apparently enough qualification for the

---

[435]    http://www.theblaze.com/stories/muslim-admits-to-attacking-atheist-over-zombie-muhammed-costume-muslim-judge-dismisses-case-lectures-atheist-on-joys-of-islam/, retrieved on 31.03.2012.

[436]http://www.youtube.com/watch?feature=player_embedded&v=Bf11F3y9 LOE, retrieved on 31.03.2012.

judicial system in Pennsylvania.[437] Having an Islamic judge place an opinion on the First Amendment is like having Chicken Little saying *the sky is falling* and the Nobel Prize Committee considering the statement as the scientific statement of the century par excellence. Judge Martin does not even know his Arabic and Islamic greeting! *Wa Alaikum as-Salam* means *And upon you be peace.* The statement has nothing to do with God. It would have nothing to do with God anyway, since it is Arabic and God is not Allah-Hubal.

<u>February 23.</u> *Muslim rams two squad cars and tries to run down a pedestrian, boards a plane and starts screaming "Allah is great", punches at a flight attendant and sings about Osama bin Laden.*

"A Continental Airlines passenger was tackled by fellow fliers and later detained after he caused a disturbance on a flight from Portland to Houston on Tuesday. ... WELL, WELL, the unruly Muslim on the plane was a Saudi national, who was arrested last Sunday for drunk driving, ramming two cop cars, and attempting to run over pedestrians. According to investigators, Yazeed Mohammed Abunayyan was smoking an electronic cigarette on a Continental Airlines flight traveling from Portland to Houston. When a flight attendant directed Abunayyan to stop smoking (or relinquish the device), he refused and began 'yelling profanities and swinging his fist at the flight attendant,' according to an indictment filed this afternoon in US District Court in Portland. Abunayyan ... also hit or attempted to hit other passengers and was 'speaking or singing about Osama bin Laden and his hatred of women,' the

---

[437] http://abusivediscretion.wordpress.com/, retrieved on 31.03.2012.

indictment charges. Abunayyan, who reportedly has been in the US visiting relatives, was charged with a felony count of interfering with flight crew members. Police reported that the intoxicated teenager led them on a 20-minute chase that ended after his Ford sedan got stuck on a dirt embankment. During the chase, Abunayyan was spotted driving in circles, attempting to run over pedestrians, and driving the wrong way on a street. He also rammed two patrol cars. Abunayyan was booked late Sunday into the Jackson County jail on a variety of charges, including driving under the influence of intoxicants, assault on a police officer, criminal mischief, hit and run, and reckless endangerment. He was freed from custody Monday around 6 PM after posting $65,000 bond. Which allowed him, a day later, to board Flight 1118, albeit briefly. ... According to Continental, though, there was no security threat."[438]

COMMENT: There was no security threat!?! "The man ... tried to light an electronic cigarette and began screaming 'Allah is great!' KHOU-TV has the report,[439] which also notes the disturbance may have started when the man and his friend were trying to sit by each other and couldn't. It also includes some emotional interviews with fellow passengers. According to KHOU, the man has not been charged with anything yet, but he was taken into custody once the plane landed in Portland. The pilot had apparently turned the plane around once the

---

[438] http://barenakedislam.com/2012/02/23/updatedcontinental-flight-1118-muslim-screaming-allahu-akbar-was-tackled-and-restrained-by-passengers/, retrieved on 31.03.2012.

[439] http://www.youtube.com/watch?feature=player_embedded&v=X-edn6-Liu8, retrieved on 31.03.2012.

disturbance ensued." Why charge him with anything? He was only obeying Allah!

<u>March 6.</u> *The Council on American Islamic Affairs and the American Civil Liberties Union invited Americans "to participate in the Second Annual Muslim Capitol Day in Jefferson City, (Missouri) on March 6, 2012".*

"Meet your representatives, create open dialogue between you and your representatives, and have your voices heard. This year hundreds of Muslims from all across the state of Missouri are expected to participate in Muslim Day at the State Capitol."[440]

COMMENT: We all know that a Muslim founded Missouri!

<u>March 18.</u> *The leftist news organization Media Matters for America cooperates with the anti-American and anti-Israeli cable news channel, Al-Jazeera, in Qatar.*

Indeed, Media Matters Action Network is part of Al-Jazeera's political arm.[441]

COMMENT: Is anyone surprised?

<u>March 23.</u> *The FBI scrubs its records at the behest of Islam.*

"...FBI Director [Robert] Mueller secretly met on February 8 at FBI headquarters with a coalition of groups including various Islamist and militant Arabic groups who in the past have defended Hamas and Hezbollah (sic) and have also issued

---

[440]  http://creepingsharia.wordpress.com/2012/03/03/terror-linked-cair-aclu-to-invade-missouri-capitol-march-6/, retrieved on 23.03.2012.

[441]  http://dailycaller.com/2012/03/18/media-matters-for-america-linked-with-anti-american-anti-israel-al-jazeera-network/#ixzz1q2jTA5ZS, retrieved on 24.03.2012.

blatantly anti-Semitic statements. At this meeting, the FBI revealed that it had removed more than 1,000 presentations and curricula on Islam from FBI offices around the country that was deemed 'offensive.' The FBI did not reveal what criteria was used to determine why material was considered 'offensive' but (that) these radical groups ... made that determination. ... FBI headquarters has banned all FBI offices from inviting any counter-terrorist specialists who are considered 'anti-Islam' by Muslim Brotherhood front groups. The February 8 FBI meeting was the culmination of a series of unpublicized directives issued in the last three months by top FBI officials to all its field offices to immediately recall and withdraw any presentation or curricula on Islam throughout the entire FBI. In fact, according to informed sources and undisclosed documents, the FBI directive was instigated by radical Muslim groups in the US who had repeatedly met with top officials of the Obama Administration to complain, among other things, that the mere usage of the term of 'radical Islam' in FBI curricula was 'offensive' and 'racist.' And thus, directives went out by Attorney General Eric Holder and FBI Director Mueller to censor all such material. Included in the material destroyed or removed by the FBI and the DOJ were powerpoints and articles that defined jihad as 'holy war' or presentations that portrayed the Muslim Brotherhood as an organization bent on taking over the world – a major tenant (sic) that the Muslim Brotherhood has publicly stated for decades."[442]

---

[442]   http://www.investigativeproject.org/3453/islamist-lobbies-washington-war-on-arab, retrieved on 23.03.2012.

COMMENT: We have met the enemy and they are us! Pamela Geller has commented on this action as follows: "Perhaps Obama can order the exhumation of hundreds of millions of victims of jihadi wars, land appropriations, cultural annihilations, and enslavements in an effort to purge the truth, the reality, from history. Over 18,000 Islamic attacks since 911, and Obama has caved to Islamic supremacists and their apologists. He ordered the purge of jihadic threat documentation. ... History will not be kind to this tool. And his grandchildren will spit when his name is uttered. This is a good day for jihad in America."[443]

<u>March 23.</u> *The Lone Star State is no longer the Lone Star State.*

It is now the Lone Star Crescent State as an advertisement for a newspaper implies.[444]

COMMENT: There is no *Yellow Rose of Texas*. There is now the Crescent Moon of Texas. This is symbolic of ever-continuing examples in the twenty-first century of creeping Islam and creeping sharia to undermine the tradition and culture and laws of the Republic of the United States of America. The daily eating away of tradition and democracy in America by the cancer of Allah-Hubal must be stopped. Already too much Islamic anti-Americanism, too much pro-Islamic and pro-sharia propaganda has occurred. Islam and

---

[443] Read http://atlasshrugs2000.typepad.com/atlas_shrugs/2012/02/obama-disarms-fbi-counter-terror-training-programs-purges-truth-about-jihad.html, retrieved on 23.03.2012.

[444] http://issuu.com/hazratamin/docs/mycrjul08, retrieved on 23.03.2012.

Muslims are brainwashing American citizens. The goal is: Stop The Islamization of America.[445]

### March 24. *Sharia law and encroachment.*

Robert Spencer at American Thinker writes that "Louisiana, Arizona, and Tennessee have already passed legislation restricting the use of foreign law in state courtrooms, and twenty-one other states are considering similar laws. These statutes are designed to halt the use of Islamic law, sharia, by American judges … ." Moreover, the threat of sharia is that it is "political and supremacist, mandating a society in which non-Muslims do not enjoy equality of rights with Muslims. And that is the focus of anti-sharia laws: to prevent this authoritarian and oppressive political and social system from eroding the freedoms we enjoy as Americans. It is plainly disingenuous to claim that anti-sharia laws would infringe upon Muslims' First Amendment rights to practice their religion. As Thomas Jefferson said, it doesn't matter whether my neighbor believes in one god or seventeen; it neither picks my pocket nor breaks my leg. It is only when my neighbor believes that his god commands him to pick my pocket or break my leg that his beliefs become a matter of concern for those who do not share them. … The purpose of anti-sharia laws is … to stop the political and supremacist aspects of Islam that infringe upon the rights and freedoms of non-Muslims."[446]

---

[445] This is the name of an organization established by Pamela Geller and Robert Spencer. They need patriotic support.

[446] See http://www.americanthinker.com/2012/03/the_necessity_of_anti-sharia_laws.html#ixzz1q2eLNLh3, retrieved on 24.03.2012.

COMMENT: Robert Spencer is correct. The purpose of anti-sharia laws and the stopping of the Islamization of America are to assure that the guarantees of freedom in the *Constitution for the United States of America* are not undermined in the first place and that a state (Islamic sharia) within a state (the Republic that is the United States of America) cannot be established.

March 27. *CIA's counterterrorism chief is convert to Islam.*

" ... The question is this: some might liken Roger to a top American official joining the Nazi Party during World War II. Others would liken Roger to a top American official marrying a German immigrant during World War II, and coming under unjust suspicion as a result. German Americans, of course, could oppose and fight against National Socialism unequivocally, without any lingering allegiance to it; Muslims who profess to reject and abhor Islamic terrorism, however, still profess belief in a book and a prophet that have inspired Islamic violence and supremacism worldwide, even among believers who have no institutional connection to al-Qaeda or any other jihad group. Whatever the truth may be in Roger's particular case, there is no doubt of one thing: if Islamic supremacists wanted to subvert the US defense against jihad terror, they couldn't do it more easily than by turning someone in a position like Roger's. The worst part of this story is that no one is even examining that as a possibility, for to do so would go against all the dogmas and pieties of the Washington establishment. ... "[447]

---

[447] http://www.jihadwatch.org/2012/03/at-cia-a-convert-to.html, retrieved on 30.03.2012. Roger's last name is not stated in the source.

339

COMMENT: Roger converted to Islam because his wife is Muslim and according to the Koran and Islam, she cannot marry an infidel. Love may be blind, but the jihadists are not. Allah-Hubal is ever-seeing, even on a crescent moon night!

<u>March 31.</u> *Virginia: Muslim owner demands disabled man with service dog leave restaurant.*

"Get this one Pam[ela],

"I have a disability which requires that I use a service dog. His name is Ray and he helps to counterbalance, alert and guide me. Under Federal Law, The Americans with Disabilities Act of 1990, a disabled person with their service dog must be allowed public accommodation and admittance. Among such places, include airplanes, public transportation, businesses which serve the general public, restaurants, etc."

"One evening two friends, myself and my service dog Ray entered a kabob restaurant in Virginia. Within seconds a man, apparently who was the owner, made a scene about my service dog and asked me to leave. I was fairly certain he was Pakistani Muslim. There were other people in the restaurant who apparently were also Muslim because of their coverings. Anyhow, I told him about the ADA, which he knew nothing about, and I told him that I was refusing to leave the restaurant and demanded that we be served the food we ordered. He was obviously very, very unhappy about it, yet he did eventually very reluctantly comply."

If he had insisted that my dog and I leave and refused to serve us in his restaurant, I would have filed a Human Relations Complaint of Discrimination or an ADA complaint with the US

Dept. of Justice. If that would ever happen I wonder if this Islamization has gone that far that it would limit me from entering a Muslim owned or operated establishment which serves the public? It's sad to see our society begin sliding down the slippery slope of making these kinds of self-serving accommodations. The people who are in favor of these kinds of accommodations as being in the friendly spirit of Freedom and Liberty are missing the point that our strong tendencies for 'cultural' and 'religious' acceptance are really being used to undermine our very freedoms and liberties in a very clandestine manner."

"The very essence of the Judeo-Christian belief is based upon 'Loving our neighbors,' but all too frequently forgotten is another teaching of our sacred writings is that if we know that someone is going to kill us 'We are "obliged" to kill them before they can kill us. In the context of this teaching, "obliged is stronger than being commanded." We are not commanded to murder someone because of their belief system or because they are different, but if they are going to kill us, self-defense is an imperative. I believe as many of our fellow Americans would like to believe, is that the majority of Muslims here in our country are not about jihad; HOWEVER, a belief system which commands its believers to deceive and lie to non-adherents about their murderous intentions is most certainly one that should be closely examined."

Respectfully submitted, Scott Sylte[448]

---

[448] This letter without spelling and syntax corrections to Pamela Geller is at http://atlasshrugs2000.typepad.com/atlas_shrugs/2012/03/muslimintolerance .html, retrieved on 31.03.2012.

COMMENT: The Koran has no suras (verses) that mention dogs. The fear of dogs is based on Mohammed's fear of dogs. The logic is interesting. If Mohammed was really a prophet, he must have known that Allah-Hubal would never have allowed his prophet to be placed in danger, let alone be placed in the dangerous position of being with a dog, man's best friend. Maybe that is the reason Mohammed did not like dogs. He was jealous that a dog is man's best friend and not Mohammed. Nevertheless, the crux of the situation is revealed in a hadith in Sahih Muslim, *Book 010, Number 3813*: "Abu Zubair heard Jabir b. 'Abdullah (Allah be pleased with him) saying: Allah's Messenger (may peace be upon him) ordered us to kill dogs, and we carried out this order so much so that we also kill (sic) the dog coming with a woman from the desert. Then Allah's Apostle (may peace be upon him) forbade their killing. He (the Holy Prophet further) said: It is your duty (to kill) the jet-black (dog) having two spots (the eyes), for it is a devil."[449]

Perhaps it is better to have a dog as man's best friend than to have Mohammed, Allah-Hubal, or a Muslim as a best friend. The restaurant owner's behavior is typical of Muslims who claim to be absolutely religious, but who do not know the core of the Koran or what X said that Y said that Z said what Mohammed said.

---

[449] Refer to http://www.cmje.org/religious-texts/hadith/muslim/010-smt.php#010.3810, retrieved on 31.03.2012. There are 30 hadiths concerning the killing of dogs in Chapter 31: COMMAND OF KILLING DOGS AND THEN ITS ABROGATION, AND PROHIBITION OF KEEPING THEM BUT FOR HUNTING AND PROTECTION OF LANDS OR CATTLE OR LIKE THAT. It seems that Mohammed could not make up his mind!

# CHAPTER TEN

# Blueprint and Prognosis

## Islamic Insurgency is Underway

Chapters Eight and Nine are only an overview of the cancer that is creeping sharia and subversive Islam. Pamela Geller, Daniel Pipes, Steven Emerson, and Robert Spencer, as well as other knowledgeable experts are convinced that a large segment of the Muslim population in the United States hates America and want violence towards the United States. Some other experts like Stephen Schwartz and Yehudit Barsky of the American Jewish Committee and even the very liberal Senator Charles Ellis (Chuck) Schumer (D-NY), have all independently of each other stated that mosques in America are financed by Islamic extremists and that the Wahhabi influence is growing.

In a press release on October 16, 2006, Senator Schumer listed the following mosques that were supported by the Wahhabi regime in Saudi Arabia:[450]

➤ Dar al-Salam Institute Fresno Mosque in California
➤ The Islamic Center in Colombia, Missouri
➤ The Islamic Center in East Lansing, Michigan
➤ The Islamic Center in Los Angeles, California
➤ The Islamic Center in New Brunswick, New Jersey

---

[450] http://web.archive.org/web/20070610042932/; http://www.senate.gov/~schumer/SchumerWebsite/pressroom/press_releases/PR02009.html, retrieved on 10 April 2012.

- The Islamic Center in New York
- The Islamic Center in Tida, Maryland
- The Islamic Center in Toledo, Ohio
- The Islamic Center in Virginia
- The Islamic Center in Washington
- The Islamic Cultural Center in Chicago
- King Fahd Mosque in Los Angeles
- The Mosque of the Albanian Community in Chicago
- South-West Big Mosque of Chicago
- Umar bin Al-Khattab Mosque in Los Angeles

This list is only the top of the proverbial iceberg. Mosques, the Islamic prayer houses, not churches, are being built and enlarged in practically every state in the union. Although almost every attempt to build a mosque is being met with resistance, the United States court system is oblivious to the ultimate goal: the undermining of American traditions, culture, and the replacement of the *Constitution for the United States of America* by sharia law. The courts undoubtedly rule in favor of the Muslim community, saying that Muslims are only exercising religious freedom. Yet the judicial system does not understand or will not understand that the Islamic system is dictatorial dogma, anti-freedom, contrary to Judeo-Christian philosophy, and anti-American. Islam is nothing more than the legitimization of a socio-political system. The strategy is to make it possible for Muslims to immigrate to non-Muslim lands. In these new lands, they are to establish communities, multiply rapidly, gain influence by becoming part of the social and political administrative structure, and induce the non-Muslim society to accept Islam. Muslims are not to assimilate into the new society. They are to legitimize Islamic law – the sharia – then claim the legal principle that in some Muslim, communal No-Go zone enclaves, sharia law can override the existing secular laws. Once this stage is achieved, the next goal is to increase the areas where sharia can become applicable. This is the Islamic immigration and integration coin: integrate without violating sharia law.

## The Penta Concepts Behind Islamic Insurgency in America as They Come From Mohammed and The Koran

It is apparent that there is a system behind Islamic insurgency in America.[451] Five duties of Islamic action (*tariqah*) that establish the *Dīn*, the way of life of the Koran, which is the direction that Muslims undertake to comply with the sharia in the umma, are as follows:

1. <u>Alertness</u> means that the course of action must be constantly aware of the true *Dīn* (*Dīn ul Huq*), which is to prevail over all other *Dīns*, the other ways and systems of life. Muslims must always be aware of and be alert to their responsibilities and duties.

---

[451] Mohammad Bayazeed Khan Panni has written an essay on *The Five Itemed Agenda for Establishing Islam*. It is a tedious, full-of-praise-for Islam-and-Mohammed writing. It is exceedingly difficult to follow, full of pathos, pseudo-intellectualism-philosophy. This author has sorted out the core five item elements. The remainder is crap, yet dangerous crap. http://www.hezbuttawheed.com/component/content/article/1-displayhome/ 6-thefiveitemedagendaforestablishingislam, retrieved on 31.03.2012.

2. Disconnection (*Hezrat*) means a cut with the majority who are in disagreement with Mohammed and Allah. The concept is expanded to include a disassociation from serving any deity other than Allah, and a disassociation from those obeying any authority, people or king or dictators etc. other than Allah or those who support Allah. Consequently, Muslims cannot integrate into secular societies because this would not allow them to continue the Islamic goal of world dominance.

3. Obedience means always following your leaders and their orders as they come from Allah and Mohammed who said, "He who obeys me, obeys Allah. He who doesn't obey me, doesn't obey Allah; he who obeys his commander obeys me, and he who doesn't obey his commander disobeys me. (Sahih Bukhari, 9:2511) Moreover, "Listen and obey (your chief) even if an Ethiopian whose head is like a raisin were made your chief." (Sahih Bukhari 1:11:662, 664)

4. Unity is stronger than division. A country can be economically, politically, and militarily powerful. A smaller country that is united and is disciplined can defeat a larger nation in a conflict if the larger, at first more powerful country, is divided. The Koran places major emphasis on unity and the fight against hostile elements in this unity. Any criticism that cuts at unity is regarded as being unfaithful to Islam.

Jihad, which means fight to the end so that the true way of life (*Dīn ul Huq*) will be supreme and prevail over all other ways of life and systems. The purpose of Alertness, Disconnection, Obedience, and Unity is to pave the way for the fulfillment of jihad, which by itself will not be successful.

It is necessary to emphasize that the number five carries important symbolical weight in Islam. Five is the Panjetan, the Five Holy Purified Ones who are the members of Mohammed's family: Muhammad, Ali, Fatima, Hasan, and Husayn. Particularly Shia Islam honors the number five. Muslims pray to Allah-Hubal five times a day. There are five pillars of Islam, just as there are five duties in establishing the *Dīn*.

This is the Islamic bond. It does not take much acumen to realize that the framework is a military concept. Therefore, Islam is not peaceful as it claims to be. It is violence based on a military strategy. Once this strategy is implemented a program will follow that will assist in sharia supplanting secular law. That strategic program is already underway.

## Islam's Twenty Point Strategy to Undermine Democratic-Republican Governments

Anis Shorrosh, the author of *Islam Revealed* and the translator of *The True Furqan*, is a Christian Arab-American. She emigrated from Arab-controlled Jerusalem in January 1967. Already on August 4, 2004, Anis Shorrosh listed twenty points that Islam uses in the peaceful undermining of democratic-republican societies and governments. They are listed below in italics, accompanied by this author's explanatory suggestions for the respective countermeasure.[452] In her short

---

[452] http://www.wnd.com/2003/08/20098/, retrieved on 31.03.2012.

introduction to the list Anis Shorrosh states, "The following is my analysis of Islamic invasion of America, the agenda of Islamists and visible methods to take over America by the year 2020," She asks, "Will Americans continue to sleep through this invasion as they did when we were attacked on 9/11?"

The Twenty Points are:

1. *Terminate America's freedom of speech by replacing it with statewide and nationwide hate-crime bills.*

COUNTERMEASURE: Those who are accused of a hate crime should make their legal arguments that hate-crimes are unconstitutional, in spite of the fact that there is some hate-crime legislation on the state and federal level. Argue that implementing sharia is a hate crime against the freedoms guaranteed by the *Constitution for the United States of America.*

2. *Wage a war of words using black leaders like Louis Farrakhan, Rev. Jesse Jackson and other visible religious personalities who promote Islam as the religion of African-Americans while insisting Christianity is for whites only. What they fail to tell African-Americans is that it was Arab Muslims who captured them and sold them as slaves. In fact, the Arabic word for black and slave is the same, 'Abed.'*

COUNTERMEASURE: Combat them with more intellectual minds like Alan Keyes (Roman Catholic), Congressman Allen West, both African-Americans and national, non-lamestream media experts. The Arab Muslims will not tell African-Americans that they have a slave heritage in the United States because the Muslims reinstituted slavery after it had been outlawed by the Roman Catholic Church and the Roman Emperor Justinian I.

3. *Engage the American public in dialogues, discussions, debates in colleges, universities, public libraries, radio, TV, churches and mosques on the virtues of Islam. Proclaim how it is historically another religion like Judaism and Christianity with the same monotheistic faith.*

COUNTERMEASURE: Confront Islam at such debates with historical facts concerning the element of its being non-virtuous. For example, there never was a golden age of Islam in Spain. Propagandize the statistics of how many people were executed by Islam in its spread throughout other countries. Ask: What virtue is there in still having slavery? Although many Islamic nations have outlawed slavery, it is still tolerated, most often under another nomenclature like *service person*. Ask: What virtue is there in killing non-believers because Mohammed says to do it because Allah-Hubal told him to do so? Show by facts that Islam is the worship of the deity moon god Allah-Hubal.

4. *Nominate Muslim sympathizers to political office to bring about favorable legislation toward Islam and support potential sympathizers by block voting.*

COUNTERMEASURE: At the first sign of a Muslim being a candidate for public office, oppose the election of all such personalities by explaining the conflicts of their oaths of office and the concept of lying – al taqiyya – for the further advancement of Islam and sharia law.

*5. Take control of as much of Hollywood, the press, TV, radio and the internet as possible by buying the related corporations or a controlling stock.*

COUNTERMEASURE: Actively call for boycotts of their products. Expose the Muslim control takeover of Hollywood, the press, television, internet and radio as far as possible. Do not believe everything the stars and the lamestream media report. Contradict them with the truth wherever they appear, whenever they give pro-Islam statements, and whatever the pro-Islamic statements are.

*6. Yield to the fear of the imminent shut-off of the lifeblood of America – black gold. America's economy depends on oil and 41 percent of it comes from the Middle East.*

COUNTERMEASURE: Use the facts that the United States of America has more oil and natural gas than all of the oil-producing countries and natural gas producing countries together. This is a fact. For example, North Dakota and Montana have an estimated 3.0 to 4.3 billion barrels of untapped oil.[453] The Marcellus Shale gas field of Pennsylvania is the most extensive gas field in America and one of the largest in the world.[454] America must not be dependent on any foreign oil. Do not believe Barack Hussein Obama and the progressives who are in the tank for Islam. They are only guaranteeing that Saudi Arabia is receiving a modern-day form of the dhimmi-jizya tax.

---

[453]    http://www.usgs.gov/newsroom/article.asp?ID=1911#.T5Zx-9nz7mc; http://205.254.135.7/naturalgas/, retrieved on 31.03.2012.

[454] http://geology.com/articles/marcellus-shale.shtml, retrieved 25.04.2012.

7. *Yell "foul, out-of-context, personal interpretation, hate crime, Zionist, un-American, inaccurate interpretation of the Quran" whenever Islam is criticized or the Quran is analyzed in the public arena.*

COUNTERMEASURE: Become your own Koran expert. It is not difficult. Expose the Koran by quoting it and asking the Muslim side to explain the contradictions. For example, what is the contradiction of Islam forbidding forced marriages. The contradiction is that the terminology is not used. It is called pre-arranged or arranged marriages, regardless of age.

8. *Encourage Muslims to penetrate the White House, specifically with Islamists who can articulate a marvelous and peaceful picture of Islam. Acquire government positions and get membership in local school boards. Train Muslims as medical doctors to dominate the medical field, research and pharmaceutical companies. (Ever notice how numerous Muslim doctors in America are, when their countries need them more desperately than America?) Take over the computer industry. Establish Middle Eastern restaurants throughout the US to connect planners of Islamization in a discreet way.*

COUNTERMEASURE: Be a candidate against them. Vote them out of office at the next opportunity. Initiate recalls against them. Name them Taqiyyas, for that is what Islam requires them to do.

9. *Accelerate Islamic demographic growth via:*

* *Massive immigration (100,000 annually since 1961).*

  COMMENT: The problem with this situation is that "US policy regarding the refugee resettlement program would shock most Americans if they only knew. The UN (United Nations) picks who become US refugees. Christians are being refused refugee status and face persecution and many times certain death for their religious beliefs under the sharia, while whole Muslim communities are entering the US by the tens of thousands per month despite the fact that they face no religious persecution. ...This is no accident. We know that the UN is driven largely by the largest bloc of countries, the OIC (Organization of Islamic Cooperation). The OIC is one of the largest intergovernmental organizations in the world."[455]

COUNTERMEASURE: Reinstate the immigration laws as they were strictly regulated in the early 1960s. After the Democratic administrations of John F. Kennedy and Lyndon Baines Johnson loosened these immigration regulations, Muslims began flowing into America in uncontrollable waves to study and stay. Investigate every person from an Islamic country concerning their homeland political status, e.g., were they persecuted, etc. Stop payment of UN dues in the proportion to which such money is used for the decisions concerning who emigrates to the US and from which country. Specifically speaking, institute strict immigration rules and regulations in the United States and deport all illegal aliens, regardless of familial situations, regardless of what human rights organizations opinionize. An illegal alien is an illegal alien and has committed a crime. The punishment for that crime is forced

---

[455] http://atlasshrugs2000.typepad.com/atlas_shrugs/refugee_resettlement_ the_quiet_jihad_tsunami/, retrieved on 31.03.2012.

deportation. Make the home country pay for their deportation. Another measure is to reduce the number of immigrants into the United States per year and per country of origin. Allow a three-year probation period before any legal immigrant can become an American citizen. Integrate the aforementioned suggestions with those provided by Newt Gingrich, which are:

1. Control the border.

2. Create a 21st Century Visa Program

- A Brazilian tourist who wants to visit Disney World and spend thousands to support American jobs should not have to wait four months to get an interview for a tourist visa.

- A foreign entrepreneur who wants to establish legal residency and immediately create American jobs should not have to spend tens of thousands of dollars in legal fees first.

- A brilliant graduate of an American engineering program should not have to go all the way home to initiate the process of applying for a high-skilled work visa.

- An American farmer in California should have efficient, legal means to hire temporary, legal labor to support the American economy.

3. "In-source" the best brains in the world.

4. Allow foreigners who want to spend money, invest and create jobs in America to do so.

5. There has to be a legal guest worker program, but its management must be outsourced to a sophisticated manager of anti-fraud systems, such as American Express, Visa, or MasterCard.

6. Create a path to earned legality for some of the 8 to 12 million people who are here outside the law.

7. Deportation of criminals and gang members should be efficient and fast.

8. Ensure that every new citizen and every young American learn American history and the key principles of American Exceptionalism.

9. English must be the official language of government.

10. Young non-citizens who came to the United States outside the law should have the same right to join the military and earn citizenship.[456]

There should be a path to legality for non-criminal immigrants, but there should not be a path to citizenship. Such persons should be allowed to remain in the United States of America, to work and to pay taxes. However, citizenship and the right to vote in elections should be reserved exclusively to those who enter the United States

---

[456] http://www.newt.org/solutions/immigration/, retrieved on 31.04.2012.

legally. All persons who become United States citizens and who previously had taken legal oaths in other countries and an oath to uphold the teachings of the Koran and Mohammed must renounce such oaths and nullify them publicly. The new citizenship oaths must be taken by swearing on the Holy Bible or the *Constitution for the United States of America*.

- *Use no birth control whatsoever – every baby of Muslim parents is automatically a Muslim and cannot choose another religion later.*

COUNTERMEASURE: Pass legislation prohibiting the automatic transfer of Muslimhood, even though the Koran says that once born a Muslim, always a Muslim. Such transfers infringe on the child's right to freedom of decision.

- *Muslim men must marry American women and Islamize them (10,000 annually). Then divorce them and remarry every five years – since one can't legally marry four at one time. This is a legal solution in America.*

COUNTERMEASURE: Propagandize such behavior and require that upon divorce, the Muslim is not able to avoid child support and all other legal costs necessary for the upkeep of the divorced families. Failure to pay such alimony must result in loss of a driver's license, business permit, passport renewal, or even voting rights or expulsion from the USA.

- *Convert angry, alienated black prison inmates and turn them into militants (so far 2,000 released inmates have joined al-Qaida worldwide). Only a few 'sleeper cells' have been captured in Afghanistan and on American soil.*

COUNTERMEASURE: Forbid the emergence of Islam in prisons as a religion by claiming and proving that it is a dogma that supports violence. Once such converted prisoners are freed, declare subversive anti-American individuals as *persona non grata* and expel them immediately if they have originated from a foreign country.

10. *Reading, writing, arithmetic and research through the American educational system, mosques and student centers (now 1,500) should be sprinkled with dislike of Jews, evangelical Christians and democracy. There are currently 300 exclusively Muslim schools in the US which teach loyalty to the Quran, not the US Constitution. In January of 2002, Saudi Arabia's Embassy in Washington mailed 4,500 packets of the Quran and videos promoting Islam to America's high schools – free of charge. Saudi Arabia would not allow the US to reciprocate.*

COUNTERMEASURE: Reduce diplomatic ties with Saudi Arabia to an absolute minimum. Establish sporadic, special quarantines for travelers from Saudi Arabia and other Islamic countries. Regulate the importation and publication of the Koran to the degree that Saudi Arabia or any other Islamic country prohibits the importation or publication of the *Holy Bible*. Expose the Koran's evil suras, all of them. Every time a Jew, an evangelical Christian or a member of a non-Muslim organization is attacked, even verbally, indict the culprits for committing a hate crime. If the law is not being enforced because the law enforcement agency is in the hands of the pro-

Muslim authorities, like in Dearborn, Michigan, get them removed from office as quickly as possible. Because they are not enforcing the law, indict them for committing a hate crime. Although this author believes that hate-crime laws are unconstitutional, hate crime laws can be used to work both ways.

11. *Provide very sizeable monetary Muslim grants to colleges and universities in America to establish 'Centers for Islamic studies' with Muslim directors to promote Islam in higher education institutions.*

COUNTERMEASURE: Regardless of the financial status of the educational institution, do not accept the grants. Yet, if they are accepted do not require that the directors be Muslim. Make yearly controls of the materials being used in the Islamic studies programs. Make sure that arguments are factual. If controls are not allowed, call for the discontinuation of the Islamic studies programs.

12. *Let the entire world know through propaganda, speeches, seminars, local and national media that terrorists have hijacked Islam, when in truth, Islam hijacked the terrorists.*

COUNTERMEASURE: Propagandize the truth in the local media about the Koran's 169 war suras against the non-believers. Do not invite Muslims as speakers at public events.

13. *Appeal to the historically compassionate and sensitive Americans for sympathy and tolerance towards Muslims in America who are portrayed as mainly immigrants from oppressed countries.*

COUNTERMEASURE: Portray Muslims as believers in a heathen dogma dedicated to a moon-god called Allah-Hubal. Use the facts of history uncovered by the recognized international historians and researchers. If this is a hate crime, then the facts of experts on the matter are also hate crimes. At every opportunity, expose Mohammed for his pedophile desires, sexual machismo, anti-female stance, psychological disorders, and criminal actions.

14. *Nullify America's sense of security by manipulating the intelligence community with misinformation. Periodically terrorize Americans with reports of impending attacks on bridges, tunnels, water supplies, airports, apartment buildings and malls.*

COUNTERMEASURE: Should the persons who manipulate the intelligence community in the above fashion be exposed, arrest them and prosecute them in a court of law for at least attempts at sedition – this is overt conduct, such as speech and organization, that is deemed by the legal authority to tend towards and demand insurrection against the established order. The Alien Registration Act, or Smith Act of 1940 is still in effect in the United States.

15. *Form riots and demonstrations in the prison system demanding Islamic sharia as the way of life, not America's justice system.*

COUNTERMEASURE: The prison authorities must quash such riots and demonstrations as quickly as possible. Place such prisoners who want riots and demonstrations off limits to the public. Should the riots and demonstrations come from outside the prison system, indict the organizations for sedition.

16. *Open numerous charities throughout the US, but use the funds to support Islamic terrorism with American dollars.*

COUNTERMEASURE: Do not give charities associated with Islamic organizations tax-free status and control their financial accounts at least once a year. Monitor their administrative personnel. If necessary, forbid the charities.

17. *Raise interest in Islam on America's campuses by insisting freshmen take at least one course on Islam.*

COUNTERMEASURE: Raise interest in American patriotism, the *Constitution*, democratic republicanism, and capitalism by requiring that freshmen students take two courses on the subjects in their first and/or second year of college, regardless of their major field of study. Give such courses three grade points. Give the Islamic courses no grade points.

18. *Unify the numerous Muslim lobbies in Washington, mosques, Islamic student centers, educational organizations, magazines and papers by internet and an annual convention to coordinate plans, propagate the faith and engender news in the media.*

COUNTERMEASURE: Call for a boycott of such internet sites and yearly conventions. As a constituent, make your representatives at local, state, and national level aware of the fact that they are not obliged to accede to Islamic interests. Islam is not America.

19. *Send intimidating messages and messengers to the outspoken individuals who are critical of Islam and seek to eliminate them by hook or crook.*

COUNTERMEASURE: Publicize such intimidating messages and messengers in the press, even if it is a local, weekly newspaper. Should the local paper refuse, publish your own information sheets and warn your fellow citizens of such messages and messengers. If one knows who the perpetrators are, accuse them of a hate crime or intent to commit a personal injury. Take them to court. This can be an expensive procedure, but if you win the case, it can be decided that the perpetrators will have to pay a fine, and the plaintiff, and the cost of the trial.

20. *Applaud Muslims as loyal citizens of the US by spotlighting their voting record as the highest percentage of all minority and ethnic groups in America.*

COUNTERMEASURE: Expose their voting record via public media as being only a steppingstone for the final implementation of sharia law in America. The behavior of Muslims as voters is an attempt to use the freedoms in the United States of America to undermine the freedoms guaranteed by the *Constitution for the United States of America.*

As far as this author is informed, none of the suggested countermeasures are anti-American and none are prohibited by United States law. It is necessary as a survival strategy to counteract attempts by Islamic organization to undermine the American cultural heritage and America's democratic-republican laws. Expose Muslims by showing that their loyalty means nothing because of the Arabic/Islamic concept of al-taqiyya. Forbid them from taking oaths of office on the Koran or any other oath process because the concept of al-taqiyya cancels out their oaths.

Every one of the points enumerated by Anis Shorrosh is being undertaken and exploited to its fullest by Muslims and their Islamic organizations in the United States of America. There are daily examples of creeping sharia and crappy Islam, as chapters eight and nine have shown. The portrayal of such developmental disasters of an Islamic tsunami in America in this book was capped at the date of March 31, 2012. Since that date new examples of Islamic undercutting of the American culture, traditions, and legal system have been posted on the various watchdog online sites. Regrettably, that is likely to continue.

Not one of these cultural jihad actions or Islamic defamations has been reported by the lamestream media. For them, such threats do not exist. They have been infiltrated and placed in an economic dependence on investments from wealthy progressives and Arabs. Therefore, the majority of citizens have absolutely no knowledge of what is transpiring with the forces of Islam in their sometimes surreptitious and sometimes overt takeover of the United States of America. This means that Americans are not prepared to counter these attacks. Yet in order to survive as a free people, Americans must take action to not only stem the waves of Islam directed against America, but to exterminate the cancerous dogma. Some of the following actions can always be undertaken by Americans for their self-defense against the creeping evil that claims its Allah-Hubal-Mohammed-ordained destiny is to rule the world.

# Measures to Combat Creeping Sharia and Islam

Regardless of what Barack Hussein Obama or the anti-American leftist and progressive elements say, the United States of America is in a protracted war. It is a war declared upon America by Islam. The goal of the *Explanatory Memorandum on the General Strategic Goal for the Group in North America,* is that Islamists are intent on "eliminating and destroying Western Civilization from within and sabotaging its miserable house", and "installing a universal caliphate."[457] The most active Islamic organizations involved in attaining this goal are Hamas, the Muslim Brotherhood, its front organizations such as the Council on American Islamic Relations, the Organization of the Islamic Conference, the Muslim American Society and the innumerable sub-front organizations of the Muslim Brotherhood. Their parameters of involvement are unlimited, encompassing elementary schools, grade schools, high schools, colleges and universities, pseudo-interfaith dialogue organizations, local, state and federal courts, the internet, working places, neighborhoods, media, government organizations, government departments like the United States Department of Defense, the Department of Homeland Security, the Department of Justice, the Department of State, the Department of the Treasury, the state legislatures, and the

---

[457] http://www.ruthfullyyours.com/2012/02/17/edward-cline-islamic-rules-for-radicals/, retrieved on 24.04.2012. See also Akram, Mohammed. *An Explanatory Memorandum on the General Strategic Goal for the Group in North America*, May 22, 1991, Government Exhibit 003-0085, U.S. vs. HLF et al., at http://www.investigativeproject.org/documents/misc/20.pdf. retrieved on 24.04.2012. The report is in Arabic. The English translation begins on page 16.

United States Congress, to name only a few, ... which is enough.[458]

The head of the cancerous organism is the Muslim Brotherhood, which in the United States of America is dedicated to "a kind of grand jihad in eliminating and destroying the Western civilization from within and 'sabotaging' its miserable house by their hands and the hands of believers so that it is eliminated and Allah's religion is made victorious over all other religions."[459] Omar Ahmad, cofounder of CAIR, made a more explicit statement in 1998 announcing, "Islam isn't in America to be equal to any other faith, but to become dominant. The Koran should be the highest authority in America, and Islam the only accepted religion on earth."[460]

The following list is intended to assist patriotic Americans in their fight against the Islamization and the mosqueing of the United States of America. The suggested actions are not listed in any specific order of importance because the person executing these operations must decide for him/herself which ones should be emphasized. Know the list,

---

[458] See also Geller, Pamela. *Stop the Islamization of America A Practical Guide to the Resistance*, WND Books, Washington, D. C.: 2011, pp. ii, iii.

[459] Spencer, Robert. *Stealth jihad: How Radical Islam Is Subverting America Without Guns Or Bombs*, Regnery Publishing Inc., Washington, D.C.: 2008, p. 16.

[460] Akram, Mohammed. *An Explanatory Memorandum on the General Strategic Goal for the Group in North America*, May 22, 1991, Government Exhibit 003-0085, U.S. vs. HLF et al , p. 7 (21).

use it well, and become involved in Stopping the Islamization of America![461]

> Stop the construction of Muslim footbaths, and prayer rooms in schools, universities, public places such as airports, train stations. They are against the Establishment Clause (The First Amendment) of the *Constitution for the United States of America.* (G viii, 43)

> Expose Islamic concepts such as *al-taqiyya* (lying, deception) (G 33), *dawah* (proselytizing) (G 7, 146), and *jihad* (to be active for the furtherance of Islam) (G 56).

> Learn Saul Alinsky's *Rules for Radicals* and use them against Islam as well as the American left, which is working hand-in-hand with Islamists in their desire to destroy America.

> Remove all tax-exempt status from any Islamic organization regardless of its stated goals.

> Stop taxpayer support for the renovation of old and the construction of new Islamic cultural centers and mosques throughout the United States and the world. (G 1-3, 15-16)

> Speak up and in so doing, fine-tune your arguments. (G 38)

> Never get discouraged.

> Learn from experience. Turn former failures into successes.

---

[461] Many of these suggestions come from Pamela Geller in her book, *Stop the Islamization of America A Practical Guide to the Resistance*, WND Books, Washington, D. C.: 2011. They are sourced as (G plus page number) and are interspersed with some suggestions from the present author.

- Learn the strategy of the enemy. It is here: Akram, Mohammed. *An Explanatory Memorandum on the General Strategic Goal for the Group in North America*, May 22, 1991, Government Exhibit 003-0085, U.S. vs. HLF et al.

- Beat the enemy at his/her own game. (G 49)

- Remember that for every verse (sura) in the Koran there is a moral logic that will confront it, expose it, and defeat it.

- Welcome adverse criticism and the adverse media. This can only propagandize your undertakings. (G 4-8, 46-48)

- Send no Muslim representatives to a foreign country. Send only conservatives and make the foreign country accept them even if this means cutting the country's foreign aid and reduction of diplomatic relations.

- Never believe Islamic sources. They will conduct al-taqiyya. Believe the opposite of what they say. (Some examples are at G 33-34.) Believe only documented sources that can be investigated.

- Never invite or allow a Muslim or a speaker from an Islamic organization to address an audience in your community, school, church, etc.

- Find out who your real opponents are, including real Muslims behind the scenes. (G 25-26)

- Find out your opponent's sympathizers. Check them and prove links to Islamic organizations, almost all of which are primary and secondary front organizations of the Muslim Brotherhood and/or Saudi Arabia. (G 26, 27, 229)

➢ Reduce diplomatic relations with all Islamic countries to the lowest level possible.

➢ Find out who is supporting your opponents with money and propagandize your findings. Most of the financial funding comes from Saudi Arabia through the reinvestment of oil money from non-believer nations into active Islamic sabotage, creeping sharia, and Islamic jihad. Most mosque funding in the United States (and Canada) comes from Saudi Arabia and King Saud's Wahhabi Islamic World Domination Movement. (G 26, 27)

➢ Protest against Islamic charity collections. The Saudis and the Muslim Brotherhood have a hammerlock on Islamic mosques and organizations in America. The worshippers of mosques and the members of Islamic organizations are encouraged to send money to Islamic organizations outside of America, which pass the funds on to jihadists for their attacks on non-believers anywhere in the world. This is nothing more than money laundering using the hadith "He who equips a raider so he can wage jihad in Allah's path ... is himself a raider."[462] The federal government must undertake measures to stop the collections of such monies.

➢ If a mosque is to be built in your area or if one already exists, research, examine, and document its literature and expose its content. Make everything you find public. For example, expose sections in their Koran that are totally opposed to free societies. Koran 9 (Repentance) concerns

---

[462]    http://hadith.al-islam.com/Display/Display.asp?Doc=2&Rec=2695, retrieved on 24.04.2012.

jihad and only jihad. Whatever claim you make to expose the Koran, Islamic sources will use al-taqiyya. (G 27)

➢ Check the zoning laws of your community as well as parking and traffic laws, and relate them to the proposed construction of a mosque. (G 31, 40)

➢ Never forget that in Islam the mosque is the state and the state is the mosque.

➢ Publicize as much true, anti-Islamic information as possible. (G 30, 43)

➢ Do not be afraid to confront liberals, progressives, and pro-Islamic organizations. (G 43, 44)

➢ If you or your protest group are brought before a court of law, find out if the judge is a Muslim or if a juror is a Muslim, and have them be relieved from the case on the grounds that they have a conflict of interest. Muslims are obliged to the Koran, Mohammed's hadiths, and sharia law only, regardless of the oath they took when they accepted their positions. It they do not uphold the Koran, the hadiths, and sharia, then they are not good Muslims and must be disciplined. The ultimate disciplinary action is being killed for the cause of Islam.

➢ Never stop the fight until you win. (G 30, 37, 38, 43)

➢ Always be ready with truthful, documented facts concerning who, what, when, where, why (G 31, 47), as well as the significance

➢ Ask pro-Islam lawyers who are not Muslim if they are upholding their oaths to the *Constitution*. Ask pro-Islam

Muslim lawyers if they are doing the same. If they say yes, accuse them of implementing al-taqiyya and demand their dismissal from the case.

➢ Support politicians who understand Islam and the Islamic threat to America. Do not support politicians like Keith Ellison who allows Islamic interest groups to pick up his tab when he speaks or makes his pilgrimage to Mecca. (G 62)

➢ Build and organize protest groups in your neighborhood. (G 38)

➢ Organize protests and rallies. (G 38)

➢ If you organize a meeting with (a) guest speaker(s), make sure that there are no Islamic plants in the audience who will interrupt the meeting. If they are present, have them removed immediately. (G 39-40)

➢ Do not give your community to the enemy. (G 38)

➢ If necessary, contact county auditors and tax assessors to audit the Islamic organization's finances. (G 40)

➢ Study your opponent. (G 42, 170-177, 180)

➢ Develop your own talking points. Do not let the enemy develop any talking points. (G 47)

➢ Do not allow media control of your statements. (G 47) If you are interviewed and the interviewer is asking pro-Islamic questions to place you on the spot, tell the interviewer that the question they are asking is not the correct question and rephrase the subject matter to fit your true, factual, documented response.

- Do not kowtow and do not let yourself be cowed by anyone. (G 75)

- Always state the truthful, documented facts. (G 53, 75)

- Never forget that Islam cannot tell the truth because the dogma is comprehensively untruthful.

- Do not shout in delivering your argumentation, but speak forcefully. Those who shout are in the wrong!

- Always maintain your freedom. The more the enemy tries to oppress you, the freer you become. Call their bluff! Document their attempts at oppressing you and publicize them. The more the enemy attempts to chain you, the more vehement you must be in exercising your freedom and attacks on them.

- Never accept the Islamic argument of assimilation. Don't ever think about assimilation. Building any kind of relationship means that a person or organization is submitting to Islam. Never forget that in Islam any Muslim who assimilates is punishable by death.

- Never forget that *there are no moderate Muslims*!

- Understand the meaning of the Arabic term *Hurriyya*, which is often translated as *freedom*. The Muslim philosopher Muhiyuddin Muhammad Ibn Arabi (1165-1240) defined freedom as *perfect slavery to Allah*. Franz Rosenthal (1914-2003), the eminent American scholar on Islam and Semitic languages wrote that the culture of Islam does not have the corresponding Western concept of freedom. ... Islamic culture historically has nothing corresponding to the Western concept of freedom as "a

369

fundamental political concept that could have served as a rallying cry for great causes." A Muslim "was expected to consider subordination of his own freedom to the beliefs, morality and customs of the group as the only proper course of behavior…" Thus "…the individual was not expected to exercise any free choice as to how he wished to be governed … In general, … governmental authority admitted of no participation of the individual as such, who therefore did not possess any real freedom vis-à-vis it."[463]

➤ Never forget that freedom in Islam is understood as *perfect slavery to Allah*.

➤ Argue against Islam on the level that Islam is bent on a clash of civilizations and your stance is that your civilization with its guarantees of human rights must survive. Muslims do not like the phrase *clash of civilizations* because they do not recognize the existence of civilizations outside of Islam.

➤ Do not question Islam's claim that it is a religion. (G 45) Yet, always be aware that Islam claims to be a *religion* that propagandizes the killing of non-believers. Is that really a religion? Moreover, should a movement that actively kills non-believers be protected by law and be allowed to supplant the *Constitution*?

➤ Constantly repeat that the goal of the Muslim Brotherhood and Islamic organizations is to destroy the United States of America from within and to "sabotage its miserable house."

---

[463] See http://www.americanthinker.com/blog/2011/02/egypt_hurriyya_vs_freedom_and.html, retrieved on 24.04.2012.

Quote the Islamists with documented evidence. (G iv, see footnote 457)

➢ Never forget that there are too many politicians in America who have sold out to the enemy that is Islam. Do not give them one inch. They will sell you out, too.

➢ Do not become a *Funktionshäftling* (A concentration camp Kapo). (G 175)

➢ Propagandize the motto of the Muslim Brotherhood: (G 104)

Allah is our goal.

The Prophet Muhammad ibn 'Abdullah is our leader.

The Qu'ran is our constitution.

jihad is our way.

And death in the way of Allah is our promised end.

➢ Do not insult Islam. (G 56) At the same time do not forget that one cannot insult Islam because Islam insults itself. Point out inconsistencies in Islam by quoting respective statements from the Koran, the hadiths, and the sharia. Do not forget that Mohammed constantly re-interpreted and changed the preaching of Allah. (G 181)

➢ Develop Islam's stance on misogyny (hatred of females) to your advantage. Never forget that the burqa is a cloth coffin, regardless of what some so-called experts say. (G 95, 112)

➢ Never accept a Muslim's redefinition of jihad. (G 107) For example, jihad is defined in the Koran 5:33, and 9:14. The

371

forms of jihad are: war jihad, litigation jihad, cultural jihad, anti-female jihad, infiltration jihad, media jihad, geographical jihad, re-writing history jihad, dawa (proselytizing) jihad, etc.

➤ Jihad is the core tradition of Mohammed. This fact is supported by centuries of scholarship. Jihad has its roots in the commands of the Koran. The purpose of jihad is to establish the sharia.

➤ Never accept the suggestion to delete some words in a debate. If you accept the Islamic position of deleting words from a debate, then you are deleting words from a language, which is controlling the language, and thus controlling the debate.

➤ Never concede your position. Always be polite, courteous, and make use of proper language. (G 40)

➤ Never forget that Islamic hate groups accuse Americans of what they themselves are guilty of. (G 165)

➤ Stop outreach activities towards Islamists. (G 158) Take them apart and thus destroy them with ethics, morals, logic, and the law.

➤ Make the most out of every opportunity to oppose Islamization.

➤ Never forget that Islam uses the legal system to destroy the legal system. It uses freedom of speech to destroy freedom of speech. It uses the American way of life to destroy the American way of life.

➢ Do not forget that Muslims maintain that where Islamic sharia law and American law collide, sharia law must prevail. (G 97)

➢ Muslims will say *Ask not what Islam can do for you, but what you can do for Islam*, which is nothing but Islamic indoctrination using John F. Kennedy's statement that he plagiarized from Kahil Gibran, himself a Muslim. (G 103, 104)

➢ Never forget that Arabic is not just a language. It is the language of Islam. As such, Arabic is an integral part of the world conversion politics of Islam. It is a vanguard language that is opposed to Western cultures and Western languages (non-Muslim cultures and non-Muslim languages).

➢ Never forget that there was never a golden culture under Islamic dictatorship anywhere. (G 106)

➢ Never forget that the bottom line of Islam is that it is barbaric. (113, 128)

➢ Never forget that the Muslim home is a concentration camp.

➢ Be aware of the deceptive definition that according to Muslims, sharia law is not law because "the obligations that sharia Law imposes are not legal obligations, but are obligations of a personal and private nature dictated by faith."[464] Yet when firmly established in the community, the state, on the national level, in the culture, it is to supplant the *Constitution*, which embodies every virtue humans have

---

[464] http://www.law.ou.edu/sites/default/files/files/common_folder/03%20 parry%20essay%20blu1.pdf, retrieved on 24.04.2012.

ever known. Notice that in the definition the terminology *sharia law* is used to say that it is not law. (G 134)

➢ Never forget that the mass lamestream media like the *New York Times are* nothing more than velvet-tongued masters of nonsense. (G 113)

➢ Never forget that the Islamic project is to destroy America and to convert it into an Islamic caliphate and make it part of the umma. (G 143, 147)

➢ Obtain information on how to stop the Islamization of America from AtlasShrugs.com; jihadwatch.org; Loganswarning.com; creepingsharia.com. (G 147)

➢ As the strategy of Islam is to take the United States apart and destroy it, let your strategy be: tell the truth and expose Islam for the cause of freedom.

➢ Support the correct political candidates. (G 181) There are still some upright politicians available.

➢ When an Islamic group has a demonstration, organize a counter demonstration. (G 181)

➢ There is no real Islamic participation in politics. Islamic presence in politics is called *siyash*: sabotage. Islam uses politics and the principles of democratic republicanism to achieve power. Islam does not want power as a form of political culture. Islam wants power to save itself.

➢ Always tell the truth. Be righteous. Set an example. (G 38)

Exactly because of the above guidelines, the reader should not forget that in 1991, Siraj Wahhaj (born Jeffrey Krease in 1950), was the first Muslim cleric to give an invocation to the Unites States Congress. He has warned America and its politicians that the United States of America will fall if it does not "accept the Islamic agenda. If only Muslims were clever politically, they could take over the United States and replace its constitutional government with a caliphate."[465] In 1992, a colleague, Imam Warith Deen Mohammed (1933-2008), gave the invocation in the Senate. He has stated that he felt that the influence of Islamic schools of law was advancing in America. "I think we are gradually getting a sense of madhabs in America, especially those like me. We are getting a sense of madhabs. And with the coming generation I think that we will be getting a much stronger sense of it. It is coming more and more."[466] *Madhab* is the Arabic word meaning *the way taken*, in *the sense of the teaching*, the *school of thought*. They are schools of Islamic law (*Fiqh* meaning *realization*) from specific sources, the Koran and the hadiths, and they compose the totality of the legal system, the sharia.

---

[465] Spencer, Robert. *The Politically Incorrect Guide to Islam and the Crusades*, Regnery Publishing, Inc., Washington, D.C.: 2005, pp. 44-45. See also the *Minneapolis Star Tribune*, April 4, 1993 and Pipes, Daniel and Chada, Sharon, *CAIR: Islamists Fooling the Establishment* in *Middle East Quarterly*, Spring 2006.

[466] http://www.patheos.com/blogs/altmuslim/2008/09/if_we_become_independent_thinkers_we_can_make_a_contribution/, which was retrieved on 24.04.2012.

Yes, America! They are coming every day! Encounter the Muslim undermining of America with a solid, patriotic, American resistance. Resistance with force and truth is what Muslims and Islam understand. This will stop the Islamization of America. The attacks must be encountered and defeated decisively. If the creeping Islamization is not defeated, there will only be one last death notice ...

# Obituary

The Caliphate States of America in 2076

Today, a man was found dead in the former capital of the former United States of America, Washington, D. C., now known to all Muslims as the caliphate capital of the world. The man's corpse was taken to the caliphate coroner's laboratory to determine the cause of death. The man was extremely old, supposedly in the range of three hundred years. The man died a natural death despite signs that he had been in an enduring struggle for survival. Across the soles of both feet in large letters was the following tattooed message in Arabic:

"This message is written in Arabic so that all persons living in the former United States of America will understand it."

*I was the last, living, original, American patriot.*

# APPENDIX I

# Benjamin Franklin's Statement on Islam

Benjamin Franklin was born in Boston, Massachusetts on January 17, 1706. He died in Philadelphia, Pennsylvania on April 17, 1790. The first writing of his *Memoirs of the Life and Writings of Benjamin Franklin* was undertaken while he was the representative of the American Colonies in London, England in 1771. When Franklin was in Paris as a representative of the United States in 1784, he began work anew on the autobiography. Although the original recount was in the form of an autobiographical letter to his son William Franklin, from 1784 on, the autobiography took on the intended appearance of a report about his personal experiences in the Age of the Enlightenment and how Benjamin Franklin was able to use moral principles and practical experiences to become a prosperous, self-made man. The third part of the autobiography was started in 1788 when he was the President (Governor) of Pennsylvania. The fourth was begun shortly before his death. It has only a few pages that differ in length according to the various editions. The first unofficial publication of the *Memoirs of the Life and Writings of Benjamin Franklin* was in French in 1791. The first incomplete manuscript publication in English was in 1817/1818. The complete English edition was published in 1868.

With Benjamin Franklin's noted memorandum "I am now about to write at home, August, 1788 ...," we can conclude that Chapter Ten of *Memoirs of the Life and Writings of Benjamin Franklin*, was written back at home in Philadelphia. In this chapter we read:

"In 1739 arrived among us from Ireland the Reverend Mr. Whitefield, who had made himself remarkable there as an itinerant preacher. He was at first permitted to preach in some of our churches; but the clergy, taking a dislike to him, soon refus'd him their pulpits, and he was oblig'd to preach in the fields. The multitudes of all sects and denominations that attended his sermons were enormous, and it was a matter of speculation to me, who was one of the number, to observe the extraordinary influence of his oratory on his hearers, and how much they admir'd and respected him, notwithstanding his common abuse of them, by assuring them that they were naturally half beasts and half devils."

"It was wonderful to see the change soon made in the manners of our inhabitants. From being thoughtless or indifferent about religion, it seem'd as if all the world were growing religious, so that one could not walk thro' the town in an evening without hearing psalms sung in different families of every street."

"And it being found inconvenient to assemble in the open air, subject to its inclemencies, the building of a house to meet in was no sooner propos'd, and persons appointed to receive contributions, but sufficient sums were soon receiv'd to procure the ground and erect the building, which was one hundred feet long and seventy broad, about the size of Westminster Hall; and the work was carried on with such spirit as to be finished in a much shorter time than could have been expected."

"Both house and ground were vested in trustees, expressly for the use of any preacher of any religious persuasion who might desire to say something to the people at Philadelphia; the design in building not being to accommodate any particular sect, but the inhabitants in general; so that *even if the Mufti of Constantinople were to send a missionary to preach Mohammedanism to us, he would find a pulpit at his service.*"[467]

COMMENTARY AND EXPLANATION

Islamic internet sites are overjoyed with this author-italicized statement from Benjamin Franklin.[468] They present this statement as Franklin's open advocacy of Islam for the United States of America. The situation deserves enumerated scrutiny.

1. The statement was made in conjunction with the appearance in the Colonies of the Irish itinerant preacher George Whitefield. Benjamin Franklin was only stating that he was proud of Philadelphia's solution in finding room for George Whitefield to deliver his sermons. This statement is typical of Benjamin Franklin's use of hyperbole to make a point.

2. Benjamin Franklin was not aware that a Mufti is a person who issues opinions on Islamic law. Neither did he know that *da'wah* or *dawah* means the preaching of Islam nor that a preacher is a *da'eah*. The more correct term would be *imam*, the worship leader of a mosque and the Muslim

---

[467] The emphasis is by the present author.

[468] http://www.muslimpopulation.com/America/USA/Islam%20in%20USA. php; http://muslimvoices.org/religious-textbook-wars/; http://pakistanlink. org/Opinion/2011/Feb11/04/01.HTM, retrieved on 24.04.2012.

381

community. The imam leads the mosque services of Islamic dogma.

3. The first English translation of the Koran is that by the English intellectual George Sale, which appeared in a quarto volume in November 1734 and in a medium octavo volume in 1764. George Sale wrote in his commentary,

"It is certainly one of the most convincing proofs that Mohammedism was no other than human invention, that it owed its progress and establishment almost entirely to the sword."[469]

We know that Thomas Jefferson bought a copy of this edition in 1765 when he was a student at the College of William and Mary in Virginia.[470] He catalogued it in his personal library not under religion, but under law. When in 1786, Thomas Jefferson, then the American ambassador to France, and John Adams, then the American ambassador to Britain, met in London with Sidi Haji Abdul Rahman Adja, the Tripolitan ambassador to Britain, Jefferson most likely bought a second copy of the Koran.

4. Benjamin Franklin never argued that Muslims should be able to preach Islam in the United States of America. The

---

[469] http://www.gutenberg.org/cache/epub/7440/pg7440.html, The Koran (Al-Qur'an) by George Sale, retrieved on 24.04.2012.

[470] http://www.saudiaramcoworld.com/issue/201104/thomas.jefferson.s.qur.an.htm, retrieved on 24.04.2012.

statement above does not have the strength of an argument. Franklin definitely read the Koran and knew its contents, as well as what some historical Muslims had said. For example, in a letter to *The Federal Gazette*, March 23, 1790, Benjamin Franklin used a statement given by Sidi Mehemet Ibrahim, a member of the Divan of Algiers, in 1687, to show the evilness contained in Islam and the Koran. It deserves to be quoted in its entirety because Islamic sites like those already mentioned take the following quotation out of context:

"Nor can the Plundering of Infidels be in that sacred Book [The Koran] forbidden, since it is well known from it, that God has given the World, and all that it contains, to his faithful Mussulmen, who are to enjoy it of Right as fast as they conquer it." (The underlined section is that which Islamic internet sites claim is Benjamin Franklin's opinion.)

Here is the whole context. The religious sect called *Erika*, or Purists, prayed for the abolition of piracy and slavery as being unjust and wanted Algiers to stop the practice.

> "*Allah Bismillah, &c. God is great, and Mahomet is his Prophet.*"

> "Have these Erika considered the consequences of granting their petition? If we cease our cruises against the Christians, how shall we be furnished with the commodities their countries produce, and which are so necessary for us? If

we forbear to make slaves of their people, who, in this hot climate, are to cultivate our lands? Who are to perform the common labors of our city, and in our families? Must we not then be our own slaves? And is there not more compassion and more favor due to us as Mussulmen than to these Christian dogs? We have now above fifty thousand slaves in and near Algiers. This number, if not kept up by fresh supplies, will soon diminish, and be gradually annihilated. If we, then, cease taking and plundering the infidel ships, making slaves of the seamen and passengers, our lands will become of no value for want of cultivation; the rents of houses in the city will sink one-half; and the revenue of government, arising from its share of prizes, be totally destroyed. And for what? To gratify the whims of a whimsical sect, who would have us not only forbear making more slaves, but even manumit those we have.

But who is to indemnify their masters for the loss? Will the State do it? Is our treasury sufficient? Will the Erika do it? Can they do it? Or would they, to do what they think justice to the slaves, do a greater injustice to the owners? And, if we set our slaves free, what is to be done with them? Few of them will return to their countries; they know too well the greater hardships they must there be subject to; they will not embrace our holy religion; they will not adopt our manners; our people will not pollute themselves by intermarrying with them. Must we maintain them as beggars in our streets, or suffer our properties to be the prey of their pillage? For men accustomed to slavery will not work for a livelihood when not compelled. And what is there so pitiable in their present condition? Were they not slaves in their own countries?"

"Are not Spain, Portugal, France, and the Italian States, governed by despots, who hold all their subjects in slavery, without exception? Even England treats its sailors as slaves: for they are, whenever the government pleases, seized, and confined in ships of war; condemned not only to work, but to fight, for small wages, or a mere subsistence, not better than our slaves are allowed by us. Is their condition, then, made worse by their falling into our hands? No: they have only exchanged one slavery for another, and I may say, a better; for here they are brought into a land where the sun of Islam gives forth its light, and shines in full splendor; and they have an opportunity of making themselves acquainted with the true doctrine, and thereby saving their immortal souls. Those who remain at home have not that happiness. Sending the slaves home, then, would be sending them out of light into darkness."

"I repeat the question, What is to be done with them? I have heard it suggested that they may be planted in the wilderness, where there is plenty of land for them to subsist on, and where they may flourish as a free State; but they are, I doubt, too little disposed to labor without compulsion, as well as too ignorant to establish a good government, and the wild Arabs would soon molest and destroy or again enslave them. While serving us, we take care to provide them with everything, and they are treated with humanity. The laborers in their own country are, as I am well informed, worse fed, lodged, and clothed."

"The condition of most of them is, therefore, already mended, and requires no further improvement. Here their lives are in safety. They are not liable to be impressed for soldiers, and forced to cut one another's Christian throats, as in the wars of their own countries. If some of the religious mad bigots, who now tease us with their silly petitions, have, in a fit of blind zeal, freed their slaves, it was not generosity, it was not humanity, that moved them to the action: it was from the conscious burden of a load of sins, and a hope, from the supposed merits of so good a work, to be excused from damnation."

"How grossly are they mistaken to suppose slavery to be disallowed by the

Alcoran! Are not the two precepts, to quote no more, '*Masters, treat your slaves with kindness; slaves, serve your masters with cheerfulness and fidelity,*' clear proofs to the contrary? Nor can the plundering of infidels be in that sacred book forbidden, since it is well known from it that God has given the world, and all that it contains, to his faithful Mussulmen, who are to enjoy it of right as fast as they conquer it. Let us, then, hear no more of this detestable proposition, – the manumission of Christian slaves; the adoption of which would, by depreciating our lands and houses, and thereby depriving so many good citizens of their properties, create universal discontent, and provoke insurrections, to the endangering of government, and producing general confusion. I have, therefore, no doubt but this wise council will prefer the comfort and happiness of a whole nation of true believers to the whim of a few Erika, and dismiss their petition."

"The Divan came to the following conclusion: 'The doctrine that plundering and enslaving Christians is unjust, is, at best, *problematical*; but that it is the interest of this State to continue the practice, is clear; therefore let the petition be rejected.'"

Benjamin Franklin notes, "And it was rejected accordingly."[471]

Benjamin Franklin knew the contents of the Koran and the pronouncements of Mohammed. He knew that Muslims plundered according to the dictates of Mohammed and the Koran. Benjamin Franklin knew that the Judeo-Christian God would never stoop to such a non-human niveau. He knew that Islam was evil, exceedingly more evil than the English monarchy under King George III of England.

---

[471] http://american_almanac.tripod.com/ffslave.htm, retrieved on 24.04.2012.

# APPENDIX II

# Dr. Youssef A. Mroueh

Dr. Youssef A. Mroueh is a mathematician and physicist living in Canada. He is an Islamic functionary and a past President of the World Union of Writers in Arabic – Canada. We can read the following about Dr. Youssef A. Mroueh:[472]

**DR. YOUSSEF A. MROUEH [Mathematician, Scientist, Researcher]**

• Born in Nabatieh, Lebanon in 1937.

• Came to Canada in 1969.

• Educated in Lebanon, Britain, Germany, the USA, and Canada. He holds a D.Sc. in radiation physics from Jackson University. (It is not known which Jackson University, or Jackson State University is meant; Jackson, Mississippi; Jackson Tennessee; San Francisco, or wherever.)

• He originated a new mathematical theorem in topology in 1954.

• Modified the Fitzgerald-Lorenz contractionfor special relativity in 1965.

• Investigated the behaviors of matter at superhuman speeds in 1972.

---

[472] http://www.canadianarabcommunity.com/makingadifferenceincanada. php, retrieved on 16.03.2012.

• He is in charge of research in radiation control, industrial radiography and ultrasonics.

• Arab Canadian researcher and author of several studies and reports of science, religion, and philosophy.

As listed, the information can be considered to be impressive. After all, there are not many doctors of radiation physics who write about religion and philosophy, and as quoted in Chapter Seven of *The Muslim Discovery of America*, cultural, historical traditions. The reader now knows that the assertions made by Dr. Mroueh, to the effect that there are hundreds of place names in the United States of America and Canada which have Arab-Islamic roots as their origin are not true. It is also the irony of fate and an etymological fact that even his name is not of Arab-Islamic origin. The origin of the name Youssef and Mroueh deserve closer examination.

**Youssef** is transliterated as Jusuf, Yossef, Youcef, Yousaf, Yousef, Yousif, Youssef, Youssif, Youssouf, Yousuf, Yusef, Yuseff, Yusof, Yussef, Yusuf. It is written in Arabic as يوسف *Yūsuf* and *Yūsif*). Written this way, the nomenclature is a male Arabic name, meaning *Allah increases in piety, power, and influence*. The name is considered the Arabic equivalent of the English name *Joseph*. The indication is that the name is Arabic. However, only the writing is Arabic. The name Youssef is not only the Arabic equivalent of Joseph,[473] it is the variant spelling of the Hebrew name Joseph, which "like all other Hebrew names beginning with the syllable 'Jo,' has Yhwh as its first element, and is a contraction, the original form being

---

[473] http://en.wikipedia.org/wiki/Yusuf, retrieved on 16.06.2012.

'Jehoseph.'"[474] The original meaning is *God shall add*. Arabic culture changed the original meaning to *Allah increases in piety, power, and influence*. Well, if Dr. Mroueh can take liberties in rewriting the history of the discovery of America, Arab culture can take liberties in redefining the meaning of the Hebrew name J(eh)oseph.

We learn from the Old Testament that Joseph is Jacob's eleventh son and Rachel's first. We learn from the New Testament that Joseph is the husband of the Virgin Mary. Additionally, in the New Testament we encounter Joseph of Arimathea, who is a disciple of Jesus. It was this Joseph who provided the tomb for Jesus' burial.

Without providing conclusive documentation, the Mroueh family contend that they have traced their lineage back to Malik Al-Ashtar (???-sometime after 659/660?), a loyal companion of Ali Ibn Abi Talib, Muhammed's cousin and son-in-law.[475] During Muhammad's time Malik Al-Ashtar converted to Islam and during Ali Ibn Abi Talib's caliphate he fought in the Battles of Jamal (656) and Siffin (657) during the first Fitna (First Muslim Civil War) in Ali's Islamic defence. For his service he was appointed Governor of Egypt in 658.

Malik Al-Ashtar was a leader from the ancient Yemeni Tribe of Al Nakhay (or Al Naghy).[476] In the 6th century, after

---

[474] http://jewishencyclopedia.com/articles/8803-joseph#1553, retrieved on 16.03.2012.

[475] http://www.mroueh.com/origins.htm, retrieved on 16.03.2012.

[476] http://www.eslam.de/begriffe/m/malik_aschtar.htm, retrieved on 16.03.2012.

expanding his kingdom into the Arabian Peninsula and portions of East Africa, King Abu-Karib Assad converted to Judaism. In the 7th century Mohammed began his conquest of the Arabian Peninsula. By Mohammed's death in 632, Yemen had come under the control of Islam. There are some indications that Malik Al-Ashtar might have originated in Hamadan, the capital city of the present Hamadan Province in the western part of Iran. Before Malik Al-Ashtar's conversion to Islam, he could have been of the Jewish faith, as was his king. If Malik Al-Ashtar originated in Hamadan, he was Persian and belonged to the faith of Zoroastrianism. Persia came under complete Islamic control in 651.

At best, the family name Mroueh is questionably quasi-Arabic, for it definitely has some genealogical reaches into Yemenite and or possibly Persian sources. The first name Youssef is Hebrew in origin. Therefore, the name Youssef Mroueh has no absolute Arab-Islamic root connection.

The appellation *Mroueh* means *honor* and *generosity*.[477] This is one side of the medal. Certainly Muslims consider Dr. Youssef A. Mroueh's attempts at documenting the existence of Muslims in America in pre-Columbian times as honorable for the furtherance of Islam. Indeed, Dr. Mroueh was very generous in his listing of place names discussed in Chapter Seven. The other side of the medal is that for a doctor of radiological science to lie as generously as he did is an insult to academia and basic principles of research. Dr. Youssef A. Mroueh has lost his honor with his lies attrributing Arabic Islamic origins to American place names.

---

[477] http://www.mroueh.com/origins.htm, retrieved on 16.03.2012.

# BIBLIOGRAPHY

The bibliography is an all-inclusive listing of the sources used in writing this book. The listing does not contain any additional sources.

## Books

A'la Maududi, Sayyid Abdul. *The Meaning of the Qur'an*, Vol. 5, Markazi Maktaba Islami Publishers, New Delhi: 2006.

Alford, Terry. *Prince Among Slaves*, Harcourt Brace Jovanovich, New York: 1977.

Ali al-Masudi, Ali. *The Meadows of Gold and Mines of Gems, The Book of Golden Meadows* in Al-Masudi *Muruj Adh-Dhahab*, Vol. I.

Allison, Robert J. *The Crescent Obscured The United States and the Muslim World 1776-1815*, Oxford University Press: 1995.

Allison, Robert J. *The Crescent Obscured: The United States and the Muslim World, 1776–1815*, Oxford University Press, Oxford: 1995.

Armbruster, C. H. *Dongolese Nubian. A Lexicon.* Cambridge University Press, Cambridge: 1965.

Armstrong, Karin. *Jerusalem: One City, Three Faiths*, Balantine Books, New York: 1997.

Austin, Allan D. *African Muslims in Antebellum America Transatlantic Stories and Spiritual Struggles*, Routledge, New York: 1997.

Beers, Frederick L. (J. B. Beers & Co.). *History of Greene County, New York: with biographical sketches of its prominent men*, Hope Farm Press, Cornwallville, N.Y.: 1969.

*Behind the Veil*, an electronic book at http://answering-islam.org/BehindVeil/index.html, retrieved on 12.01.2012.

Bostom, Andrew G. editor. *The Legacy of Islamic Antisemitism From Sacred Texts to Solemn History*, Prometheus Books, Amherst, New York, 2008.

Bostom, *Sharia versus Freedom The Legacy of Islamic Totalitarianism*, Prometheus Books, Amherst, New York: 2012.

Bostom, Andrew G. editor. *The Legacy of Jihad Islamic Holy War and the Fate of Non-Muslims*, Prometheus Books, Amherst, New York: 2005.

Campo, Juan E. *Encyclopedia of Islam*, Facts on File, New York: 2009.

Chisholm, Hugh, ed. Barbary Pirates in *Encyclopædia Britannica*, 11th ed., Cambridge University Press, Cambridge: 1911.

Coon, Carleton S. *Southern Arabia*, Smithsonian Institute Washington, D.C.: 1944.

Cooper, James, *Salih Bilali* in William Brown Hodgson's *Notes on North Africa*, Wiley and Putnam, New York: 1844.

Crone, Patricia. *Meccan Trade and the Rise of Islam*, Georgia Press, Piscataway, New Jersey: 2004.

Curtis IV, Edward E. *Encyclopedia of Muslim-American History*, Facts on File Inc., New York: 2010.

Curtis, Edward E. *Muslims in America A Short History*, Oxford University Press, Oxford: 2009.

Dilts, Howard E. *From Ackley to Zwingle: The Origins of Iowa Place Names*, Iowa State University Press: Ames, Iowa: 1993.

Dwight, Theodore Jr. *Condition and Character of Negroes in Africa, Methodist Quarterly Review*, January 1864, pp. 77-90.

*Ebony Pictorial History of Black America*, Vol. I, *African Past to Civil War*, Johnson Publishing Company, Inc., Chicago: 1971.

Eilts, Herman Fredrick. *The visit of Ahmad bin Na'aman to the US in the Year 1840*, Embassy of Oman: 1962.

*Encyclopaedia Britannica, Micropaedia*, Vol. 1, William Benton, Chicago: 1974.

Evanz, Karl. *The Judas Factor: The Plot to Kill Malcolm X*, Thunder's Mouth Press New York: 1992.

Farah, Caesar. *Islam: Beliefs and Observations*, Barrons, New York: 1987.

Fell, Barry. *Saga America*, Times Books, New York: 1980.

Fell, Barry. *Vermont's Ancient Sites and the Larger Picture of Trans-Atlantic Visitations to America, B. C.* in *Ancient Vermont, Proceedings of the Castleton Conference, Castleton State College*, October 14-15, 1977, edited by Warren L. Cook, published for Castleton State College by the Academy Books of Rutland, Vermont: 1978.

Fell, Howard Barraclough (Barry). *America B. C.: Ancient Settlers in the New World*, Quadrangle Books, New York: 1976.

Fell, Howard Barraclough (Barry). *Bronze Age America*, Little, Brown, Boston: 1982.

Fell, Howard Barraclough (Barry). *Saga America*, Times Books, New York: 1980.

Gaubatz, David P. and Sperry, Paul. *Muslim Mafia*, WND Books, New York: 2009.

Geller, Pamela. *Stop the Islamization of America A practical Guide to the Resistance*, WND Books, New York: 2011.

Geller, Pamela. *Stop the Islamization of America A Practical Guide to the Resistance*, WND Books, Washington, D. C.: 2011.

Ghanea Bassiri, Kambiz. *A History of Islam in America: From the New World to the New World Order*, Cambridge University Press; 2010, chronicles the Muslim presence in America across five centuries.

Gibbon, Edward. *The History of the Decline and Fall of the Roman Empire*, David Womersley, editor, 3 Vols., Penguin, New York: 1994, Chapter 50.

Gilbert, William Harlen. *Surviving Indian Groups of the Eastern United States: Annual Report Smithsonian Institution*, Library of Congress: 1948.

Glassé, Cyril. *The new encyclopedia of Islam*, Rowman & Littlefield, Lanham, Maryland: 2008.

Goddard, Ives. *The Delaware Jargon* in *New Sweden in America*, edited by Carol E. Hoffecker et al, University of Delaware Press, Newark: 1995.

Grunebaum, G. E. von. *Classical Islam: A History 600 A.D. - 1258 A.D.,* Aldine Publishing Company, Chicago: 1970.

Guillaume, Alfred. *Islam*, Penguin, Harmondsworth, England: 1990, p.7.

Guillaume, Alfred. translator. *The Life of Mohammed*, Oxford University Press, Karachi, tenth impression, 1995.

Hall, Mark. 1985, *A Study of the Sumerian Moon-god, Nanna/Suen*; University of Pennsylvania Press, Philadelphia: 1985.

Hamidullah, Mohammad. *Muslim Discovery of America before Columbus*, in *Journal of the Muslim Students' Association of the United States and Canada*, 1968.

Hawass, Zahi A.; Brock, Lyla Pinch *Egyptology at the Dawn of the Twenty-First Century: Archaeology* (2nd ed.). Cairo: American University in Cairo: 2003.

Hill, Samuel S. and Lippy, Charles H. Charles Reagan Wilson *Encyclopedia of religion in the South,* Mercer University Press, Macon, Georgia: 2005.

Hoobler, Dorothy and Thomas. *Images Across the Ages: Chinese Portraits*, Raintree Publishers, Austin Texas: 1993.

*Institutiones Iustiniani*, Title III, Book I, paragraph 2.

Ives Goddard, Ives, ed., *Handbook of North American Indians*, volume 17: *Languages*, Smithsonian Institution, Washington, D.C.: 1996; and Bruce Trigger, ed., *Handbook of North American Indians*, volume 15: *Northeast*, Smithsonian Institution, Washington, D.C.: 1978.

Jeffreys, M. D. W. *Pre-Columbian Maize North of the Old World Equator*, in *Cahiers d'études africaines*, 1969, Volume 9, Numéro 33.

John A. Holm, *Pidgins and Creoles*, volume 1: *Theory and Structure*, Cambridge Language Surveys, Cambridge University Press, Cambridge, U.K. & New York: 1988.

Joseph Needham, Joseph and & Colin A. Ronan, Colin A. *The Shorter Science and Civilisation in China*, Cambridge University Press, Cambridge: 1986.

Khai, Tabish. *Other Routes: 1500 Years of African and Asian Travel Writing,* Signal Books, Oxford: 2006.

Kidd, Thomas. S. *American Christians and Islam - Evangelical Culture and Muslims from the Colonial Period to the Age of Terrorism*, Princeton University Press, Princeton, NJ, 2008.

Koszegi, Michael A., and Melton, J. Gordon, eds. *Islam In North America A Sourcebook*, Garland Publishing, New York: 1992.

Krakow, Kenneth K. *Georgia Place-Names*, 3$^{rd}$ ed., Kenneth K. Krakow and Winship Press, Macon, Georgia: 1975.

Lambert, Frank. *The Barbary Wars American Independence in the Atlantic World*, Hill and Wang, New York: 2005.

Lesne, Emile. *Histoire de la propriété ecclésiastique en France*, Vol. I, Facultes Catholiques, Lille: 1938.

Lewis, Bernard. *The Arabs in History*, Oxford University Press, Oxford, England, reissued in 2003.

Li, Hui-lin. *Mu-lan-p'i: A Case for Pre-Columbian Transatlantic Travel by Arab Ships*, in the *Harvard Journal of Asiatic Studies*, (Harvard-Yenching Institute), 1960-1961.

Lincoln, C. Eric. *The Black Muslims in America*, Third Edition, Eerdmans Publishing Company Grand Rapids, Michigan: 1994.

London, Joshua E. *Victory in Tripoli: How America's War with the Barbary Pirates Established the U.S. Navy and Shaped a Nation*, John Wiley & Sons, Inc., New Jersey: 2005.

Madden, Robert. *Twelve Months in Jamaica*, Carey Lea and Blanchard, Philadelphia: 1835.

Mattu, Ayesha and Nura, Maznovi. *Love InshAllah: The Secret Love Lives of American Muslim Women*, Soft Skull Press, Berkeley, California: 2012.

M'Bow, Amadou Mahtar; Kettani, Ali. *Islam and Muslims in the American continent*, Center of Historical, Economical and Social Studies, Beirut: 2001.

McCarthy, Andrew C. *The Grand Jihad How Islam and the Left Sabotage America*, Encounter Books, New York: 2010.

McCarthy, Andrew C. *Willful Blindness A Memoir of the Jihad.* Encounter Books, New York: 2008.

Meacham, Jon. *American lion: Andrew Jackson in the White House*, Random House New York: 2008.

Menzies, Gavin. *1421: The Year China Discovered America*, William Morrow, New York: 2003.

Momen, Moojan. *An introduction to Shi'i Islam*, Yale University Press New Haven, Connecticut: 1985.

Moshay, G.J.O. *Who Is This Allah?* Dorchester House, Bucks, United Kingdom: 1994.

Murata, Sachiko. *The Tao of Islam: a sourcebook on gender relationships in Islamic thought*, State University of New York Press, Albany, New York: 1992.

Murrell, William Meacham. *Cruise Of The Frigate Columbia Around The World Under The Command Of Commodore George C. Read.* Benjamin B. Mussey, Boston, Mass.: 1840.

Newman, N. A. editor. *Three Early Christian – Muslim Debates*, Ibri, Hatfield, Pennsylvania: 1994, p. 719.

Newman, Stanley. *Zuni dictionary*, Indiana University Bloomington: 1958.

Obregon, Mauricio. *The Columbus Papers, The Barcelona Letter of 1493, The Landfall Controversy, and the Indian Guides*, McMillan Co., New York: 1991.

O'Leary, De Lacy. *Arabic Thought and Its Place In Western History*, Routledge & Kegan Paul, Ltd., London: 1954.

O'Neill, John. J. *Holy Warriors Islam and the Demise of Classical Civilization*, Felibri Publications, jonplotinus@googlemail.com.

Pipes, Daniel and Chada, Sharon, *CAIR: Islamists Fooling the Establishment* in *Middle East Quarterly*, Spring 2006.

Pipes, Daniel. *Slaves, Soldiers and Islam The Genesis of a Military System*, Yale University Press, New London, Connecticut: 1981.

Pirenne, Henri. *Mohammed and Charlemagne*, translated from the French by Bernard Miall, Barnes and Noble, New York: 1956.

Potts, Austin. *The Hymns and Prayers To The Moon-god, Sin*, Dropsie College, Philadelphia Pennsylvania: 1971.

Prentiss, Craig R. *Religion and the creation of race and ethnicity: an introduction.* NYU Press, New York: 2003

Pritzker, Barry M. *A Native American Encyclopedia: History, Culture, and Peoples.* Oxford University Press, Oxford: 2000.

Purnell, Isabelle S. *History of Mahomet: Mahomet Methodist Church Centennial*, Mahomet Methodist Church, 1955.

Queen, Edward L., Prothero, Stephen, and Shattuck Jr., Gardiner H. *The Encyclopedia of American Religious History*, Facts on File, New York: 1996.

*Report of the Secretary of War, communicating, in compliance with a resolution of the Senate of February 2, 1857, information respecting the purchase of camels for the purposes of military transportation.* United States. War Dept., Davis, Jefferson, 1808-1889., Colombari, F., Wayne, Henry C. tr. (Henry Constantine), 1815-1883.

Richardson, Don. *Secrets of the Koran Revealing Insights Into Islam's Holy Book*, Regal Books, Ventura, California: 2003.

Sarwar, Hafiz Ghulam. *Muhammad: the Holy Prophet*, Muhammah Ashraf, Lahore, Pakistan: 1961.

Savage, Tom; Horton, Loren N. *Dictionary of Iowa Place-Names*, University of Iowa Press: Iowa City: 2007.

Seuren, Pieter A. M. *Western Linguistics an historical introduction*, Blackwell, Oxford: 1998.

Sezgin, Fuat. *The Pre-Columbian Discovery of the American Continent by Muslim Seafarers*, Institute for the History of Arabic-Islamic Studies, Johann Wolfgang Goethe University, Frankfurt am Main: 2005, at www.uni-frankfurt/fb13/igaiw, retrieved on 16.01.2012.

Smith, Jane I. *Islam in America*, Columbia University Press, New York: 1999, 2009.

Sonneck, Oscar George Theodore. *A Bibliography of Early Secular Music*, "*ALGERINE CAPTIVE. Song by Raynor Taylor.

Spencer, Robert, *The Politically Incorrect Guide to Islam and the Crusades*, Regnery Publishing, Inc., Washington, D.C.: 2005.

Spencer, Robert. *Did Mohammed Exist? An Inquiry into Islam's Obscure Origins*, ISI Books, Wilmington, Delaware: 2012.

Spencer, Robert. *Stealth Jihad: How Radical Islam Is Subverting America Without Guns Or Bombs*, Regnery Publishing Inc., Washington, D.C.: 2008.

Sperl, Stefan; Shackle, C.; Awde, Nicholas. *Qasida Poetry in Islamic Asia and Africa: Classical traditions and modern meanings - Volume 20 of Studies in Arabic literature*, E. J. Brill, Leiden: 1996.

St. Jerome, *Epistle* lxxvii.

Stark, Rodney. *The Victory of Reason*, Random House, New York: 2005.

Stevens, Michael and Allen, Christine *State Records of South Carolina. Journals of the House of Representatives*, 1789-90, University of South Carolina Press: 1984.

Stewart, H. F. *Thoughts and Ideas of the Period* in *The Cambridge Medieval History: The Christian Empire*, Vol. I, Cambridge University Press, Cambridge: 1936.

Tanselle, Thomas. in *Royall Tyler*, Harvard University Press, Cambridge, Massachusetts: 1967.

Taylor, Colin F. editor. *The Native Americans The Indigenous People of North America*, Smithmark, New York: 1991.

Temple, Robert. *The genius of China: 3,000 years of science, discovery & invention*, 3rd ed., Andre Deutsch, London: 2007.

Thacher, John Boyd. *Christopher Columbus*, New York: 1950.

Thackston, Wheeler McIntosh. *Album prefaces and other documents on the history of calligraphers and painters: Volume 10 of Studies in Islamic art and architecture*, E. J. Brill, Leiden, 2001.

*The American Annual Register for 1827-28-29*, E. and G. W. Blunt, New York, 1830.

*The New Encyclopædia Britannica*, 15th Edition, Encyclopædia Britannica, Inc., Chicago, Illinois: 1998, Vol. 10.

Tibbetts, Gerald R. *The Beginnings of a Cartographic Tradition*, in: John Brian Harley, David Woodward, *Cartography in the Traditional Islamic and South Asian Societies*, Chicago: 1992.

Turner, Richard Brent. *Islam in the African-American Experience*, Indiana University Press, Bloomington, Indiana: 2003.

van Donzel, E. J. *Islamic Desk Reference, compiled from the Encyclopaedia of Islam*, E. J. Brill, Leiden: 1994.

Van Sertima, Ivan. *They Came Before Columbus*, Random House, New York: 1976.

von Wuthenau, Alexander. *Unexpected Faces in Ancient America*, Crown Publishers, New York: 1975.

Waldman, Carl. *Encyclopedia of Native American Tribes*, Checkmark Books, New York: 2009.

*Wall Street Journal*, Vol. CIV, NO. 6, Friday, July 9, 1999.

Wallon, H. A. *Histoire de l'esclavage dans l'antiquité*, 3 vols., Paris: 1879, Vol. III.

Warraq, Ibn, editor and translator. *The Quest for the Historical Muhammad*, Prometheus Books, Amherst, New York: 2000.

Warraq, Ibn, editor and translator. *What the Koran Really Says: Language, Text, and Commentary*, Prometheus Books, Amherst, New York: 2002.

Warraq, Ibn, editor. *Leaving Islam: Apostates Speak Out*, Prometheus Books, Amherst, New York: 2003.

Warraq, Ibn, editor. *The Origins of The Koran: Classic Essays on Islam's Holy Book*, edited by Ibn Warraq, Prometheus Books, Amherst, New York: 1998.

Warraq, Ibn. *Defending the West: A Critique of Edward Said's Orientalism*, Prometheus Books Amherst, New York: 2007

Warraq, Ibn. *Which Koran?: Variants, Manuscripts, and the Influence of Pre-Islamic Poetry*, Prometheus Books Amherst, New York: 2007.

Warraq, Ibn. *Why I Am Not a Muslim*, Prometheus Books, Amherst, New York: 1995.

Warraq, Ibn. *Why I Am Not A Muslim*, Prometheus, Amherst, New York: 1995.

Warraq, Ibn. *Why the West is Best: A Muslim Apostate's Defense of Liberal Democracy*, Encounter Books, New York: 2011.

Webb, Muhammad Alexander Russell. *Islam in America and Other Writings*, Magribine Press, Chicago: 2006.

Weslager, Clinton Alfred. *Delaware's Forgotten Folk, The Story of the Moors & Nanticokes*, University of Pennsylvania Press, Philadelphia: 1943.

Weslager, Clinton Alfred. *Forgotten Moors* in *The Nanticoke Indians*, University of Delaware Press, Newark: 1983.

Wiener, Leo. *Africa and the Discovery of America*, Philadelphia: 1920, Vol. 2.

Wilson, Peter Lamborn. *Pirate Utopias: Moorish Corsairs & European Renegadoes*, Autonomedia, New York: 1996,

Wilson, Peter Lamborn. *Sacred Drift: Essays on the Margins of Islam*, City Lights Books, San Francisco: 1993.

Ye'or, Bat. *Eurabia: The Euro-Arab Axis*, Fairleigh Dickinson University Press, Madison, New Jersey: 2005.

Ye'or, Bat. *Islam and Dhimmitude: Where Civilizations Collide*, Fairleigh Dickinson University Press, Madison, New Jersey: 2001.

Ye'or, Bat. *The Decline of Eastern Christianity: From Jihad to Dhimmitude; seventh-twentieth century*, Fairleigh Dickinson University Press, Madison, New Jersey: 1996.

Ye'or, Bat. *The Dhimmi: Jews and Christians Under Islam*, Fairleigh Dickinson University Press, Madison, New Jersey: 1985.

## Internet Sites

http://30mosques.com/archive2010/2010/09/day-22-ross-north-dakota-a-leap-in-time/.

http://abusivediscretion.wordpress.com/.

http://adamholland.blogspot.de/2010/05/alan-sabrosky-large-majority-of-us-jews.html.

http://afifichestclinic.ning.com/profiles/blogs/a-collection-of-islamic.

http://allaboutMohammed.com/islamic-jurisprudence.html.

http://allaboutmuhammad.com/islamic-jurisprudence.html.

http://american_almanac.tripod.com/ffslave.htm.

http://answeringislam.org/Authors/Arlandson/ultimate_goal.htm.

http://answering-islam.org/BehindVeil/btvintro.html.

http://answering-islam.org/BehindVeil/index.html.

http://answering-islam.org/BehindVeil/index.html. (*Behind the Veil*).

http://answering-islam.org/Quran/Themes/jihad_passages.html.

http://answering-islam.org/Silas/suicide.htm.

http://answering-islam.org/Terrorism/by_the_sword.html.

http://archive.frontpagemag.com/readArticle.aspx?ARTID=13221.

http://archive.frontpagemag.com/readArticle.aspx?ARTID=297.

http://archive.frontpagemag.com/readArticle.aspx?ARTID=5236.

http://articles.chicagotribune.com/2009-03 21/news/0903200518_1_bomb-threat-jewish-school-google-search.

http://atgsociety.com/2011/03/muslims-aim-at-reconquering-spain/.

http://atheism.about.com/od/islamic sects/a/wahhabi.htm.

http://atlasshrugs2000.typepad.com/. All contemporary articles and archived articles.

http://atlasshrugs2000.typepad.com/atlas_shrugs/2010/07/nyc-mosque-forcing-muslim-call-to-prayer-on-neighborhood-.html.

http://atlasshrugs2000.typepad.com/atlas_shrugs/2010/10/full-text-wilders-in-berlin.html.

http://atlasshrugs2000.typepad.com/atlas_shrugs/2011/10/mosquei ng-the-workplace-hertz-suspends-34-muslim-workers-for-abusing-special-prayer-break-times-refu.html.

http://atlasshrugs2000.typepad.com/atlas_shrugs/2011/10/muslim-attacks-wisconsin-man-with-tire-iron-accusing-him-of-criticizing-his-islamic-religion.html.

http://atlasshrugs2000.typepad.com/atlas_shrugs/2011/12/all-american-muslim-dawah-show-to-highlight-how-911-hurt-muslims.html.

http://atlasshrugs2000.typepad.com/atlas_shrugs/2011/12/bni-shut-down-again-hamas-tied-cair-does-victory-dance.html.

http://atlasshrugs2000.typepad.com/atlas_shrugs/2011/12/hamas-hizballah-and-al-qaeda-flags-at-obama-endorsed-occupy-dc.html.

http://atlasshrugs2000.typepad.com/atlas_shrugs/2011/12/hezballa h-laundering-drug-money-in-us-banks-.html .

http://atlasshrugs2000.typepad.com/atlas_shrugs/2011/12/nyc-taxpayer-funded-childrens-museum-to-hold-muslim-program-.html.

http://atlasshrugs2000.typepad.com/atlas_shrugs/2011/12/nyc-taxpayer-funded-childrens-museum-to-hold-muslim-program-.html.

http://atlasshrugs2000.typepad.com/atlas_shrugs/2011/12/obama-defense-dept-allows-muslim-cadets-to-wear-hijabs-or-turbans-hamas-tied-cair-thrilled.html.

http://atlasshrugs2000.typepad.com/atlas_shrugs/2011/12/oic-driven-un-adopts-anti-free-speech-resolution-championed-by-obama-administration.html.

http://atlasshrugs2000.typepad.com/atlas_shrugs/2011/12/palestini an-liberation-army-mufti-caliphate-will-return-and-west-will-pay-jizya-or-else-you-will-bri.html.

http://atlasshrugs2000.typepad.com/atlas_shrugs/2011/12/puffho-trumpets-another-anti-muslim-hate-crime-that-wasnt.html.

http://atlasshrugs2000.typepad.com/atlas_shrugs/2011/12/raising-money-for-lady-al-qaida-i-want-to-kill-americans-and-death-to-america.html.

http://atlasshrugs2000.typepad.com/atlas_shrugs/2011/12/tarek-mehanna-guilty-devout-muslim-found-guilty-of-conspiring-against-us.html.

http://atlasshrugs2000.typepad.com/atlas_shrugs/2011/12/there-goes-the-nabe.html.

http://atlasshrugs2000.typepad.com/atlas_shrugs/2011/12/the-shocking-truth-about-lowes-and-all-american-muslim.html.

http://atlasshrugs2000.typepad.com/atlas_shrugs/2012/01/michael -coren-family-threatened-by-muslim.html.

http://atlasshrugs2000.typepad.com/atlas_shrugs/2012/01/muslim-football-players-in-dearborn-heights-arrested-for-assault-on-christian-quarterback-.html.

http://atlasshrugs2000.typepad.com/atlas_shrugs/2012/02/hamas-cair-organizing-support-for-lady-al-qaeda-hearing-i-want-to-kill-americans.html.

http://atlasshrugs2000.typepad.com/atlas_shrugs/2012/02/muslim-gang-sex-trafficking-trial-in-tennessee-unusual-in-scope-30-on-trial.html.

http://atlasshrugs2000.typepad.com/atlas_shrugs/2012/02/obama-disarms-fbi-counter-terror-training-programs-purges-truth-about-jihad.html.

http://atlasshrugs2000.typepad.com/atlas_shrugs/2012/02/sionafdi
-counters-muslim-brotherhoods-icna-ad-campaign-to-mainstream-
shariah.html.

http://atlasshrugs2000.typepad.com/atlas_shrugs/2012/02/sionafdi
-counters-muslim-brotherhoods-icna-ad-campaign-to-mainstream-
shariah.html.

http://atlasshrugs2000.typepad.com/atlas_shrugs/2012/02/what-
the-headline-isnt.html.

http://atlasshrugs2000.typepad.com/atlas_shrugs/2012/03/muslimi
ntolerance.html.

http://atlasshrugs2000.typepad.com/atlas_shrugs/islam-in-
america.html.

http://atlasshrugs2000.typepad.com/atlas_shrugs/refugee_resettle
ment_the_quiet_jihad_tsunami/.

http://babynames.fortunebaby.com/meaning_of_the_name_ameer
a.html.

http://babynamesworld.parentsconnect.com/meaning_of_Ebo.html.

http://barenakedislam.com/2012/02/05/have-your-schools-been-
indoctrinated-with-whitewashed-islamic-propaganda-yet/.

http://barenakedislam.com/2012/02/23/updatedcontinental-flight-
1118-muslim-screaming-allahu-akbar-was-tackled-and-restrained-
by-passengers/.

http://bigpeace.com/ndarwish/2010/08/26/sharia-for-
dummies/#more-20945.

http://blog.seattlepi.com/hottopics/2011/03/22/2-2-million-fatwa-
on-terry-jones-after-quran-burning/.

http://blogs.cbn.com/stakelbeckonterror/archive/2012/01/10/alaba
ma-muslim-opens-fire-on-police-wanted-to-draw-attention.aspx.

http://books.google.de/books?id=5XfxzCm1qa4C&pg=PA32&dq
=%22AliMolina%22&hl=de&sa=X&ei=yk86T5r4As3Nswbpg92

nBg&ved=0CEcQ6AEwBA#v=onepage&q=%22Ali-Molina%22&f=false.

http://books.google.de/books?id=5XfxzCm1qa4C&pg=PA32&lpg
=PA32&dq=little+field+in+O%27odham&source=bl&ots=ZSeuk
3hios&sig=FM86WvfZmHmNlggv5LMN5brsak&hl=de&sa=X&
ei=tNRITOXDoLl4QTehKXhDg&ved=0CCUQ6AEwAA#v=one
page&q=little%20field%20in%20O%27odham&f=false

http://books.google.de/books?id=9lCM_c35aJAC&pg=PA277&lp
g=PA277&dq=meaning+of+AliChuk&source=bl&ots=tF5qtLSW
19&sig=WpsQNhmxyG0c0wKVxSIZkmNeoMc&hl=de&sa=X&
ei=hk06T5e4BMXMtAbtm_TOBg&sqi=2&ved=0CCAQ6AEwA
A#v=onepage&q=meaning%20of%20Ali-Chuk&f=false.

http://books.google.de/books?id=ranPAAAAMAAJ&printsec=fro
ntcover&hl=de#v=onepage&q&f=false. (*Graham's Illustrated
Magazine*, 1857).

http://books.google.de/books?id=T5d5wS7so14C&pg=PA81&lpg
=PA81&dq=meaning+of+Zilwaukee&source=bl&ots=VcJhvYSq
zw&sig=nPInI2y03CdlN6my_pRMg9m4uf8&hl=de&sa=X&ei=
OVc6T5i9HcPOsgbI0KjzBg&ved=0CCIQ6AEwAA#v=onepage
&q=Zilwaukee&f=false.

http://canadachannel.ca/HCO/index.php/Mathieu_Da_Costa_and_
Early_Canada,_by_A._J._B._Johnston.

http://cartographicimages.net/Cartographic_Images/212_Masudi.h
tml.

http://circanceast.beaufortccc.edu/BCCC/articles/Spring%201984/
PDF/Story3.pdf.

http://counterjihadreport.com/tag/islamist-lobbies/.

http://creepingsharia.wordpress.com/ All contemporary articles
and archived articles.

http://creepingsharia.wordpress.com/2012/01/19/clinton-
announces-kareem-abdul-jabbar-as-cultural-ambassador/.

http://creepingsharia.wordpress.com/2012/02/03/philadelphia-city-council-passes-bill-oking-sharia-law/.

http://creepingsharia.wordpress.com/2012/03/03/terror-linked-cair-aclu-to-invade-missouri-capitol-march-6/.

http://dailycaller.com/2012/03/18/media-matters-for-america-linked-with-anti-american-anti-israel-al-jazeera-network/#ixzz1q2jTA5ZS.

http://de.althistory.wikia.com/wiki/Ard_Marjhoola.

http://de.wikipedia.org/wiki/Ahmedabad.
http://en.wikipedia.org/wiki/List_of_countryname_etymologies.

http://de.wikipedia.org/wiki/Amira.

http://de.wikipedia.org/wiki/Bagdad;;http://yahuwah-is.net/.

http://de.wikipedia.org/wiki/Gamaliel.

http://de.wikipedia.org/wiki/Sabina.

http://de.wikipedia.org/wiki/Toledo.

http://de.wikipedia.org/wiki/Zulu_%28Volk%29.

http://destituterebel.instablogs.com/entry/does-america-have-muslim-roots/.

http://divine-ripples.blogspot.com/.

http://divine-ripples.blogspot.com/2011/02/obama-saudi-operative-to-facilitate.html.

http://dnaconsultants.com/_blog/DNA_Consultants_Blog/tag/Cajuns/.

http://docsouth.unc.edu/nc/omarsaid/omarsaid.html.

http://edughoni.blogspot.com/2011/08/muslim-sailors-first-discovered.html.

http://en.alukah.net/Thoughts_Knowledge/0/412/.

http://www.thenational.ae/news/uae-news/tariq-ibn-ziyads-legacy-stands-as-a-reminder-to-reject-failure#full.

http://en.wikipedia.org/wiki/Ahuimanu,_Hawaii.

http://en.wikipedia.org/wiki/Alakanuk,_Alaska.

http://en.wikipedia.org/wiki/Alhambra.

http://en.wikipedia.org/wiki/Arawak_peoples.

http://en.wikipedia.org/wiki/Ashtabula_River.

http://en.wikipedia.org/wiki/Assyria.

http://en.wikipedia.org/wiki/Assyria.

http://en.wikipedia.org/wiki/Babylon.

http://en.wikipedia.org/wiki/Battle_of_the_Trench

http://en.wikipedia.org/wiki/Chav%C3%ADn_culture.

http://en.wikipedia.org/wiki/Cree.

http://en.wikipedia.org/wiki/Damascus.

http://en.wikipedia.org/wiki/Early_world_maps.

http://en.wikipedia.org/wiki/Hagar.

http://en.wikipedia.org/wiki/Hagar.

http://en.wikipedia.org/wiki/Hague,_New_York.

http://en.wikipedia.org/wiki/Hohokam.

http://en.wikipedia.org/wiki/Hopi.

http://en.wikipedia.org/wiki/Islamorada,_Florida.

http://en.wikipedia.org/wiki/Itta_Bena.

http://en.wikipedia.org/wiki/John_Allen_Muhammad.

http://en.wikipedia.org/wiki/Jumbo.

http://en.wikipedia.org/wiki/Kanaranzi,_Minnesota.

http://en.wikipedia.org/wiki/Lebanon.

http://en.wikipedia.org/wiki/Liberia.

http://en.wikipedia.org/wiki/List_of_countryname_etymologies

http://en.wikipedia.org/wiki/Madrid.

http://en.wikipedia.org/wiki/Mahican.

http://en.wikipedia.org/wiki/Masonic_manuscripts.

http://en.wikipedia.org/wiki/Medes.

http://en.wikipedia.org/wiki/Media,_Illinois.

http://en.wikipedia.org/wiki/Media,_Pennsylvania.

http://en.wikipedia.org/wiki/Medinah,_Illinois.

http://en.wikipedia.org/wiki/Mingo,_Iowa.

http://en.wikipedia.org/wiki/Muhammad_%28name%29.

http://en.wikipedia.org/wiki/Nazca_culture.

http://en.wikipedia.org/wiki/O%27odham_language.

http://en.wikipedia.org/wiki/Quamba,_Minnesota.

http://en.wikipedia.org/wiki/Ramadan#cite_note-1.

http://en.wikipedia.org/wiki/Salt_Lake,_Hawaii.

http://en.wikipedia.org/wiki/Samaria_%28ancient_city%29.

http://en.wikipedia.org/wiki/Shabbona

http://en.wikipedia.org/wiki/Shabbona,_Illinois.

http://en.wikipedia.org/wiki/S-L-M.

http://en.wikipedia.org/wiki/Tallahassee,_Florida.

http://en.wikipedia.org/wiki/Tallulah,_Louisiana.

http://en.wikipedia.org/wiki/Tama,_Iowa.

http://en.wikipedia.org/wiki/Toledo,_Ohio.

http://en.wikipedia.org/wiki/Unadilla_%28town%29,_New_York.

412

http://en.wikipedia.org/wiki/Yusuf.

http://en.wikipedia.org/wiki/Zuni_language.

http://genesisden.musicdot.com/genealogy.htm.

http://genesisden.musicdot.com/genealogy.htm.

http://geology.com/articles/marcellus-shale.shtml.

http://global-security-news.com/2011/09/16/40-terror-plots-foiled-since-911-combating-complacency-in-the-long-war-on-terror/.

http://hadith.alislam.com/Display/Display.asp?Doc=2&Rec=2695.

http://hauns.com/~DCQu4E5g/koran.html#Koran.

http://hewit.unco.edu/DOHIST/puebloan/begin.htm.

http://holgerawakens.blogspot.de/2010/10/florida-pastor-receives-death-threat.html.

http://islam.wikia.com/wiki/Al-Masudi.

http://islamexposed.blogspot.com/.

http://islaminaction08.blogspot.de/2009/06/christians-oppressed-in-islamic.html.

http://islaminaction08.blogspot.de/2009/07/michiganmuslim-mob-surrounds-and.html.

http://issuu.com/hazratamin/docs/mycrjul08.

http://issuu.com/hazratamin/docs/mycrjul08.

http://jewishencyclopedia.com/articles/8803-joseph#1553.

http://kitmantv.blogspot.com/2010/06/first-comes-saturday-then-comes-sunday.html.

http://kjmatthews.

http://loganswarning.com/ All contemporary articles and archived articles.

http://m.wired.com/dangerroom/2012/02/hundreds-fbi-documents-muslims/.

http://marychristinalove.wordpress.com/muslims-in-the-workplace/.

http://members.tripod.com/~Glove_r/Hapgood.html.

http://memory.loc.gov/ammem/collections/jefferson_papers/mtj prece.html. (Gawalt, Gerard W. *America and the Barbary Pirates: An International Battle Against an Unconventional Foe*)

http://michellemalkin.com/2010/11/27/just-another-bomb-plotting-jihadist-yelling-allahu-akbar/.

http://middlesborodailynews.com/bookmark/1407025-Islam-convert-gets-35-years-in-plot-to-attack-mall.

http://midnightwatcher.wordpress.com/2012/04/23/education-in-america-textbooks-are-being-systematically-rewritten-to-include-lies-half-truths-and-misleading-narratives-to-promote-islamist-agenda/.

http://minnesotaindependent.com/38101/cultures-collide-somali-youth-harass-gay-man-at-pride.

http://mozadded1924.wordpress.com/2011/12/01/muslim-exploreres-over-the-past-untill-the-u-s-instead-of-colombus/.

http://muslimvoices.org/religious-textbook-wars/.

http://muslimwiki.com/mw/index.php/Islamic_place_names_in_A merica.

http://myafrica.wordpress.com/2006/10/02/is-ishmael-the-father-of-prophet-Mohammed/.

http://news.bbc.co.uk/2/hi/africa/1068950.stm.

http://news.bbc.co.uk/2/hi/americas/4461642.stm.

http://news.smh.com.au/breaking-news-world/two-arrested-in-nyc-synagogue-bomb-plot-20110513-1ekyf.html.

http://niger1.com/?tag=abu-bakari-ii.

http://niger1.com/?tag=sundiata-keita.

http://obit.staff.umm.ac.id/files/2011/01/Lec-10.pptx. (Kennedy, Brent. *Islamic Horizons* November/December 1994, in *Early Contact of Muslims in America*).

http://online.wsj.com/article/SB100014240527487035898045754 45841837725272.html.

http://pakistanlink.org/Opinion/2011/Feb11/04/01.HTM

http://pioneercity.com/history.html.

http://pluralism.org/reports/view/75http://en.wikipedia.org/wiki/American_Jews;.

http://projectshiningcity.org/fp518.php.

http://quod.lib.umich.edu/cgi/t/text/textidx?c=moa&cc=moa&iew =text& rgn=main&idno=AGX7642.0001.001.

http://religionresearchinstitute.org/mecca/construction.htm.

http://reviewofcubanamericanblogs.blogspot.com/2008/10/columb us-saw-mosque-in-cuba-now-its.html.

http://righttruth.typepad.com/right_truth/.

http://rupeenews.com/usa/california-was-named-after-calif-haronia-caliph-haroon-rashid-al-hambra-was-also-from-muslim-spainmore-than-500-american-town-have-muslim-origins/.

http://s.michellemalkin.com/wp/wpcontent/uploads/2009/02/1aaaa saud.jpg.

http://sipseystreetirregulars.blogspot.com/.

http://sipseystreetirregulars.blogspot.com/2012/02/jesse-trentadue-talks-to-lew-rockwell.html.

http://spiritualchange.blogsome.com/2010/12/18/muslim-contacts-with-american-indians-before-columbus/.

http://sultanknish.blogspot.de/2011/12/unlimited-muslim-entitlement.html.

http://sun.cair.com/AboutUs/VisionMissionCorePrinciples.aspx.

http://sunnah.org/history/precolmb.htm

http://sunnah.org/history/precolmb.htm.

http://surnames.meaning-of-names.com/Cushman/.

http://theopinionator.typepad.com/my_weblog/2009/11/muslim-major-shouts-allahu-akbar-as-he-massacres-13-soldiers-injures-30.html.

http://topics.nytimes.com/topics/reference/timestopics/organizations/n/nation_of_islam/index.html.

http://unmyst3.blogspot.com/2011/03/hadji-ahmed-map.html.

http://userpages.bright.net/~kcc/kalida/history.htm.

http://vladtepesblog.com/?p=24380.

http://washoevalley.org/wv/wv%20history.htm#Jumbo_Grade.

http://web.archive.org/web/20070610042932/.

http://web.archive.org/web/20070610042932/http://www.senate.gov/~schumer/SchumerWebsite/pressroom/press_releases/PR02009.html. (Schumer: *Saudis Playing Role in Spreading Main Terror Influence in United States* – Original Charles Schumer Press Release September 10, 2003).

http://wikiislam.net for further information.

http://wikiislam.net/wiki/Bestiality.

http://wikiislam.net/wiki/Main_Page, and the links and articles therein.

http://wikiislam.net/wiki/Music_and_Singing:_Wisdom_Behind_Its_Prohibition_by_the_Shari%27ah.

http://wikiislam.net/wiki/Qur%27an,_Hadith_and_Scholars:Women.

http://wn.com/Islam_in_America_Thomas_Jefferson%27s_Quran.

http://work949.wordpress.com/2010/11/28/michelle-malkins-jihadist-mugshot-collection-worthy-of-viewing-what-say-you-now-portland/.

http://www.abarimpublications.com/Meaning/Asshur.html#.TzuIxFHz7mc.

http://www.abarim-publications.com/Meaning/Asshur.html.

http://www.abarimpublications.com/Meaning/Salem.html#.T0YxPHlGTmc.

http://www.abarimpublications.com/Meaning/Solomon.html#.TzpWElHz7mc.

http://www.accessgenealogy.com/native/tribes/cherokee/cherohist.htm.

http://www.aish.com/jw/s/48969486.html.

http://www.akdart.com/med14.html.

http://www.alabamaheritage.com/vault/UAburning.htm.

http://www.al-huda.com/Article_13of42.htm.

http://www.al-islam.org/encyclopedia/chapter6b/1.html.

http://www.almoltaqa.ps/english/showthread.php?t=6604.

http://www.americanthinker.com/2012/03/the_necessity_of_anti-sharia_laws.html#ixzz1q2eLNLh3.

http://www.americanthinker.com/blog/2011/02/egypt_hurriyya_vs_freedom_and.html.

http://www.amp.ghazali.net/html/mosques_in_us.html.

http://www.amp.ghazali.net/html/mosques_in_us.html.

http://www.answering-islam.org/Silas/slavery.htm.

http://www.answeringmuslims.com/2010/06/in-dearborn-we-were-arrested-for-having.html.

http://www.answeringmuslims.com/2011/07/christian-preacher-harassed-and-bullied.html.

http://www.answers.com/topic/aliquippa.

http://www.answers.com/topic/medina-1.

http://www.anti-cair-net.org/AhmadStateScanned.pdf.

http://www.aolnews.com/2010/09/15/molly-norris-artist-behind-everybody-draw-mohammad-day-cartoo/.

http://www.archive.org/stream/minnesotageogra00uphagoog/minnesotageogra00uphagoog_djvu.txt.

http://www.babynames.com/name/ZULU.

http://www.baby-vornamen.de/Jungen/Y/Ya/Yaro/.

http://www.barkati.net/english/#01.

http://www.bchistory.org/beavercounty/BeaverCountyTopical/NativeAmerican/IndianNamesinBCMA97.html.

http://www.beforebc.de/Related.Subjects/Queen.Califia.and.California/AfricansPredateColumbusTheAbundantEvidence.html.

http://www.berkeleydailyplanet.com/issue/2002-07-06/full_text.

http://www.bible.ca/islam/islam-allah-pre-islamic-origin.htm.

http://www.bible.ca/islam/islam-photos-moon-worship-archealolgy.htm.

http://www.bibletopics.com/biblestudy/96a.htm.

http://www.biblical-baby-names.com/meaning-of-zuzu.html.

http://www.bibliotecapleyades.net/egipto/fingerprintgods/fingerprintgods00.htm.

http://www.bigorrin.org/makah_kids.htm.

http://www.bostani.com/Discovered.

http://www.british-israel.ca/Islam.htm. (Salemi, Peter. *The Plain Truth About Islam*)

http://www.canadianarabcommunity.com/makingadifferenceincanada.php.

http://www.carolmoore.net/sfm/jdl.html.

http://www.caroun.com/Calligraphy/aCalligraphyGeneral/Kufic/KuficScript.html.

http://www.catholicnewsagency.com/news/us-free-speech-faces-islamic-blasphemy-law-pressure-analyst-says/.

http://www.cbsnews.com/2100-201_162-5030167.html.

http://www.celestialnavigation.net/instruments.html.

http://www.chinesediscoveramerica.com/.

http://www.cis.org/articles/2002/back802.html.

http://www.citytowninfo.com/places/hawaii/maili.

http://www.cmje.org/religious-texts/hadith/muslim/010-smt.php#010.3810.

http://www.coachisright.com/ag-eric-holder-responsible-for-168-deaths-in-1995-oklahoma-city-bombing%E2%80%A6and-more/.

http://www.colony14.net/id41.html, *The Obama Timeline*, wherein there are monthly news reports as well as respective essays.

http://www.courthousenews.com/2011/01/12/33268.htm.

http://www.coveredbridges.com/index.php/poi_detail?poiID=46.

http://www.csmonitor.com/USA/Politics/2011/0810/President-Obama-to-hold-iftar-dinner-Five-facts-about-the-Muslim-ceremony/What-s-the-purpose-of-Ramadan.

http://www.cyberistan.org/islamic/mamerica.html.

http://www.dailymail.co.uk/news/article-1385083/Rageit-Almurisi-Family-defends-Yemeni-man-stormed-cockpit-San-Francisco-flight.html.

http://www.dailymail.co.uk/news/article-2084551/Sami-Osmakac-Terror-suspect-caught-camera-brawling-Christian-protesters.html.

http://www.danielpipes.org/blog/2003/06/cairs-legal-tribulations.

http://www.danielpipes.org/blog/2003/06/cairs-legal-tribulations; June 23, 27, and May 2, 2010.

http://www.danielpipes.org/blog/2005/11/muslim-taxi-drivers-vs-seeing-eye-dogs.

http://www.debbieschlussel.com/archives/2008/10/religion_of_tol_1.html.

http://www.definition-of.net/abeyta.
http://wiki.name.com/en/Abeyta.

http://www.dreamscape.com/morgana/larissa2.htm.

http://www.enchantedlearning.com/explorers/page/e/estevanico.shtml.

http://www.encyclopedia.com/doc/1O40-Isham.html. (A. D. MILLS. "Isham." A Dictionary of British Place-Names. 2003,Encyclopedia.com.).

http://www.epodunk.com/cgibin/genInfo.php?locIndex=20806.

http://www.epodunk.com/cgibin/genInfo.php?locIndex=21144.

http://www.eslam.de/begriffe/m/malik_aschtar.htm.

http://www.everyculture.com/Ge-It/Guinea.html.

http://www.faithfreedom.org/.

http://www.faithfreedom.org/Articles/skm 30804.htm.

http://www.faithfreedom.org/Articles/SStephan/islamic_slavery.htm.

http://www.faithfreedom.org/Articles/SStephan/islamic_slavery.htm.

http://www.faithfreedom.org/index.htm.

http://www.familysecuritymatters.org/publications/id.9606,css.print/pub_detail.asp.

http://www.familysecuritymatters.org/publications/id.9606,css.print/pub_detail.asp.

http://www.fas.org/sgp/crs/misc/RS21695.pdf.

http://www.fas.org/sgp/crs/misc/RS21695.pdf.

http://www.fas.org/sgp/crs/terror/R41416.pdf, p. 48.

http://www.flex.com/~jai/satyamevajayate/index.html.

http://www.flickr.com/photos/mikewoodfin/4607874292/in/photostream/.

http://www.freerepublic.com/focus/f-news/1440602/posts.

http://www.glencoe.com/qe/qe98columbus.php?qi=3990.

http://www.godlikeproductions.com/forum1/message1534398/pg1.

http://www.godtube.com/watch/?v=JE01BMNU.

http://www.google.com/hostednews/ap/article/ALeqM5hDlRkRffovJlX8OT05h89h3zfgWwD9BS4ETO3.

http://www.gutenberg.org/cache/epub/7440/pg7440.html The Koran (Al-Qur'an) by George Sale.

http://www.hezbuttawheed.com/component/content/article/1-displayhome/6-thefiveitemedagendaforestablishingislam.

http://www.hezbuttawheed.com/component/content/article/1-displayhome/6-thefiveitemedagendaforestablishingislam.

http://www.historyofmecca.com/.

http://www.historyworld.net/wrldhis/PlainTextHistories.asp?historyid=aa51#ixzz1nPFl79eB.

http://www.huffingtonpost.com/jay-rubenstein/crusade-vs-jihad-was-one-_b_1146871.html.

http://www.humnet.ucla.edu/aflang/Hausa/Language/dialectframe.html.

http://www.imamreza.net/eng/imamreza.php?id=2028. (Pimienta-Bey, Jose V. *Muslim Legacy in Early Americas*)

http://www.imamreza.net/eng/imamreza.php?id=3932.

http://www.imamreza.net/eng/imamreza.php?id=6683htm.

http://www.inquiryintoislam.com/2010/07/why-is-islam-so-successful.html.

http://www.investigativeproject.org/3453/islamist-lobbies-washington-war-on-arab.

http://www.investigativeproject.org/documents/misc/20.pdf. (Akram, Mohammed. *An Explanatory Memorandum on the General Strategic Goal for the Group in North America*, May 22, 1991, Government Exhibit 003-0085, U.S. vs. HLF et al.).

http://www.iol.ie/~afifi/BICNews/Personal/personal1.htm.
http://www.wafin.com/articles/23/index.phtml.

http://www.ishamcemetery.org/.

http://www.ishof.org/black_history/pdf/mamoutYarrow.pdf.

http://www.islamhelpline.com/node/5780.

http://www.islamicawareness.org/Quran/Sources/Allah/moongod.html.

http://www.islamicity.com/forum/printer_friendly_posts.asp?TID=16191.

http://www.islammonitor.org/.

http://www.islammonitor.org/index.php?option=com_content&task=view&id=3897&Itemid=67.

http://www.islam-watch.org/articles.htm.

http://www.islamwatch.org/Nosharia/PreventEuropeIslamization1.htm.

http://www.islam-watch.org/Warner/Taqiyya-Islamic-Principle-Lying-for-Allah.htm.

http://www.islamweb.net/emainpage/index.php?page=articles&id=134284. All of it is a form of al-taqiyya.

http://www.islandcityharbor.com/History/index.htm.

http://www.islandcityharbor.com/History/index.htm.

http://www.isna.net/.

http://www.isna.net/ISNAHQ/pages/Mission--Vision.aspx.

http://www.jewishencyclopedia.com/articles/11305-names-of-god#164.

http://www.jewishencyclopedia.com/articles/11305-names-of-god#164.

http://www.jihadwatch.org/. All contemporary and archived articles.

http://www.jihadwatch.org/2004/01/hizballah-entering-us-through-mexico.html.

http://www.jihadwatch.org/2004/04/andalusian-myth-eurabian-reality-print.html. (Ye'or, Bat and Bostom, Andrew. *Andalusian Myth, Eurabian Reality.*).

http://www.jihadwatch.org/2004/09/boston-suit-challenges-city-on-mosque-project.html.

http://www.jihadwatch.org/2005/01/new-jersey-an-islamic-murder-of-coptic-christians.html.

http://www.jihadwatch.org/2006/01/fitzgerald-take-a-tour-of-dawanet.html.

http://www.jihadwatch.org/2006/12/muslims-seek-prayer-room-at-airport.html.

http://www.jihadwatch.org/2007/03/minneapolis-some-muslim-workers-at-target-refuse-to-handle-pork.html.

http://www.jihadwatch.org/2007/09/our-followers-must-live-in-peace-until-strong-enough-to-wage-jihad.html.

http://www.jihadwatch.org/2009/06/christian-and-muslim-get-in-religious-argument-in-bar-muslim-shoots-christian.html.

http://www.jihadwatch.org/2009/06/hijab-wearing-islamic-supremacist-woman-crashes-memorial-for-arkansas-jihad-victim-shouting-jesus-wa.html.

http://www.jihadwatch.org/2009/06/hijab-wearing-islamic-supremacist-woman-crashes-memorial-for-arkansas-jihad-victim-shouting-jesus-wa.html.

http://www.jihadwatch.org/2010/07/sharia-in-new-jersey-muslim-husband-rapes-wife-judge-sees-no-sexual-assault-because-husbands-religio.html.

http://www.jihadwatch.org/2011/08/obama-spreads-false-claim-that-thomas-jefferson-hosted-first-ramadan-iftar-dinner-at-white-house.html.

http://www.jihadwatch.org/2012/01/florida-jihad-suspect-brawled-with-christians-warned-on-youtube-to-convert-to-islam-before-it-is-too.html.

http://www.jihadwatch.org/2012/02/would-be-capitol-jihad-bomber-wanted-to-target-synagogue-military-gathering-place.html.

http://www.jihadwatch.org/2012/03/at-cia-a-convert-to.html. Roger's name is not stated in the source.

http://www.jihadwatch.org/cgi-sys/cgiwrap/br0nc0s/managed-mt/mtsearch.cgi?blog_id=1&tag=New%20York%2FColorado%20bomb%20plot&limit=20.

http://www.jpost.com/MiddleEast/Article.aspx?id=207415.

http://www.justice.gov/opa/pr/2008/June/08-nsd-492.html.

http://www.law.ou.edu/sites/default/files/files/common_folder/03%20parry%20essay%20blu1.pdf.

http://www.leaderu.com/wri/articles/islam-singh.html.

http://www.let.rug.nl/usa/P/aj7/speeches/ajson3.htm.

http://www.letusreason.org/islam6.htm.

http://www.liveleak.com/view?i=1ea_1294982297.

http://www.liveleak.com/view?i=dfb_1255153840.

http://www.livius.org/ctcz/cyrus_I/babylon02.html#Chronicle%20 of%20Nabonidus.

http://www.makah.com/.

http://www.mathaba.net/news/?x=66517.

http://www.mce.k12tn.net/indians/reports2/apache.htm.

http://www.meaning-of-names.com/spanish-names/alameda.asp.

http://www.medindia.net/news/Despite-Its-Muslim-Majority-WHO-Names-Malaysia-as-Worlds-10th-Largest-Alcohol-Consumer-85415-1.htm.

http://www.medterms.com/script/main/art.asp?articlekey=6992.

http://www.mhanation.com/main/history/history_arikara.html.

http://www.middle-east-studies.net/?p=2755. http://sunnah.org/history/precolmb.htm.

http://www.mideastweb.org/islamhistory.htm.

http://www.militantislammonitor.org/article/id/3507.

http://www.militantislammonitor.org/article/id/3604.

http://www.militantislammonitor.org/article/id/3673.

http://www.militantislammonitor.org/article/id/3770.

http://www.militantislammonitor.org/article/id/383.

http://www.militantislammonitor.org/article/id/3830.

http://www.militantislammonitor.org/article/id/457.

http://www.monticello.org/site/research-and collections/tunisian-envoy.

http://www.moonbattery.com/archives/2007/06/boston-mosque-f.html.

http://www.mostlymaps.com/mapmakers/gerardus-mercator.

http://www.mroueh.com/origins.htm.

http://www.mroueh.com/origins.htm.

http://www.multilingualarchive.com/ma/enwiki/de/Khashkhash_I bn_Saeed_Ibn_Aswad.

http://www.multilingualarchive.com/ma/enwiki/de/Rodrigo_de_T riana.

http://www.muslimpopulation.com/America/USA/Islam%20in%2 0USA.php

http://www.muslimsinamerica.org/index.php?option=com_content &task=view&id=17&Itemid=28.

http://www.muslimsinamerica.org/index2.php?option=com_conte nt&do_pdf=1&id=15.

http://www.muslimsinamerica.org/index2.php?option=com_conte nt&do_pdf=1&id=14.

http://www.muslimsunrise.com/index.php?option=com_content&t ask=view&id=134&Itemid=1.

http://www.nationalreview.com/articles/243587/ban-burqa-claire-berlinski.

http://www.nationalreview.com/articles/244803/muslims-mainstream-media-madness-clifford-d-may?page=1.

http://www.newt.org/solutions/immigration/.

http://www.nps.gov/sagu/forteachers/upload/Unit%208%20-%20Water%20in%20the%20Desert.pdf.

http://www.nundahistory.org/shorthistory.html.

http://www.nysun.com/national/dont-bring-that-booze-into-my-taxi/41264/.

http://www.nytimes.com/2009/06/02/us/02recruit.html.

http://www.onenesspentecostal.com/nameofgod.htm.

http://www.onenewsnow.com/Culture/Default.aspx?id=1528354.

http://www.onlineutah.com/monahistory.shtml.

http://www.oocities.org/mutmainaa/history/muslim_caribbean.html.

http://www.outwestnewspaper.com/camels.htm.

http://www.palestinefacts.org/pf_early_palestine_name_origin.php, and http://en.wikipedia.org/wiki/Palestine.

http://www.past2present.org/own/counties/Allamakee.htm.

http://www.patheos.com/blogs/altmuslim/2008/09/if_we_become_independent_thinkers_we_can_make_a_contribution/,

http://www.pbs.org/programs/prince-among-slaves/.

http://www.pbs.org/wgbh/pages/frontline/shows/saudi/analyses/wahhabism.html.

http://www.pkviews.com/forum/showthread.php/706-Does-America-Have-Muslim-Roots-SUPPRESSED-HISTORY.

http://www.pleasantonweekly.com/news/show_story.php?id=2916.

http://www.politicalislam.com/.

http://www.politicalislam.com/blog/statistical-islam-part-5-of-9-abrogation-and-dualism-dec-3-2010/.

http://www.presidency.ucsb.edu/ws/index.php?pid=29521&st=moslem&st1=#axzz1mAc1ie7R.

http://www.presidency.ucsb.edu/ws/index.php?pid=29536#axzz1pStBOxw6.

http://www.presidency.ucsb.edu/ws/index.php?pid=29537#ixzz1p Swv44go.

http://www.pressandguide.com/articles/2012/01/14/news/doc4f10 672d3e47d004412938.txt.

http://www.prophetofdoom.net/Prophet_of_Doom_Letter_to_the_ Reader.Islam.

http://www.pvv.ntnu.no/~madsb/home/war/vegetius/. (Vegetius [Flavius Vegetius] *De Rei Militari*, III)

http://www.quickbabynames.com/meaning-of-Zaidee.html.

http://www.renewamerica.com/columns/zieve/070111.

http://www.reuters.com/article/2008/11/06/us-usa-election-muslims-idUSTRE4A57ZC20081106.

http://www.ruthfullyyours.com/2012/02/17/edward-cline-islamic-rules-for-radicals/.

http://www.sabrizain.org/malaya/potomac.htm.

http://www.sacklunch.net/placenames/L/Liberia.html.

http://www.sage-ereference.com/abstract/terrorism/n185.xml.

http://www.sageereference.com/view/terrorism/pdfs/Reading_d10 .pdf.

http://www.san.beck.org/1-12-NorthAfricato1700.html.

http://www.saudiaramcoworld.com/issue/201104/thomas.jefferson .s.qur.an.htm.

http://www.scribd.com/doc/71994512/Sundry-Free-Moors-Act-2012.

http://www.senate.gov/~schumer/SchumerWebsite/pressroom/pre ss_releases/PR02009.html.

http://www.serbianna.com/news/2007/01377.shtml.

http://www.shiloahbooks.com/download/Muslim%20History.

http://www.shiloahbooks.com/download/Muslim%20History.pdf.

http://www.shiloahbooks.com/download/Muslim%20History.pdf.

http://www.spanish-town-guides.com/Salamanca_History.htm.

http://www.splcenter.org/get-informed/intelligencefiles/groups/nation-of-islam.

http://www.stormfront.org/forum/t746826-14/#post8648916.

http://www.sultan.org/articles/wahabism.html.

http://www.telegraph.co.uk/news/worldnews/northamerica/usa/3515658/US-based-Muslim-charity-guilty-of-funding-terrorism.html.

http://www.theatlantic.com/international/archive/2011/10/the-man-behind-pakistani-spy-agencys-plot-to-influence-washington/246000/.

http://www.theblaze.com/stories/muslim-admits-to-attacking-atheist-over-zombie-muhammed-costume-muslim-judge-dismisses-case-lectures-atheist-on-joys-of-islam/.

http://www.thegatewaypundit.com/2011/06/marine-reservist-yonathan-melaku-arrested-in-connection-to-dc-military-building-shootings/.

http://www.thegatewaypundit.com/2012/02/colorado-high-school-choir-forced-to-praise-allah/.

http://www.thememriblog.org/.

http://www.theologyweb.com/campus/archive/index.php/t-52114.html.

http://www.thereligionofpeace.com/.

http://www.therightscoop.com/walid-shoebat-explains-islamic-muruna-strategy/.

http://www.thinkbabynames.com/meaning/0/Sallee.

http://www.thinkbabynames.com/meaning/1/Hayes.

http://www.thinkbabynames.com/meaning/1/Malak.

http://www.thinkbabynames.com/meaning/1/Malcolm.

http://www.uaf.edu/anla/collections/search/files/KO972J-PN-04/f.08VillageProf.pdf.

http://www.umanet.org/cms.cfm?fuseaction=articles.viewThisArticle&articleID=263&pageID=159.

http://www.usgs.gov/newsroom/article.asp?ID=1911#.T5Zx-9nz7mc; http://205.254.135.7/naturalgas/.

http://www.vbgov.com/government/departments/libraries/research/lawlibrary/pages/wahab-public-law-library.aspx.

http://www.voanews.com/english/archive/2005-10/2005-10-20-voa14.cfm?CFID=432813&CFTOKEN=38573615.

http://www.washingtonpost.com/ac2/wpdyn/A128232004Sep10?Language=printer.

http://www.washingtonpost.com/wpdyn/content/article/2009/03/24/AR2009032402818.html.

http://www.webcitation.org/query?url=http://www.ansamed.info/en/news/ME.XEF93985.html&date=2011-02-25.

http://www.websters-online-dictionary.org/Chinook/illahee.

http://www.wfaa.com/news/local/Possible-terror-incident-in-Fort-Worth-84316367.html.

http://www.whyMohammed.com/es/Contents.aspx?AID=4626.

http://www.wiroots.org/wimarquette/marqplaces2c.html.

http://www.wisemuslimwomen.org/about/shuracouncil/.

http://www.witnesspioneer.org/vil/Articles/politics/muslims_in_the_americas_before_columbus.htm.

http://www.wnd.com/2002/07/14478/.

http://www.wnd.com/2003/08/20098/.

430

http://www.wnd.com/2005/04/29850/.

http://www.wnd.com/2006/10/38376/.

http://www.wnd.com/2008/02/57141/.

http://www.wnd.com/2009/07/105227/.

http://www.wnd.com/2011/01/250597/.

http://www.world-mysteries.com/mpl_1_2.htm.

http://www.yahuwah-is.net/Files/yahuwshua.html.

http://www.youtube.com/watch?feature=player_embedded&v=43I NJy_cf3M.

http://www.youtube.com/watch?feature=player_embedded&v=Bf 11F3y9LOE.

http://www.youtube.com/watch?feature=player_embedded&v=FF W3ZNC8sjw.

http://www.youtube.com/watch?feature=player_embedded&v=n2 uwtk6Isxk#!.

http://www.youtube.com/watch?feature=player_embedded&v=X4 mbTL0d4fs.

http://www.youtube.com/watch?feature=player_embedded&v=X-edn6-Liu8.

http://www.youtube.com/watch?feature=player_embedded&v=yJ vGGuLrVzo.

http://www.youtube.com/watch?v=FMh3IYfuwf4.

http://www.youtube.com/watch?v=Ib9rofXQl6w&feature=player_ embedded.

http://www.youtube.com/watch?v=TfW9inRkTpU&feature=playe r_embedded.

http://www.zeriyt.com/islam-in-the-united-states-albanians-t15098.0.html.

http://zionsake.tripod.com/MuD-No_prophecies.html#D.

http://en.wikipedia.org/wiki/Salt_Lake,_Hawaii.http://en.wikipedia.org/wiki/Maili,_Hawaii.

http;www.parenting.com/baby-names/girls/Zuzu.

https://islamquotes.org/?p=d&d=v&k=1711.

https://theislamicstandard.wordpress.com/tag/asabiyyah/.

www.airforcetimes.com/news/2007/09/ap_binladen_070911/.

www.Al-islam.org., (*The Term* Shia *in Quran and Hadith*)

**The Holy Bible**

Deuteronomy 4:19; 17:3.

II Kings 21:3-5.

Second Book of Moses 10:25.

The Gospel According to St. Mark 25:31-46.

**Newspapers**

*Minneapolis Star Tribune*, April 4, 1993.

*Wall Street Journal*, Vol. CIV, NO. 6, July 9, 1999.

# INDEX

The index should be used in conjunction with the chapter divisions. For example, generally, speaking, there are no index listings for names of individuals that appear in Chapter Three or the items and individuals in Chapter Four. The same is true of Chapters Five and Six. Geographical names that appear in Chapter Seven are not listed in the Index either. Once the reader examines Chapter Seven, the raison d'être will be apparent. These subjects are handled separately in the respective chapters.

442